GORDON WRIGHT
Professor of History, Stanford University
ADVISORY EDITOR TO DODD, MEAD & COMPANY

EUROPE IN THE GLOBAL AGE:

1939 to the Present

EUROPE IN THE

F. Roy Willis

University of California, Davis

DODD, MEAD & COMPANY

GLOBAL AGE:

1939 to the Present

NEW YORK   TORONTO   1974

Preface

THIS book is a history of Europe from the beginning of the Second World War to the present day. It is intended to be of use to all, in college or out, who feel the need of a coherently organized, detailed presentation of the major developments in Europe during the last three decades. Historians have traditionally been chary of treating recent events as part of the past, preferring to wait for the patina of time to dull the immediacy of events investigated; but this caution has less justification than it used to have. Documentation is made available today with a speed and proliferation unheard of before the Second World War. Excellent monographs abound. Moreover, students, aware that the past thirty years of European history have had a profound influence upon their own lives, are demanding that historians prove their claim that the study of the past enables them to see the present in perspective.

I followed three principles in writing this book. First, concentration was placed upon political and economic history. Military events were sketched in only for their relevance to political and economic change. Second, an attempt was made to cover the history of all Europe "from the Atlantic to the Urals," with equal emphasis being given to developments in Eastern and Western Europe. Third, the vast impact on Europe of its changing relations with Asia and Africa was dealt with at length, while Latin America, whose influence on recent European events has been slight, was excluded.

The book owes much to the students in my courses in Contemporary European History at the University of Washington and at the University of California, Davis. Their discussions have been of great value in the unending task of sorting the relevant from the ephemeral, a more than usually thorny task for the historian attempting to see patterns of development in the events of his own lifetime.

F. R. W.

Contents

Polish National Communism; Slight Liberalization in Kádár's Hungary; Rumania's National Road to Communism. DISUNITY IN THE WEST, 411. *Territorial Disputes in Western Europe; De Gaulle's Veto on British Membership in the Common Market; Failure of de Gaulle's Plans for European Political Union; Battles over Agricultural Policy in EEC; Disorder in the Atlantic Alliance.*

MAPS

Chapter One THE ORIGINS OF THE SECOND WORLD WAR

THE First World War and the peace treaties that followed it made a mockery of the idealism of a generation of young men who had been induced to believe that one particular war could put an end to all war. By 1939 there were few Europeans who sincerely believed that war would henceforth be impossible, and there were even some who thought a new war necessary and desirable. The Europeans who had experienced the horror of the First World War pondered on its aftermath and lived for twenty years in the constant awareness that a second holocaust was a probability. When war finally came in September 1939, there was a curious similarity in the gloomy acceptance of its inevitability in Berlin, Paris, and London. Europeans knew they had failed to meet their problems for twenty years and believed that the new war was their punishment for this failure.

This Second World War grew directly out of the First. (1) The First World War left economic and political chaos in Europe; the Paris Peace Conference failed to restore stability. (2) The internal weakness of the line of new or remodeled states in Eastern Europe, from Finland to Bulgaria, invited the intervention of their stronger neighbors, the Soviet Union and Germany. (3) The establishment of Communist control in Russia gave to world communism a base from which to expand, and it gave to Russian expansion into Eastern Europe an ideological justification as an extension of the proletarian revolution. (4) Economic breakdown combined with fear of Communist revolution brought to power in Italy and Germany Fascist governments that intended to use military aggression to advance their territorial expansion. (5) The democratic governments of the United States, France, and Britain did not make effective preparation for the deterrence of aggression. (6) In the Far East, the expansionist aims of the militarist government of Japan were encouraged by the incapacity of the Nationalist government of China and the weak-

1

ness of the European powers, whose control of their colonial possessions in Asia was being challenged from within by nationalism and communism. (7) In 1931–39, the Western powers met the aggression of Japan, Italy, and Germany with weak protest or with appeasement, thereby encouraging the Soviet Union to join Nazi Germany in expanding into Eastern Europe. Full-scale European war began when Britain and France belatedly decided to halt German expansion into Eastern Europe by defending Poland.

THE LEGACY OF WORLD WAR ONE

Achievements of the Nineteenth Century. The First World War was an unexpected climax to a century of astounding progress in almost every sphere. As a result of the eastward advance of the industrial and agricultural revolutions across the Continent, Europe's economic productivity had vastly increased. This extraordinary increase in material wealth, which in the early days of the Industrial Revolution had produced glaring contrasts of wealth and poverty, was slowly being shared with the working classes as they came, through use of the vote, of trade unionism, or of direct violence, to make their strength known. The national governments, too, had increasingly come to recognize their own responsibility for the well-being of their populations. By 1914, state social security systems were already in force in Germany, Britain, and Scandinavia, and democratic socialist parties were active from Portugal to Russia.

Political advances had accompanied the material gains. Parliamentary democracy based on universal manhood suffrage was the form of government in Britain, France, Italy, Belgium, Holland, Switzerland, and Scandinavia. The three great empires that dominated Central and Eastern Europe—Germany, Austria-Hungary, and Russia—had all adopted the façade at least of parliamentary monarchy, and seemed likely to be forced to concede the realities of political power to their restive middle classes. The national minorities within the Austrian Empire were gaining greater autonomy, if independence was still refused them. The Magyars had divided the Habsburg Empire with the Austrians in 1867; a similar concession to the Czechs was being considered in 1914; the Poles of Galicia controlled their own administration. Nation after nation had emerged from centuries of Turkish oppression—Greece and Serbia in 1830, Rumania in 1862, Bulgaria in 1878, and

Albania in 1913. The forces of nationalism and liberalism, which the statesmen of the Congress of Vienna in 1815 had tried to repress, had made enormous gains.

Even the wars of the century had been short and isolated. The bloodiest war of all, the Crimean War, in which four great powers had participated, had cost only 500,000 lives; and, partly as a result of German Chancellor Bismarck's role as an honest broker, the division of the globe among the colonial empires of Britain, France, Belgium, Portugal, Italy, and Germany had not provoked any important armed conflict. In the golden glow of the Edwardian era, Europe preened itself upon the inevitability of its progress and failed to recognize the gravity of the dangers that it faced.

The First World War (1914–18) grew out of the very optimism that a century of peace and prosperity had engendered. In 1914 no government recognized that the development of industrial technology had changed the nature of war; they were still prepared to believe, with Clausewitz, that war is diplomacy carried on by other means. War appealed to national minorities like the Poles, the Czechs, the South Slavs, and the Italians of Dalmatia, as a means of restoring their national independence or of rejoining their homeland; to revolutionaries like Lenin, as a means of destroying the capitalist system and the forms of government that upheld capitalism; to nationalists of the Treitschke type, as the surest method of stimulating the highest energy and ideals of the nation; and to the misled masses in every nation in Europe, as a method of "settling once and for all" the national quarrels that their governments had presented to them as moral conflicts.

Immediate Results of World War One. Few realized in the euphoria of 1914 that they would still be paying the price of their enthusiasm fifty years later. First, the cost of the war, in lives and wealth, was beyond any expectation. Eight and a half million soldiers died; one soldier out of five was killed, and one out of three was wounded. The Allied powers spent $156 billion on the war, and the Central powers $63 billion. Second, the war destroyed the great empires of Central and Eastern Europe. In November 1917, the Communist party under Lenin's leadership seized control of Russia; on November 9, 1918, Kaiser Wilhelm II of Germany fell from power and Germany declared itself a Republic; on November 11, 1918, the Austro-Hungarian Emperor, Charles I, abdicated. By the end of 1918, a line of small, weak states stretched across Europe from the Arctic to the Mediterranean—Finland, Estonia, Latvia, Lithuania, Poland, Czechoslovakia, Austria, Hungary, the Serb-Croat-Slovene state (later called Yugoslavia), Rumania, Bulgaria, Albania, Greece. Third, social revolution threatened. Communist uprisings took place in Germany and in Hungary which for six months remained in the hands of Béla Kun. Fourth, war had changed the character of the Western democracies themselves. Embittered nationalism had replaced the humane liberalism of the prewar years; defeatism rather than optimism was the keynote of the thinking of the war-scarred generation. The Treaty of Versailles was a dangerous compromise between the idealistic world design of American President Wilson and the realistic nationalism of British Prime Minister Lloyd George and French Premier Clemenceau.

The Paris Peace Conference, 1919. The negotiators in Paris began, apparently on Wilsonian lines, by accepting the national independence of the newly proclaimed states of Eastern Europe, and thus the demise of the three great empires of Germany, Russia, and Austria-Hungary. Austria and Hungary were compelled to recognize the cession of Galicia to Poland, Transylvania to Rumania, Bohemia, Moravia, Slovakia, and Sub-Carpathian Ruthenia to Czechoslovakia, and Croatia and Bosnia-Herzegovina to Yugoslavia. The Treaty of Versailles with Germany granted to Poland the province of Posen and parts of West Prussia. Although the Allies did not negotiate with Communist Russia on its future boundaries in the west, they continued to recognize the independence of Finland, Estonia, Latvia, and Lithuania as decreed by the Germans in the Treaty of Brest-Litovsk of March 1918, and later attempted to define the eastern boundary of Poland along the Curzon Line, which passed on a north-south line through Brest-Litovsk. Between the might of Germany and Russia, the Paris negotiators thereby accepted the creation of a line of unstable states that were to prove a major source of the political upheavals of interwar Europe.

The Treaty of Versailles imposed upon Germany terms that were harsh without being crippling. Germany lost its colonies, its fleet and merchant marine, and 13 per cent of its prewar European territory, including half of its iron ore and one-fifth of its steel industry. With its productive capacity thus impaired, the new Republic was saddled with a crippling reparations bill of $32 billion, part of which was to be paid in coal, chemicals, and other goods. The German Army was to be restricted to 100,000 men, the German Navy to ships of less than 10,000 tons, and the area from the western border to fifty kilometers east of the Rhine was to be permanently demilitarized. The idea that the treaty of Versailles was a *Diktat,* or dictated peace, was to be used by German demagogues to keep Germans in a continual state of outraged nationalism.

The Allies failed to meet the problem of the communization of Russia or indeed of the appeal of communism to peoples disillusioned and tormented by a war in which they had no stake. Direct military intervention by Britain, France, the United States, and Japan in the Russian Civil War against the Reds was ineffective, although French aid was of importance in permitting the Poles to attack Russia in 1920 and to seize and hold large areas of White Russia and the Ukraine, with a Russian population of four million. The possibility of remedying the social and economic grievances, on which communism thrived, was not even considered at the Paris Peace Conference.

Finally, the peace treaties, as English economist John Maynard Keynes complained, "impaired . . . the delicate, complicated organization" of the European economy. By paralyzing the German economy, Keynes argued in *The Economic Consequences of the Peace,* the Allies were destroying the industrial and commercial unit around which the whole of the European economy was organized. The result could only be the economic decline of the victors as well as the vanquished, bringing with it political chaos and the resort to dictatorship.

THE COLLAPSE OF THE NEW STATES OF EASTERN EUROPE

The redrawing of the map of Eastern Europe on national lines brought neither prosperity nor political freedom to the new or reshaped states of that region. Instead, it created in the vital buffer region between Russia and Germany, thirteen states that were overburdened by economic difficulties, racked by internal conflicts both of classes and national groups, and misgoverned first by pseudo-democracies and then by dictatorships. The weaknesses and the injustices of the new states made them the obvious prey of Fascist expansion from the West and of Communist expansion from the East. Their history in the three decades after Versailles is a gloomy recital of their submission first to internal authoritarianism, then to fascism, and finally to communism.

Economic Problems. Economic weakness was the primary cause of all the internal problems of the area. There was low yield in all basic crops, owing to fragmentation of holdings and the lack of fertilizer, equipment, and technical knowledge. In many areas, half of the agricultural workers were redundant; in parts of the Balkans, agricultural workers produced only one-ninth the yield of workers in the intensely farmed areas of Denmark. After 1919 every government attempted to deal with the problem of land reform by instituting programs for redistributing the great estates among the peasantry. In Finland and the Baltic states, the program was successful in bringing much new land into cultivation and in increasing production. In Rumania, Czechoslovakia, and Yugoslavia the reforms succeeded in reducing the economic, and thereby the political, power of the landowning class. But productivity remained low, and not enough land was made available to satisfy the demands of the rural proletariat. In Poland and Hungary, halfhearted programs were quickly dropped by the politically powerful landowning class; as a result, bitter social conflict continued between landless agricultural laborers and small landholders and the landowning classes. A situation existed in which the appeal of communism was both natural and revolutionary.

As for industry, large-scale development took place only in Poland, the Czech areas of Czechoslovakia, and in western Hungary. Every state drew up industrialization plans, but these were intended above all to safeguard its own military needs by the creation, for example, of native iron and steel industries. All these efforts were hampered by lack of capital and raw materials, by the unwillingness of the intellectual class to engage in business rather than in law or bureaucracy, by the erection of tariff barriers, and by the instability of the currency. National rivalry thus prevented the adoption of any natural economic trade pattern in the area. Finally, the depression of the 1930's hit the small East European countries particularly hard, causing widespread unemployment and making it easy for Nazi Germany to increase its influence by grant of favorable trade treaties.

Collapse of Democratic Government. In all these countries, democratic constitutions had been adopted after the war, with elected parliaments, independent judiciaries, and guarantees of civil rights, and, for varying lengths of time, each maintained the semblance of a working democracy. In only one, however, did democracy take root. Hungary,

EASTERN EUROPE BETWEEN THE WARS

after experiencing a Communist revolution under Béla Kun, followed by a Rumanian occupation, fell again under the control of the Magyar landowning aristocracy, which turned increasingly toward fascism. Poland's government was seized by the military in 1926. In Yugoslavia, Rumania, and Bulgaria, royal dictatorship was established on the pretext that it was the only alternative to internal disorder. Authoritarian regimes were set up in Austria in 1932, in all the Baltic states by 1934, and in Greece in 1936. Backward Albania was first ruled by its clans, and then, after 1928, by the conservative King Zog I. Only Czechoslovakia seemed to be able to avoid the universal slide into totalitarianism, through the beneficent leadership of President Thomas Masaryk and Foreign Minister Eduard Beneš.

Attitude of Neighboring States. Thus, by the mid-1930's, the states of Central Europe invited the intervention of their neighbors. To Communist Russia, the region was not only its buffer against German expansion but a natural area for the expansion of Communist control. Rural and industrial poverty, class conflict between industrial proletariat and capitalist gentry and between peasantry and landowners, and injustice at every level of administration provided a situation ripe for exploitation. To Nazi Germany also, the states of Central Europe were inviting. Not only were they the *Lebensraum* (living space) for the German people, but in many cases the ruling groups had already embraced anti-Semitism and the methods of the police state and, indeed, were prepared to accept fascism as the natural safeguard against the advances of communism. To the Western democracies, however, Central Europe, in spite of its decline into totalitarianism, represented a last hope for democracy. France returned to its centuries-old policy of maintaining a line of client-states between Germany and Russia, signing treaties of alliance with Poland in 1921, Czechoslovakia in 1924, Rumania in 1926, and Yugoslavia in 1927, and accepting the formation of the Little Entente of 1921 between Czechoslovakia, Yugoslavia, and Rumania. As Fascist sympathizers gained the upper hand in more and more of the East European states in the 1930's, France, joined by a reluctant Britain, came to regard the maintenance of an independent Czechoslovakia and Poland as a major necessity for their own security.

THE RUSSIFICATION OF COMMUNISM

To the east of these weak states loomed the enigmatic bulk of Russia. Here again the First World War had brought a transformation of enormous importance in the seizure of the country by the Bolshevik party and of international communism by the Bolshevik government of Russia.

The Price of Communist Victory. In March 1917, the tsar's government was overthrown by an uprising of workers and soldiers in Petrograd. The Provisional Government, headed first by the liberal aristocrat Prince Lvov and then by the Social Revolutionary leader Alexander Kerensky, had made the fatal errors of continuing the war and of failing to carry out an immediate redistribution of the land. In November 1917, in a carefully planned insurrection, the Bolshevik or Communist party, led by Lenin and Trotsky, won control of Petrograd, Moscow, and the other major cities of Russia, dissolved the Provisional Government, abolished private ownership of land, and appealed to all the belligerent powers for an immediate end to the fighting. Attacks on the new regime were broken by force; a popularly elected Constituent Assembly was dismissed after one meeting; a completely new Red Army numbered 800,000 men by the end of 1918 and 3 million by 1919; and in December 1917, the new Communist government, the Council of People's Commissars, opened peace negotiations with the Germans at Brest-Litovsk.

It was four years, however, before the survival of Communist control of Russia was assured; and the price paid affected Russian policy for the following twenty years. To win peace from the Germans, the Russian negotiators had to accept one of the harshest peace treaties of modern times. By the Treaty of Brest-Litovsk of March 3, 1918, the Communist government agreed to give up all Russia's territorial gains of the past two hundred years. It recognized the full independence of Finland, Georgia, and the Ukraine. Estonia, Latvia, Lithuania, and Russian Poland were declared independent of Russia, but remained under German military control. Kars, Ardahan, and Batum on the Black Sea were granted to Turkey. By the Treaty of Bucharest of May 1918 the Germans permitted Rumania to take the province of Bessarabia from Russia. Russia thus lost one-quarter of its territory, 62 million of its people, three-quarters of its coal, and half of its industrial plant. Although it renounced the treaty nine months later, the Communist government was able to bring only Georgia and the Ukraine back under its control. When the end of the Civil War in 1923 brought a final stability to its borders, Russia could make its own irredentist claims. The Finnish border lay within forty miles of Petrograd, threatening the security of Russia's largest city; Estonia, Latvia, and Lithuania, which had been Russian for two centuries, now blocked its access to the Baltic, and in the 1930's were governed by anti-Communist regimes; Poland, after intervening in the Civil War against the Bolsheviks, had ended the war in control of a four-hundred-mile-long strip of the Ukraine and White Russia; and Rumania retained its hold on Bessarabia and thus on the mouth of the Danube. Russia's territorial expansion a generation later was to be, in large part, the reversal of its losses of 1918–23.

In spite of opposition within his own government, the losses were not immediately disturbing to Lenin because he saw that the urgent task was to ensure the survival of his regime and because he believed that Communist revolution was imminent in the industrialized states of Europe, notably in Germany. Counterattacks on the Communist regime began in mid-1918 in the Ukraine, the Caucasus, Siberia, and the Baltic states. By 1924, however, the Red Army was triumphant on all fronts. The minority nationalities, like the Ukrainians and the Georgians, had been brought under control; the White armies of former imperial generals like Wrangel and Yudenich had been defeated; and intervention forces of Britain, France, Japan, the United States, Greece, Rumania, and Poland had all been withdrawn. The Civil War, however, was to mark the future policy of Russia. Distrust of its immediate neighbors was to be expected, since the Poles had captured Kiev, the Rumanians had shared in the taking of Odessa, and the Japanese of Vladivostok. The British, French, and Americans had aided the Whites. The Soviet Union would therefore feel free, in 1939, to spurn the alliance of the Western democracies in favor of a profitable deal with Nazi Germany at the expense of Poland.

Communist Failures outside Russia. Even more significant in Lenin's view than Russia's immediate danger was the imminence of continent-wide revolution. Lenin was convinced in 1918 that Central Europe was ripe for proletarian revolution. In Germany, he misjudged the opposition's strength. However, Socialist President Ebert concluded a secret agreement with the army high command for the suppression of Bolshevism and, when the Communists, or Spartacists, attempted to seize Berlin in January 1919, he permitted his minister of the interior to use the independent armed bands of demobilized soldiers to destroy them. By the summer of 1919, the *Freikorps* had savagely suppressed uprisings in many of the major cities of Germany, ending any Communist hope of a violent seizure of power. In Hungary, a Communist regime under Béla Kun, which held power from March to August 1919, was dislodged by an invasion of the Rumanian Army. In northern Italy, where the workers seized control of their factories in 1919, the Communists were never able to gain leadership of the movement that, from lack of determination to seize political power, quickly petered out. Lenin attempted to coordinate the various Communist movements of Europe by forming the Third International, the Comintern, in March 1919. In 1920, he forced Comintern members to adhere to "Twenty-One Conditions," which excluded mere sympathizers and reformers. Following the failure of the spontaneous Communist uprisings, Lenin thus disciplined, under Russian direction, the remaining movements. International communism became a weapon of the Soviet Union.

Stalin's Russia. While communism was proving its inability to seize control of the industrialized states of Europe, power in Russia was falling into the hands of the only Bolshevik leader who had not been in exile for most of his life—Joseph Stalin. Lenin, who had been wounded by an assassin in 1920 and largely incapacitated by a paralytic stroke in 1922, died in 1924. Trotsky, his logical successor and the principal proponent of immediate world revolution, found that Stalin, as secretary-general of the Communist party, was able to edge him out of all positions of importance. First he was ousted from the Council of Commissars, then from the Policy Bureau, then from the party, and finally in 1929 he was driven into exile.

Once in control, Stalin declared that Russia's aim must be to consolidate communism in Russia through a policy of "Socialism in one country." In 1928, he put an end to the New Economic Policy (NEP), Lenin's partial return to the capitalist system, and in the first Five-Year Plan (1928–32), brought about a "second revolution" in the whole economic and political life of Russia. Stalin explained the urgency of the program in 1931 in words that were prophetic: "We are fifty or a hundred years behind the advanced countries. We must make good this distance in ten years. Either we do it or they crush us." Exactly ten years later, 146 German divisions invaded Russia. During those ten years, however, Russia was transformed. Forced industrialization was transferring the center of industry from western Russia to the Ural Mountains and Siberia, beyond the line of Nazi advance. Coal production tripled, and over-all production quadrupled. Russia by 1941 possessed the industrial capacity to fight off an invading army of three million men. Moreover, it presented to the world the impressive picture of a country that had transformed itself from backwardness into a major world power in ten years. Great canals like those linking the White and Baltic seas and the Volga and Moscow rivers, dams like that at Dniepropetrovsk, and huge new industrial complexes like the steel plants at Kuznetsk and Magnitogorsk were visible symbols of what could be achieved without the aid of the capitalist governments. The personal price paid by the Russian people was enormous—the shortage of consumer goods and housing, the long working hours, and the prison camps of up to two million laborers. But the whole vast effort was presented to the Russian people as a temporary struggle in which they were creating the economic bases of a society in which the wealth would be shared equally.

Agriculture, too, was completely transformed by the Five-Year Plans, whose purpose was to wipe out the well-to-do kulak class and change the landowning peasantry into an agricultural equivalent of the industrial proletariat. Stalin ruthlessly overrode the desperate opposition of the peasantry to the collectivization of agriculture, although the peasants fought back by killing their animals, burning their houses, and destroying their machinery. Between 1928 and 1932 the number of horses and cattle in Russia fell by half. Famine hit Russia in 1932–33. Collectivization and famine together killed some five million peasants. Only by 1939 did Russian agriculture attain the level of production of a decade earlier. But by then over 90 per cent of Russian farms were collectivized.

For the Communist party, the industrial and agricultural changes had succeeded in their major objective—the power of the state over its citizens was universal. With the efficient apparatus of the secret police, the OGPU, the party had eliminated political dissenters, within and without the party; suspect groups, like the NEP-men or the kulaks, had been wiped out. And in the 1930's, Stalin embarked on a series of purges of the highest ranks of the Communist party itself. Old-time Bolsheviks like Zinoviev, Kamenev, and Bukharin, as well as top Red Army leaders were tried for treason and executed. By 1940, every member except Stalin of Lenin's original Politburo was dead, as were fifty of the seventy-one members of the Communist Party Central Committee. The Communist party had created a totalitarian state, and that responsive instrument was in the power of Stalin alone.

The completion of Communist control of Russia and of Russian control of the world Communist movement thus ensured that future Russian expansion into Eastern Europe would have a double aim: to extend the territorial boundaries of Russia, at the very least by regaining the territories lost at the Treaty of Brest-Litovsk, and to replace the capitalist societies of Eastern Europe with Communist regimes. Stalin's aims consequently ran counter to those of both Nazi Germany and the Western democracies.

THE RISE OF FASCISM

While Stalin was concentrating on rebuilding the power of the Soviet Union, a more immediate threat to the stability of Europe was caused by the rise of fascism. Probably the major reason for the successes of fascism in the interwar years was unemployment. The seizure of power by Mussolini followed the economic breakdown in Italy in the immediate aftermath of the First World War. The rise of Hitler in Germany and of many lesser dictators in Central Europe was the direct result of the Great Depression of 1929–33. Unemployment in each case had a double effect. First, it pauperized many middle-class people, who should have been the stable element in a democratic society, and it made them the basis of support for extreme right-wing leaders. Second, it caused vast suffering among the industrial working classes, who either supported the right-wing extremists or turned in even greater numbers to socialism and communism, and thus, by holding out the specter of left-wing revolution, increased the commitment of the middle classes to the right-wing elements.

Between 1920 and 1923 the whole of Europe was plunged into an economic recession brought on by a multitude of causes—failure to absorb returning soldiers back into the economy, inflation due to faulty wartime financing, war debts and reparations, shortage of capital for reconstruction, agricultural inefficiency, collapse of faulty new industrial empires created immediately after the war. The economic disaster was at its worst in Germany, owing to the internal disorders caused by the continual skirmishing of the *Freikorps* and left-wing insurrectionists, to the inability of the government to enforce a firm monetary policy, to the creation and collapse of such huge industrial combines, and above all to the French pressure for payment of reparations that culminated in French occupation of the Ruhr in 1923. In November 1923, when the mark stood at 25 billion to the dollar and there were over two million unemployed in Germany, Hitler made his first attempt to seize power, in Munich. Insufficiently known and poorly supported, he failed against the firmness of the Bavarian police. In Italy, however, Benito Mussolini was able to use the economic distress to bring himself to power.

Mussolini's Italy. Mussolini, a blacksmith's son who had trained himself to be an elementary-school teacher, had become a socialist and pacifist agitator. On the outbreak of war in 1914, however, he had suddenly proclaimed his conversion to what became the central theme of fascism, the value of action: "It is necessary to act, to move, to fight, and if necessary, to die." Serving in the army as a private and then corporal until he was demobilized as a result of a wound from a trench mortar, he acquired that kinship with the fighting soldier from which, in 1919, he was able to create a political movement. The ex-soldiers, responding to the magnetism of his oratory and to his chauvinistic nationalism, flocked to his action groups, the *fasci di combattimento.* For the next three years, everything favored the movement. When half a million workers seized their factories in the north in 1919–20, the Fascist strong-arm groups posed before the middle classes as the saviors of society from the Red terror. The Paris Peace Conference was depicted as a national humiliation, since Italy failed to win the territorial compensation it expected for its loss of 700,000 men on the Allied side. And the political parties did their utmost to discredit the democratic process, overthrowing five weak governments in the period 1919–22. By 1922, Mussolini's National Fascist party had mastered the techniques of political terrorism. When on October 27, 1922, Mussolini proclaimed the March on Rome, a wildly improbable threat to seize power, the politicians collapsed. Mussolini was summoned to Rome by King Victor Emmanuel III to become premier.

Within six years, the characteristics of the first Fascist state were formed. It was a one-party state, recognizing the supreme power of the Leader (*Il Duce*). The old political parties, labor unions, the municipal self-government, and civil rights had all disappeared. The secret police and Fascist Militia enforced the will of the Leader. Mussolini, too, had patched together an ideology for his movement, although admitting rather proudly that "fascism was not the nursling of a doctrine worked out beforehand with detailed elaborations." This ideology was, however, to be of extreme importance, since its destruction was to become the proclaimed aim of his opponents in the Second World War. According to Fascist ideology, the nation-state was the supreme good, and the individual was significant only as a member of the state. Within the state, only an elite group could rule, and at the head of the elite there was to be a leader who, since he embodied the state, could not do what was wrong for the state. War alone brought out the best in the human beings who composed the state; and progress was brought about by the struggle of state with state, a struggle in which the higher form of state would triumph. Fascist Italy, Mussolini added, would be a new Rome, "wise, strong, disciplined and imperial." Yet Mussolini's dictatorship was but a poor foretaste of what was to come. Before Hitler took power in Germany in 1933, Mussolini's imperialism consisted of a minor quarrel with Greece, infiltration of Albania, and the acquisition of Juba as a gift from Britain. His vaunted army of one million men was mostly for show; it was badly armed, untrained, and unused. At home, he had come to a settlement with the Pope in the Lateran Agreements of 1929; he also stabilized the currency and began an ambitious, long-term program of economic development.

While Mussolini was establishing firm control in Italy, the prosperity that resulted from the Dawes Plan between 1926 and 1929 was proving unpropitious for the further success of right-wing extremists in Germany. The prosperity of the United States helped increase world trade and made possible its loans of $3.5 billion to Europe, largely to Germany. The great chemical trust I. G. Farben and the steel trust Vereinigte Stahlwerke were impressive examples of modern industrial organization. A new confidence in the stability of national currencies was indicated by the return of most European countries to the gold standard. International tensions were eased by the "spirit of Locarno," when in 1925 Germany, Britain, and France agreed to regard Germany's western borders as finally established. Democracy seemed to be taking root in the Germany of Foreign Minister Stresemann, the Czechoslovakia of President Masaryk, the Austria of Chancellor Seipel.

The Trend to the Right. Nevertheless, even during the period of prosperity the movement to the right continued. In 1923, General Primo de Rivera was installed as premier of Spain by a military coup, and for the next seven years he sought to strengthen his dictatorship. In 1926, in the neighboring state of Portugal that had endured sixteen years of political instability as a republic, the army created a military dictatorship, calling in as minister of finance a Coimbra University professor of economics, Antonio de Oliveira Salazar, who soon became also premier, minister of war, and minister of foreign affairs. Working through the church and the army, Salazar transformed Portugal into a "clerical-fascist state." In 1926 also, an authoritarian government had been set up by the Nationalist Party of Lithuania under President Smetona, and in Poland First World War hero Marshal Pilsudski, wearying of his country's political chaos, used the army to make himself premier. From then on until the outbreak of the Second World War, Poland was governed by a clique of army officers.

The Great Depression of 1929–33 provided the Fascist movements with their greatest opportunity. The Wall Street crash and the American recession that followed brought a drastic curtailment to American lending, led to the recalling of the short-term loans that constituted 40 per cent of the total American credit to Europe, and helped bring about a contraction in world trade that was particularly damaging to the manufacturing countries of Europe. The depression was worsened in 1931 by an international monetary crisis that began when the French withdrew their short-term loans from Austria to pressure the Austrian government into withdrawing its demand for a customs union with Germany. In May 1931, the largest Austrian bank, the Kreditanstalt, which held two-thirds of Austria's assets, was found insolvent. From Austria, the crisis spread to Germany, with a run on gold in the Reichsbank, and the collapse of the great Danat bank. In June 1931 the German stock exchange closed for two months. The mark again collapsed, destroying the savings of the lower middle classes, many of whom were forced to sell their property or personal possessions, often to profiteers who paid in depreciated currency. Farmers were hit by the worldwide fall in prices of agricultural produce. By 1932, there were five and a half million unemployed in Germany.

National Socialism in Germany. Hitler had used the five years of prosperity to prepare for just such a crisis. By 1929, the Nationalist Socialist Workers party, or Nazi party, had 178,000 members, a propaganda machine organized by Josef Goebbels, a terrorist wing in the brown-shirted SA of Ernst Röhm, and an efficient electoral machine that extended not only through Germany but into Austria, the Sudetenland of Czechoslovakia, and Danzig. Hitler did not, however, intend to seize power illegally. In 1932, with the financial support of the

400,000 in Danzig, and 134,000 in Memel. He intended to incorporate into Germany all the territory where these native Germans lived. But Hitler had a further territorial aim, which he had laid down in *Mein Kampf* in 1924 and which British prime ministers like Baldwin and Chamberlain seemed totally unaware of—namely, the acquisition of "room to live" (*Lebensraum*) for the German people at the expense of the Slavic peoples to the east. Restoration of prewar Germany was not Hitler's ultimate aim, although he was able to persuade the gullible that it was. Perhaps the most significant result of Western acquiescence in Hitler's toppling of the Versailles Treaty was to persuade him that there would be similar passivity when he embarked upon his eastward expansion.

THE VACILLATING DEMOCRACIES

Only wholehearted and continual intervention by the three great democracies—the United States, Britain, and France—in the international crises of the 1920's and 1930's could have prevented the tensions created by the First World War and the Peace of Paris from involving the states of Europe in another war. For twenty years the United States refused to commit itself to the responsibilities of world leadership, which its decisive intervention in the First World War and its unchallenged economic strength showed to be both its right and its duty. Britain, debilitated by social conflict, economic backwardness, and myopic leadership, indulged itself in twenty years of dream-hunting. France alone accepted the realities of political leadership, appearing for a decade as the arbiter of the European scene until its illusory hegemony was shattered by the reappearance of German and Russian might and its alliance structure was shattered by the indifference of the United States and Britain.

American Refusal of European Responsibilities. The major responsibility for the failure of the democracies to avert the Second World War lay with the United States. If only because of its preponderant power in a ruined world, the United States was the main hope for a preservation of democracy and peace. In 1919, the population of the United States reached 105 million, compared with 39 million in France, 38 million in Britain, and 59 million in Germany. During the war, the British and French had not only sold investments in the United States of about $4 billion, but they had contracted loans of $4.2 billion and $3.4 billion, respectively. In all, Europe owed the United States $10 billion at the end of the war. The necessity of American involvement in international politics was emphasized by the significance of international trade to the United States. As early as 1904 American exports were greater than those of Britain or Germany, whereas its imports totaled only one-third of Britain's and about two-thirds of Germany's. After both the First and Second World Wars, European countries were to ask themselves whether the major aim of American foreign policy was to safeguard that favorable trade balance.

President Wilson returned from the Paris Peace Conference convinced that, in spite of the Republican majority in the Senate, he had committed the United States to continue its responsibility for the maintenance of a peaceful world order both by making the creation of a League of Nations the first article of the Treaty of Versailles and by signing a Treaty of Assistance with France, guaranteeing it against future German aggression. The Senate refused to ratify both treaties, however, and in 1921 the United States made separate peace treaties with Germany, Austria, and Hungary. The League of Nations, Wilson's prize creation, was doomed to impotence from the start, since it lacked the support of Russia, Germany, and the United States. The Republican administrations of Presidents Harding (1921–23), Coolidge (1923–29), and Hoover (1929–33), in spite of their promises of a return to isolationism, far from severed their ties with the rest of the world. Disarmament conferences, like the Washington Naval Conference of 1921–22 and the London Naval Conference of 1930 were supported; Coolidge's secretary of state, Frank B. Kellogg, joined with French Foreign Minister Briand in proposing the Paris Peace Pact for the renunciation of war as national policy, an innocuous declaration subscribed to by sixty-two nations; and the United States government was the principal influence in introducing the Dawes Plan of 1924 and the Young Plan of 1929 to prevent the reparations burden from destroying the German economy. But these measures were either clearly designed to save American investments and trade, in particular with Germany, or were merely ingenuous statements of good faith. In a world where fascism and communism were gaining strength daily, the power of the United States could be felt only if it were thrown behind the League of Nations or into "entangling alliances" with Britain and France in defense of the small countries of Eastern Europe that President Wilson had done so much to bring into being. Not even President Roosevelt, who succeeded Hoover in 1933, could persuade the American people to accept either of these distasteful policies.

Britain's Debility. The responsibility for the maintenance of the peace settlement of Paris, or at least for ensuring that changes in that settlement would be peaceful, fell upon Britain and France. Britain showed itself incapable of shouldering this burden. Lloyd George had seen to it that Britain and its Dominions enjoyed the spoils by the acquisition of German East Africa, German Southwest Africa, half of German Togoland and the Cameroons, and a share of the German Merchant Marine; and, when the Turkish Empire was divided, Britain had taken control under mandate of the League of Nations of Palestine, Transjordan, and Iraq. But although the Empire was increasing in size, Britain itself was entering a period of chronic economic weakness. The war had cost Britain 700,000 dead, and 1.5 million wounded, as well as a quarter of the overseas investments it had accumulated over the past two centuries. Concentration on war production had brought about the loss of many of its overseas markets, especially to American competition. The obsolescence of many British factories and mines made it increasingly difficult for Britain to compete with American and German production. Poor working conditions embittered the trade unions in their struggle with managers and owners, whom they regarded as totally unresponsive to their needs, with the result that strikes continually increased in number and violence. In 1919 alone an average of 100,000 men were on strike every day, amounting to a loss of 32 million working days. The appalling conditions in the mines provoked the most determined strikes—a month in 1920, three months in 1921, and six months in 1926. At the beginning of the 1926 strike, the miners were joined by the railroad and transport workers in a general strike that lasted nine days. The general strike was a genuine class struggle, in which students and white-collar workers ran the buses, trucks, and railroads to help break the strike, and warships were stationed off the industrial coasts of Wales, Merseyside, and Tyneside. After hundreds of strikers had been jailed, the Trade Union Congress capitulated to the businessman's government of Conservative Stanley Baldwin, which added injury to injury by passing a Trade Disputes Act declaring general strikes illegal in the future. The social antagonisms helped prevent any Conservative government from taking any strong foreign-policy stand that demanded the support of the whole country. But continual unemployment was probably the greatest cause of apathy in international affairs. By 1921, Britain had two million unemployed, 17 per cent of the work force. In the most prosperous conditions of the mid-1920's, the number fell only to one million, and when the Great Depression hit in 1930, it rose to two and a half million. In 1936, when Hitler gambled on Western inaction after he remilitarized the Rhineland, there were still one and a half million unemployed in Britain.

In this period of continual depression none of the political parties showed the dynamic leadership needed. The Liberal party was split and moribund, its great wartime leader Lloyd George unable to deal with the problems of economic reconstruction. The Labour party, which might have profited from working-class misery, lost support by taking office in 1924 and 1929 as a minority government dependent upon Liberal support and thus unable to put through a Socialist program. The coup de grâce to the party's hopes was dealt by its own leader, Ramsay MacDonald, a vapid old egoist, who split his party in 1931 in order to remain prime minister as a Conservative puppet. The Conservative party remained the party, as Lord Keynes wrote, "of the past, vested interests, the Upper Classes, the City, the Army and the Church." Its economics were orthodox: retrenchment, high tariffs, and imperial preference. It was led by businessmen-politicians, like Stanley Baldwin and Neville Chamberlain, who completely failed to understand the mentality of the new rulers of Germany and Italy. As a result, their foreign policy declined into appeasement.

Conservative Foreign Policy. Disarmament, which accorded well with Britain's economic weakness, was a major aim of British foreign policy between the wars. The British government accepted the naval-limitation agreements of the conference of Washington in 1922 and of London in 1930; it took a leading role in the disarmament negotiations in the League of Nations; and Ramsay MacDonald joined with French Premier Edouard Herriot in proposing the Geneva Protocol of 1924, for the "Pacific Settlement of International Disputes." In 1925, Foreign Minister Austen Chamberlain went much further, in signing the Locarno Treaty with Germany and France, by which Britain guaranteed the western frontier of Germany. And in 1928, after its "reservations" had been satisfied, the British government signed the Paris Peace Pact. Unfortunately, the Conservative governments of the 1930's seemed to believe that the same methods of diplomacy could be used in dealing with Fascist states.

A second constant in Conservative foreign policy was distrust of the French alliance system. Considerable relief was felt when the Treaty of Assistance given France in 1919 lapsed through America's nonratification, and an attempt to negotiate a similar treaty in 1921 failed. Britain refused to guarantee Germany's eastern borders at Locarno, and France was compelled to act alone in promising Poland and Czechoslovakia aid should Germany attempt to change their common borders. Not until 1939 did the British government make a definite commitment to defend any Eastern European state.

A third, and what was to prove the most vital, theme was distrust of Communist Russia. In 1918–20, there had been direct interference on the White side in the Civil War, and aid had been supplied to the Poles for their invasion of Russia. After the Labour government of 1924 recognized the Soviet government, signed a trade treaty, and granted a loan, it was badly defeated in an election dominated by the Red scare conjured up by Conservative propaganda. The new government ignored the Soviet trade treaty; and, after two Soviet agencies in London had been ransacked in 1927 in a government search for propaganda and espionage, the Soviet government broke off diplomatic relations. The Second Labour Government restored diplomatic relations in 1929; and in 1934, the Soviet government, influenced by the growing danger of German Nazism and Japanese imperialism, shifted its tactics completely and made overtures of friendship to the democratic powers. The French government welcomed the possibility of Soviet aid against Germany and in 1935 signed the Franco-Soviet mutual assistance treaty. The following year, French Communists, Socialists, and Radical Socialists fought the elections in alliance as a Popular Front. The British, however, continued to remain aloof. Not until 1939 did the British seriously contemplate a military alliance with Russia, and then they were to find that the Germans had forestalled them by persuading the Russians to sign the Nazi-Soviet Non-Aggression Pact of August 1939. There seems little doubt that the leading members of the Conservative party were seriously influenced by the skillful Nazi self-portrayal as the main enemy of Soviet communism. (Nazi Ambassador Ribbentrop was a welcome weekend guest in the country homes of many English aristocrats.) As late as March 1939, Chamberlain rejected a Soviet proposal for a six-power conference on the German situation; he noted in a private letter: "I must confess to the most profound distrust of Russia. I have no belief whatever in her ability to maintain an effective offensive, even if she wanted to. And I distrust her motives. . . ." Thus, adherence to traditional Conservative principles of foreign policy made Baldwin and Chamberlain incapable of dealing with Hitler.

France's Postwar Problems. The defection of the United States and Britain from the role of peace-keepers left to France the onerous burden of preventing new aggression in Europe, particularly from Germany; and France was not even as well equipped as Britain for this task. France had lost 1.3 million killed in the war, and twice as many had been wounded. Its eastern provinces had been devastated by trench warfare. Six hundred thousand buildings had been totally or partly destroyed, including many textile and steel factories, as well as the road, rail, and canal system in the five million ravaged acres; and it took seven years before the destruction was repaired. More significant were the economic and social problems that France, like Britain, inherited from the past century. Unlike the new factories that were set up in the war-devastated areas, the majority of French industry was backward in technology. The small- and medium-sized firm, often owned and managed by one family, kept prices high, avoided the risks involved in expansion, competition, and merger, and induced the few large and progressive companies to indulge in the same philosophy. The industrial federation, the General Confederation of French Production, acted as a drag on French productivity throughout the generation. Conflict with the workers' unions was frequent and, with the growing influence of Communist leadership, was far more violent than in Britain. As early as 1924 the Communist party polled almost a million votes in the elections for the Chamber of Deputies. For twelve years after the war France suffered from a manpower shortage; then, when the Depression hit in 1932, unemployment resulted. By 1936 there were almost a million unemployed. The most glaring economic weakness, however, lay in the currency. Inflation became the ogre it has remained to this day, partly because of inadequate financial methods of the government, inequitable and inefficient taxation, and the costs of the occupation of the Ruhr in 1923–24. When Poincaré, the darling of the well-to-do, stabilized the franc in 1926 at one-fifth its prewar value, the left-wing parties added to their other grievances the belief that financial manipulation by France's "two hundred families," the great banking aristocracy, was responsible for wiping out the savings of the poor and of the lower middle classes (and, incidentally, for erasing most of the national debt at the same time).

The politicians in this last generation of the Third Republic were even more dispiriting than those of Britain. No coherent government policy was ever formulated and put into force because the multitude of large and small parties ensured that every government would be a short-lived coalition. Strong premiers, like Clemenceau or Poincaré, were wanted only for times of crisis; weak premiers, like Painlevé or Sarraut, were overturned for trifles. The left wing was divided, except for the brief experiment of the Popular Front in 1936–38, between the Communists and Socialists; the center between the Radical Socialists and the Socialist Republicans; and the right was a continually varied group of alliances, from independents to outright Fascists. By 1939, there was a universal disgust with the politicians of the Third Republic, which partly accounted for the low morale of the French people when those politicians led them into war again.

France's Four Answers to the German Question. In foreign policy, however, the numerous governments of this generation were able to muster some popular support and pursue a fairly continuous line of policy. The key to the whole of French policy was fear of Germany; and, in meeting the German problem, the French attempted four different solutions. First, under Clemenceau and Poincaré, the French attempted to destroy Germany's capacity for aggression, through territorial annexations and exaction of reparations in the Treaty of Versailles, and through the occupation of the Ruhr when Germany defaulted on its reparations payments. The failure of the Ruhr occupation made the French unwilling later to attempt similar sanctions against Hitler for his infringement of the Versailles Treaty, notably in 1936, when he remilitarized the Rhineland, for it left the majority of French people with a fear that military intervention in Germany was not only ineffective but that it was damaging to the French economy. Consequently, between 1924 and 1932, largely through the diplomacy of perennial Foreign Minister Aristide Briand, the French tried a second method, conciliation, in signing the Locarno Pact, welcoming Germany into the League of Nations, and seeking to bring Germany into a European Federal Union. Unfortunately, the French, like the British, were to attempt to pursue with Hitler this policy of reasonable compromise they had begun with Stresemann. The third, and most significant, of the French methods for meeting the German danger was the construction of an alliance system in Eastern Europe. The aid given to the Poles in their invasion of Russia led to the signing of the Franco-Polish treaty in February 1921 and was followed by treaties of friendship and alliance with Czechoslovakia, Rumania, and Yugoslavia; and the Little Entente of 1921 between Czechoslovakia, Yugoslavia, and Rumania soon received France's blessing. The French did not, however, unconditionally guarantee any of these states against aggression, and in the 1930's the alliance system began to fall apart. The Poles signed a nonaggression pact with Germany on January 26, 1934. Foreign Minister Barthou, who had attempted to revivify the alliances with the Little Entente powers, was assassinated in Marseilles on October 9, 1934, with France's reliable friend, King Alexander of Yugoslavia; his successor, Pierre Laval, was inclined to seek an accommodation with Germany and Italy. Laval hoped in particular to use Mussolini as a curb on Hitler and attempted to win his friendship by granting him a few small strips of French colonial territory in Africa. Results of a sort were seen when the British, French, and Italian governments joined in the so-called Stresa Front in 1935, announcing their disapproval of German rearmament and their intention of maintaining the independence of Austria. By the next year, however, German support of Mussolini's invasion of Ethiopia was bringing the "Axis" alliance into being, and the Popular Front government in France was looking to Russia for support.

France, unlike Britain, had never discounted the importance of Soviet intervention in Europe. The slavish obedience of the French Communist party to the Comintern was a reminder of the power Russia could exert on France's internal affairs—supporting rearmament under the Popular Front, for example, and paralyzing it with strikes after the Munich agreement of 1938. Most frightening was the possibility of a Soviet-German understanding, which began with the commercial Treaty of Rapallo in April 1922, and took a sinister form in the military agreements by which the new Reichswehr was given technical assistance and the use of tank and air force facilities by the Red Army. In the 1930's, however, faced with the growing strength of fascism in Central Europe, Russia and France moved closer together. Foreign Commissar Litvinov posed as a supporter of collective security; and in 1932 he negotiated a nonaggression treaty with France. French Foreign Minister Barthou worked for Russia's admittance to the League of Nations in 1934, and attempted to construct a kind of Eastern Locarno, which would guarantee the security of most East European nations. When Poland refused to join, the Franco-Soviet Pact was signed in May 1935, by which each nation promised the other aid in the case of unprovoked aggression. In July, the French Communists, on instructions from Moscow, concluded the first Popular Front agreement with the Socialists and shortly after extended it to include the bourgeois party of the Radical Socialists. In May 1936, the Socialist leader Léon Blum was made premier as a result of the electoral triumph of this alliance.

It might have seemed, therefore, that in the crucial years of Hitler's first gambles, the friendship of France and Russia could be converted into the necessary deterrent to German ambition. But many factors prevented the conclusion of a strong military agreement between France and Russia. The British Conservative government expressed great distrust of the Franco-Soviet Mutual Assistance Pact of 1935 and was disinclined to make any commitment itself to Soviet Russia. The French right wing, led by Fascist-style movements like the Action Française and the Cagoulards, was using the Communist threat as an excuse for demanding an understanding with Hitler. The French Communist party refused to take office in the Blum government; there was disagreement over the policy to take in the Spanish Civil War; and Communist-led strikes in 1936–37 helped bring Blum down after only a year in power. The Poles were opposed to any understanding with Russia, especially one that would give the Red Army the right to cross Polish territory, as the Russians were to demand in the negotiations of May 1939. Finally, as a result of the great purges of the Red Army leadership, the French government suspected, like the British, that Stalin had gravely weakened the military effectiveness of Russia and thereby made an alliance of dubious value.

The fourth measure, the construction of the Maginot Line of fortifications along the German border, showed the lack of confidence France felt in its other security precautions. The Maginot Line, which cost over half a billion dollars to construct, was intended to defend France along the German border with Alsace-Lorraine. To the north, the French High Command considered, lay the impassable Ardennes hills and the defense positions of Belgium along the Albert Canal anchored on the fortress-city of Liège, which the French would help defend. The tank was regarded only as a support for infantry and not as a mobile striking force. While Hitler's Panzer generals were building up this instrument for rapid exploitation of a sudden breakthrough in static defenses, the French were lulled by the feeling that their defense line and their army of regulars and reserves, which in 1939 numbered five million men, could hold the borders of France inviolate.

French foreign policy, therefore, showed similar weaknesses to that of Britain. Internal pressures of social conflict, and especially weariness of military responsibility, combined with the feeling of the security of France's own defenses to discourage direct intervention against Mussolini or Hitler. The French alliance system of the 1920's was a façade, impressive only during the weakness of Russia and Germany. The rapprochement with the Soviet Union was never developed into a useful military alliance. By 1939, the balance of power had shifted decisively in favor of Germany.

THE ASIATIC CAULDRON

Obsessed with dangers in Europe, the democratic powers seemed only dimly aware that in Asia new forces were arising that would not only contribute to the outbreak of a second world war and to their difficulties in winning it but would remain to plague them for generations after the war was won. In 1919 the victorious powers accepted the birth of seven new nations in Europe but assumed that in the world beyond Europe the era of colonialism could continue. The German and Turkish empires were parceled out among the victors. The only recognition paid to Wilsonian liberalism was the stipulation that these territories be held under mandate of the League of Nations, which thus assumed a weak responsibility for the welfare of the colonial peoples. The comfortable domination of the imperial powers of Europe was, however, to be seriously challenged in the generation between the two world wars by three forces of enormous impact—nationalism, communism, and Japanese imperialism.

The British Colonial Empire. Britain had long recognized the national aspirations of those of its colonies inhabited by Europeans; and, by granting "dominion status," it had given self-government to many of its colonies before the First World War—Canada in 1867, Australia in 1900, New Zealand in 1907, and South Africa in 1909. The total legal independence of these Dominions was formally recognized in the Statute of Westminster of 1931, which defined Britain and the Dominions as "autonomous communities within the British Empire, equal in status, in no way subordinate one to another in any aspect of their domestic or external affairs, though united by a common allegiance to the Crown and freely associated as members of the British Commonwealth of Nations." It was in the subcontinent of India, 1.7 million square miles in area with a population in 1919 of 315 million, that non-European subjects of Britain first made a powerful demand for national independence. The Hindus, who constituted about two-thirds of the population, were led by the Indian National Congress party under Mohandas K. Gandhi, the Mahatma (Holy One), who preached nonviolent opposition to British rule. The Moslems, rather less than one-third of the population but a majority in the provinces of the northwest and northeast, supported the All-India Moslem League under a tough-minded lawyer, Mohammed Ali Jinnah. In spite of the introduction of partial self-government in the India Act of 1919, demands for home rule continued to be pressed with strikes and noncooperation, which were met with force. Worse, however, the rivalry of the Moslem and Hindu populations became more vicious, making more difficult the British task of assuring peaceful transition to the independence both Moslems and Hindus were demanding. When the Second World War began, a new India Act, passed in 1935, had still not come into force as a result of disagreements within India itself. But much had been achieved by the British. Many Indians had received higher education, especially in law and medicine; a large share of Indian administration was carried on by Indians themselves; and much experience had been gained in both provincial and central self-government. Among the leaders of the independence movements, socialism of the Fabian type rather than communism predominated.

The British were also faced with demands for national autonomy in Ceylon and Burma. In Ceylon, the British gave in to nationalist demands of the predominant Buddhist groups and in 1931 greatly enlarged the suffrage and gave important responsibilities to the Ceylonese ministers in the Executive Council. Until the First World War, Burma had been regarded by the British as in many ways a model colony. After the local dynasty was removed from power in 1885, Britain introduced railways, steamboats, and roads; constructed schools and a University; and developed rice into the country's main export. The Burmese, however, resented the economic exploitation of their country, not only by the

British, but by the Indians and the Chinese. Agitation became strong after the First World War; and, as in India and Ceylon, the British responded by associating Burmese in administration. In 1935 Burma was separated from India, with which it had previously been united, and was given considerable powers of self-government. Agitation redoubled, however, and the nationalist leaders, led by Aung San and the future military dictator Ne Win began to look to Japan for aid in their anti-British campaign. When the Japanese armies appeared in Burma in 1942, they were regarded as liberators.

In the other British colonies, there was little unrest. Malaya, prosperous from the British development of tin and rubber and from the activity of the great port of Singapore, had little feeling of nationalism, especially as about two-fifths of its population consisted of Chinese, who thought of China as their permanent home, and one-sixth consisted of Indians, who espoused Indian rather than Malayan nationalism. Communism, however, had made progress among the Chinese population, especially in Singapore; and the Japanese were later to attempt to appeal half-heartedly to the nationalism of the Malays against the Chinese. Malaya was a prize, not a powder keg. In the East Indies, the British colonies of North Borneo, Brunei, and Sarawak were governed paternally, either as personal fiefs or as possessions of a British trading company.

French Indochina. In the rich French colony of Indochina (present-day Vietnam, Laos, and Cambodia), which was brought under French control in the second half of the nineteenth century, demands for independence became strong after 1919. The French had made little effort to foster experience in self-government. French companies dominated the economy, virtually excluding the Indochinese from such activities as banking, insurance, and mining. The mass of the population lived in rural poverty, untouched by the veneer of French culture acquired by a small elite. Among this group of Vietnamese, nationalism and communism united. Nguyen Ai Quoc, better known by his pseudonym of Ho Chi Minh, had gathered a Marxist group among the Indochinese students in Paris in 1917. After ten years of political activity throughout Southeast Asia, he founded the Communist party of Indochina at Hong Kong in 1930. Six years later, his party joined with other left-wing nationalists to form a "Democratic Front," an Indochinese equivalent of the Popular Front then in power in Paris. When the

Japanese danger threatened, the 40,000 Frenchmen in the colony found themselves isolated.

The Dutch East Indies. The Dutch East Indies (present-day Indonesia), consisting principally of the islands of Sumatra, Java, Bali, southern Borneo, the Celebes, the Moluccas, and western New Guinea, throughout the nineteenth century had endured the ruthless exploitation of the so-called culture system, by which the natives had been compelled to produce such goods as sugar and coffee, which the colonial government sold directly in Holland. Even the adoption of the "ethical policy" in 1905, by which the Dutch proposed to increase the colony's self-government and its economic well-being, had little success. Nationalist movements became strong just before and during the war, and the Dutch were compelled to make more concessions in the face of riots on Java and Sumatra. They turned to force to hold down the growing revolts, imprisoning such leaders as Sukarno, and banning the Communist party of the Indies, which had been created by Dutch Communists in 1920. Repression broke the power of the Communists temporarily, but nationalist agitation, especially emphasizing the oppression by the white race, created a situation that the Japanese were to profit from later.

The Philippine Islands under United States Rule. The fourth colonial power in east Asia, the United States, was a relative newcomer, since it had only acquired the Philippine Islands in 1898 at the end of the Spanish-American War. A nationalist movement, opposed to Spanish rule in the 1890's turned against the new occupier, and fought bitterly against a large American army for four years before being finally quelled in 1902. The American occupation brought great economic development to the islands, as a result of American investments, road and railway building, extensive schooling, and medical improvements. The vast landholdings of the Catholic friars had been sold on easy terms to fifty thousand Filipinos. But the promise of independence given in 1916 was shelved when the Republicans took power in 1921, and the efficient regime of the new governor-general, Leonard Wood, did little to soften the nationalist demands. Partly to satisfy those demands, partly under pressure of interest groups in the United States who wished to push the Philippines outside the American tariff wall, Congress passed the Hare-Hawes-Cutting Bill promising independence in ten years, which was rejected by the Philippine legislature. Finally, in 1934, the Tydings-McDuffie Act proved acceptable, and the Commonwealth of the

Philippines was created in 1935, under President Manuel Quezon. The islands were promised their independence in 1946. These acts did not create any great affection for the United States among the majority of Philippine nationalists, some of whom proved willing to collaborate with the Japanese occupation; nor did it weaken the power of the Communist-led Workers' Party of the Philippines, created in 1927 and permitted freedom of activity from 1938. The condition of the poor peasantry was such that during the war the Communists were able to equate national opposition to the Japanese with the overthrow of the moneylenders and absentee landlords.

Although the United States had promised independence to the Philippines, it was still deeply involved in the affairs of east Asia in the interwar years. The building of the Panama Canal, the acquisition of the Hawaiian and Philippine Islands, the vast growth of American imports of such raw materials as rubber, tin, and copper from the colonies of Britain, France, and Holland, had given the United States a great economic and political stake. For the United States, however, as for the other colonial powers, the center of involvement lay in the rising nationalism of China and Japan.

Nationalists and Communists in China. China, in the nineteenth century, had become the prey of the colonial powers and of its immediate neighbors, Japan and Russia. The Manchu dynasty, which had governed China since 1644, was decrepit and incompetent. The form of government, then two thousand years old, was quite unsuited to the age of industrialism. The provinces were uncontrollable; the coasts were dominated by pirates; and the army was rent with mutiny. Britain had led the incursion into China, taking Hong Kong in 1842 and forcing the opening of five Chinese ports to foreign trade. The next year it gained for its citizens the privilege of extra-territoriality, which freed them from the control of Chinese law. By the end of the nineteenth century, British ships were carrying one-third of China's foreign trade, British investments totalled 30 per cent of all foreign investment in China, and more than 1,000 British companies had offices in China. The total British investment in China was over $1.25 billion. The British example had been followed by the French, the Russians, and at the turn of the century the Germans and Japanese. By the time of the First World War, about two-thirds of the country had been divided into "spheres of influence." The Europeans had their own settlements in fourteen cities.

Britain, Russia, Germany, and France had all been granted, or had "leased," important seaports. Collection of the customs was in European hands. And a series of defeats in war at the hands of the European powers had created a widespread hatred of the "barbarians." The greatest shock the Chinese suffered, however, was to be disastrously defeated in 1894–95 by another Asian power—Japan. The Chinese fleet was destroyed, and the Chinese Army was driven from Korea and parts of Manchuria. By the Treaty of Shimonoseki China was forced to recognize the independence of Korea, thus leaving it open to Japanese expansion, and to cede to Japan the Liaotung Peninsula, Formosa, and the Pescadores. Under pressure from the Western powers, however, Japan was forced to give up her claim to Liaotung—a peninsula of enormous strategic importance that opened the way to Manchuria and covered the sea approaches to Peking from the ports of Dairen and Port Arthur.

So great was China's humiliation that it appeared for some time after its defeat that it might be partitioned by the European powers. In 1899, however, Secretary of State John Hay laid down the "Open Door policy," demanding for the citizens of the United States the same privileges as those of other nations; and the next year he declared that it was the policy of the United States "to preserve Chinese territorial and administrative integrity." America's commitment to China grew throughout the twentieth century, with the result that it came to appear to Japan the principal obstacle to its expansion in Asia. The Chinese themselves were determined to end their humiliations. One reaction to Western influence was seen in the Boxer Rebellion of 1899–1900, when foreigners throughout the country were slaughtered and the foreign legations in Peking were besieged for four months until relieved by an army from Britain, France, Germany, Russia, Japan, and the United States. But many Chinese also felt that their country should learn from Western civilization. Under the last two Manchu emperors a few feeble reform attempts were made, particularly in education and the introduction of the machinery of representative government. In 1911, anti-imperial insurrections broke out in Wuchang. A professional revolutionary, Sun Yat-sen, was chosen Provisional President of the Chinese Republic and was inaugurated in Nanking on January 1, 1912. Sun was from a poor peasant family in south China. His brother had put him through school in Hawaii. He later studied Western medicine in Hong Kong and Canton, but forsook medicine to devote himself to bringing about the revolution he believed to be the only way to rid China of the Manchus and to remodel its whole society. His aim seemed to be achieved when the last Manchu emperor abdicated in February 1912.

The infant Republic was soon in trouble, however. To bring unity to the country, Sun gave up the presidency to an imperial general, Yuan Shih K'ai, who for four years attempted to rule as a dictator (1912–16). After Yuan's death, the provincial warlords ruled without reference to the central government, and China was plunged in chaos. The parliament, dominated by the Kuomintang, or Nationalist party, of Sun Yat-sen, broke with the president and set up a rival government in Canton in 1917, which Sun himself headed from 1921–25. The reunification of the country was finally carried out by the armies of the Kuomintang under Sun's most forceful disciple, Chiang Kai-shek, whose armies began a triumphant drive north in 1926, one year after the death of Sun. By the spring of 1927, however, when most of the Yangtze valley had been taken, the forces of the Kuomintang were beginning to split apart. Sun, though above all a nationalist and indeed an admirer of the West, had turned to Lenin's Russia for aid when, at the Paris Peace Conference, the Western powers had refused to give up their concessions in China. From 1923 on, Russian advisers were reshaping the Kuomintang, organizing its propaganda, and on Sun's death portraying him as the image of a Chinese Lenin. The tiny Chinese Communist party, founded in 1921, increased rapidly in size, and, as the Kuomintang Army advanced, was able to gain control of vast areas taken by the northern prong of the drive. Chiang himself, however, under great pressure from the bankers who were financing his armies and personally increasingly distrustful of his Communist allies, began to remove Communists from prominent positions. After taking Shanghai in April 1927, he destroyed the Communists there. He then set up a government in Nanking, while the Communists set up a rival one in Hankow, which was broken within a few months. The Russian advisers fled, and when Chiang entered Peking in June 1928 he was an open enemy of the Communists. In 1929, he broke diplomatic relations with Russia.

The years of Chiang's "extermination campaigns" against the Communists were of major importance for the development of Asian communism. Chiang, from his remodeled capital at Nanking, was attempting to westernize his country through railroads, schools, and industrialization, and was satisfying Chinese nationalism by slowly throwing off the privileges of the Western powers. The Communists, freed of the compromises of the earlier Popular Front with the Kuomintang, were preaching class war to the Chinese peasantry in the huge areas of central China, centered on Kiangsi, which they controlled until they were finally driven out in 1934. The new leader of the "Chinese Soviet Republic," Mao Tse-tung, born into a peasant family and a librarian-turned-revolutionary, then led his followers on the famous "long march," a six-thousand-mile–one-year-long trek through frightful mountain country, to establish a new center in Yenan, beyond the reach of Chiang's armies. Only twenty thousand out of ninety thousand survived the journey, but these survivors created a virtually autonomous Communist state, from which the Communist conquest of China was eventually to come. A general agreement between Chiang and the Chinese Communist party was reached in February 1937, however, in face of the Japanese invasion of China. The Chinese Soviet government and the Chinese Red Army were abolished, and Mao declared that the Communists had accepted the doctrines of Sun Yat-sen. With their slogan "Chinese do not fight Chinese," the Communists appeared to be calling for national unity in face of foreign attack. They had ended the civil war on their own terms, and forced the unwilling Kuomintang to face the invader. Communist popularity was enormously strengthened. But it was still difficult to predict whether the war with Japan would strengthen the Communists or the Kuomintang. Both were hopeful.

Japanese Expansion before 1939. While China was thus engaging in a painful and disruptive process of modernization that was changing every aspect of its life—political, economic, social, religious, and cultural—the Japanese had succeeded in adopting Western technology without changing the character of their society or their culture. In 1853, the famous expedition of the American Commodore Perry put an end to the almost total isolation that the Tokugawa Shoguns, or military governors, had enforced for two and a half centuries. The arrival of Europeans and Americans brought lasting changes to Japan. Observing this impressive display of Western naval force, the Japanese concluded that the only way to meet the threat of the foreigner was to learn from him the advanced military techniques, both naval and military, that were enabling him so easily to enforce his will in Asia. Secondly, the knightly class of samurai and the feudal lords of the western region, adopting the slogan

"Honor the Emperor—Expel the Barbarian," used the excuse of the foreign incursion to overthrow the Shogunate in 1867 and to proclaim the absolute emperor as the force that would modernize Japan.

The reign of the new Emperor Mutsuhito, better known as the Meiji emperor, 1868–1912, saw the transformation of Japan carried out from the top. Feudalism was abolished in 1871. The army was reorganized with the help of German advisers, conscription was begun, and the samurai code of honor, *bushido,* was inculcated in the officer class. British naval officers aided in the creation of a modern navy. A new legal system was based upon the French. A constitution was granted by the divine emperor in 1889, which set up a parliament of two houses but made the government responsible to the emperor, whose sanction was required for passage of all laws. Vast impetus was given to economic development, by building of railroads, creation of an enormous merchant marine, founding of banks, and aid to a group of outstanding commercial families known as the *Zaibatsu*. Population grew at a steady rate, almost doubling between 1870 and 1930. To Japanese leaders, particularly in the military, it became increasingly urgent for Japan to seek outlets for her population, and the raw materials needed for her industry, such as coal, rubber, iron ore, and tin, by expansion on the Asian continent. Thus, economic needs provided a pretext for military expansion at the very time when Japan was acquiring the arsenal that would enable it to expand.

The nearby Pacific islands were first annexed—Hokkaido, the Kuriles, the Bonin group, which included Iwo Jima, and the Ryukyus with the strategic outpost of Okinawa. After the quick defeat of China in 1894–95, Formosa was taken; and following the almost equally easy victory over Russia in 1904–5, Japan took over the Russian leases on the Chinese ports of Port Arthur and Dairen and the Russian railroad property in south Manchuria, and annexed south Sakhalin. By one of history's ironies, President Theodore Roosevelt presided over Japan's discomfiture of Russia at the peace conference in Portsmouth, New Hampshire; forty years later, President Roosevelt was to agree at the Yalta Conference to the reversal of that treaty in return for Stalin's promise to aid in the invasion of Japan!

The south Manchurian commercial holdings were organized as the South Manchuria Railway Company, with an administrative body called the Government-General of Kwantung, which disposed of its own section of the Japanese Army, called the Kwantung Army. This was to be the driving force in future Japanese expansion into China. In Korea, whose independence had been recognized by China in 1895, the Japanese had strengthened their political controls; and in 1910, they annexed the peninsula outright. Entering the First World War on the Allied side, they devoted their efforts to seizing the German holdings in the Chinese province of Shantung, and the German territory in the Pacific—the Marianas (except Guam), the Caroline and Marshall Islands, all of which the Japanese were granted by the Treaty of Versailles.

For the next twenty years the principal rein on Japanese expansion was to be American interference. When Japan sent troops into eastern Siberia in ostensible support of the Whites in the Russian Civil War, President Wilson sent American troops as well, to keep watch on the Japanese. Under strong American pressure at the Washington Naval Disarmament Conference, 1921–22, the Japanese agreed to give up the former German holdings they had taken in Shantung, to pull out of eastern Siberia, and to give up northern Sakhalin to the Russians. They even accepted the limitation of the size of their navy to three-fifths that of the United States and of Britain, and the prohibition of fortification of their Pacific islands. Relations were made worse in 1924 when Congress finally cut off all immigration from Japan, thus giving great offense to a people deeply sensitive to affronts inflicted on it by Occidental races.

The growing strength of nationalism in China, evidenced in the disappearing privileges of the Western powers and in the Kuomintang's military successes, perturbed the Japanese military with the belief that China might soon be strong enough to repel further Japanese incursions. The impetus to renewed aggression came from the Japanese forces in Manchuria, the Kwantung Army. On September 18, 1931, following an explosion on the tracks of the Japanese-owned South Manchuria Railway, which was alleged to have been set off by Chinese, the Kwantung Army occupied the whole of Manchuria without serious opposition from the Chinese armies. China appealed to the League of Nations, which took no action against Japan. American Secretary of State Stimson, however, promised American cooperation if the League acted and announced the Stimson Doctrine—that the American government would not recognize any situation in Japan's relations with China brought about by force, or violating the integrity of China or the Open Door policy. When the Japanese set up the former Manchu emperor of China as the puppet emperor of Manchuria, now called Manchukuo, the United States refused to recognize the new state, and its example was universally followed. Japan's reaction was to withdraw from the League of Nations and to expand into Inner Mongolia and north China. In an armistice in 1933, the Japanese agreed to pull back their troops from north China on condition that the Chinese maintain that area demilitarized.

For the next five years, militarism gained force in Japan. The effects of world depression hit the Japanese export trade and caused vast unemployment. The need of "living space" for a population expanding at over 700,000 a year became a popular theme. The unemployed and the pauperized, as in Germany and Italy, looked to right-wing extremists for their salvation and sought to blame the business aristocracy and the politicians for their misfortunes. The army increasingly reflected the ideals of the "Young Officer Group," extremists in sympathy with many of the ideals of European fascism. The ultra-patriots, particularly among the military, indulged in a series of assassinations of leading civilian politicians, professors, and newspaper editors suspected of liberalism or even of moderation. The worst incident was an attempt by a group of army officers at the head of 1,400 soldiers to seize the state on February 26, 1936. Before they were put down they had murdered several of the country's most respected statesmen and had held the main government buildings in Tokyo for several days. Among the military rose a demand for a "Showa Restoration," with which the emperor, restored to power by the military, would put an end to parliament, drive the Western powers out of Asia, and create an Asian "co-prosperity sphere" dominated by Japan.

Serious preparation for this goal was undertaken in both Japan and Manchukuo. The military budget was increased to 50 per cent of the national revenue. Further expenditure was financed by forced loans. Manchukuo was forcibly and uneconomically industrialized to provide the war materials demanded by the military. A propaganda campaign was begun to whip up chauvinism at home, while harsh censorship prevented the expression of opposition. In this mood of aggressive nationalism, the Japanese used the excuse of a skirmish between Japanese and Chinese troops at the Marco Polo Bridge outside Peking to embark upon an attempt to subjugate the whole of China. In bloody fighting, the

Chinese armies were driven back from the major cities—Peking, Nanking, Shanghai, Hankow, and Canton. Chiang Kai-shek retreated progressively westward, taking with him as much industrial equipment as could be transferred, and accompanied by large numbers of officials, businessmen, professors, and students. The Nationalist capital was finally established at Chungking; and there Chiang waited for the world war that would eventually bring about Japan's defeat. The Chinese Communists, however, profiting, as Mao Tse-tung had planned, from the Japanese sweep of the Kuomintang from the major part of China, settled into guerrilla warfare behind the Japanese lines, establishing themselves in large parts of the country as the sole surviving Chinese administration. The Japanese, meanwhile, attempted to stabilize their rule by setting up a puppet government in Nanking in March 1940.

In November 1936, Japan joined with Germany and Italy in signing the Anti-Comintern Pact. Yet its enemies were not the Russians but the democratic powers, Britain, France, the Netherlands and the United States, whose colonies in east Asia it eventually proposed to annex. The West European powers, involved as they were with the problems of German and Italian expansion, were not willing to take action on behalf of China in 1937, even though they joined the other members of the League of Nations in condemning Japanese aggression. The attitude of the United States, which for the last half century had been to support the integrity of China, was crucial. While the Japanese armies were committing outrages against all white foreigners in China, as well as against the Chinese, and had even machine-gunned American shipping and sunk and American gunboat, the "Panay," in the Yangtze River, President Roosevelt was unable to bring the American people to feel the need for armed intervention. His "quarantine speech" in October 1937, clearly aimed at the Japanese as well as the European Fascists, had been a flop; and the American government settled the "Panay" dispute by accepting indemnification and apologies. The only direct action taken by the American government was to renounce the treaty of commerce with Japan on July 26, 1939 as a preparatory step to cancelling the supply of strategic materials, and to suggest to airplane manufacturers a voluntary embargo on supply of planes to Japan. It seemed in 1939 as though the Japanese advance in China and American opposition to Japanese advances had both been stalemated. The outbreak of war in Europe was to renew Japan's opportunity for aggression.

Thus, in the interwar years, nationalism in varying forms had affected almost every part of Asia. In every country it had been expressed in opposition to the domination, colonial or otherwise, of the Western powers. Communism, too, had taken root more or less strongly in almost every country of Asia, profiting on the one hand from the national opposition to the Western powers and on the other from the misery of the rural proletariat and their hatred for the rich of their own nationality. Japanese expansion complicated the whole picture, through its attempt to substitute domination by an Asian power for colonial domination. The nationalists of those countries occupied by, or even merely threatened by, Japan, would find themselves faced with important choices. First, should they ally with the Japanese invader in order to throw off the domination of the colonial powers? At one extreme would be the Burmese, who welcomed the Japanese; at the other would be the Filipinos, who took to the mountains to expel them. Second, should they ally with their native Communist party to overthrow the aggressor, or should they wage a dual war against both native Communists and Japanese invaders? In every country except China the Nationalists allied with the Communists.

APPEASEMENT AND WAR

In 1933, the holocaust that Europeans had feared or desired since the guns had fallen silent in 1918 seemed again to be imminent; and the region where the *casus belli* would be found was Eastern Europe.

Hitler's First Goals. As chancellor of Germany, Hitler at once began to prepare the economic and military arsenal that would enable him to achieve the goals of his foreign policy. As he had repeated so often in his speeches and in *Mein Kampf,* he wanted the overthrow of the Treaty of Versailles, the incorporation in a Greater Germany of all people of German blood, and the acquisition of living space for the German race in Eastern Europe. All three aims were directed at that quarreling band of states that stretched between Russia and Germany from the Baltic to the Mediterranean. The abolition of the Treaty of Versailles implied the return to Germany of Danzig and the Polish Corridor, as well as an end to the ban on the union of Austria with Germany. Greater Germany was to include the Lithuanian port of Memel and the Sudetenland of Czechoslovakia. Living space for this German people was to be found in Poland, Lithuania, and Russia. The natural allies of Hitler in this drive to the east were the states of southeastern Europe, whose rulers were turning to fascism, either of a military, clerical, or monarchical type, in face of growing discontent among a miserable and increasingly revolutionary peasantry and proletariat—above all, Horthy's Hungary, Carol's Rumania, and Boris' Bulgaria.

The situation in Eastern Europe was complicated by the Soviet government's dual aims: the irredentist desire to recover the lost lands of Imperial Russia—Bessarabia from Rumania; parts of White Russia and the Ukraine from Poland; and independent Finland, Estonia, Latvia, and Lithuania—and the ideological drive to establish communism in Russia's border states and, even better, in the industrialized countries of Western Europe. In Eastern Europe, Russia's natural allies were those lower classes that could be won over from smallholder parties or from socialism to communism; it was in Bulgaria, Yugoslavia, Hungary, and Poland that the greatest progress was made.

The key areas in the defense of Eastern Europe were Poland and Czechoslovakia. As the richest states of the central tier they were the most tempting prizes; they were also the most strongly armed, Czechoslovakia with thirty-five divisions and Poland with forty. The ultimate test of the Western democracies' determination to halt Hitler's aggressions and, as it turned out, of their ability to halt Soviet communism, lay in the defense of Poland and Czechoslovakia.

Hitler's early goals were, however, less ambitious. For five years, the only attempt to bring any part of Eastern Europe under Nazi administration was an abortive coup by the Austrian Nazis in 1934, which Hitler rapidly disavowed. Instead, he played the role of reliable friend in the dual struggle of the Eastern European countries against economic recession and Soviet communism. On January 26, 1934, he signed a ten-year non-aggression pact with Poland, with which he made great propaganda capital in his play upon the Western desire for peace. Fascist influence inside Poland was strengthened, as was Poland's hostility to Russia; and Poland helped itself to Teschen when Hitler began the dismantling of Czechoslovakia in October 1938. Hitler next turned to the Balkan states. After the murder of King Alexander in 1934, German influence increased greatly in Yugoslavia, aided by grant of a favorable trade treaty and by the appointment in 1935 of German sympathizer Milan Stojadinović as premier. Similar trade treaties were concluded with Rumania and Bulgaria, by which Germany took the agricultural surplus of these countries at high prices in return for the supply of manufactured goods, and often of armaments. Only Czechoslovakia held out firmly against Hitler's blandishments, ignoring hints that a treaty similar to that with Poland might be concluded. Instead, Czechoslovakia relied on its alliance with France and on a new treaty of mutual assistance signed with Russia in 1935. It thereby made itself one of the first objectives of Nazi expansion.

While Eastern Europe was being linked in this way with Germany, Hitler began, step by step, to test the willingness of the democratic powers to take action against him. Showing extraordinary understanding of the longing for peace in Britain and France, two countries he had never visited, and of the advances that had been made there and in the United States by "revisionism"—the belief that the Treaty of Versailles had been an unjust and dangerous settlement that needed revising—he accompanied each infringement of the Versailles Treaty with the assurance that he was merely remedying injustice. In October 1933 he withdrew Germany from the League of Nations and from the Disarmament Conference on the grounds that Germany was the only country that had shown its willingness to disarm. When the Saar plebiscite of January 1935 had given a 90 per cent vote for the return of that territory to Germany, he assured the French that no quarrel remained between them. Two months later he used the occasion of the increase in French conscription to announce that Germany was reintroducing conscription and creating a peacetime army of 550,000 men.

This was Hitler's first direct infringement of the Treaty of Versailles; but he already had good reason to believe that no action would be taken against him. When the Japanese occupied the Chinese province of Manchuria in 1931, China appealed to the League of Nations, which condemned Japanese action. Japan thereupon withdrew from the League. No sanctions were imposed. The League's powers were thus shown to be mere moral recommendations, of little value when opposed by resolute force; and the League, the first instrument of the democratic powers in restraint of aggression, was seen to be worthless. The second instrument, the French alliance system in Eastern Europe, had already been weakened by Hitler's diplomatic advance, and the fear that the West could not be trusted in a conflict with Germany had already been planted by the French government's rejection of Marshal Pilsudki's two proposals, made in 1933, for common preventive action against Hitler. The third instrument, collective action by Britain, France, and perhaps the United States, seemed to Hitler improbable. He had already been able to create in the minds of the British and French governments the attitude that culminated in the Munich Conference. Even in 1935 the British and French were asking Hitler what concessions he required from them for the maintenance of peace. Although German rearmament was condemned by the British, French, and Italian governments at Stresa in April and by the Council of the League of Nations, the British immediately afterward concluded a naval pact with Germany, allowing Germany to begin naval rearmament up to 35 per cent of British strength and even, in the case of submarines, to equal British strength. The agreement, concluded without consultation, was regarded as a betrayal by the French. The British replied by criticizing France's attempt at finding its own safeguard in the Franco-Soviet treaty.

Italian Conquest of Ethiopia. The British and French were therefore divided when their partner in the Stresa Front, Mussolini, began to make preparations for an invasion of the independent African state of Ethiopia. Until 1935, Mussolini's imperialism had been largely verbal, even though he had declared prophetically in 1927 that "between 1935 and 1940 will come the tragic moment in Europe's history, and we can let our voice be heard." In 1896, Italy had been badly defeated in a first attempt to conquer Ethiopia. With tanks and poison gas, Mussolini now determined to reverse that defeat. War began in October 1935. Eight months later Ethiopia was in Italian hands. This open and successful aggression had several baleful consequences. The League of Nations, led by Britain and France, condemned Italy and, for the first time, voted for the application of economic sanctions; but since the embargo on Italy did not include oil, on the grounds that the private American companies would have supplied Italy's needs, nor the closing of the Suez Canal, the sanctions did not paralyze Italian war efforts. Their failure was the final blow to the League of Nations. The invasion of Ethiopia also transformed Mussolini's relations with Hitler because it destroyed the Stresa Front, showed Mussolini that in an aggressive foreign policy only Nazi Germany would support him, and thereby ended his role as the supporter of the independence of Austria.

Remilitarization of the Rhineland. Two months before the Italian Army entered Addis Ababa, Hitler had profited from the embroilment of the British and French in the Ethiopian affair to destroy another clause of the Treaty of Versailles. On March 7, 1936, he had moved into the demilitarized area of the Rhineland token forces of one division, three battalions of which were stationed on the French border at Aachen, Trier, and Saarbrücken. On March 9, the Polish government offered military support to France, in the intervention it assumed the French would mount. Together, the French and Poles could have mustered ninety divisions. It was little wonder that Hitler admitted that "the forty-eight hours after the march into the Rhineland were the most nerve-wracking of my life," for his generals had informed him that the German forces had no chance of standing against the power of France. At this last point when Hitler might have been stopped without a general war, all the weaknesses of the democratic powers came into play. In France, the Fascist sympathizers and the Communists were in unison in denouncing a resort to force. The military leaders persuaded the cabinet that the army was unprepared for any limited campaign but only for general mobilization. The indecisive Premier Sarraut and his foreign minister, Flandin, decided not to act without British support. Stanley Baldwin's government, convinced, according to Neville Chamberlain, that "public opinion would not support us in sanctions of any kind," urged caution. *The Times* of London, whose editor was a prime advocate of appeasement, declared that "it is the moment, not to despair, but to rebuild." The British people as a whole regarded the episode, in a favorite phrase, as no more than the Germans "going into their own back-garden." In the United States, congressional investigations had just turned up startling evidence of the profits made by armaments manufacturers during the First World War, giving a great boost to both isolationism and antiwar sentiment. In 1935, 1936, and 1937 Congress enacted neutrality legislation, prohibiting the sale of arms to both sides whenever the President recognized a state of war in any area, banning Americans from traveling on the ships of belligerents, and preventing the grant of a government loan to belligerents. Events in Europe encouraged rather than diminished American fear of involvement.

With the successful remilitarization of the Rhineland, Hitler was ready to move against Eastern Europe. His attacks on the Versailles Treaty were no longer directed at the inequality it had imposed on Germany, but at the separation of German blood from the German Reich. Austria was his first objective. Mussolini's remaining opposition to the union of Germany and Austria was overcome by a skillful campaign of flattery, Hitler describing him as the "leading statesman in the world, to whom none may even remotely compare himself." In November 1937, Italy joined the Anti-Comintern Pact that Hitler had concluded a year earlier with Japan. And in the same month Mussolini announced that Italy no longer intended to safeguard Austrian independence, since its ambitions were now in the Mediterranean and the colonies. More significant, however, in weakening Italy's ability to defend Austrian independence, Mussolini had become deeply embroiled in the Spanish Civil War, another conflict that was to prove of inestimable value to Hitler in preventing the formation of a united front against him.

Spanish Civil War. Civil war began in Spain on July 17, 1936, with an army revolt in Spanish Morocco under the leadership of General Francisco Franco. The revolt spread quickly throughout the south and west of Spain and was intended to overthrow the government of the infant Spanish Republic. This Republic had been founded in 1931, a year after King Alfonso XIII had dismissed the military dictator Primo de Rivera; and, under moderate liberal leadership, it had begun a slow program of reforms, notably by granting autonomy to Catalonia and the Basque provinces of the northeast and by imposing controls over the army. After three years of reactionary conservative government, 1933–36, a Popular Front coalition of moderate Republicans, Socialists, Communists, and Anarchists won a slight majority in the elections of February 1936, a victory that provided the excuse for revolutionary groups among the industrial workers and peasantry to indulge in wild excesses against the church and the propertied classes. In this chaos, Franco's Nationalist forces posed as the defenders of religion, property, and the army. The Republican forces stood for social reform of many kinds, from the moderate liberalism of the right-wing Republicans to the revolutionary syndicalism of the Anarchists. At first both sides seemed equally matched. The Nationalists held the rural south and west, but included most of the trained military forces. The Republicans held the industrial triangle between Madrid, Valencia, and Barcelona, and the Basque provinces in the northern mountains; their armies consisted largely of armed workers.

What transformed the character of the war was the intervention on ideological grounds of the German, Italian, and Russian governments. Mussolini was involved before the war was ten days old, with the dispatch of twelve airplanes to Franco; by 1937 he was exhausting Italy to provide 70,000 troops and vast quantities of military equipment and aircraft. Hitler dispatched only the Condor Air Legion, technical supplies, and experts who used the war to try out Germany's new inventions and techniques. For Hitler, a long war in Spain would prevent Britain and France from seeking a rapprochement with Italy, distract them from his ambitions in Eastern Europe, and further their internal dissensions. Stalin's intervention on behalf of the Republicans undoubtedly served Hitler admirably. Large-scale Russian aid in the form of military equipment, supplies, and technical experts reached Spain from October 1936 on. From November, the International Brigades, recruited from foreign Communist refugees in Russia and other volunteers from Europe and America, joined in the defense of Madrid. This military aid was followed by the ruthless seizure of control of the Republican administration by Spanish, and even in places by Russian, Communists. By 1938, the Communists were powerful throughout the Republican-held area of Spain; they had cynically and brutally wiped out the Catalan Trotskyite and Anarchist leaders; political commissars had indoctrinated the whole Republican Army, particularly the International Brigades; and sections of the Russian secret police, the NKVD, were operating independently in purging opposition. In November 1938, however, realizing that Nationalist victory was imminent, Stalin suddenly put an end to Soviet intervention, withdrew the International Brigades, and ended the dispatch of military equipment. Three months later Barcelona fell, followed in March 1939 by the fall of Madrid and the flight of thousands of Republican refugees into France. Franco at once established a semi-Fascist regime.

The Popular Front government of Léon Blum was put in a particularly difficult position by Franco's attack on the Popular Front government in Spain. To the amazement of most Frenchmen, Blum proclaimed a policy of nonintervention, forbidding even the sale of armaments to the Republican government. He had bowed to pressure from the right in France, and to the persuasion of the British government, which feared a conflict with Italy. The Non-Intervention Committee established in September 1936 was joined by twenty-seven European states, including the blatantly interventionist Italy, Germany, and Russia. Only the Conservative government of Britain observed strict nonintervention, with the result that many Republican sympathizers in Britain became convinced that it secretly hoped for the victory of the Nationalists. This distrust became more pronounced when the Conservatives made over- tures to Mussolini that culminated in the signing of the "Gentleman's Agreement" of January 1937, in which both countries agreed to respect the status quo in the Mediterranean, and the Anglo-Italian Agreement of April 1938 by which Neville Chamberlain agreed to seek international recognition of Italian annexation of Ethiopia in return for the phased withdrawal of Italian forces from Spain at the end of hostilities.

Absorption of Austria. While the Spanish War was distracting all the major powers, Hitler turned to completion of his plans for Austria. Although Austria had been controlled by a "clerical-fascist" government since 1932, both Chancellors Dollfuss and Schuschnigg had opposed union with Nazi Germany and had attempted to suppress the Austrian Nazi party, while the semi-autonomous city of Vienna with its large Jewish and Socialist population was even more bitterly opposed to a Nazi takeover. With the loss of Mussolini's protection in 1936, the Austrian government agreed to give cabinet posts to the Nazi sympa- thizers known as the National Opposition, in return for a Nazi promise of nonintervention. In 1938, however, in a blustering interview with Schuschnigg in his mountain retreat at Berchtesgaden, Hitler demanded that Nazi sympathizers be given three of the most important ministries in the Austrian government and that the ban on the Nazi party be lifted. On returning to Vienna, Schuschnigg attempted to destroy Hitler's claim that most Austrians wanted union with Germany by holding a plebiscite on Austrian independence. In reply, Hitler ordered the German Army to invade Austria on March 11, Schuschnigg was replaced as chancellor by a Nazi nominee, Seyss-Inquart, and Hitler entered Vienna in triumph on March 14. The plebiscite, held by the Nazis on April 10, gave a 99.75 per cent majority in Austria in favor of union with Germany. Yet an- other clause of Versailles had thus been destroyed.

The Betrayal of Czechoslovakia. Once again, Britain and France accepted this move with apparent equanimity. France was in a cabinet crisis and had no government. Chamberlain told Parliament that "nothing could have arrested what actually has happened—unless this country and other countries had been prepared to use force." When Stalin approached Britain and France on March 18 with a proposal for a conference on their collective security against German aggression, Chamberlain rejected it on the grounds that such a grouping would "be inimical to the prospects of European peace." He had completely swallowed Hitler's assertions that his only aim was to bring into the German Reich those of German blood; and six months before Hitler moved against Czechoslovakia, Chamberlain and the appeasers in Britain were already prepared to satisfy his demands for the Sudetenland, with its more than three million German-speaking people. The government of Radical Edouard Daladier was also dominated by the appeasers, notably Foreign Minister Georges Bonnet, and was willing to follow Chamberlain's lead. Together, the British and French governments put pressure on the government of President Beneš to accept the demands of Hitler and of the Nazi Sudeten German party. Chamberlain himself twice flew to see Hitler in September, to be told finally that the Czechs must evacuate the Sudetenland by October 1, a demand that the British government as well as the Czech government declared to be unacceptable. The threat of war was averted, however, by the intervention of Mussolini, whose proposal for a conference was immediately accepted by the German, British, and French governments. Meeting at Munich the next day, September 29, Daladier and Chamberlain accepted Hitler's demands with only a few face-saving changes and returned home to be feted as the saviors of the peace. German troops occupied the Sudetenland on October 1; the Poles were ceded Teschen on October 10; and the Hungarians took a strip of Slovakia on November 2.

The peaceful acquisition of the Sudetenland was one of Hitler's greatest triumphs. He had been informed by his generals that they opposed the invasion of Czechoslovakia because the fortification on the western border, the Westwall, was still weak and because the German Army could only deploy twelve divisions against France's sixty-five. He was unaware that a group of generals led by General Ludwig Beck were preparing a conspiracy to seize him by force upon the outbreak of war. The Czech Army of one million men was well trained and equipped; it was supplied by the Skoda armaments works, the second largest in Europe; and it had in the fortified mountain bastion of the Sudetenland an ideal defensive position. Of all the states in Eastern Europe, it was the only surviving and prosperous democracy, and thus it was apparently the state most likely to be chosen by Britain as the place where fascism must be stopped. Chamberlain, however, aghast, as he told the British people in a radio broadcast, that "we should be digging trenches and trying on gas-masks here because of a quarrel in a far-away country between people of whom we know nothing," gave in to, or encouraged, the forces of appeasement in both Britain and France.

The dismemberment of Czechoslovakia quickly followed. In March 1939, the German army invaded the main body of Czechoslovakia—the provinces of Bohemia and Moravia—after terrifying the Czech government into ordering its army not to resist, and made these provinces into a German protectorate. Slovakia was recognized as an independent state, whose government, however, requested that it also be made a German protectorate. Sub-Carpathian Ruthenia, the easternmost tip of the country that had strong national ties with the Ukrainian population of Russia, after one day of independence, was annexed by Hungary. The next month, Mussolini followed Hitler's example by annexing Albania. Only now, with the acquisition for the first time of an area that was clearly non-German, did Chamberlain realize that Hitler's ambitions were limitless. On March 31, 1939, he told Parliament that the British and French governments would come to the aid of Poland "in the event of any action which clearly threatened Polish independence and which the Polish government accordingly considered it vital to resist with their national forces." And this guarantee was followed two weeks later by similar pledges to Rumania and Greece.

The only hope that remained for the democratic powers to avoid war, or at least to win an early victory, was to spend the next months in the creation of the Grand Alliance, which Winston Churchill had long called for. Again, the obvious ally was the United States. But antiwar sentiment in America was stronger than ever. A resolution to change the constitution to make a nationwide referendum necessary for the declaration of war was barely defeated in the House of Representatives in 1938; Roosevelt's speech of October 5, 1937, in which he had called for a "quarantine" on the "epidemic of world lawlessness" had been bitterly denounced throughout the country; and his request in 1939 for a revision of the Neutrality Acts to enable him to help the victims of aggression was denied. His only direct attempt to restrain the aggressors was his demand on April 14, 1939, that Hitler and Mussolini declare that they would respect the independence of thirty countries, which he named—a request that Hitler used to keep the German Reichstag rocking with laughter. Much more serious, in Hitler's view, was the chance that the Western powers would make common cause with Russia.

Nazi-Soviet Non-Aggression Pact and the Invasion of Poland. By

March 1939, however, Stalin had probably lost faith in the value of an alliance with Britain and France. His offer to come to the aid of Czechoslovakia in September 1938 had been turned down. The Munich Conference, to which he had not been invited, frightened him as creating a possible nucleus for an anti-Soviet alliance, or at the very least as guaranteeing the neutrality of the West in the event of a German attack on Russia. On March 10, 1939, Stalin told the Eighteenth Party Congress that the West need not expect Russia to get embroiled with Germany in a "new imperialist war." On May 3, he replaced Foreign Commissar Litvinov, the proponent of collective security, by Molotov; and for the next six months, he negotiated concurrently with Britain, France, and Germany. In these negotiations for a military alliance against Germany, the British and French showed more than usual obtuseness. Low-level delegations were sent, rather than foreign ministers. Their distaste for such contacts with a Communist regime was made obvious, as were their doubts about the value of the newly purged Red Army. Their hands were tied by the refusal of the Polish government, which feared the Russians almost more than the Germans, to allow the passage of Soviet troops through Poland. It became clear in August that Stalin was negotiating to see whether the Western powers or Germany would give him a free hand in Eastern Europe, especially in the Baltic states and eastern Poland. On August 23, 1939, Hitler gave him that assurance, and in the early hours of August 24 the two governments signed the Nazi-Soviet Non-Aggression Pact. By its published clauses, the two countries entered into a ten-year non-aggression agreement. By the Secret Additional Protocol, Eastern Europe was divided into spheres of influence, that of Russia including Finland, Estonia, and Latvia. Poland was to be partitioned between them. Germany was to disinterest itself in the fate of Bessarabia.

The attack on Poland was scheduled for dawn on September 1. Even the increasing evidence that Britain intended at last to oppose him with force did not deter Hitler, who was convinced that a quick victory in Poland would persuade the Western powers to make an early peace themselves. A Polish attack on a German radio station just over the border was faked. An army of a million and three quarters swept into Poland before war had been declared. On the evening of September 1, both the British and French ambassadors warned Hitler that their countries would come to the aid of Poland unless hostilities were immediately suspended. An angry debate in the House of Commons on September 2 warned Chamberlain that he risked being thrown out of office unless he declared war. At 9 A.M. on the morning of September 3, British Ambassador Nevile Henderson informed the German Foreign Office that unless Britain was satisfied that the German attack on Poland were ended by 11 A.M., a state of war would exist between their two countries. The same afternoon, the French also declared war. The British and French thus went to war ill-prepared, without the aid of Russia or the United States, in defense of the military despotism of Poland, a state notorious for its oppression of racial minorities, for its social and economic injustices, and for its recent participation in the dismemberment of Czechoslovakia. It was, Winston Churchill wrote later, a decision "taken at the worst possible moment and on the least satisfactory ground, which must surely lead to the slaughter of tens of millions of people." It was better only, he concluded, than a decision "to fight when there is no hope of victory, because it is better to perish than live as slaves."

Chapter Two   # THE TRIUMPHS OF THE AXIS, 1939-1942

FOR three years after the attack on Poland, the advance of Nazi Germany and of its allies in aggression, Italy and Japan, continued almost unhindered. By the end of 1942, Germany and Italy controlled almost the whole of Europe from the Pyrenees to the Volga and from the Arctic to the Mediterranean, while Japan was in possession of half of China, most of Southeast Asia, and most of the islands of the western Pacific Ocean. The initial campaigns, in which Britain and France had fought solely for the independence of Poland, were transformed into a world war by the continuing aggressions of the Axis powers—Hitler's invasion of Western Europe, the Balkans, and Russia; Mussolini's attack on Greece; and the Japanese attack on the United States at Pearl Harbor, followed by its invasion of the British and Dutch colonies of Southeast Asia. The Grand Alliance that was to defeat the Axis powers was thus created, not by any skillful diplomacy on the part of Britain, Hitler's only remaining opponent in June 1940, but by the aggression of June 22, 1941, when Hitler invaded Russia, and of December 7, 1941, when the Japanese bombed Pearl Harbor. The entry of the United States into the war, while of enormous importance militarily, did not affect the ideological basis of the British and French entry into the war—namely, the commitment of democratic powers to curb aggression. But the entry of Communist Russia transformed the nature of the conflict. Russia intended to use the war for the advance of communism in Eastern Europe, in that very area where Britain and France had ostensibly fought for the preservation of democracy. For the last two and a half years of the war, therefore, Britain and the United States were faced by a second ideological challenge—that of their Communist ally. They were to prove far less capable of meeting this challenge than that of fascism.

52

THE OPENING CAMPAIGNS
IN EASTERN EUROPE

The Invasion of Poland. When the German Army invaded Austria in March 1938, Hitler was outraged to find that a large proportion of the armored vehicles and troop transports had broken down on the road to Vienna. By contrast, the Polish campaign was a model of the new blitzkrieg tactics. Using 1,500 planes, the German Air Force destroyed Polish communications by bombing roads, railroads, and bridges. Crowds of refugees along the highways were strafed. The Polish Air Force was incapacitated by the destruction of its airfields, and its planes were destroyed before they could leave the ground. Against deep thrusts by nine fast tank divisions, the Poles could raise only one tank brigade and twelve brigades on horseback. Forty-nine German divisions of motorized infantry followed. Cracow fell on September 6, and the capital, Warsaw, fell after a heroic defense on September 27. The original pincer movement on Warsaw closed on the demoralized Polish divisions caught between the two army groups of Generals von Bock and von Rundstedt; between September 9 and 17, a second pincer movement struck one hundred miles farther east on the remaining Polish forces. A few isolated groups of Polish troops held out vainly for a few more days. The Polish government managed to get across the border into Rumania. Poland collapsed before a single detachment of British or French troops reached the country they had entered the war to defend.

The Russian government, which had been temporizing on the invitation by the German foreign minister to see if "it did not consider it desirable for Russian forces to move at the proper time against Polish forces in the Russian sphere of interest and for their part to occupy this territory," now suddenly decided to act. On September 17, on the pretext that the Polish state had disintegrated and that Russian intervention was necessary for the safety of the Ukrainian and White Russian population of eastern Poland, the Red Army entered Poland, meeting no resistance from the Polish Army. On September 18, they met the German Army at Brest-Litovsk. Stalin then demanded, and received on September 29, a revision of the Secret Additional Protocol of August 24, by which Lithuania was to be considered within the Russian sphere of influence, and the two exclusively Polish provinces of Lublin and eastern Warsaw within the German sphere. Stalin thereby strengthened his claim to be incorporating only people of Russian stock in the Soviet Union, especially as the new boundary line followed very closely that proposed to the Allies by British Foreign Minister Curzon in 1920. Germany retained control of the exclusively Polish region, an area less than half that of prewar Poland inhabited by 22 million people. Western Poland was annexed directly to Germany. The rump, one quarter the area of prewar Poland, was made into a protectorate on the pattern of Bohemia-Moravia, called a Government-General, and placed under Gauleiter Hans Frank, but under the direct supervision of SS chief Himmler. The desperation of Polish resistance to the Nazi invasion was soon to be justified by the horrors of Nazi occupation.

The Phony War. Following the defeat of Poland, Hitler ordered the attack on France to begin two weeks later, on November 12, a move his generals regarded as suicidal, in view of their estimate of French military strength. Bad weather, the generals' procrastination, and the accidental betrayal of the entire invasion plan when a German plane made a forced landing in Belgium, brought a postponement of the westward attack until the following spring, however, and to the surprise of the British and the French, no attack came by land or by air (although there was intermittent submarine warfare) during the strange six months of what came to be called the "phony war." The French Army, which at the outbreak of war had numbered one million men, was now increased to five million by calling up the reservists. Of all this vast army, there were, however, only four armored divisions, which, though equipped with excellent tanks, were untrained in the techniques necessary to meet the deep infiltration of the German Panzer divisions. Unfortunately, too, the Belgian King Leopold had determined in 1937 that Belgium should revert to its traditional policy of neutrality, thereby preventing any coordination of military planning with Britain and France in defense of northeastern France, to which the Maginot Line had not been extended. It also precluded the possibility of a Franco-British thrust through Belgium at the industrial heart of Germany in the Ruhr. The British Expeditionary Force, which numbered ten divisions by March 1940, was sent to strengthen the Franco-Belgian border. The major British activity was on the sea, however, where the German Navy succeeded in sinking half a million tons of Allied shipping by the end of 1939. In reply, the British introduced the convoy system, began a blockade of the German coast and of German ships in neutral ports, and succeeded in forcing Germany's pocket battleship, the "Graf Spee," to flee to Montevideo where it was scuttled.

The Russo-Finnish War. The Russians displayed their distrust of their Nazi ally by establishing their influence over the Baltic republics. On September 28, 1939, Estonia signed a mutual assistance treaty, giving Russia the right to use key bases in Estonia. Similar treaties with Latvia and Lithuania were signed in October. Soviet land, sea, and air forces took over the principal military installations. Leningrad thus seemed to be protected against a German advance from the south. The Soviet government then demanded a rectification of the Russo-Finnish borders, by which Finland would cede the section of Karelia near Leningrad, which included the fortifications of the Mannerheim Line, and would lease the port of Petsamo on the Arctic and the naval base of Hangö on the Gulf of Finland. The Finns, although advised by Germany to give in and refused aid by Sweden, mobilized on November 13. On November 30, the Russians invaded Finland and bombed Helsinki. Upon the appeal of Finland, the League of Nations expelled Russia, thereby ensuring that the League itself would not survive the world war. Finland, however, fought alone, and, to the amazement of the world, succeeded in holding the Russian attack in the deep snow of central Finland and along the Mannerheim Line, which was not breached until February 1940. By then the British and French were congratulating themselves for not having overestimated the value of a Russian military alliance in 1939, while Hitler and the German generals had concluded that an invasion of Russia would be far easier than had been anticipated. Before British and French volunteers could be sent to the aid of the Finns—a step that might have prolonged the Finnish war uselessly and embroiled the French and British in a war with Russia—the Finns accepted the Russian armistice terms on March 12. Finland ceded the Karelian Isthmus, including the port of Viipuri, several islands in the Gulf of Finland, and strips of territory to the north and west of Lake Ladoga, in central Finland, and near Petsamo. Hangö was leased for thirty years, giving Russia a vital base controlling the entrance to the Gulf of Finland. But Russia withdrew its support from a puppet Communist government it had created under Otto Kuusinen, which it would undoubtedly have placed in control of Finland had its initial expectations been realized. Three months later Stalin ordered the military occupation of Estonia, Latvia, and Lithuania, which were all incorporated into the Soviet Union as constituent republics in July. In June, on receipt of a Soviet ultimatum and with German persuasion, Rumania ceded Bessarabia and northern Bukovina to Russia. By July, 1940, therefore, Stalin had garnered all the promised gains of the Nazi-Soviet Non-Aggression Pact. Except for Finland, the promised "sphere of influence" had been annexed to the Soviet Union. Stalin would henceforth refer to this new boundary as Russia's "prewar" frontier, beyond which Russia had no territorial ambitions. The only additional territory in Europe that Russia annexed in 1945 was part of East Prussia and Sub-Carpathian Ruthenia, an insignificant area in comparison with its gains in 1939–40.

German Invasion of Denmark and Norway. The Finnish war had emphasized the significance of the northern Norwegian port of Narvik and of the railroad that linked it to the iron-ore mines of Sweden. To forestall British occupation of Norway as a method of sealing the Baltic and closing Germany's ore supply route through neutral Norwegian waters, Hitler ordered the "Weser Exercise," the occupation of Denmark and Norway, which began on April 9. The Danes offered almost no resistance. The king and cabinet ordered fighting to stop within a few hours and were permitted to remain in office under a German "protectorate." The Norwegians, who the Germans hoped would rally to a native Nazi, Vidkun Quisling, resisted. King Haakon VII and his government fled, with the gold reserves, first to the northern mountains and then to England. But within six weeks the Norwegian forces, even bolstered by a Franco-British expeditionary force in Narvik, were defeated. Norway, like Denmark, was placed under German "protection," with a façade of self-government under a Norwegian Administrative Council and then under Quisling, but was in fact governed directly by a Reich commissioner for Norway. In a model operation, the Germans had gained control over the entrance to the Baltic, the whole North Sea coast of Europe, and over the ore supply routes. Two more neutral countries had been overrun. Neither Denmark nor Norway was to forget this lesson in the postwar world.

VICTORY IN THE WEST

German Invasion Strategy. With Norway and Denmark prostrate, Hitler turned again to the often-postponed plan for his attack on the Western democracies. To enter France, the German Army had the choice of three principal routes: through Alsace-Lorraine and down the river Marne to Paris, the choice of Bismarck in 1870, an opening now blocked by the Maginot Line; across the North European Plain, through neutral Holland and Belgium, with the main wing of the attack hugging the Channel coast until it could swing south on Paris up the Seine River, the choice of the German General Staff's Schlieffen Plan in 1914; or up the Moselle Valley, across neutral Luxembourg and through the wooded Ardennes Hills of Belgium to Sedan, and thence down the Somme River to the Channel coast, a route never previously tried and now considered impassable for tanks. The British and French expected the Germans to attack across the Belgian Plain and massed their main forces between the Channel and Valenciennes along the Belgian border so that they could advance quickly to the aid of Belgium if the Germans infringed its neutrality. Hitler's original intention in the fall of 1939 had been to attack in precisely that way; but, adopting as his own a plan suggested by General Erich von Manstein for an assault through the Ardennes, Hitler ordered a pincer attack, with one wing attacking from Aachen along the expected invasion route to Brussels and the sea, but with the main body of the armored divisions emerging unexpectedly from the Ardennes to break the French line and to trap the British and Belgian and a good portion of the French Army on the Channel coast as the pincers closed. This plan was at first strongly opposed by most of the German High Command, who considered that, in judging whether tanks could pass through the Ardennes, their technical knowledge was better than Hitler's famed "intuition." The astounding success of the plan, which convinced Hitler of his own superiority as a military strategist over the accumulated wisdom of the German officer corps, was to have fatal consequences later.

The Defeat of the Low Countries. The invasion began with simultaneous attacks on the Netherlands, Belgium, and Luxembourg on May 10, 1940. The Netherlands, which had been neutral since 1815, had only been included in the invasion plans when the German Air Force insisted on its need for Dutch airfields for the coming attack on England; and a small force was assigned for its conquest. Airborne troops quickly seized the important bridges that opened the route to Rotterdam and The Hague; but after four days of fighting Rotterdam was still holding firm. On May 14, to break Dutch resistance by terror, Hitler and Goering ordered the destruction of the center of Rotterdam

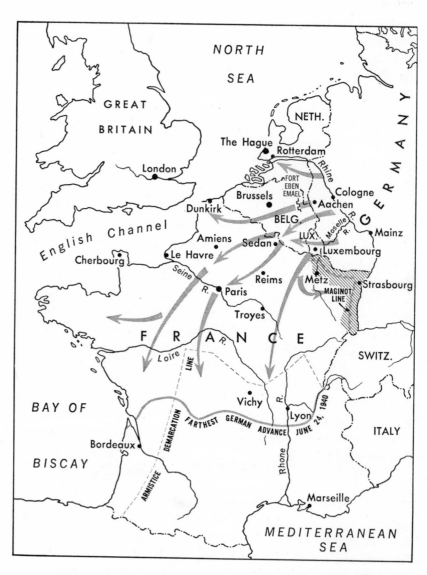

GERMAN VICTORIES IN THE WEST, 1940

by dive bombers. That evening the Dutch royal family and government fled to England, and the next morning the Dutch Army capitulated. Resistance had lasted five days.

Meanwhile, a stronger force entered Belgium from Aachen. Parachute troops captured the important bridges near Maastricht, and eighty German soldiers in gliders, equipped with a new explosive and flame throwers, captured the greatest fortification in Europe, Fort Eben Emael, by landing on its roof. General von Bock then pushed on toward Brussels. The British and French, who assumed that this was the main German attack, rushed forward and established a strong defensive line with the Belgian Army between Antwerp and Namur along the Dyle River. They thus walked into the trap that had been planned for them. On May 14 seven Panzer divisions appeared from the Ardennes Mountains, established bridgeheads across the Meuse between Dinant and Sedan, broke the French line at Sedan, and fanned out behind the Allied lines. General Heinz Guderian's two tank divisions then swung north toward the Channel to close the trap on the nine British, twenty-two Belgian, and ten French divisions facing von Bock's army group. The armored columns, then seven divisions strong, reached the Channel at the mouth of the Somme River on May 20, thus completing the encirclement.

That evening Hitler began work on the armistice terms, for the annihilation of the principal forces opposing him seemed certain. The trapped Allied forces might still have broken out, had there not been a change of command on May 19. It took General Maxime Weygand, the new commander-in-chief, three days to decide what to do, and by then it was too late to strike south. The only hope for the trapped armies was to evacuate by sea. By May 24, the one port left to them was Dunkirk; and there, and on the surrounding beaches and sand dunes, half a million French and British troops awaited rescue. To their amazement, on that day the Germans halted at the Aa Canal only twenty miles from Dunkirk and did not attempt to advance again until the evening of May 26. The order to pause, which Hitler had given because he was saving the armor for the attack on the French armies defending Paris and because he believed the German Air Force and von Bock's group could wipe out the trapped divisions, was a disastrous error. The two-day delay gave the British and French time to construct defensive positions behind which the troops could be evacuated by the amazing armada of tugs, pleasure cruisers, sailboats, and navy ships that was rushing to and fro across the Channel, loaded to the gunwales with Britain's only trained soldiers. Of this motley fleet, a third was sunk. But by June 4, when Dunkirk finally fell, 338,226 British and French soldiers had been transferred to England. Forty thousand French troops, who had fought to the end to keep the evacuation going, fell into German hands. The nucleus of the British Army had been saved, however; and the British fighter planes, the Spitfire and the Hurricane, had proved that they were superior to anything the Germans possessed. Dunkirk had been a British air victory.

Belgium, in whose defense the troops at Dunkirk had been trapped, capitulated before Dunkirk fell. On May 28, King Leopold III, against the unanimous advice of his government, had agreed to unconditional surrender, and as commander-in-chief, had ordered the Belgian armies to lay down their arms. Like the Danish king, he determined to remain through the German occupation; but his government fled into exile, and Premier Pierlot told the Belgian people by radio broadcast that Leopold had forfeited his right to rule. Leopold's action, taken without consultation with the British and French, permitted the German forces along the Belgian channel coast to sweep south toward Dunkirk. Belgium had held out for eighteen days.

The Fall of France. When the Germans resumed their attack on the main body of the French Army on June 5, the morning after Dunkirk's surrender, they had already won the battle of France. Against their 143 divisions, the French could raise only 65 and the British 2. The French Air Force was already powerless, and the British refused to transfer any important section of the Royal Air Force to France with Britain itself gravely threatened. The French premier, Paul Reynaud, who had replaced Daladier in March 1940, was unable to stir either the country or his own cabinet to a major effort. The Communist party denounced the war against Moscow's new ally, Germany; the party was banned, its press closed down, and its leaders arrested. The working classes in general found that the war was being used to end collective bargaining and strikes, to freeze wages, to destroy the power of the unions, and to suppress civil liberties. At the other political extreme, many right-wing leaders were demanding an accommodation with Hitler. Even among members of the government parties, there were pacifists, like the Socialist Paul Faure or appeasers, like the Radical Bonnet, or, most damaging of all, defeatists, like the First World War hero Marshal Philippe Pétain, who was serving in Reynaud's cabinet as vice-premier. Reynaud himself, though brave and determined, lacked the strength needed to reverse the almost universal lack of will to struggle that the French people was beginning to display.

Two weeks after Dunkirk the French campaign was over. Nowhere did the French succeed in holding back the German onslaught. Paris, undefended and abandoned by the government, was taken on June 14. On June 16, Reynaud resigned and Marshal Pétain became premier, with the avowed intention of seeking an immediate armistice. All thought of carrying on the struggle from a redoubt in Britanny or from Algeria was dropped. On June 18, Pétain called for a cease-fire. On June 21, the armistice terms were presented by Hitler and his military leaders to a French delegation in the railroad car in the forest of Compiègne where a German delegation had received from Marshal Foch the armistice terms of November 11, 1918. Hitler completed the parallel by sitting in Foch's chair! The terms, as accepted the next day, were surprisingly lenient. France was to be divided—the Germans would occupy the north and east, with the whole Channel and Atlantic coast; south and central France, including the whole Mediterranean coast, and the French Empire would be unoccupied and independent, ruled by the legal French government. The French fleet, which the British had begged the French to send to British ports, was to be demobilized and disarmed in its home ports. Hitler thus ensured that there would be no government-in-exile carrying on the struggle from the French colonies and that the French Navy should not be added to the already superior British Navy. But it is also possible that he believed that what he considered leniency would persuade the British to make peace, thereby making it unnecessary for him to destroy the British Empire, an institution he considered of value to the world. Mussolini, who had not entered the war until June 10, 1940 and had been ignominiously held back along the French borders, was permitted to seize only a few small patches of French territory and to insist upon creation of a fifty-mile demilitarized zone along the French border and on the Tunisian-Libyan border.

For Hitler, the defeat of France and Britain was still only a necessary prelude to satisfaction of his ambitions in the East. Yet the defeat of France was by far his greatest military triumph yet. The French had mobilized five million men. With the British, they had approximately the same number of tanks as the Germans, including many of better quality. They had 500 first-line planes. Security from attack over a long portion of their frontier, if not the whole length, was assured by the Maginot Line. They were not defeated because their soldiers refused to fight— 100,000 were killed in the six-week war—but because they were unable to meet the new form of attack of the Nazi blitzkrieg. When Guderian's armored columns broke through the line of the French Second Army at Sedan, they were not immediately counterattacked because the French had dispersed their armor throughout the front in support of the infantry and because, as Churchill was appalled to discover, the French had kept no strategic reserves at all. Thus, lack of technical preparation, failure to understand the nature of the coming war (and indeed even to learn when it was demonstrated in Poland), had weakened the French far more than internal divisions, economic weakness, or lack of political leadership. Where Britain was to be saved by radar and the fighter plane, France might have been saved by the armored divisions recommended to it in the 1920's by its own General d'Estienne and in the 1930's by Colonel Charles de Gaulle.

THE BATTLE OF BRITAIN

Before July 1940, Hitler had given no serious thought to the method by which England could be invaded. He assumed that after the defeat of France England would make peace, since his only demand was that it leave him a free hand on the Continent. Hitler reasoned, according to his chief of staff, Halder: "If we smash England militarily, the British Empire will disintegrate. Germany, however, would not profit from this. With German blood we would achieve something from which only Japan, America and others will profit." He waited for a month for Britain to take up the peace feelers that were reaching it from the Pope, the king of Sweden, and various American sources, and he remained incredulous and uncertain when no response came. Only on July 16, 1940, in "Directive No. 16 on the Preparation of a Landing Operation against England," did he declare: "Since England, despite her militarily hopeless situation, still shows no sign of willingness to come to terms, I have decided to prepare a landing operation against England, and if necessary to carry it out." The assault was to be called OPERATION SEA LION.

Winston Churchill. For the British people, the situation was by no means as hopeless as it seemed. The British Navy was in command of the Channel, a narrow but notoriously treacherous body of water, which made not only crossing but the amassing of an invasion fleet difficult. The British Air Force was technically superior not only to the slow Stuka dive bombers but even to the finest German fighters; and by their radar network the British were able to follow the flight of any German planes and direct the Spitfires and Hurricanes to them exactly. And even on land, the British had raised an army of sixteen divisions of fighting caliber, four of them armored, by the expected invasion date of mid-September. Best of all, in Winston Churchill the British had found one of the greatest war leaders of all their history. Churchill, a direct descendant of the Duke of Marlborough, was born in Blenheim Palace, which had been given to the Duke after his great victories over the armies of Louis XIV at the head of one of the earliest grand alliances that Britain had put together. His father, Randolph Churchill, was a Conservative leader who had ruined his own career by an ill-timed protest resignation; his mother was Jennie Jerome, an American. After Harrow and the Royal Military College at Sandhurst, he had managed to see, and often take part in, almost every military action around the globe—the Cuban rebellion of 1895, the uprising on the Northwest frontier of India in 1897, the great charge of Omdurman in the Sudan in 1898, and the Boer War in 1899–1900. On his return from Boer captivity, he entered Parliament as a Conservative, became a Liberal four years later, and by 1908 was a member of Lloyd George's cabinet. In 1911, at the age of thirty-six, he was appointed first lord of the admiralty, and he remained in charge of Britain's naval operations until the failure of the Gallipoli expedition in 1915, which he had supported as a sure method of breaking the deadlock on the Western front. In the 1930's, the Conservative party, to which he had returned in 1924, found him an unwelcome critic of British appeasement and military unpreparedness, and a realistic proponent of the need of a Soviet alliance against Hitler. Only in September 1939 did Chamberlain admit Churchill to the cabinet, in his old position of first lord of the admiralty; but his ascendancy was such that when Chamberlain was finally driven from power after the defeat of Norway, Churchill was his natural replacement not only in the eyes of the Conservatives but of the Labour and Liberal parties, which agreed to enter a national government only on condition that it be headed by Churchill.

The new government took office on May 10, the day of the German attack on the West; and one of Churchill's first duties was to announce, on June 4, the evacuation from Dunkirk. He used the occasion not only to bolster Britain's resolve but to remind the United States of its responsibilities in this struggle:

> Even though large tracts of Europe and many old and famous States have fallen or may fall into the grip of the Gestapo and all the odious apparatus of Nazi rule, we shall not flag or fail. We shall go on to the end, we shall fight in France, we shall fight in the seas and oceans, we shall fight with growing confidence and growing strength in the air, we shall defend our island, whatever the cost may be, we shall fight on the beaches, we shall fight on the landing-grounds, we shall fight in the fields and in the streets, we shall fight in the hills; we shall never surrender, and even if, which I do not for a moment believe, this island or a large part of it were subjugated and starving, then our Empire beyond the seas, armed and guarded by the British fleet, would carry on the struggle, until, in God's good time, the New World, with all its power and might, steps forth to the rescue and the liberation of the Old.

Air War over Britain. By the end of July the German Navy was convinced that the invasion of England should be postponed until 1941, and was particularly concerned at the army's demand that the invasion front stretch along a full two hundred miles of the English south coast. It was decided, however, that the key to a successful invasion was the destruction of the Royal Air Force by Goering's *Luftwaffe.* The invasion of Britain was to take place on September 15 if, in Hitler's opinion, the first eight to fifteen days of the air offensive proved to be successful.

In August the *Luftwaffe* had in France and the Low Countries 929 fighters, 875 bombers, and 316 Stuka dive bombers. Against them the British had 700–800 fighters and only 1,434 pilots, on whom the defense of Britain rested. On August 15, Goering launched OPERATION EAGLE. A fleet of 100 bombers and 34 fighters sent from Norway against the northeast of England, which Goering expected to find undefended, was driven back with heavy losses. Four consecutive attacks, each of 200 planes, were sent against the south coast, and two managed to get through as far as Croydon, on the edge of London, where they bombed aircraft factories and airfields. But the Germans lost 76 planes to only 34 fighters of the RAF. It was necessary, Goering concluded, to destroy the British radar stations and their underground intelligence centers; for the German pilots, as one of them later explained, "realized that RAF fighter formations must be controlled from the ground by some new procedure, because we heard commands skilfully and accurately directing Spitfires and Hurricanes on to German formations. We had no radio fighter control at the time . . . and no way of knowing what the British were doing with their forces as each battle progressed." Through September 6, Goering sent over 1,000 planes almost every day, inflicting heavy damage on the British fighters by protecting bombers with three or four times as many fighters and on the radar-sector stations by bombing. The situation for Britain was desperate by the beginning of September. Only 1,023 fighter pilots and only 704 planes remained, even though 465 new planes had been manufactured during August alone. But the strength of the British Army had increased so greatly during August that the Germans were compelled to increase the scale of, and thus render almost unachievable, their invasion plans.

At the beginning of September, however, Hitler decided that the air attacks on Britain should be directed against the large cities, and especially at London, both to retaliate for the bombing of Berlin, which had begun on August 24, and to destroy the British will to resist. At the same time, the concentration of the invasion fleet in the Channel ports off Britain began; and on September 3, Hitler fixed a tentative date of September 21 for the beginning of the invasion. On the afternoon of September 7, 372 German bombers and 642 fighters struck at London in two successive waves. The second wave got through, setting aflame large sections of the London dockland and housing along the Thames River; a third wave of bombers, attacking after dark, used the flames of London as a beacon. Similar attacks were mounted every night for the next week, with such apparent success that on September 15 the *Luftwaffe* again attacked by day. That battle, in which the RAF broke up the successive waves as they approached, 800 strong, proved that the fighter and radar protection of Britain was still intact, and the Germans were compelled to return to night bombing. Two days later, Hitler decided to postpone the invasion of Britain indefinitely; the dispersion of the invasion fleet began. It was announced formally on October 12: "The Führer has decided that from now on until spring, preparations for 'Sea Lion' shall be continued solely for the purpose of maintaining political and military pressure on England. Should the invasion be reconsidered in the spring or early summer of 1941, orders for a renewal of operational readiness will be issued later."

Nevertheless, the air attacks on Britain's cities continued throughout October and November. Two hundred bombers attacked London every night, using delayed-action bombs that had to be found and rendered harmless and incendiary bombs that spread destruction through vast areas of homes. The British adjusted themselves with remarkable cheer to the nightly ritual of the air-raid shelter, the scream of the air-raid siren, the red glare of the night sky lit up by burning cities, and the sorrow of so many civilians killed—30,000 in London alone. From London, the blows spread to the great industrial cities of the north— Liverpool, Manchester, Birmingham, Sheffield; and, on the night of November 14–15, the heart of Coventry was wiped out. After November, however, the German attacks began to lessen, although there was a last major blow in the incendiary raid on London on the night of December 29, which left many of the capital's finest monuments, among them eight Wren churches and the Guildhall, in ruins. But Britain was no longer Hitler's principal target. Already he had turned toward the east.

THE CONQUEST OF THE BALKANS

For Hitler, the defeat of the Western powers had always been a preliminary to the invasion of Russia. On November 23, 1939, he had told his generals that "we can oppose Russia only when we are free in the West," for it was a two-front war that he feared most. In September 1940, he had taken the same decision about the invasion of England as Napoleon in 1805—that undefeated England, though inaccessible, could not attack him—and that therefore he was free to lunge eastward. As early as July 31, 1940, Hitler announced to his generals that he intended to defeat Britain by first defeating Russia. "If Russia is smashed, Britain's last hope will be shattered. . . . In view of these considerations Russia must be liquidated. Spring, 1941. The sooner Russia is smashed, the better." The General Staff at once went to work on the detailed invasion plans, while the Operations Staff was given the job of

Aufbau Ost (Buildup East) to transfer large numbers of German divisions into Poland without rousing Russian suspicions. Hitler approved the General Staff's plan in December, and on December 18, 1940, he issued Directive No. 21, OPERATION BARBAROSSA, in which he ordered that preparations for the invasion of Russia should be completed by May 15, 1941.

Mediterranean Strategy. Meanwhile, however, Admiral Erich Raeder, commander of the German Navy, was attempting to persuade him to make the Mediterranean the scene of the next major German offensive. Raeder could see that Britain's economic and strategic interests were vitally involved in the area of the eastern Mediterranean, Suez, and the Red Sea route to the Mid Eastern oil fields and to India, while Germany and Italy could be directly threatened by British, and possibly American, seizure of Northwest Africa, following landings in the Atlantic island groups of the Cape Verde, the Azores, Madeira, and the Canaries. In September 1940, Raeder attempted to persuade Hitler to enter military alliances with Spain for the seizure of Gibraltar and with Vichy France for the protection of French North Africa, and to cooperate with Italy in capturing Suez and driving north through Palestine and Syria toward Turkey. Hitler certainly considered features of this plan useful; in October he attempted to enlist the support of Franco, Pétain, and Mussolini. His nine-hour meeting with Franco at Hendaye, on the Franco-Spanish border, on October 23, was one of the most frustrating interviews Hitler ever endured—"I would sooner have three or four teeth pulled out than go through that again," he told Mussolini. Franco not only declined German aid in capturing Gibraltar, and avoided committing Spain to enter the war, but demanded a large share of the French colonial empire and vast supplies of armaments and foodstuffs from Germany. At Montoire the next day, Pétain agreed that "the Axis Powers and France have an identical interest in seeing the defeat of England accomplished as soon as possible," but did not agree that their collaboration should involve France in the fighting. Worse yet, on his return journey even Mussolini had a disagreeable surprise for Hitler.

Italian Debacle in Greece. For the past year, Mussolini had become increasingly incensed at the minor role to which his partner had relegated him. At their meeting on March 18 on the Brenner Pass, Hitler had not said a word about his intention of invading Norway three weeks later. Mussolini's demands on France in June had been refused by the

Germans. In the middle of August Hitler had told him not to get involved in military adventures in Yugoslavia or Greece and had then highlighted German predominance in the Balkans by sending Ribbentrop to dictate to Hungary and Rumania a settlement of their territorial dispute, returning to Hungary the northern half of the province of Transylvania, which it had lost in 1919. At the same time, the Germans compelled Rumania to cede southern Dobrudja to Bulgaria. When the Rumanian foreign minister saw the partition line drawn by Ribbentrop, he collapsed onto the map. A week later, the Rumanian King Carol abdicated, but Hitler's position was strengthened when General Ion Antonescu, a Fascist admirer, became dictator. Antonescu brought Rumania into the Tripartite Pact and requested the sending of German troops to guarantee Rumanian security against Russia. Mussolini was particularly furious that Hitler had not mentioned his intention of sending these troops to Rumania when they met again at the Brenner Pass on October 4. "Hitler always faces me with a *fait accompli*," Mussolini raged to his foreign minister, Ciano. "This time I am going to pay him back in his own coin. He will find out from the newspapers that I have occupied Greece." His letter to Hitler explaining his intention was deliberately back-dated three days, and Hitler only received the news in his special train as he was returning from Montoire. He at once demanded a special meeting with Mussolini, which was arranged for Florence on October 28. Two hours before arriving, Hitler learned that the Italians had invaded Greece that morning.

"Führer, we are on the march!" Mussolini greeted him jubilantly. "Victorious Italian troops crossed the Greco-Albanian border at dawn today!" Three weeks later, they were returning across the border in defeat, demoralized by winter rains and constant ambush by Greek mountain troops. The British, answering the Greek appeal that they honor the guarantee Chamberlain had given in April 1939, had profited from this opportunity to occupy Crete and other Greek islands and had aided the Greek Army with money, arms, and troops. Other disasters for Italy followed. In December 1940, General Wavell's British and Commonwealth forces counterattacked the forces of Marshal Graziani, three times their number, which had advanced from Libya into Egypt, flung them back 500 miles during the next two months, and captured 130,000 prisoners. Between January and May 1941, other British forces drove the Italians out of Italian Somaliland and Eritrea along the Red Sea and liberated the whole of Ethiopia. Finally, the Italian Fleet was heavily damaged by British attacks on Taranto Bay in southern Italy and off Cape Matapan in southern Greece.

The Mediterranean debacle required Hitler's attention before he could launch the attack on Russia. In November, he gave orders that Gibraltar was to be captured, but failing again to win Franco's cooperation, he dropped the plan and with it any ambition in the western Mediterranean. To bolster the Italian forces in Libya, he sent General Erwin Rommel with a light armored division and a few air force units to command the German and Italian forces; and the Desert Fox, faced by a British Army weakened by dispatch of a large part of its strength to Greece, was by the middle of May again threatening Egypt. Finally, to deal with the Greeks, who held one quarter of Albania by the end of 1940, he ordered OPERATION ALPINE VIOLETS, an attack through Albania, and OPERATION MARITA, for a major thrust from Rumania through Bulgaria toward the Thracian coast of Greece. His order of priorities was clear from the size of forces he assigned: The Mediterranean and North Africa were not regarded as a major battleground.

German Conquest of Yugoslavia and Greece. To send troops to Greece, Hitler had first to ensure the collaboration of Yugoslavia, Hungary, Rumania, and Bulgaria. Rumania's Antonescu was cooperating willingly, and that winter 700,000 German troops were massed in Rumania. Hungary permitted free troop movements across its territory, and like Rumania, agreed to join the Tripartite Pact. Bulgaria, which was under strong Russian pressure, held out longer, but in February 1941, permitted German troops transit from Rumania to Greece and itself joined the Tripartite Pact. It seemed at first that Yugoslavia, too, would present no difficulty, after the Yugoslav regent, Prince Paul, had been summoned to the Berghof to be both browbeaten and offered the Greek port of Salonika as compensation for joining the Tripartite Pact. On March 25, the Yugoslav premier and foreign minister made a secret journey to Vienna to sign the pact. Two days later, however, the Yugoslav Army overthrew the regent, declared Peter, heir to the throne, king, and offered Germany a non-aggression pact.

The coup d'état threw Hitler into a rage, blunting his judgment at a time when he was planning the most grandiose military adventure of his career. Not content to overcome Yugoslav opposition to his invasion of Greece, he decided that evening that the Yugoslav state itself was to be partitioned, its army annihilated, and the spoils distributed among its neighbors. To give himself time to deal with Yugoslavia he ordered a month's delay in the attack on Russia. On April 6, 1941, Hitler's armies attacked Yugoslavia from Hungary and Greece from Bulgaria. In three days of bombing, Belgrade was laid in ruins, and 17,000 civilians were killed in what Hitler called OPERATION PUNISHMENT. A week later, the remnant of the Yugoslav Army surrendered at Sarajevo, and the king and government fled first to Greece and then to England. The Greeks held out only until April 23; the four British divisions that had been sent to their aid carried out a desperate evacuation by sea; and the island of Crete was captured by German paratroopers. The Greek government in turn fled to London. The whole of the Balkans had thus become either obedient satellites or occupied rump states. On April 30, Hitler ordered the invasion of Russia to begin on June 22.

THE INVASION OF RUSSIA: THE ADVANCE TO STALINGRAD

Russo-German Tension. Stalin had always suspected, even in the cordial days of the Nazi-Soviet Non-Aggression Pact, that Hitler would eventually turn his armies against Russia. As Churchill had clearly perceived as early as October 1, 1939, the advance of Russian troops into Poland was necessary for the safety of Russia. A German advance into the Balkans would bring war.

> I cannot forecast to you the action of Russia. It is a riddle wrapped in a mystery inside an enigma; but perhaps there is a key. That key is Russian national interest. It cannot be in accordance with the interest or the safety of Russia that Germany would plant herself upon the shores of the Black Sea, or that she should overrun the Balkan States and subjugate the Slavonic peoples of Southeastern Europe. That would be contrary to the historic life-interests of Russia.

The German victories in France, ending the danger for Hitler of a two-front war if Germany attacked Russia, were the occasion for Stalin's annexation of the Balkan states, of Bessarabia, and northern Bukovina, a clear indication that he was not relying on Hitler's protestations of friendship. At the same time, however, the Russians were assiduously fulfilling their trade treaties with Germany, shipping fooodstuffs and raw

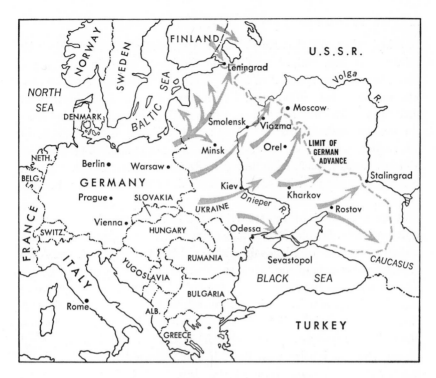

THE INVASION OF RUSSIA

materials promptly until the very day of the German invasion; and Stalin seemed to be going out of his way to display his friendship for German envoys and ambassadors on every public occasion. He did not even reply to a warning Churchill sent him in June 1940 of the danger to Russia of German hegemony in Europe. Tensions grew, however, as Hitler proceeded to turn the Balkan states into Nazi satellites; and when Germany, Italy, and Japan signed the Tripartite Pact on September 27, 1940, Molotov demanded to be given the text before it was signed, and any secret protocols attached, as well as the text of a German agreement with Finland for the transit of German troops across Finnish territory. To allay Russian suspicions and to direct Russian aims away from Eastern Europe, Molotov was invited to visit Berlin on November 12–13. The extraordinary talks that followed, in which Hitler and Ribbentrop attempted to persuade the Russians to share in the imminent partition of the British Empire, were dampened by Molotov's persistence in asking probing questions on German intentions. "Which sea?"

he asked, when told that Russia should turn south to her natural outlet on the open sea, and he persisted in displaying more interest in the Black Sea and the Baltic than in the Persian Gulf and the Arabian Sea. The meetings were interrupted for frequent descents into the air-raid shelters; and Molotov savored the irony of German assertions that Britain was defeated: "If that is so," he asked Ribbentrop, "why are we in this shelter, and whose are these bombs that are falling?" The proposal Molotov brought back, for a four-power pact of Russia, Germany, Italy, and Japan, was met with such untenable demands that Hitler dropped his plan.

Stalin attempted to oppose Hitler in the Balkans throughout the spring of 1941. He objected to the entry of German troops into Bulgaria and signed a pact of friendship with Yugoslavia on April 4. On April 13, he freed Russia of the fear of a two-front war by signing a neutrality pact with the Japanese foreign minister, Matsuoka, who knew from hints just given him in Berlin that an attack on Russia was imminent. "We are both Asiatics," Stalin told Matsuoka. "I am a moral communist," the Japanese minister replied! As German divisions multiplied on the Russian border with Poland, Stalin massed a slightly greater number of Red Army divisions, 170 to 146; the May Day parade was a more than usually impressive display of Russian military might; and on May 6, Stalin himself became chairman of the Council of People's Commissars, the equivalent of prime minister, thus personally becoming head of the government as well as of the Communist party. But apparently he still hoped for another bargain with Hitler. In the last days before the invasion, he publicly abused the British, expelled the envoys of Belgium, Norway, and Yugoslavia, and took up diplomatic relations with the pro-German government in Iraq. When the attack came, the Russian Army had mobilized only half its strength. Even Russian industry had not been put on a war footing. Stalin was to claim later that the Nazi-Soviet Pact of 1939 had given Russia two years to prepare for invasion and a territorial buffer against such an attack. But these two years had been far more advantageous to Germany than to Russia, giving Hitler control of the resources of most of Europe and forging his army into the finest fighting machine Europe had ever seen; the second front in the West, which was in existence in 1939–40, no longer remained in 1941; and the territorial acquisitions of Russia of 1939–40 were overrun by the Germans in a few days. In the nine months before the German assault, Stalin was, Churchill wrote, "a callous, a crafty and an ill-informed giant."

The Invasion of Russia. The German invasion plan had been formulated in December 1940. Its main aim was to encircle and destroy the Russian armies in western Russia, ensuring that they could not retreat into the vast spaces of Asiatic Russia. Russia was to be occupied from the Volga River to Archangel. The attack was to have three main prongs—two army groups driving north of the Pripet marshes through the Baltic states and White Russia were to take Leningrad and encircle the Russian armies on the Baltic; one army group was to attack through the Ukraine and capture Kiev, giving Germany control of the vast agricultural resources of the "black-soil" region; and in the extreme south, German and Rumanian troops were to take Odessa, the Black Sea coast, and the Caucasus, including the great Donets mining and steel region. The attack that began at dawn on June 22 seemed to go off just as planned for the first five months. German bombers destroyed much of the Russian Air Force before the planes left the ground. The North Army Group, under Field Marshal von Leeb, pushed rapidly through the Baltic states and by mid-September was in the suburbs of Leningrad, and in close contact with the Finnish forces of Marshal Mannerheim who were delightedly taking revenge. Field Marshal von Bock's Center Army Group, of thirty infantry and fifteen armored divisions, reached the Dnieper River on July 5, and Smolensk, only two hundred miles from Moscow, on July 16. At that point, von Bock and his tank commander Guderian begged Hitler to let them strike at Moscow, profiting from the speed and striking power of their armored divisions. Hitler's refusal, on the ground that he wished to encircle the Russian armies near Kiev and seize the agricultural and industrial resources of the Ukraine while the northern armies took Leningrad, was probably his most significant error in the war. Moscow was the center of Russian administration and transportation as well as a major industrial center. Guderian's divisions could have reached it easily while the summer weather lasted. Instead, Hitler halted the Center Army Group until the beginning of October and sent part of its armored divisions to the aid of both the northern armies of von Leeb and the southern group of von Rundstedt. Kiev fell on September 20, and Guderian's Panzers, joining up with those of South Army Group, encircled and made prisoner 600,000 Russian troops. Von Rundstedt pressed eastward, capturing Kharkov and Taganrog on the Sea of Azov. By the end of September, the Germans held the whole of the Ukraine. The Center Army Group, after their two-month halt, was then permitted to move north toward Moscow. They captured Orel on October 8 and encircled another 600,000 Russians near Viazma. On October 15 they were sixty-five miles from Moscow, and by the end of November they were within twenty miles of the Russian capital. But the rains that had begun to hamper operations in September had turned in November to snowy slush; and in December the harshness of the Russian winter made further advances impossible. When the German Army withdrew into its winter "hedgehogs," fortified defense centers, neither Moscow nor Leningrad had fallen, nor had the Russian armies been destroyed. Hitler's fortunes had turned decisively.

The Russian Counterattack. Meanwhile, the Russians were growing in strength and confidence. In June, Stalin had streamlined the government, creating a five-man State Defense Committee to control the war effort and postponing the Third Five-Year Plan. The front had been divided into three parts, with Voroshilov commanding the north, Timoshenko the center, and Budenny the south. Stalin himself took supreme command and personally supervised the strategy of the war in detail. To prevent the appearance of a fifth column, the half million Volga Germans were deported to the east, with terrible losses of life. And, on July 3, when his armies were retreating rapidly, Stalin called for a "scorched-earth" policy in the territory left in German hands:

> All rolling stock must be evacuated, the enemy must not be left a single engine, a single railway car, a single pound of grain or gallon of fuel. . . . All valuable property, including metals, grain, and fuel, that cannot be withdrawn, must be destroyed without fail. . . . In areas occupied by the enemy, guerrillas, mounted and on foot, must be formed; sabotage groups must be organized to combat the enemy, to foment guerrilla warfare everywhere, blow up bridges and roads, damage telephone and telegraph lines, set fire to forests, stores and transport. In occupied regions conditions must be made unbearable for the enemy and all his accomplices.

Perhaps most important of all, the transfer of war factories to the Urals and Siberia was begun and soon reached such a scale that in the period September–December 1941 over a thousand factories were transferred from the area later taken by the Nazis. Finally, aid was at once forth-coming from Britain and the United States. On the evening of the invasion, Churchill told his radio listeners: "No one has been a more consistent opponent of Communism than I have. I will unsay no word that I have spoken about it. But all this fades away before the spectacle which is now unfolding. . . . Any man or state who fights on against Nazi-dom will have our aid. Any man or state who marches with Hitler is our foe. . . . It follows therefore that we shall give whatever help we can to Russia and the Russian people." On July 12, 1941, an Anglo-Soviet Mutual Assistance Pact was signed in Moscow. Large quantities of weapons and supplies of oil and rubber vitally needed in Britain were sent through the Arctic to Russia, in British convoys at great risk; but Stalin's immediate demand that Britain create a second front by invading Europe was shelved as unrealistic. President Roosevelt declared Russia eligible for Lend-Lease aid and agreed that the United States would supply Russia with $1 billion worth of goods in 1942.

When the Soviet government evacuated Moscow in November, Stalin remained in the Kremlin, restoring confidence in the panic-stricken Moscow population. Speaking from the top of the Lenin mausoleum to the troops and volunteer-workers brigades going out to meet the Germans at the edge of Moscow, he told them to remember the heroes of old Russia—Alexander Nevsky, Dimitry Donskoy, Kuzma Minin, Dimitry Pozharsky, Alexander Suvorov, and Mikhail Kutuzov. And, just when the Germans were digging in for the winter, he unleashed the first major Russian counteroffensive. On December 6, when the temperature had fallen more than thirty degrees below zero, one hundred divisions of infantry, cavalry, and tanks under General Georgi Zhukov struck along a two-hundred-mile front. For the next two months, the Germans withdrew with enormous losses, to between 75 and 200 miles from Moscow. According to the German chief of staff, Halder, the Germans lost a third of the invading army by the end of February—over one million men.

When his most trusted generals demanded permission to retreat, Hitler began wildly to dismiss his most expert leaders. Kluge, Guderian, Hoeppner, Sponeck, and von Rundstedt were allowed to resign or were dismissed; on December 17, Hitler personally took over from Field Marshal von Brauchitsch, commander-in-chief of the army. Thus, the war in Russia became in a real sense a personal duel between two dictators who each, as commander-in-chief, insisted on controlling the fighting front down to the smallest details. But now Stalin was to be faced not with the subtly calculating leader of the early war years but with a megalomaniac who increasingly lost touch with reality as the defeats poured in upon him. In Russia, it became clear that Hitler was serious when he promised that if defeated he would take the world down with him in flames.

Stalingrad. With the coming of spring, Hitler set his goal for 1942 as the taking of the Caucasus oil fields, the Donets industrial basin, and the great river port of Stalingrad on the Volga. During the winter, his army had been reinforced with fifty-two divisions drawn from Rumania, Hungary, Italy, Slovakia, and Spain. In May, the Crimea was taken; in July, the German armies were divided, with one force sent to attack Stalingrad and another to penetrate the Caucasus. The latter reached the Maikop oil fields, which the Russians had destroyed, but was held back before the oil center of Grozny. The drive on Stalingrad, however, which began on September 15, ran into desperate Soviet resistance. Shelling and bombing reduced the city to ruins, through which the armies fought from building to building. Finally, when Hitler, convinced the battle was won, returned to Munich for his annual Beerhall rally with the "Old Fighters" of his 1923 Putsch, the Russians counterattacked, driving without difficulty through the Rumanian and Italian divisions on either side of Stalingrad and encircling the German Fourth Army of General von Paulus. A relief force under Field Marshal von Manstein could probably have relieved von Paulus and enabled his forces to break out; but Hitler, wildly determined to hold the symbolic city of Stalin, did not allow von Paulus to retreat. On December 23, the relief army was withdrawn, and the 200,000 soldiers trapped in Stalingrad were left to die of frostbite, wounds, starvation, and continual Russian attacks, without supplies, ammunition, medicine, or reason. The Russians twice offered honorable surrender terms, but Hitler categorically refused to allow von Paulus to surrender. His troops fought on until January 31, when he surrendered with the remaining 91,000 soldiers, of whom 24 were generals. By then, the German Army in the Caucasus had narrowly avoided a similar encirclement, but had been closely followed by the Russian armies, which took Rostov on February 14 and Kharkov on February 16. The Germans had at last lost the initiative. After Stalingrad, it was not a question of whether the Nazis would win the war but of when they would be beaten.

JAPANESE AGGRESSION
FROM PEARL HARBOR TO MIDWAY

The German victories in Europe convinced the Japanese that the time was ripe for the extension of their New Order to include all the east Asian colonies of the West European powers and of the United States —the British colonies of Hong Kong, Malaya, Burma, and North Borneo; French Indochina; the Netherlands East Indies; the Philippine Islands of the United States—as well as the independent kingdom of Thailand (Siam). For the first year of the European war, Japan had maintained its neutrality; but the defeat of France in June 1940 convinced it that the Axis powers were close to final victory. On September 27, 1940, the Japanese signed the Tripartite Pact with Germany and Italy, and in April 1941 concluded a neutrality pact with Soviet Russia. The Vichy governor of French Indochina was compelled in September 1940 to permit the stationing of Japanese troops in northern Indochina, and in July 1941, a similar agreement extended the occupation to the whole country. By then Britain was facing the Nazis alone and could do nothing to stop the Japanese advance.

Japanese-American Tension. The United States was still the only possible obstacle to Japanese aggression; but Roosevelt was moving step by step toward open belligerency. In 1940, the sale of high-grade gasoline and scrap metal to Japan was banned, since they were of direct use in Japanese war production. When the news was announced of Japan's advance into Indochina, Roosevelt ordered the freezing of all Japanese assets in the United States. At the same time, naval production was stepped up, with a $4 billion appropriation from Congress; large-scale fortifications were built on the American-held islands of Guam, Midway, and Wake; and naval and air facilities were developed in the Aleutian Islands, Alaska, Hawaii, and the Philippines. In September 1940, the Selective Service Act was passed. Growing amounts of aid were sent to Chiang Kai-shek.

The American people were, however, still slow in learning the lessons of the European war; and Roosevelt's increasing opposition to the Nazi regime was meeting considerable criticism. In April 1940, he denounced

JAPANESE EXPANSION, 1941–1943

the German invasion of neutral Denmark and Norway; in July he ordered shipped to Britain a large consignment of rifles and artillery of First World War vintage, and followed this in September with the exchange of fifty overage destroyers for lease or cession of a number of British naval bases in North America and Bermuda. After winning election to a third term as president in November 1940, Roosevelt told the American people in a "fireside chat" that the peril of the democratic nations was their own peril: "We must be the great arsenal of democracy." In his State of the Union message the following January, he appealed to Congress to aid the nations defending the Four Free-doms—of speech, of religion, from want, and from fear. In March, Congress met this appeal by voting the Lend-Lease Act, which allowed the President to lease or lend armaments to nations whose defense he considered vital to the interests of the United States. Beginning with a first appropriation of $7 billion, Lend-Lease was eventually to supply $50 billion of aid to the Allied powers. To ensure that the goods reached Europe, the United States became involved in the sea war in the Atlantic. In April, Greenland was taken under American protection, followed in July by Iceland. American warships began to form convoys as far as Iceland and South Africa. In September, after two American merchant ships were torpedoed, Roosevelt ordered American ships to "shoot on sight" at German submarines and warships. Hitler, however, was wisely determined to keep the United States out of war, at least until Russia had been defeated, and he refused the pleas of his naval commanders that unlimited submarine warfare be begun on American ships. He also pressed the Japanese not to provoke war with the United States, but instead to attack Russia in Siberia and the British at Hong Kong and Singapore. With his uncanny ability to sense the mood of foreign nations he had never visited, Hitler was convinced that the American people would not fight unless its own territory or its citizens were directly attacked. Unknown to Hitler, the Japanese were planning just such an attack.

The American embargo on trade with Japan, followed by similar embargoes by Britain and the Dutch East Indies, cut off Japan from its much-needed oil supplies, as well as from strategic raw materials like rubber and scrap iron. The Japanese government replied by simultaneously preparing for all-out war and seeking better relations, on its own terms, with the United States. All political parties were fused in the Imperial Rule Assistance Association. Labor unions were united in the Patriotic Industrial Society, and government control was extended over all industrial activity, in what was called The New Economic Structure. Strict rationing and substitute goods were introduced to meet the shortages of food and clothing. The final supremacy of the military was achieved when Konoye, a member of the old court nobility, was replaced as premier on October 17, 1941 by General Hideki Tojo, one of the most bellicose of the army leaders. Two weeks later the cabinet decided that it would wage war on the United States if no satisfactory conclusions had been reached in the talks with the American government by November 25, a deadline extended later by four days. Plans were completed for simultaneous attacks on the British, Dutch, and American colonial possessions in east Asia and for the destruction of the American Pacific fleet. The talks in Washington had begun in February; but by November it was obvious that the positions of the two countries were irreconcilable. The Japanese demanded that the United States end the trade embargo, especially on oil, recognize the Japanese New Order in Asia, and withdraw help from Chiang Kai-shek if he refused to make peace. In return, Japanese expansion would be halted. Hull's final ultimatum in November was nothing less than a demand that Japan withdraw from all its territories acquired since 1937. War was obviously about to begin, as the American government was well aware, not only from the Japanese military preparations, but from deciphered code messages being received at the Japanese Embassy.

Pearl Harbor. A Japanese task force of aircraft carriers set off for Pearl Harbor on November 25, and had still not been discovered by American ships or planes two weeks later when it was within striking distance of Pearl Harbor. On December 7 at 7:55 A.M. a wave of 189 Japanese bombers attacked the moored American warships, airfields, and barracks at Pearl Harbor. Two waves followed, only the last sustaining any important damage from artillery fire of the ships and the shore batteries. The Japanese lost about sixty planes. They destroyed five battleships, fourteen other ships, many planes, and killed 2,403 Americans. America was left with only three capital ships in the Pacific. On December 8, the United States declared war on Japan; three days later, Germany and Italy declared war on the United States. On December 7, Japanese forces also struck at Guam, the Philippines, Malaya, Hong Kong, and Thailand. With surprisingly small forces—13 divisions and about 1,600 planes—they had soon subjugated most of east Asia. The whole of Malaya and the supposedly impregnable city of Singapore fell by February 1942. Hong Kong capitulated on Christmas Day 1941, to be followed soon after by the British colonies in North Borneo. British Burma fell in May 1942. The Dutch East Indies were taken by March 1942. Independent Thailand, occupied shortly after Pearl Harbor, signed a treaty of alliance with Japan, and in January 1942 declared war on Britain and the United States. The American islands of Guam and Wake fell in a few weeks, and the forces of General Douglas MacArthur in the Philippines were soon driven into the narrow Bataan Peninsula near Manila and the island-fortress of Corregidor, until finally forced to surrender in May 1942.

Japanese Expansion Halted. MacArthur himself was ordered by the

President to retire to Australia to take command of the Allied forces in the western Pacific. He at once established a strong base at Port Moresby on the south shore of New Guinea, and there in the late summer of 1942 he turned back a Japanese invading force that was attempting to complete the conquest of the island, probably as a preparatory step to the invasion of Australia. In September, the American and Australian forces in Port Moresby began the counterattack that three years later was to bring General MacArthur to Tokyo itself. Even more decisive fighting was taking place on the sea. Australia was saved from invasion in May when, in the Battle of the Coral Sea, a large Japanese naval force was forced to retreat with heavy losses. On June 4, a Japanese fleet, followed by a landing force, approached the American Midway Island, which could have become a stepping-off point for the invasion of Hawaii. American air power crippled the Japanese fleet in one of the most decisive battles of the war, establishing a supremacy of air power over both the Japanese Air Force and fleet that was never to be lost. In three days of fighting the Japanese lost four aircraft carriers and two large cruisers. Shortly after this defeat the United States began the long, bloody process of retaking the Pacific islands. Between August 1942 and January 1943, small American forces fought for control of Guadalcanal, Tulagi, and Florida, in the Solomon Islands, while the rival navies skirmished continually along the coasts. By January 1943, when the German surrender at Stalingrad occurred, both southern New Guinea and the Solomon Islands were cleared of the Japanese. Japan's aggression had been turned back.

FORMATION AND AIMS
OF THE GRAND ALLIANCE

The German invasion of Russia and the Japanese attack on Pearl Harbor ended the months of British isolation under German attack and brought into being the Grand Alliance whose victory, though far distant, was certain. "All the rest," wrote Churchill, "was merely the proper application of overwhelming force." But the place and the time for the application of that force had to be determined by agreement between these disparate allies; and, as became ever more clear, the decisions taken on military strategy were to have lasting importance for their influence upon the postwar world. Whereas Churchill and Stalin were constantly aware of the long-term political results that would follow from their military decisions, both Roosevelt and Truman believed that military strategy should be judged for its effectiveness in defeating the Axis powers rather than for its putative political benefits. They attempted to ignore the fact that while the war of the Grand Alliance was being fought to remove the Axis yoke from Europe, Asia, and Africa, a second struggle was being waged—of communism and Western democracy—to fill the vacuum created by the expulsion of Fascist control. To this should perhaps be added a third conflict, that of nationalism against colonialism in Asia, a struggle in which the Communists played at first only a minor role. In this third struggle, the sympathies of the United States government, though not its policy, ran counter to that of Britain.

The Atlantic Charter. Churchill and Roosevelt, in the Atlantic Charter of August 1941, had already made a general statement of their postwar aims before the United States had even become a belligerent. Meeting on board ship off Newfoundland, the President and Prime Minister had made known "certain common principles in the national policies of their respective countries on which they base their hopes for a better future for the world." Their countries had no desire for territorial gain. They desired that all peoples should have the right of self-government, greater freedom of trade and access to raw materials, and the chance to live in freedom from fear and want. Nations threatening aggression should be disarmed, "pending the establishment of a wider and permanent system of general security." At the Arcadia Conference in January 1942 it was decided that every nation joining in the Grand Alliance against the Axis powers should subscribe to its principles; and eventually every founding member of the United Nations did so. It is ironic how few of these principles were actually enforced by the nations that paid lip service to them.

Even in the Atlantic Charter one can see, in germ, disagreements between Churchill and Roosevelt. First, capitalist America, the most efficient and best-endowed power, saw free trade as a basis for a better future for the world. For twenty years after the signing of the Atlantic Charter American statesmen found difficulty in understanding that, in completely free competition with either American agriculture or industry, the economy of any other country would suffer. Yet, at the same time, American business and agriculture continued to demand the protective tariffs necessary to safeguard them in those few economic areas where competition from the outside might be harmful to American interests. This paradoxical thinking on international economics dogged American policy makers from the Atlantic Charter to the Kennedy Round of tariff negotiations with the Common Market. Churchill reminded Roosevelt that during eighty years when Britain had espoused free trade, the United States had responded with protectionism, and that he had no intention now of disbanding the system of empire preference built up during the 1930's. Second, Roosevelt believed that the "right of all peoples to choose the form of government under which they will live" implied that the Allied powers would have no right to impose governments of their own nomination on the peoples they would liberate from Axis rule. He believed General de Gaulle's claim to be handed the administration of the French colonies and of France itself to be as little justified as the claims of the Communist Lublin Committee that Stalin was to impose on Poland. For Roosevelt, the responsibility of the Allied powers was primarily to ensure the conduct of free elections. For Churchill, the Old World realist, such aims would only be achieved where the Western democracies actually could enforce them militarily. He did not believe that in areas where the Red Army was supreme, elections of the kind Roosevelt envisaged would take place. For that reason, he pressed for the invasion of Italy in 1943; for an invasion through Yugoslavia into Austria, Hungary, and Czechoslovakia; and for the British liberation of Greece. And he was also prepared to accept that these ideals were not attainable when they ran directly counter to Russian force; in those circumstances he was willing to bargain with the Russians to delimit respective spheres of interest. Such bargaining was repugnant to the American government, which intended, as Secretary of State Hull said, to create a world where there would "no longer be any need for spheres of interest, for alliances, for balance of power, or any other of the special arrangements through which, in the unhappy past, nations strove to safeguard their security or promote their interests." Third, Roosevelt believed that the wish "to see sovereign rights and self-government restored to those who have been forcibly deprived of them" should apply not only to the victims of Axis expansion but to the inhabitants of the colonies of the West European powers, whom he believed to be exploited more or less thoroughly by their overlords. Roosevelt deliberately avoided committing the United States to restore the European colonies in the Far East, but hoped that it would be possible to grant them independence as the United States was pledged to do in the Philippines. Had Roosevelt's vision been realized, the West European countries might well have been saved enormous and vain expenditures of lives and money in the attempt to hold onto their possessions after the war; but Churchill had not "become the King's First Minister in order to preside over the liquidation of the British Empire" or indeed of the French or Dutch empires. Fourth, the Americans regarded the Soviet annexations in Eastern Europe in 1939–40 as unacceptable territorial aggrandizement and throughout the war refused to give their sanction to those changes. Churchill, however, was willing to do so, but deferred to American pressure.

These disagreements were to emerge more openly in the military planning in the later stages of the war. For the moment, however, the British and American governments were in agreement on strategy, notably that the major American war effort should be directed to the defeat of Germany and Italy in Europe and not to the defeat of Japan in Asia. This decision was made as early as January 1941, when the possibility was considered that America might become involved in war with both Germany and Japan at the same time; throughout 1941, Anglo-American staff talks were conducted on that basic supposition. Even Pearl Harbor did not alter the American decision. When the British and American military staffs met in Washington in January 1942, during the Arcadia Conference, General Marshall reaffirmed "that Germany is still the prime enemy and her defeat is the key to victory."

Anglo-American Relations with the Soviet Union. Coordination of planning of Britain and the United States with Russia presented few political problems before 1943. While the German armies were driving into the heart of Russia, neither the British nor American governments asked themselves whether their aid was making possible the survival of Soviet communism. When Foreign Minister Anthony Eden reported, after his trip to Moscow in December 1941, that the Soviet government intended to restore the "prewar" European boundaries, that is, those of June 22, 1941, and thus to retain its territorial gains from Finland, Estonia, Latvia, Lithuania, Poland, and Rumania, the British and American governments refused to give their consent. But at the same time they could not prejudice their relations with Russia at so crucial a time by openly opposing Russia's claims. As a result, the West was later to be presented with a *fait accompli,* when behind the advancing Red Army the Russian government simply reincorporated those territories into Russia.

Stalin was not satisfied by the mere sending of supplies, however. As early as July 18, 1941, Stalin asked Churchill for the creation of a second front in northern France, which the British at once dismissed as impossible. On September 4, Stalin told Churchill that the "Germans consider danger in the West a bluff, and are transferring all their forces to the East with impunity, being convinced that no second front exists in the West, and that none will exist." Such a front should be established that year, Stalin concluded, either in France or in the Balkans, to draw away thirty or forty German divisions from Russia. Again Churchill pointed out Britain's inability to put together such a force, and the dangers of a disaster should such a landing be attempted. With the entry of the United States into the war, Stalin became more than ever convinced that such a front could rapidly be created. He had paid deference to American sentiment, by subscribing to the United Nations Declaration of January 1, 1942, and to British demands, by signing the Anglo-Soviet Treaty of May 1942, a twenty-year agreement of mutual aid and alliance. He was delighted when Roosevelt assured Molotov in May 1942 that a second front could be expected this year. General Marshall and the American Chiefs of Staff were indeed convinced that such an invasion of France was possible in 1942, and certain in 1943; but German advances in Libya and the Caucasus and Japanese successes in east Asia, as well as the enormous shipping losses due to submarine attack, persuaded the British and finally the Americans that a frontal attack in France in 1942 would be suicidal folly. Instead, it was decided in July to launch an assault on French North Africa that autumn. Churchill broke the news personally to Stalin, who "said a great many disagreeable things" but had to be satisfied with the assurance, soon to be broken, that a major cross-Channel invasion would take place in 1943.

Anglo-American Invasion of French North Africa. The Anglo-American landings in Algiers, Oran, and Casablanca were planned for the night of November 7–8, 1942. Meanwhile, the British Eighth Army, under the command of General Montgomery, had begun to attack Rommel's German and Italian forces in Egypt at El Alamein, only eighty miles from Alexandria. After twelve days of fighting, the Eighth

Army had driven the Germans and Italians back in flight to Libya, and was in rapid pursuit. Egypt was saved, and Libya was almost defenseless. Should the landings in Algeria be successful, the two Allied armies could meet in Tunisia and complete their control of the whole of the North African shore, from Tangier to Suez. The Allies had hoped that the Vichy forces would cooperate with the British and American armies; but French resistance was strong, especially in Casablanca and Oran. For that reason, General Dwight D. Eisenhower, commander of the operation, decided to make a deal with Admiral Jean Darlan, the commander-in-chief of the Vichy armed forces, who happened to be in Algiers visiting his sick son and who therefore was the highest authority in the French colonies. Darlan was recognized by Eisenhower as high commissioner of the North African Territories, and he in turn, on November 10, ordered the French forces to cease fire and the French fleet in Toulon to sail for Algeria. Fighting stopped in Algeria and Morocco; but German forces poured into unoccupied France, the Toulon fleet was scuttled and thus lost to the Allies, and vast German reinforcements were sent into Tunisia. It was to require bitter fighting throughout January, February, and March 1943 before Montgomery's Eighth Army could unite with the Anglo-American forces from Algeria in control of Tunisia. Only in May 1943 was Tunisia brought finally under control. The lateness of the invasion of Algeria and Morocco and the failure to secure Tunisia made it impossible for the Allies to mount a cross-Channel invasion in 1943. It remains, therefore, an open question whether this venture was an unnecessary diversion, particularly since it was not followed up with an invasion of the Balkans.

The deal with Darlan, one of the most notorious collaborators in Vichy and an outspoken Anglophobe, was strongly criticized in Britain and France as a sordid betrayal of the ideals for which the Allies were fighting. More important, it raised for the first time the question of the form of government that the Allied armies would impose upon territories liberated by them. Darlan was assassinated on Christmas Eve, however, and the Allies were given a second chance to pick the authority they would support in the French colonies. Both Roosevelt and Churchill had their own candidates. Roosevelt supported General Henri Giraud, a First World War hero with no political ambitions, who had escaped from captivity in Vichy France. Churchill's candidate was General Charles de Gaulle, a theorist of tank warfare who had been under-secretary of war for eleven days in the cabinet of Paul Reynaud.

De Gaulle had fled to London when Pétain became premier, and on June 18, 1940, had proclaimed himself the center of continuing French resistance to the Germans. With Churchill's aid, he had put together a small French fighting force, known as the Free French; and by November 1942 several French colonies in central Africa and the Pacific had rallied to his movement. De Gaulle regarded his own French National Committee as the nucleus of a future French government, and indeed his more enthusiastic supporters were claiming that in some mysterious way he incarnated the spirit of France. This type of reasoning had little appeal to Franklin Roosevelt, who felt that de Gaulle was a usurper who wanted to ride to power in France on the backs of the Anglo-American armies. To settle this dispute and to determine military aims for 1943, Churchill and Roosevelt decided to meet in the newly liberated city of Casablanca in January 1943.

The Casablanca Conference. After a long discussion, the Chiefs of Staff concluded that the Tunisian campaign would not be over before May and that it would therefore be necessary to postpone the landing in northern France until spring of 1944, in view of the enormous scale of the operation. The British view, that the Germans should be kept occupied in the Mediterranean by an attack on Sicily and subsequently on southern Italy in the spring of 1943, was finally adopted, over the opposition of some American chiefs who felt that the main American effort in 1943 should be directed against the Japanese-held islands in the Pacific. To prepare for the invasion of France, the antisubmarine war was to be stepped up, troops and supplies were to be massed in England, and bombing of German industrial cities was to be increased. The French situation was temporarily settled after both Giraud and de Gaulle had been brought to Casablanca, by their agreement to cooperate; this was implemented in June by the formation of a French Committee of National Liberation (CFLN), of which they were to be joint chairmen, which took over the administration of French North Africa. By then, the CFLN had at its disposal a well-equipped army of 256,000 men who were training for the invasion of Sicily. This appreciable force, which increased to a million men by the end of the war, introduced an entirely new political factor into the international situation. France, as General de Gaulle never ceased to claim, was again in a position to assert its right to be considered one of the great powers and to be included in making the decisions that would affect the nature of the postwar world. The revival of France produced a new conflict within the Allied side, for Roosevelt and Stalin were both rigidly opposed to giving France the status of a great power and were determined not to invite de Gaulle to the conferences of the Big Three. De Gaulle's animosity toward Roosevelt for this relegation of France to a minor world role was to be lasting and, indeed, was to assume great significance when de Gaulle returned to power as president of France in 1958. De Gaulle never forgot the shock of discovering at Casablanca that "Roosevelt intended that the peace should be an American peace, and that in particular France should have him for her savior and arbiter."

At the conclusion of the conference, Roosevelt and Churchill met the press; and Roosevelt cheerfully made the first momentous statement of the Allied terms for the end of the war—nothing less than "unconditional surrender." While surprised that the phrase had been given to the press, Churchill had previously agreed that this should be Allied policy, and Stalin himself later concurred. Yet the statement obviously implied that the Atlantic Charter's principles need not be extended to the Axis powers. Nazi propagandists seized upon the statement to stiffen resistance in Germany. As a result, it has often been claimed that this demand for unconditional surrender may have discouraged opposition to Hitler in Germany and lengthened the war. This is most unlikely, for the plots against Hitler continued, and as Churchill pointed out, peace terms written out in detail seemed far more terrible than the formula of unconditional surrender.

Thus, by the end of 1942, certain features of the postwar world were already determined. Russia for its part had made clear that its postwar boundaries would extend at least as far as those of June 1941. The French colonies in North Africa had not been promised their independence, in spite of Roosevelt's anticolonialism. By permitting de Gaulle and Giraud to establish the CFLN, the question of the future government of France had already been settled, for de Gaulle would have no difficulty in establishing his precedence over Giraud and, within a few months, of driving his rival into retirement. The predominance of de Gaulle would imply the eventual return of France to great-power status, with its corollary, the right to share in the postwar settlement with Germany and its allies. The decision to invade Italy offered hopes, not to be realized, for Anglo-American penetration into southern Europe, especially into the Balkans.

Chapter Three

THE AXIS
NEW ORDER
IN EUROPE
AND ASIA

DURING the period of Axis control, Europe and Asia were transformed, politically, socially, economically, and even culturally. The drama of military events on the moving peripheries of the Axis empires should not cause one to lose sight of the fact that Belgium, the Netherlands, and northern France, for example, were in Nazi control for almost five years, Poland and Czechoslovakia for six years, and Austria for seven; nor of the fact that the Japanese held the East Asian colonial possessions of Britain, France, the Netherlands, and the United States for almost four years, half of China for eight years, and Korea for thirty-five years. Even the minor partner, Italy, wrought lasting changes in its own restricted sphere. The future development of all the peoples within the Axis empires, including that of the ruling peoples themselves, was vitally affected by these years of conquest. What, then, was the nature of the New Order imposed by the Axis powers? What changes in the character of the countries in these empires were brought about? And what new forces arose in those countries in opposition to the Axis regime?

WARTIME GERMANY

At the time of the Battle of Stalingrad, German and Italian control extended over the whole of the Continent of Europe from the Pyrenees to a line stretching across Russia from the Gulf of Finland to the Sea of Azov, with the exception of neutral Switzerland, Sweden, and Turkey. Italy had been relegated to a minor role in the control of this empire, being responsible only for a small area of France on its Alpine border, Croatia and Montenegro, Albania, and Greece (which it controlled jointly with Germany). The rest of Europe was Germany's, either annexed directly, occupied by German troops, or in satellite status.

In 1943, the German state itself was much larger than the country Hitler had come to rule ten years before. Territories of German stock, or which could be easily made so, had been annexed directly—Austria, Sudetenland, western Poland; Memelland; Bialystok; Alsace and Lorraine; Luxembourg; Eupen, Malmédy and Moresnet (Belgian towns Germany had lost in 1919); and part of Slovenia. Within this area lived the *Herrenvolk,* the "master race," whose superior blood in Hitler's view, gave them the right to rule Europe. For the benefit of this people the whole empire was organized.

Nazi Racial Policy. In Germany itself, the Nazis set out to ensure the purification of the blood of the German race. Large-scale deportations of non-Germans took place in the territories annexed, particularly from Memelland, western Poland, and Alsace-Lorraine; and colonization by Germans was begun. Such racially suspect groups as the gypsies were systematically exterminated; programs were begun to raise the quality of the German "race" itself by so-called mercy killing of the insane and the chronically ill and by mating selected SS men with Aryan women. Thousands whom the Gestapo suspected of disaffection were worked to death in the labor camps, died in the concentration camps, or were summarily shot or hanged. Above all, the Jews were regarded as the impurity in the Aryan blood that had to be removed. From the pogrom of November 1938 on, violence was used against them on an increasing scale until, in January 1942, Hitler determined upon the "final solution"—genocide, the extermination of the Jews as a people. Thus, the Nazis killed thousands who, at least in 1933, were German citizens. Of 600,000 Jews in Germany in 1933, almost half emigrated before 1939. Of those who remained, only 131,800 were still alive in 1942 and only about 12,000 in 1945. Among those lost to Germany through the brutality of its own rulers were many of the most talented, honorable, and liberal of its citizens. Their loss would be grievously felt in the postwar years.

Economic and Social Problems. Population losses were high throughout Germany. By 1945, 3 million German soldiers and civilians were known to be dead from the fighting or the air raids, and another 1.7 million were missing. The losses naturally occurred particularly among men between the ages of twenty and forty, the first to be recruited into the armed forces. In this age-bracket, there was a drop in numbers of 1.4 million. There was correspondingly an increase in the proportion of women, which rose from a ratio of 105 women to 100 men in 1939, to

ATLANTIC

OCEAN

NORTH

SEA

GREAT

BRITAIN

NORWAY

SWEDEN

FINLAND

DENMARK

BALTIC SEA

Leningrad

GERMANY

Berlin

NETH.

BELG

LUX

Paris

FRANCE

Vichy

SWITZ.

BOHEMIA–
MORAVIA

AUSTRIA

SLOVAKIA

POLAND
(GEN. GOV.)

Bialystok

U. S. S. R.

HUNGARY

BESSARABIA

RUMANIA

CROATIA

SERBIA

BULGARIA

ITALY

ALBANIA

GREECE

TURKEY

BLACK
SEA

SPAIN

CRETE

	Annexed by Germany
	Occupied by Germany
	Satellite States
	Occupied by Italy

HITLER'S EUROPE, 1942

125 women to 100 men in 1945. Millions of women of marriageable age had no chance of finding husbands.

The mobilization of 8 million men into the German armies caused vast labor shortages at home. These were partly made up by institution of compulsory labor, from 1943 on, of men from sixteen to sixty-five and of women from seventeen to forty-five. Even children were put to work on light jobs and in the fields. But the main supply of labor was from the prisoners of war, of whom 2 million were utilized, and from the conquered and even satellite countries. Fritz Sauckel, named the Nazi commissioner-general for manpower on March 21, 1942, employed any method, from collaboration with regimes like Marshal Pétain's to mass deportation, to supply Germany with 8.5 million foreign workers. Although workers from Western Europe were at first quite well treated, those from Poland and Russia were always regarded as *Untermenschen* (sub-humans); they were barely fed and clothed, were worked to the point of collapse, and were treated with inhuman brutality. The legacy of hatred for Germany taken back to their home countries can hardly be estimated. Indeed, one of the greatest fears of the average German when the Allied armies invaded was of the vengeance that the forced laborers would take, if they were set loose on the German population. A final source of labor was from the concentration camps, many of whose inmates were deliberately worked to death rather than being exterminated. Krupp, for example, used 35,000 foreign laborers, 18,000 prisoners of war, and 5,000 concentration inmates. A synthetic rubber factory was constructed at Auschwitz.

This mobilization for war worked well in keeping up German productivity, especially in war materials. Only in the last year of the war did armaments or airplane production flag, in spite of incessant Allied bombing. The supply of consumer goods and food was ensured by exploitation of the rest of the empire. The livestock and farm machinery of Alsace and Lorraine, for example, were shipped into the neighboring provinces of Baden and the Palatinate; and it was laid down as a matter of principle that the inhabitants of the Ukraine and eastern Poland should be allowed to starve while the foodstuffs of the area were shipped to Germany. Throughout the war, the food ration of the German people was almost twice that of the conquered peoples. The German economy was also buttressed by the confiscation of the gold and foreign-currency reserves of the conquered countries; by vast "occupation costs," which brought in about $15 billion; by compulsory levies on production; and by artificial exchange rates. Large German trusts, like I. G. Farben and Vereinigte Stahlwerke, which were already prospering at home from government favor, were not only able to enjoy the trade secrets of their rivals abroad but to set up subsidiaries or forcible mergers with companies in those countries, with the aim of making permanent their hold over desirable foreign markets.

Popular Attitudes to Nazism. The lasting effects of the Nazi regime upon the mentality of Germans who lived through it are hard to estimate. Hitler had done things that many Germans regarded as positive —ended unemployment, carried through many public works, including the autobahns, overthrown the Treaty of Versailles, and provided the heady excitement of conquering most of Europe. His educational and propaganda machine had indoctrinated many young people, especially in the Hitler Youth, in the Nazi ideology. What is most curious, however, is the reaction of the German people to the negative sides of the regime. The anti-Semitism of the regime never roused widespread or even isolated protest. Before 1939 most Germans regarded the emigration of some of their best minds, like Einstein, with equanimity; after 1939 they persuaded themselves that the Jews were merely being "regrouped" or "re-educated." The destruction of political liberty and the establishment of the totalitarian state was met with criticism from only a very few university students and political leaders. The decision to wage aggressive war was greeted first with resignation and, after early success, with enthusiasm. Even the Allied bombardments, which were deliberately directed against civilian targets to break the population's morale, had little effect in rousing the German people against their government. Only a few religious leaders dared protest the regime's treatment of the churches; fewer yet dared object to its inhumanity. Yet all this could be explained by the efficiency of Nazi totalitarian controls. To live in the Third Reich, a leading German professor once explained, was comparable to looking through the windows of a lonely house on a moor and seeing terrible things being done inside. To intervene would only invite one's own destruction.

Hitler and the Army. Only one group possessed the power to overthrow Hitler—the generals of the army. They present the most fascinating problem in understanding Hitler's Germany. How could such a large group of well-educated, cultured, apparently decent men put themselves at the service of a man they saw to be a megalomaniac and a sadist, in order to extend over the whole of Europe the unparalleled horror of Nazi rule? The German Army had a tradition of political neutrality, of unquestioning obedience, and of discipline, reinforced by the significance placed upon the soldier's oath of loyalty to the head of the state, which went back over three hundred years in Prussian history, and was something few raised in reverence of German military customs even thought to question. Hitler was careful, for the most part, to permit the army to maintain its own standards of honor in methods of warfare and treatment of prisoners, except perhaps on the Eastern front. Most German generals were able to think of themselves as fighting a traditional kind of war on behalf of Germany rather than on behalf of the Nazi regime. Resistance in the army hierarchy became important only when Hitler's political decisions seemed to them militarily unfeasible. In 1938, when Hitler seemed to be risking war with Britain and France over Czechoslovakia, a group of courageous anti-Nazi civilians, led by Karl Goerdeler, the former mayor of Leipzig, and including Socialists, trade-union leaders, diplomats, aristocrats, and a few well-placed officers, began to plot to overthrow Hitler. General Ludwig Beck, the former army chief of staff, who was the center of opposition in the army, was able to gain promises of collaboration from General Halder, the new chief of staff, General von Witzleben, and General Hoeppner. The Munich Agreement led to the abandonment of that plot. Beck and Goerdeler tried again in November 1939, but army Commander-in-Chief Brauchitsch soon disavowed his early interest in a conspiracy, without, however, revealing the existence of a conspiracy to Hitler. (It is interesting to note that the army officers contacted by the conspirators never revealed to the Nazis the existence of a conspiracy in the army.) Between 1943 and 1944, without being able to persuade any field commanders to join the plot, the conspirators made seven unsuccessful attempts on Hitler's life. On July 20, 1944, a bomb placed at Hitler's feet by Colonel Claus von Stauffenberg killed four people but only bruised Hitler himself, who then carried out a vicious purge of all conceivable opposition. The principal military conspirators who were not fortunate enough to be shot the evening of the plot's failure were tried and killed by slow hanging. Trials continued for months, until almost five thousand were killed, and thousands of others who had no connection at all with the plot, were sent to concentration camps. Rommel, who had agreed to take command of the armed forces if the conspiracy were successful, later chose to commit suicide rather than be tried. After the plot's failure Hitler put an end to the army's political neutrality. On July 29, General Guderian, the new chief of staff, ordered all officers to cooperate in indoctrinating the army with National Socialist ideology.

The German Resistance. The German resistance was always feeble, disorganized, and insignificant in numbers. Hitler's opponents could never count on the solid support of any organization, such as churches, trade unions, university faculties, or even in the Army General Staff, and especially not among the people as a whole. Germany was to suffer serious consequences after the war, not only for the obvious fact that the opposition failed, but because it had been so small. In Germany itself, the younger generation felt divorced from their parents whose support of, or supine acquiescence in, Nazism, they felt, had brought appalling destruction upon them. The majority of the nation, who had not taken a personal part in the Nazi atrocities and who did not suspect the detail or magnitude of them until the Allies brought it home to them, were left without the salve to their conscience that a widespread resistance movement would have been; and for a time the nation undoubtedly sought a catharsis by its immersion in what the philosopher Karl Jaspers called the "guilt question," seeking a moral cleansing for a guilt many felt they indirectly shared. Moreover, many Germans were horrified by the experiences of war and felt quite honestly that they never wished to bear weapons again; and with this antimilitarism went a distrust never before felt in Germany of the General Staff that had sent millions of young Germans to their death in obedience to the orders of a madman. Outside Germany, the lack of resistance confirmed long-standing hatreds among Germany's neighbors. It was felt by many that Nazism was the expression of the German national character, that it was futile to make distinctions between good and bad Germans, and that the nation as a whole needed a long period of re-education under a harsh military occupation. The schools, universities, law courts, police, local and central government, and great industrial trusts were seen as institutions requiring thorough purging and remolding. Above all, German militarism, typified by the General Staff, the Officer Corps, the veterans organizations, and, as the Potsdam Conference concluded, "all clubs and associations which serve to keep alive the military tradition in Germany," was felt to need total eradication.

Nazism did lasting damage to the German people. It not only brought upon Germany destruction only equaled in the Thirty Years' War, and the death of five million Germans. It destroyed the most gifted of its people; perverted the organizations upon which a healthy democracy could be based, such as the trade unions, law courts, schools, churches, and even the family; and permitted a minority to indulge in sadism on a scale never before seen. When the Allies invaded Germany, there existed no political group who could be regarded as an alternative to the Nazis. The administration of Germany had to be carried out by the invading armies; and the foundations of self-government had to be constructed again from the very beginning.

WARTIME ITALY

Character of Mussolini's Rule. In comparison with Hitler's, Mussolini's dictatorship was mild. There were some glaring exceptions, such as the murder of the Socialist deputy Matteotti, but most political opponents had emigrated, had been imprisoned or had been sent to detention camps on isolated islands rather than executed. Anti-Semitism only became part of the policy of fascism in 1938, under Hitler's influence. The definition of "Jewish" in Italian law was much narrower than in German, the Italians were far less conscientious than the Germans in applying the law, and as a result, 30,000 of Italy's estimated prewar population of 50,000 Jews survived. Moreover, Mussolini's first expansionist adventures, in Ethiopia and Albania, were quickly carried out against enemies carefully chosen for their inability to resist; and Italian losses in manpower were not heavy. His intervention in the Spanish Civil War, to which he contributed 70,000 troops, had, however, already strained Italy's resources, and the Italian people were well aware of the cost that war with Britain and France would bring, although Mussolini was somewhat irked at the enthusiastic welcome he received as a peacemaker on his return from the Munich Conference. He was realistic enough, however, to keep Italy neutral when Hitler attacked Poland, and only declared war on Britain and France on June 10, 1940, after being convinced the war was already won. Although Italian troops made little headway in the fighting on the French Alpine border, casualties were light; and, in spite of Hitler's humiliating refusal to allow him to take Nice, Tunisia, Corsica, or French Somaliland, Mussolini might have come out of the struggle with some gain in prestige if Hitler had succeeded in defeating Britain.

The abandonment of the invasion of Britain meant more immediate disaster for the Italians than for the Germans. Mussolini had over-extended Italian resources by attacking Greece in October 1940 and by participating in the Nazi invasion of Russia. The first British counterat-tack came against the Italian armies of Marshal Graziani in Libya; and, in spite of German reinforcements sent under Rommel, Axis losses in North Africa were largely Italian. This one campaign would have been enough to drain Italian strength; but Italian East Africa was also under attack and fell in May 1941 to the British and South Africans. In 1942, the nine Italian divisions in Russia began to receive the blows of the great Soviet offensive north of Stalingrad. Disaffection spread through-out the Italian armies, which were only too pleased to be able to sur-render in safety, and hatred of the war reached even the highest ranks of the Fascist party and the Italian court. In 1943 it became evident that Hitler, who had been prepared to lose North Africa in order to win in Russia, had allowed Italy to become the main target for Allied invasion from North Africa and that he was envisaging unlimited destruction in Italy, in order, he said, that its defense might keep "the war as far away as possible from the heart of Europe and thereby from the frontiers of Germany."

The fear of Allied invasion, magnified by the bombing raids on south-ern Italy and, in July, on Rome itself, finally destroyed the will to fight of a people whose living conditions had become more and more miser-able as the war progressed. Italy had not even been able to exploit its meager share of the Axis empire to keep up the standard of living in Italy, since the German armies were stripping the nominally Italian-controlled Croatia and Greece. Production was hampered by lack of man-power, especially as more than 700,000 laborers were shipped to Ger-many. The Fascist party itself, which had been for so long the personal tool of Mussolini, lost most influence in the country, especially as the evidence of its corruption became increasingly notorious. Mussolini himself, who was the only person that could infuse the party with vigor, was slumping into a kind of fatalistic stupor, brought on by gastric ulcers and nervous collapse. In the spring of 1943, with Allied armies obviously poised for the invasion of Sicily, there was an almost universal feeling in Italy that Mussolini should be sacrificed to win peace from the Allies.

The Fall of the Duce. The problem was to find the means to overthrow him, an alternative government to replace him, and a miracle to prevent the Germans from occupying Italy. One center of opposition was the industrial cities of the north, where the Communist party had been able to keep a few cells of resistance in being, particularly in the automobile factories of Turin. Industrial strikes broke out in Milan and Turin in March 1943 and were followed by the appearance of underground resistance to fascism, complete with newspapers, weapons, and coordinated strategy. In 1934 the Communists had formed a Unity of Action Pact with the Socialists in exile in Paris, to conduct underground activity jointly; this Popular Front agreement was still in existence in 1943. Another political group created in Paris, the Action party, espoused a mild brand of socialism popularized in the underground newspaper *L'Italia Libera*. It remained, however, a party of intellectuals whose principles were to be embodied in the Italian constitution of 1947, but which never enjoyed great popular support. A third group, the Liberal party, which had governed Italy during the first decades of the Republic's existence, from 1860 to 1922, had, under Benedetto Croce's lead, maintained a critical attitude to the regime; but, as the party of the middle classes and of the ineffectual parliamentarism that had opened the way to Mussolini, they lacked popular support. The fourth possibility was the Church. In spite of the Lateran Agreements of 1929, relations between the Papacy and the Fascist government had been disturbed by Mussolini's educational policy and by his persecution of the Jews. In 1942 the Pope had suggested that Rome be declared an open city; and seeing the collapse of the Fascist state imminent, the former leaders of the Catholic Partito Popolare began to organize a new party under Alcide De Gasperi, which would become the Christian Democratic party. Although the Christian Democrats were later able to use the Church's administration to organize as a party, in 1943 they had barely begun to gather strength. None of these political groups possessed the force to overthrow Mussolini. However, in Italy, unlike Germany, there was disaffection among the leading members of the Fascist party itself; and there remained the monarchy, to which the army and police were loyal. The overthrow of Mussolini was to be carried out by these two groups.

In the execution of the coup d'état, the mildness of Italian fascism played an important role. Whereas almost every leader of the Nazi hierarchy knew that he would be executed for war crimes if the Allies won, few of the Fascist leaders feared Allied vengeance personally, nor were they afraid of Mussolini himself. Even though Count Grandi took two hand grenades with him to the final showdown meeting of the Grand Council, he told Mussolini quite openly beforehand that he intended to demand his resignation. On the night of July 24–25, 1943, the Fascist Grand Council, in Mussolini's presence, voted nineteen to seven for the restoration of all constitutional and military authority to the king; Mussolini ignored the demand of several associates that he arrest the critics. The vote would not have meant Mussolini's downfall, however, had the king not decided to use the army and police to arrest him after the vote. The king had been approached by the anti-Fascist political parties that spring; but, fearing that his association with fascism would lead to his own overthrow after Mussolini's, and believing that the British wished to maintain the monarchy in Italy, he determined to act without the support of these parties. On the afternoon of July 25 the king told Mussolini that he had already replaced him as premier by Marshal Pietro Badoglio, and as the Duce was leaving the royal villa, he was arrested by the Italian military police. Neither the Fascist party secretary nor the head of the Fascist militia made any move. Mussolini was overthrown without a single person being killed. Throughout Italy there was rejoicing. A few Fascist leaders were arrested, and the movement collapsed.

At the time of Mussolini's downfall the Allies were already in control of Sicily, and there were only seven German divisions in the whole of Italy. The obvious course for both the Allies and the new Italian government was to conclude an armistice immediately, before the Germans could rush troops into the peninsula. However, the Italians sought to impose conditions on the future of the Italian colonies and on the size of the army, while the Allies would accept only unconditional surrender and would not give any promise of reward for Italian participation in the war against Germany. Negotiations continued for six weeks. Only on September 8 did Badoglio and Eisenhower broadcast that the armistice had been signed and that the Italian forces should cease hostilities against the Allies but be prepared "to resist any attack from any other source." Hitler had already acted. On the evening he received news of Mussolini's overthrow, Hitler ordered eight divisions assembled to hold the Alpine passes; and on July 27 he had plans prepared for the military occupation of the whole of Italy, which were put in force on the day of the armistice. Five Italian divisions near Rome surrendered to the Germans almost at once; Allied landings, which the Germans feared might be north of Rome, were made at Salerno, south of Naples; and no Allied paratroops were dropped near Rome. On September 13, Mussolini himself was rescued from comfortable captivity in a ski resort in the Apennines by an SS glider rescue team and taken to East Prussia to Hitler. Two days later, he was proclaimed head of a new Italian state, the Italian Social Republic. Thus, Italy found itself divided into two states. When winter came, the Germans controlled the whole of Italy north of the heavily fortified Gustav Line from the Garigliano River on the Mediterranean to the Adriatic. The worst hardships of the war were still in store for the Italian people, and the Allies had let slip an opportunity to seize the whole of Italy and penetrate the heart of Europe by the end of 1943.

Italy's War with Germany. On October 13, 1943, the Badoglio government declared war on Germany. Fighting in Italy continued until May 20, 1945. Italy's second war, against its former ally, had more lasting effects than its first. The creation of a new Fascist government at Salò, on Lake Garda, with nominal powers and under strict German supervision, did not bring about a resurgence of support for Mussolini, nor did the social program of the new Republic win over the workers; but its mere existence brought about a state of civil war in Italy. Northern Italians were enlisted to fight against southern Italians, or to aid the Germans by factory work or in military construction; and an even more bitter social struggle occurred behind the German lines, when the Germans and their Italian supporters were attacked by a resistance movement of unexpected strength and organization. The separation of north and south Italy for so long a period—the Gustav Line south of Rome was broken only in May 1944, and the Gothic Line north of Florence only in April 1945—further sharpened the already enormous contrast between north and south. In the rural, poverty-stricken South, the Catholic Church was able to aid the new Christian Democratic party. In the north, the resistance movement was dominated by the Socialists and Communists who gained a popularity they were never to lose. The resistance movement numbered 250,000 members, of whom some 70,000 paid with their lives. Strikes, sabotage, propaganda, and guerrilla attacks, which kept eight German divisions away from the front line, were pressed with heroic skill.

Revival of Political Activity. As the resistance movement became more organized, the partisan groups tended to identify with political parties, including the Christian Democrats, the Action party, the Socialists, and above all the Communists. The left-wing groups were well aware of the political significance of their activity and proclaimed themselves a revolutionary force that would remodel Italian society. For a brief period in the Ossola Valley near the Swiss border, they proclaimed a Democratic Republic. The left-wing resistance groups were naturally dissatisfied with the conservative character of a government dominated by King Victor Emmanuel III and Marshal Badoglio, which had been recognized not only by the British and American but even, on March 12, 1944, by the Soviet government. They found allies in the anti-Fascist Committees of National Liberation and in the organized political parties in the south who, with the exception of the Liberals and Conservatives, were demanding the abdication of the king and of the Crown Prince Umberto. These political parties, whose participation in the Badoglio government had been demanded by the British and American governments, finally accepted a compromise by which the king passed his powers over to Umberto as lieutenant-general, the decision on the monarchy's future was postponed to the end of the war, and all the political parties, including the Communists, entered the government.

The Communist party made major gains in 1943–45. In the north, it gained a controlling interest in the labor movement and in much local government; in the Italian General Confederation of Labor, a union of Communist, Socialist, and Christian Democratic workers, formed in January 1944 at Bari, it was soon supreme. Its party leader, Palmiro Togliatti, as a minister without portfolio, was able to facilitate Communist appointments throughout the administration. The Allies discredited themselves somewhat by their apparent desire to uphold the monarchy and the existing class structure in Italy at a time when a majority of the people were crying for major changes. However, the popularity of the Catholic Church also increased during these years, for, particularly in Rome, the clergy took an active role in aiding the victims of the Germans, offering political fugitives hideouts, food, and shelter in churches. In this way, the fortunes of the Christian Democratic party were aided.

Unfortunately, the political instability of the postwar years was already foreshadowed in party squabbles. The taking of Rome on June 4 was followed by the transfer of constitutional powers to Crown Prince Umberto as lieutenant-general, and by the resignation of the second Badoglio cabinet. The new government, of Labor Democrat and resistance leader Ivanoe Bonomi, lasted only four months, owing to a conflict between the left-wing and the conservative parties on the degree to which the purge of former Fascists should be pushed. A second Bonomi cabinet, formed in November 1944, lasted until the end of the war. But the period was marked by bitter fighting between seven major political parties—Communists, Socialists, Christian Democrats, Liberals, Action party, Republicans, and Labor Democrats—and several minor ones. The precedent of short-lived coalition governments was being set.

Two final results of this period should be noted—the fearsome destruction and the lasting hatred of Germany. Italy was a battleground for two years. Its roads, railroads, bridges, factories, airfields, ports, and homes were bombed, blasted by artillery, or destroyed in street fighting. Terrible losses of manpower occurred in the support of both the Allies and the Germans, in the resistance, or in deportations to Germany. When the war ended, Italy was a ruined country. The blame for this devastation was assigned above all to the Germans. Even during the years of alliance, the overweening attitude of Germans toward Italians at every level from the Duce down had roused resentment. This was transformed into loathing after the armistice. In the Balkans, the Germans wiped out thousands of Italian soldiers and deported the rest to Germany—40,000 in all. Vast numbers of workers were forcibly taken from the north to work in Germany. Savage reprisals were executed after partisan raids, as in the shooting of 1,500 civilians in the little village of Marzabotto. The hatred of Germany, which was so potent a factor in the postwar history of Europe, was fully shared by its former ally.

WESTERN EUROPE
UNDER THE NAZI YOKE

Hitler's plans for German expansion, as elaborated before 1939, had not included the conquest of Western Europe. The decision of Britain and France to aid Poland, however, had led him to defeat Denmark, Norway, the Netherlands, Belgium, Luxembourg, and France itself. In these countries, a pragmatic approach was taken in determining the form of administration to be set up. Territories considered of German heritage—Eupen, Malmédy, and Moresnet from Belgium, Alsace and Lorraine from France, and Luxembourg—were fused with neighboring German provinces. Norway, Denmark, and the Netherlands were known as "autonomous" territories where native governments continued to function and German control was exercised by civilians. Military administrations were set up in Belgium and occupied France.

Alsace-Lorraine. Alsace and Lorraine suffered heavily from their intermediary position between Germany and France. Compulsory military service was introduced in August 1942, but German citizenship was only given to those who served in the armies. Germanization was carried out by ordering use of the German language and place names, and even of German family names, by large-scale expulsions of such "non-Germans" as Jews, gypsies, and French-speaking people, and by the settlement, especially in Lorraine, of Germans from the East. About 200,000 were deported to Germany when resistance to the extension of German citizenship was shown. While serving in the German forces, citizens of Alsace and Lorraine found themselves forced to fight against the resistance forces and even to take part in reprisals such as the shooting of French hostages. French purge courts after the war had great difficulty in determining the blame to be laid upon these unfortunate people; and, as happened after the Treaty of Versailles had restored Alsace and Lorraine to France in 1919, it was found that the forcible separation had created animosities between the French-speaking and the German-speaking Alsatians. The higher standard of living that Germany enjoyed was not shared with these provinces, which were stripped of their farm animals and machinery and of many of their industrial goods; and the separation from France caused a breakdown of their normal pattern of trade, without a corresponding increase in trade with Germany. The effect was to make Alsace and Lorraine almost more distrustful of Germany than the rest of France and to make of their inhabitants the most convinced supporters of all movements of European integration. The city of Strasbourg provided the headquarters for several of the new federal institutions of Western Europe—the Council of Europe in 1949, the Common Assembly of the European Coal and Steel Community in 1950, and the European Parliament in

1958—and for long competed to be chosen as the federal capital of a United States of Europe.

Luxembourg. The Grand Duchess Charlotte of Luxembourg and her government had fled to London when the Germans invaded, and maintained a government-in-exile there throughout the war. The Luxembourg Parliament approved her action on May 11, 1940 and was soon dissolved by the new German chief of the civil administration, who had been ordered by Hitler to "recover the former German Reichsland Luxembourg for the German Reich." German became the official language; the law courts and administration were converted to the German pattern; local collaborators were found to run branches of the Hitler Youth and German Labor Front. Acquaintance with German rule intensified resistance to Germanization. The professional classes were decimated by imprisonment and deportation to Germany; 15,000 Luxembourgers were forcibly incorporated into the German armies; families of deserters or resistance fighters were deported to Poland, as were 2,000 Luxembourg Jews. By 1944, a well-organized resistance movement was functioning in the Ardennes Mountains, causing considerable trouble to the retreating German armies. German rule in Luxembourg therefore solidified the Luxembourg people. There was no social conflict within the resistance movement, which was unified in support of the return of the grand duchess and the government-in-exile. Yet Luxembourg drew two important conclusions from the bitter experience— neutrality was worthless; European integration was the sole salvation of the small nations.

The Netherlands. The Germans always claimed that the "autonomous" states of the Netherlands, Norway, and Denmark deserved special treatment because they were related to Germany by blood, their populations being either Germanic or Nordic. In the Netherlands, the Germans hoped to be able to use the Dutch Nazis, who numbered 100,000. Reich Commissioner Seyss-Inquart constantly proclaimed his "special responsibility for the peoples of Germanic blood" and for the "Germanic" Dutch people. But the customary repression accompanied these declarations. Over 100,000 Dutch Jews were deported to Polish concentration camps; 350,000 Dutch workers were sent to Germany; and thousands were taken to settle the agricultural lands of the Ukraine and to join the German armies. Conditions of life deteriorated as German exactions of food and industrial goods grew, and by the end of the war large parts of the country were near starvation. The flat fields of the Netherlands did not lend themselves to the formation of a resistance movement like those of France or Luxembourg, however. Opposition to the Germans was expressed by strikes, sabotage, even by open protests, and by such solidarity that 300,000 persons, including 30,000 Jews, were hidden, mostly in the cities. The Dutch, like the people of Luxembourg, were strengthened in their loyalty to their queen by German oppression. Although the Communist party gained ground by its strong share in the Dutch resistance movement, it found its gains minimized by the growth of progressive sentiment among the other political parties, which gave new life to a political system that had become archaic. Reformist groups in the resistance formed the Popular Dutch Movement, whose leader William Schermerhorn was named premier by Queen Wilhelmina in May 1945; and from this movement was formed the important new Labor party, in February 1946. In spite of terrible suffering, therefore, the Dutch emerged from the ordeal with a better political system and without the wounds of collaboration or class war. Like Luxembourg, they were to see their future security in Benelux, the Coal and Steel Community, the Common Market, and NATO. But, as we shall see later in the chapter, they were to face one enormous problem as a result of the war—the development of nationalist aspirations in the Dutch East Indies—from which 15 per cent of the Dutch national income was drawn.

Denmark. Denmark was proclaimed by the Germans to be their "model protectorate." The popular King Christian X, determined to spare his people as much suffering as possible, had ordered that the German armies should not be opposed, and decided himself to remain in Copenhagen through the occupation. The Germans thereupon declared Denmark to be a "sovereign state under German protection" and permitted the Danish Constitution to remain in force. German pressure, however, forced the admittance to the cabinet of Erik Scavenius, a well-known German sympathizer, who became foreign minister in July 1940 and premier in November 1942. The king was compelled to make numerous concessions to the Germans, including acceptance of Danish signature of the Anti-Comintern Pact in November 1941 and the beginning of measures against Danish Jews, and constitutional liberties were slowly whittled away. Nevertheless, for the first two years of the occupation, Hitler insisted that efforts be made to conciliate the Danes, and he refused to allow the SS to indulge in taking hostages or mass terrorism. Free elections were permitted on March 23, 1943 and disappointed the Germans by resulting in only 43,000 votes for the Danish Nazis who won 3 seats out of 150 in the Parliament. This challenge could hardly be tolerated; and in August 1943, when the king and his government re-- fused to impose martial law and apply the death penalty for sabotage, the Germans took over direct administration of the country, dissolved the government, and made the king a virtual prisoner. Resistance spread widely. Most Danish Jews were smuggled into Sweden to prevent their arrest and deportation. German military installations, communications, and industries supplying Germany, were sabotaged; hundreds of re- sistance newspapers came into being; organization became so efficient that a general strike on June 30, 1944 forced the Germans to com- promise. Sabotage bred German terrorism. The Gestapo took over the destruction of the Danish resistance movement. Danish property was destroyed as "countersabotage"; and a series of political assassinations was carried out. As in the Netherlands, German brutality helped unite the country. At war's end the country was able to resume its normal political life, with the same king, political parties, and virtually the same leaders as before the war.

Norway. In the Norwegian Vidkun Quisling, Hitler found a tool who gave his name to all collaborators. The Norwegian King Haakon VII and his government, unlike that of Denmark, had ordered the Nor- wegian armies to resist the Germans; and the hopeless struggle had dragged on for sixty-two days. Meanwhile, the Germans had permitted Quisling to form a government, without the king's consent, on the opening day of the invasion. Quisling himself, an ex-army officer who had veered from extreme left-wing sympathies to Nordic racism, was despised in Norway, however, and his Nazi party had never received more than 2 per cent of the vote. After six days the Germans decided to use an Administrative Council, made up of a more respectable group of Norwegians, who were willing to work with the Germans to reduce the hardships of the occupation; but six months later this council was dis- missed, the king dethroned, and Parliament abolished. Provisional state councillors, mostly Norwegian Nazis, were set up as a façade govern- ment; and in February 1942, Quisling himself was brought back as minister-president. The dismissal of the Administrative Council proved a major factor in bringing an organized resistance movement into being.

Two of its members set up the first resistance group; and the church, trade unions, professional organizations, and the political parties united to plan opposition to the occupying power. *Milorg* (Military Organization), the armed resistance, was formed at the end of 1941 and soon was carrying out sabotage throughout the country, supplied by a regular fishing-boat service between the Shetland Islands and northern Norway that came to be called the Shetland Bus. Faced with the resistance, the Germans made no further attempts to conciliate the population. About 8,000 political prisoners, including 1,000 Jews, were sent to concentration camps in Germany and Poland. Compulsory labor service was initiated for some 75,000 Norwegians, but only about 2,000 were sent to Germany. Deportation was largely avoided by flight across the border to Sweden, where some 58,000 refugees found safety. Thus, in a small way, Sweden repaid its refusal to sell Norway armaments or gasoline at the time of the German attack. With the Russian liberation of the most northerly province of Norway in October 1944, German brutality increased. Hostages were shot, villages burned, mass executions carried out, university professors and students arrested in the hundreds. When liberation came on May 7, 1945 the country was united. Even Quisling and his supporters received fair trials, and only about sixty were charged with major offenses. The king was welcomed back, and Norway returned to its Socialist traditions with the formation of a coalition government under Einar Gerhardsen, leader of the Labor party. The Communists, who had run their own resistance movement, had lost the chance to infiltrate the major organizations of the country, as had happened in most other countries; the reckless nature of their sabotage had not won them much popularity.

Belgium. The Belgians were already a divided nation before the German attack. The inhabitants of the northern half of the country, Flanders, spoke Flemish, a language akin to Dutch, and were Catholic and conservative, while the French-speaking Walloons of the southern part of the country, Wallonia, were Socialist and anticlerical. A Flemish nationalist movement in the 1930's was influenced by fascism, and the Nazis determined to weaken opposition in Belgium by playing up the racial affinity between Flemings and Germans. Even though there was a Walloon Quisling group, the Walloons were convinced that the Flemings had provided the majority of Quislings while they, the Walloons, had been the main strength of the resistance movement. The equivocal position of King Leopold III exacerbated these conflicts. Leopold, after ordering the Belgian Army to capitulate on May 28, 1940, against the advice of his government, had remained in Belgium as a prisoner of war, while the government had fled to France, and later to England. His action had at first been welcomed by the Belgians, especially in Flanders, but he later forfeited that popularity by going to see Hitler, refusing to support the resistance movement, and, most effectively, by marrying a commoner in September 1941, thus forfeiting the reflected popularity of his late wife, Astrid. At the end of the war, the king himself was a source of national division, with the Flemings united in wanting his return and the Walloons, led by the Socialist leader Paul-Henri Spaak, equally fervent in wanting his ouster.

The Germans did not profit fully from these divisions because they regarded Belgium as primarily of military importance in launching the invasion of England and later in repelling an invasion from England, and as a rich source of industrial goods and raw materials. They placed the country under military administration of General Alexander von Falkenhausen and joined to it the great French coal and steel basin of the Nord/Pas-de-Calais. The Belgian civil service continued to function, although many of its leading positions were filled by pliable collaborators. For the first two years, Belgium was relatively well treated; but with the reverses in Russia, 500,000 workers were deported to Germany, and exactions from Belgian industry grew greatly. This helped magnify the resistance movement and led in turn to German terrorism. In the resistance movement, the Communists played an extremely active role, and they succeeded in dominating the largest resistance group, the Independence Front. The Catholic Church, however, aided the work of the non-Communist groups, who were united in The Secret Army. Belgium emerged from the war with its industrial plant in fairly good shape and seemed to have avoided many of the harsher consequences of the struggle. But the first five postwar years showed that the linguistic, religious, and political divisions between Flemings and Walloons had been dangerously sharpened by the occupation. The question of the future of King Leopold eventually brought the two groups into open battle.

Exploitation of France. In all Western Europe, however, it was France that suffered the most immediate as well as the most lasting consequences of Nazi occupation. In spite of the apparent leniency of the armistice terms, the Germans never hesitated to exploit the riches of France. France, as the major agricultural producer of Western Europe, was expected to supply Germany with vast quantities of livestock and cereals. In August 1940 alone, the Germans demanded half a million head of cattle and a million and a half pigs from the Unoccupied Zone; and Nazi theorists toyed with the idea of making France a peasant community, in an interesting parallel to the Morgenthau Plan later proposed for Germany. By the end of the war it was estimated that 150,000 French people had died as a direct result of undernourishment. High proportions of all manufactured goods and raw materials were taken—34 per cent of chemicals, 60 per cent of rubber, 90 per cent of airplane construction, 75 per cent of aluminum, 74 per cent of iron ore, and so on. These goods were paid for by the French themselves, by various ingenious financial schemes. Occupation costs rose from 300 million francs a day in 1940 to 700 million a day in 1944. The exchange rate was artificially set at 20 francs to a mark, about 30 per cent above the mark's actual value. The property of Jews, and of members of the resistance and other condemned groups was confiscated. By the end of the war, the French estimated their loss due to the direct transfer of French goods to the Germans at 2,318 billion francs. Manpower was also exploited. In January 1944, there were 870,000 French prisoners of war working in Germany, many in armaments works, and over a million laborers, who had been deported by the Obligatory Labor Service. Although conditions in Germany for these workers were abominable, they of course did not compare with the fate reserved for the 120,000 Jews, mostly foreign refugees, or the 112,000 political prisoners, most of whom never returned to France.

The Vichy Regime. The French had not, however, been united in their opposition to the invader. Indeed, when Marshal Pétain had offered himself as a "shield" to protect them from direct German rule, most Frenchmen rallied to him with a feeling of relief. Pétain, not de Gaulle, represented the "real physical France," Stalin commented later. Only twenty-one parliamentarians had embarked on the "Massilia" to carry the government to French Morocco, and they had been arrested on arrival in Casablanca. Most of the other members of the French Parliament had found their way to Vichy where, on July 10, 1940, a joint session of the two houses, by a vote of 569 to 80, had given Pétain power to draft a new constitution. The members of the two houses were assured that they would continue in office, and they drew their salaries without the houses ever being called back into session. Their vote effectively killed the Third Republic, and its death was little mourned in France. Pétain promised a national revolution on the lines of Mussolini's Italy or of Salazar's Portugal. This revolution never advanced very far. Pétain became head of the French State; "Liberty, Equality, Fraternity" was replaced as a national motto by "Work, Family, Country." Corporate organization of economic life was begun with an agricultural corporation for the peasantry, but was never applied seriously in industry, although organization committees did replace the employers' associations. What was significant about Pétain's rule was its absolute reliance upon the professionals of the state bureaucracy, especially the famous Inspecteurs des Finances. In the Occupied Zone in particular, where Pétain's decrees were enforced in principle only, the French bureaucracy governed directly under the supervision of the German military government. It was this willingness of the French civil servants to remain in office during the German occupation rather than the collaboration of the principal politicians at Vichy that provoked the greatest division in French society. At war's end it was quite possible to condemn Pétain, Laval, or Darnand as Quislings, or to reject such French Nazis as Doriot or Déat. But in the vast ranks of the state civil service and in the upper levels of industrial administration, Germany had been aided by the cooperation of thousands of Frenchmen. The problem to be faced was whether these men should be condemned as traitors and ejected from the mainstream of national life, pardoned as men who had had no other choice but to continue in their jobs, or perhaps even be praised as having courageously interposed themselves to modify the exactions of the Germans. No answer to these questions was satisfactory; and the problem of the purges remained to plague French society for years after the Liberation.

Pétain's government declined into ever greater collaboration after April 1942 when Laval became head of the government for the second time. Laborers were rounded up for the Germans, although Laval did try to set up an exchange scheme by which one prisoner of war was returned for every three laborers sent to Germany. A vicious Militia was created on the model of the Gestapo and took its share in arresting and torturing French resistance leaders. Most foreign Jews were handed over for extermination. Yet even this phase of collaboration produced its own ferment for the future; for Laval attempted to ennoble his movement with the ideals of Franco-German conciliation in a unified Europe. In the Nazi New Order, he claimed to see an end to the centuries of national rivalry that had racked Europe. "A new Europe will inevitably arise from this war," Laval declared. "We often talk of Europe. It is a word to which we are not yet very accustomed in France. We love our country because we love our village. As for me, a Frenchman, I could wish that tomorrow we should be able to love a Europe in which France will have a worthy place." From 1943 on this attractive idea was voiced more frequently by the Germans, too, whose propagandists claimed that the Third Reich was in fact a great new European community. In the mouths of these men, the ideas were sullied, and by war's end, the only people who dared to speak of Franco-German rapprochement or of European unification were those who had a clear record of opposition to the Nazis.

The French Resistance. Fortunately, within the resistance movements throughout Europe, and particularly in France, these ideas were also being voiced. Underground opposition groups had sprung up from the moment Pétain announced the cease-fire, particularly in the Unoccupied Zone where organization was easier. In Lyon, the center of the southern resistance movement, Captain Henri Frenay, who was later to become a passionate supporter of European federalism, gathered around himself a group called Combat, which included several of the postwar political leaders of France. A more revolutionary group, Liberation, attempted to combine the Socialist and Communist political parties and trade unionists to plan a popular uprising. In the north, where the German Army exercised strict controls, the groups tended to be more fragmented and shorter-lived. Students at the Sorbonne organized Defense of France; Jean-Paul Sartre had his own group, Socialism and Freedom; the Communist party flung itself wholeheartedly into the National Front; Socialists supported Liberation-North; and military and professional men joined the Civilian and Military Organization. The activities of these groups ran the gamut from newspaper and book publishing, supplying of information to the Allies, and aiding downed pilots to escape, to sabotage and finally to direct attack by the military groupings of the Maquis. While serving at first largely to demoralize the occupying troops, the underground was of direct assistance to the Allies just before and after the D-Day invasion; and in 1944, 137,000 of the resistance troops, the French Forces of the Interior, were united with the regular French Army. The resistance movement did far more for France than harass the Germans. It helped restore national self-confidence and self-respect, which had been endangered in the debacle of 1940. It produced a new generation of leaders who simply took over the administration of the country from the bureaucrats of Vichy in 1944. Above all, it stimulated a revolutionary ferment, which was expressed as a demand for a wholesale renovation of French society. The Charter of the National Council of the Resistance, a unifying committee for the Resistance movement founded in 1943, laid down a minimum program of reforms, including nationalization of "all the great monopolized means of production, which are a product of common labor, of the sources of power, of mineral wealth, of insurance companies, and of big banks"; a national plan for the increase of production; social security benefits for the workers; and "the granting of political, social and economic rights" to the native populations of the French colonies. In foreign affairs, the resistance leaders demanded an end to the narrow nationalism that had brought about the Second World War, and many saw an alternative in federalism of various kinds. In the postwar years, the resistance leaders were in the forefront in the drive to unite Western Europe. The European Union of Federalists, The French Committee for Exchanges with the New Germany, and the French Council for United Europe were all headed by former resistance leaders.

Charles de Gaulle. The force that unified these disparate groups was the personality of General Charles de Gaulle. De Gaulle, a graduate of the French military academy St. Cyr, served with distinction in the First World War, but found advancement slow in the postwar years owing to the unorthodoxy of his military ideas, which he insisted on publicizing in a series of small, superbly written books. In *The Edge of the Sword* (1932), he had suggested that a great officer should know when to disobey his superiors. In *Toward a Career Army* (1934), he had proposed the creation of six armored divisions trained in rapid mobility as a substitute for the static defense of the Maginot Line. These ideas had brought him to the attention of Paul Reynaud who made him undersecretary of war in June 1940, a position he held for only eleven days. During that time, however, on two missions to London, he made contact with Churchill who recognized in him, he said, "the man of destiny." On June 16, in Bordeaux, learning of Pétain's appointment as premier with the avowed aim of seeking an armistice from the Germans, de Gaulle put into practice the theory he had announced in *The Edge of the Sword,* deserted Pétain's army, and fled to London on a British plane. Churchill at once placed at his disposal the services of the B.B.C.; and, in a famous speech on June 18, de Gaulle called upon the French people to join him in continuing the struggle against the Germans: "The flame of French resistance must not go out, and shall not go out." On June 19, he went further: "The ordinary forms of power have disappeared. . . . I, General de Gaulle, French soldier and leader, feel that I am speaking in the name of France." De Gaulle thus declared himself the leader of French resistance; and within a few months, he was joined in London by several thousand French soldiers and civilians, and several French colonies in the Pacific and central Africa rallied to him.

By the end of 1941, de Gaulle had transformed himself from a soldier refusing to recognize his country's defeat to the head of a government-in-exile, the French National Committee. Unlike the Norwegian or the Dutch governments-in-exile, however, he had received no parliamentary mandate; and for that reason the American government refused to recognize his political demands. With no power, constitutional or physical, to enforce them, de Gaulle fell back on personal intransigence and moral loftiness. His three weapons, wrote resistance leader Emmanuel d'Astier, were:

> prestige, secrecy, and cunning. His cunning is mediocre, but his secrecy, supported by a natural, icy prestige, takes him a long way. I have often wondered what his prestige derives from: his height? . . . Or from his appearance, which is always so typical of himself, a picture showing a lack of sensitivity to the warmth of life? Or from his inspired voice, its broken cadences emerging from an inanimate body lacking in all animal warmth, a voice issuing from a waxwork? Or from his aloofness from his fellow men? Or from his language, always too infallible when his thought is not, approximating in certain of his utterances to the great sermons of the eighteenth century? Or from his remoteness, the expressionless body and his few gestures which, in the last analysis, are as solemn and inevitable as his adjectives? . . . I do not know. He remains a mystery: this man, motivated by one historical idea, the greatness of France, and whose single voice seems to replace all others. . . .

In an astounding feat of personal magnetism, de Gaulle succeeded in winning the allegiance of the French Empire, the army and the resistance movement. By his broadcasts, he slowly came to embody for most French people the very spirit of an undefeated France. His agents, armed with British funds, parachuted into France to organize the dispersed efforts of the underground movements which were finally, through the courageous efforts of a young ex-prefect, Jean Moulin, united in the National Council of the Resistance, which recognized de Gaulle as the leader of the French resistance movement. Although he agreed to act as a joint president with General Giraud of the French Committee of National Liberation, formed in Algiers in June 1943, he was soon able to force Giraud from the committee and into retirement. He then transformed the committee into a cabinet, assigned ministries to the major political parties and resistance groups, and created a representative, if not an elected, parliament, known as the Consultative Assembly.

The supreme test of de Gaulle's strength came after the D-Day landings, since the American government had still refused to agree to recognize him as ruler of liberated France. To Roosevelt's amazement, de Gaulle's representatives installed themselves, with popular acclamation, in every region liberated. Instead of the chaos and the possible Communist attempt at a coup d'état that the American government had been led to expect, the turnover in administration went through with few incidents. Violence that did occur was individual revenge-taking with no over-all political aim. De Gaulle entered Paris on August 25, to be acclaimed the next day by a crowd of two million as he strode down the Champs Elysées, amid the crackle of the shots of the last rooftop snipers. The Provisional Government of the French Republic, with de Gaulle as provisional premier, was recognized by the Allies in August as the *de facto,* and by October as the *de jure,* government of France. De Gaulle had thus succeeded in founding an entirely new political force, Gaullism, whose doctrines, until then a satisfactorily vague reassertion of French unity and resistance, had to be tailored to meet the problems of a country shattered but in ferment. It was perhaps too much to expect de Gaulle to carry off a similar triumph in the post-liberation era as that he had just enjoyed.

Western Europe, then, was greatly changed during the years of German occupation. All the countries were exploited to the point of economic disruption by the Germans; in all, resistance movements, usually reformist if not revolutionary in their attitude to their country's political and social structure, sprang into being; existing weakness and tensions were accentuated, as in the Fleming-Walloon rivalry in Belgium and the class conflict in France; new social and political problems were created by the increase in the Communist party's influence and by the need to deal with collaborators, to write new constitutions, or to determine the status of monarchy. But there was also a bright side to the picture. The resistance movements had for a brief while overcome social and political divisions; a new idealism saw in a unified and reconciled Europe a method of ending national wars; and the less privileged were being promised a fairer deal in society.

THE AXIS SATELLITES

The authoritarian regimes of Rumania, Bulgaria, and Hungary saw considerable advantages to be derived from alliance with Germany and Italy. They were to pay an unexpectedly heavy price for that allegiance.

Rumania. Rumania was Hitler's most willing ally, in spite of resentment at the Germans for compelling it to cede Bessarabia and northern Bukovina to Russia, northern Transylvania to Hungary, and southern Dobrudja to Bulgaria. After the abdication of King Carol in September 1940, the regular army under the leadership of General Ion Antonescu had dominated the government. For a time, Antonescu's government included the Iron Guard, a Nazi-style anti-Semitic band of toughs that indulged in political murders and outrages against the Jews. But in January 1941 Antonescu called upon the regular army to destroy the Guard, which it did in a few days of street fighting. Hitler made no objection, although he welcomed the Guard's leaders to refuge in Germany. In Antonescu, he found a man he admired, particularly as Antonescu was anxious to join in the war against Russia. "You can always count upon Rumania," Antonescu told Hitler, "when the Slavs are to be fought." Antonescu, now aping Hitler by calling himself the Conducator, or Leader, welcomed German troops to train the Rumanian Army, allowed the passage of German divisions on their way to the conquest of Greece, and joined the attack on Russia on June 22, 1941. Within five weeks, the Rumanian armies had regained northern Bukovina and Bessarabia.

Up to this point, Antonescu had enjoyed almost unanimous approval, except for the small Communist party. Maniu, the Peasant party leader, and Brătianu, the Liberal leader, had both seen the return of the provinces lost to Russia as essential. With the defeat of the Iron Guard, the outrages against the Jews had been modified. A certain muted opposition could be expressed. Vested interests of landowners and businessmen were protected. But after July 1941, Maniu and other opposition leaders demanded an end to the war on Russia, and concentration instead on the return of northern Transylvania from Hungary. Antonescu, however, with Hitler's approval, seized the northern Black Sea coast, including the port of Odessa, and annexed it to Rumania as the province of Transnistria. By 1943, after the Battle of Stalingrad, Rumanian casualties were almost half a million. The Rumanian people were war weary and sickened by the German alliance, especially as Russian air attacks were increasing, while shortages of all necessities of life were being felt by all save the well-to-do. The Court, Maniu, and even the vice-premier, Mihai Antonescu, began to consider how best to withdraw Rumania from the German alliance. Fear of Allied invasion of the Balkans, the example of the overthrow of Mussolini in July 1943, and growing German intransigence, strengthened the determination of King Michael to act against the Conducator.

Rumania's future development was determined during the next twelve months. Conducator Antonescu's solution to Rumania's dilemma, which he presented to Hitler on April 16–17, 1944, was for the Axis powers to make peace with the West and to concentrate on eliminating Russia. Meanwhile, Vice-Premier Mihai Antonescu was working to persuade Hitler's allies, especially Italy, to make a separate peace with the West and to desert Germany. Neither of these plans had any chance of acceptance by the West. Maniu, however, who was well-known and respected in the West, and indeed was the best hope for the restoration of true democracy in Rumania, began sending his own emissaries to meet Western representatives in Cairo, to discuss how Rumania could leave the war. He proposed that Rumania cease fighting against Russia, but that the Western Powers guarantee Rumania against Russian demands and send troops to Rumania by air at the moment of the surrender. Neither the British nor the American governments even considered negotiating without the Russians, especially as the Red Army had taken Bessarabia and northern Bukovina in March 1944. Maniu's emissaries therefore found themselves faced with a joint delegation of British,

American, and Soviet representatives; and the armistice terms, presented in April, were drawn up by Russia. But, while demanding that Rumania join the war against Germany and recognize Russia's right to Bessarabia and the northern Bukovina, Molotov emphasized that the Soviet government did "not pursue the aim of acquiring any part of Rumanian territory or of changing the existing social order in Rumania."

With no other guarantee than this promise but with no other hope of averting Russian military occupation, Maniu and the king concerted for the overthrow of the two Antonescus. On August 23, when they came to the royal palace to report on their recent talks with Hitler, the two were arrested by the royal guard. That evening the king proclaimed that Rumania was no longer at war with the Allies, including the Russians, and two days later he declared war on Germany. Unresisted, the Red Army swept into Rumania, reaching Bucharest on August 30, and the northern border of Bulgaria on September 1. The new Rumanian government, headed by General Sănătescu, was made up largely of regular army officers, but the leaders of the four main political parties— Peasants, Liberals, Socialists, and Communists—were named ministers without portfolio. The armistice terms, signed on September 12, gave Russia the right to station troops in Rumania, to supervise the Rumanian press, to incorporate twelve Rumanian divisions in the Red Army in the struggle against Germany, and to receive $300 million worth of commodities as reparations during the next six years. The significance of King Michael's revolution, according to Hugh Seton-Watson, was enormous: "Rumania's change of front, together with the Teheran decision not to open a front in the Balkans, decided the fate of Central Europe, decided that the Soviet Union should dominate the whole region, that its new order should be a communist new order."

Bulgaria. Unlike Rumania, Bulgaria suffered relatively little from its satellite status. This was partly due to the character of King Boris, a tough negotiator who refused to be cowed by Hitler's blustering, secure in his own personal hold over Bulgaria since the royal coup in 1934. Boris, authoritarian and opportunistic rather than Fascist in inclination, was determined to gain the greatest benefit at least cost for Bulgaria from the German alliance. He shared in the dismemberment of Rumania, taking the southern Dobrudja, and he joined the attack on Yugoslavia and Greece to annex large areas of western Thrace and of both Greek and Yugoslav Macedonia. He refused to declare war on

Russia, even though Bulgaria had joined the Tripartite Pact in March 1941, on the grounds that Pan-Slav tradition was too strong in Bulgaria for his people to support such a war. Bulgaria's principal aid to the Germans was in permitting free transit for German troops across Bulgaria, and, as Germany's war losses mounted, in taking over more of the garrisoning duties in the occupied Balkan states.

The German alliance, however, was not popular with the mass of the Bulgarian people, nor with the opposition political parties. As early as 1942, the Bulgarian Communists joined with representatives of the Socialist, Agrarian, and *Zveno* parties in the formation of a Fatherland Front. *(Zveno* was a group of intellectuals with strong army support.) Throughout 1943, with the encouragement of radio broadcasts from Russia by the veteran Bulgarian Communist Georgi Dimitrov, then a deputy of the Russian Supreme Soviet, of the Russian legation in Sofia which remained open throughout the war, and of the Fatherland Front, underground opposition developed. Political assassinations were carried out. Armies of partisans were formed in the mountains, dominated to a large extent by the Communists. After the mysterious death of Boris three days after a stormy visit to Hitler, Bulgarian politicians were divided between the pro-German Regency Council, acting on behalf of the six-year-old King Simon, the Liberal and Conservative parties who were in opposition but refused to collaborate with the Communists in the Fatherland Front, and the four left-wing parties of the Fatherland Front, whom it was Russian tactics to install in power.

The opportunity came as the Red Army occupied Rumania in August 1944. Since May, the Bulgarian government, headed by a former Agrarian, Bagrianov, had been emphasizing its pan-Slav ties, and reminding Russia of its neutrality in the Russo-German War. Bagrianov fell from power on September 1, when two Russian armies were already stationed on the Bulgarian border; and the new government of the Democrat Mushanov invited the Russians to liberate Bulgaria from the Germans, opened peace discussions with British and American representatives in Cairo, and broke relations with Germany. It was too late, however, because on September 5 the Russians suddenly declared war on Bulgaria, invaded without opposition, and four days later accepted the Bulgarian demand for peace. Their move gave them the right to occupy the whole country and to impose their armistice terms on Bulgaria. Moreover, on the night of September 8-9, the Fatherland Front, which had refused to join a pro-Western government put together by the right-wing Agrarian, Muraviev, organized a popular uprising, and set up a new government under the *Zveno* leader Georgiev. An armistice similar to that imposed on Rumania was signed in Moscow on October 28. It remained to be seen what use the Soviet government would make of its predominant position.

Hungary. In Hungary, there was considerable sympathy for Nazi aims. Anti-Semitism was strong, as was fear of both Russia and of communism. The Magyar ruling classes, the landed gentry and the industrial magnates, were aware of the dangerous social discontent among the peasantry, who had been refused land reform, and among the industrial proletariat; and they had the specter of the Béla Kun regime to look back upon. The only demands that seemed to unite the country were for the revision of the Treaty of Trianon, which had dismembered Hungary's empire. Hence, there had been widespread support for the seizure of Sub-Carpathian Ruthenia from Czechoslovakia in March 1939, and for the taking of northern Transylvania from Rumania in August 1940. Hitler was determined to have Hungarian military aid in the defeat of Russia, however, and used the pro-German Hungarian General Staff to pressure the Hungarian government into declaring war on Russia on June 27, 1941. In 1942, the Germans forced them to send one third of the Hungarian Army to the Russian front, where they were to be decimated in the defense of Stalingrad. Thus, with worsening economic conditions at home due largely to German demands for Hungarian wheat, with bitterness at German willingness to sacrifice badly equipped Hungarian troops to save German troops on the Russian front, and particularly with the death in Russia of his son and probable heir to the Regency of Hungary, Horthy became disenchanted with the German alliance. In March 1941, he had appointed as Premier Kállay, a personal friend and an aristocrat, who was to act as a brake on German exactions. The most effective anti-German pressure was, however, exerted by the opposition parties, notably the Socialists, the Smallholders, and the Liberals, who used the demand for land reform to gain support of the peasantry in their assault on the German alliance. Many peasants and workers were, however, looking toward Russia to remedy their social grievances, and the Hungarian Communist party began to develop strength during the war years. As in Bulgaria it adopted the tactic of allying with the well-established peasant and workers' parties, the Smallholders and the Social Democrats, in a Hungarian Front that would be able to take over the government at the end of the war.

Throughout 1943, Hungarian enthusiasm for the German alliance waned. Kállay dissolved the parliament in May to prevent pro-Nazi opposition to his government. He approached Mussolini on withdrawing their countries from the war. The Hungarian divisions remaining were withdrawn from Russia to defend Hungary along the Carpathian Mountains. And in August, in a secret message to the British ambassador in Turkey, a representative from Kállay offered to let British and American planes fly over Hungary without opposition if they would not bomb Hungary itself. By September 1943, the Hungarian government was determined to make peace. Unfortunately for the Hungarian people, however, Hitler's General Staff was preparing to make Budapest the key fortress in the inner defense line to which German troops would withdraw when the Russians took the Balkans. While Horthy was visiting Hitler at Salzburg, on March 19, 1944, German troops carried out the occupation of Hungary, installed a new pro-German government, and placed real control in the hands of the SS.

Hungary was thus in the miserable position of being at the mercy of all the belligerents. While the British and Americans were bombing the major industrial cities, and the Russian armies were penetrating its eastern borders, the SS was making up for Horthy's failure to adopt thoroughgoing Nazi policies. An immediate roundup of Hungarian Jews was begun, and by the end of the war about 180,000 had died and 180,000 were in captivity in Poland, out of a prewar Jewish population of 400,000. Politicians known for anti-German sympathies were arrested, and many were sent to Mauthausen concentration camp in Austria. Between August and October 1944, however, Horthy managed to set up a fairly autonomous regime in order to organize the country in the war against Rumania, which was now allied with the Russians and fighting to get back northern Transylvania. On October 15, however, Horthy asked the Russians for an armistice. The German SS intervened at once, and Horthy was seized by the same SS adventurer, Skorzeny, who had rescued Mussolini. The misery of the Hungarians was intensified. A puppet government organized the last-ditch resistance of Budapest, during which the major part of the old city was destroyed. On

October 10, the Russians were within forty-five miles of Budapest; the city did not fall until the middle of February. During this period, the Nazis wiped out all the remaining resistance groups headed by the old political parties. The future of Hungarian government thus lay with the Red Army, which, as in Rumania and Bulgaria, was in physical control of the country.

Finland. Whereas Bulgaria had attempted to maintain the fiction that it was fighting a war against Britain and the United States only, Finland had sought to limit its participation to the war on Russia, which it had begun with the Germans in June 1941. Moreover, the Finnish government declared that it intended only to recover the territories lost to Russia in the Winter War of 1939–40, and it refused to join in the German attack on Leningrad in August 1942. German defeats in Russia, particularly the Battle of Stalingrad, convinced the Finns, as the other satellites, that Germany had lost the war and that they had better consider how to pull out of the war as soon as possible. Large numbers of German troops stationed in north Finland held the threat of a German occupation similar to that in Hungary, however, and there was widespread reluctance to accept the Russian demand that Finland return the territories Russia had been given at the peace treaty of 1940. Nevertheless, negotiations with the Soviet ambassador in Sweden began in February 1944, but Russian preconditions were so severe that the Finns rejected them in April. Such obstinacy merely provoked a full-scale Russian attack on the Mannerheim Line in June 1944 and the occupation of Viipuri, the capital of Finnish Karelia. In August, Marshal Mannerheim again became the country's president, with the distressing task of making peace with the Russians. An armistice was finally accepted on September 19, re-establishing the 1940 frontier, giving Russia a fifty-year lease for a naval base at Porkkala, and granting Russia the Arctic port of Petsamo. Finland was to pay $300 million worth of commodities as reparations over the coming six years. Finland was not, however, to be occupied by Soviet troops. Finland lay at the mercy of Russia, fully aware that its policy must be never to endanger Soviet security or even Soviet susceptibilities. But the Russians, too, had learned the difficulty of subduing Finland. From this double realization was to come the uneasy independence Finland enjoyed after the war.

THE OCCUPIED STATES OF THE BALKANS:
YUGOSLAVIA, ALBANIA, GREECE

The occupied states of the Balkans—Yugoslavia, Albania, and Greece —suffered deeply from German and Italian exploitation, although Italian squeamishness at times moderated the cold efficiency of German inhumanity. The widespread resistance movements that arose in opposition to this tyranny not only fought to drive out the occupying powers but also fought for a new social organization in their countries after the war. The Communists, who were the most powerful of the resistance groups, quickly ceased to cooperate with the other organizations and eventually turned their weapons against them. In Yugoslavia and Albania they were successful in destroying their internal enemies and in taking power as the Germans and Italians withdrew. In Greece, only British military intervention prevented a similar Communist takeover of power.

German Policy in Yugoslavia. Yugoslavia, which had dared to thwart Hitler's drive on Greece by the coup d'état of March 1941, was torn apart. Slovenia, the strategically important northern province on the borders of Austria and Italy, was first divided between Germany and Italy and then, after the Italian surrender in 1943, taken wholly by Germany. Its intellectuals were deported or murdered, and its peasants were told that they were originally of German nationality and thus eligible for military service. Other northern border areas were either handed to Hungary or placed under an autonomous regime dominated by their native German minority. Macedonia was incorporated into Bulgaria, with no attention paid to its nationalist aspirations. Montenegro was made autonomous under Italian supervision. Finally, the Germans attempted to profit from the old rivalry between Catholic Croatia and Greek Orthodox Serbia. Croatia, occupied by Italy, was made a Fascist state under a well-known terrorist, Pavelić, whose armed bands, the Ustash, carried out horrible massacres of Serbs and Jews. At first, Pavelić was popular, but the benefits of Croatian autonomy were soon seen to be illusory, as atrocities and exploitation increased. Within two years, a strong resistance movement had sprung up. In Serbia, the Germans, after a short period of military government, set up a native government under General Milan Nedić, an honest Serbian patriot who believed that he was acting like Marshal Pétain to save his people from the excesses of German occupation, but who was finally compromised by aiding the Germans in suppressing the resistance forces and in supplying Germany with forced labor. The Germans attempted to worsen relations between Serbs and Croats as a method of holding down the country more easily. Much of the bitterness of Serbs against the Croats who had collaborated with Pavelić carried over into the postwar years, and was to play its part in the show trial of the Croat Archbishop Stepinac in 1946.

The Rivalry of Mihailović and Tito. The Yugoslav situation was complicated by the division in the resistance forces between those who wished to restore the prewar political and social regime and those who wished to transform the country, the latter themselves being divided between the Communists and the democratic parties from Socialists to Peasants. The conservative forces found their leader in Colonel Draža Mihailović, a royalist career officer who had taken to the mountains in April 1941 with his unit. With the support of the so-called illegal Chetniks, members of the army organization trained in guerrilla warfare who refused to join Nedić, and made popular by the praise of the B.B.C., Mihailović was soon joined by many who wished to fight back against the Germans. He was, however, strongly anti-Croat and anti-Communist, and he soon subordinated the struggle against the Axis powers to his struggle against the Communist partisans. The government-in-exile in London, which represented a wide spectrum of the Yugoslav democratic parties, was, however, dominated by authoritarian military and civilian officials. Mihailović was appointed war minister through their influence in January 1942, and in 1942–44 he was accompanied by a British mission. The government-in-exile had entered what was nothing less than a Yugoslav civil war on the losing side.

The partisan movement under the leadership of Josip Broz, better known as Tito, was a genuinely popular Communist revolution. Yugoslav communism had its roots as far back as the Populist movement in Serbia in the 1870's, and Marxist parties were active in Serbia and Croatia just before and after the First World War. Suppressed during the royal autocracy, the party remained small, but concentrated on forming its cadres. Tito himself, a tough, proud peasant's son, born in Croatia in 1892, was captured by the Russians in 1915 while serving in the Austrian Army, and saw with his own eyes the Bolshevik takeover in Russia. He returned to Yugoslavia in 1920 a convinced Communist, took part in subversive activities for which he was several times jailed, and in 1937 became secretary-general of the Yugoslav Communist party. Putting together a team of reliable young revolutionaries, including Milovan Djilas and Edo Kardelj, he built up an efficient, if small, corps of party workers. Following the Moscow line, the Yugoslav Communists declared themselves strictly neutral in the opening of the war; but with Hitler's invasion on April 6, 1941, and particularly after his attack on Russia in June, Tito called upon the Yugoslav people to take up arms against the Germans who "like mad dogs, are attacking the Soviet Union, our dear Socialist fatherland." The resistance was at first spontaneous, and all groups worked together. But within a few months, Tito and Mihailović had become enemies. Tito was determined that his partisans should make Yugoslavia Communist, and he organized the resistance to that end. The peasantry were enlisted in his movement, as were many other groups formerly passive in politics, such as the mountaineers of Bosnia and Macedonia and Moslem women. Home rule within a federal state was promised to the various national groups, particularly the Macedonians who were chafing under Bulgarian domination, and to the Croats, to win them away from Pavelić. National Liberation Committees were set up in all the liberated areas, which took over local administration and promised the peasantry a more just social order. In November 1942, Tito called a conference at his headquarters in Bihać, in the Bosnian Mountains, of delegates of the resistance from all over Yugoslavia, most of whom were Communist sympathizers; this congress formed the Anti-Fascist Council of National Liberation of Yugoslavia as the central governing organ for the areas taken by the partisans.

Tito Triumphant. The partisan bands found themselves under great German and Italian pressure and faced seven major offensives against their mountain strongholds. In the fourth of these, in January 1943, Mihailović's Chetnicks cooperated with the Axis troops and lost a long, bloody battle against Tito's forces in the Neretva Valley. That spring, the British decided that Tito was serving the Allied cause more usefully than Mihailović and sent a mission and material aid to him, although support was not finally withdrawn from Mihailović for another year. At this point, Tito broke with the government-in-exile, declaring that the Council was now the "supreme executive and legislative body of the Yugoslav State" and setting up a provisional government, the National

Committee of Liberation. Thus, the Yugoslav partisans, like the Free French under de Gaulle, had proclaimed themselves the government in place of the legally constituted authorities. With the appointment of Dr. Šubašić as premier of the government-in-exile in June 1944, Tito moderated his stand, however, and permitted two members of the National Committee of Liberation to enter the Šubašić cabinet. The government-in-exile then called upon all Yugoslavs to rally to Marshal Tito.

As the Red Army swung into Yugoslavia from Rumania and Bulgaria in September, the partisans, now a quarter million strong, emerged from the mountains and took a major role in the expulsion of the Germans from the plains of Serbia. At Moscow on September 22, Tito insisted, to Stalin's surprise, that Russian troops should remain in Yugoslavia for a limited period only and that the partisans should be under Tito's command. Belgrade itself fell to the First Proletarian Division of Tito's forces, aided by Russian tanks, on October 20; the main forces of the Red Army continued northwest toward Hungary, leaving the rest of Yugoslavia to be liberated by the partisan forces, in fighting that continued until May 1945. As the Germans retreated, the Yugoslav collaborationist forces disbanded or fled with them to Germany. On March 7, 1945 Tito dissolved the National Committee of Liberation and took office as premier of a united government including representatives of the government-in-exile. In this new government, Tito's Communists were already supreme. But, unlike the Communist regimes that were to be imposed upon the other countries of the Balkans, this government owed little to Moscow, was supported by the majority of the Yugoslav people, and in Tito had a leader who was capable of standing up to any pressure from Stalin. The emergence of a unique and independent brand of communism in Yugoslavia was made possible by the nature of Yugoslavia's liberation.

Communist Victory in Albania. Tito's success in Yugoslavia ensured the triumph of communism in Albania. Still the most backward country in Europe after twenty years of Italian influence, Albania was ripe for social revolution. In the north, the Ghegs were organized in a Moslem tribal society; in the south, the Tosks held their land in semifeudal tenure from the great landowners, the beys. The tribal chieftains of the north and the landowners of the south controlled the wealth and the political power of the country. Leadership and ideology for a resistance movement against the Italians, which was also to carry out a social revolution, was provided by a few intellectuals who were trained mostly in Belgrade or Paris, whereas the nucleus of proletarian support was found in the few cities—Tirana, Durazzo, and Valona. With the help of Yugoslav Communists from the region bordering on Albania, a Communist party was founded in November 1941, and its leaders agreed to join with some of the beys opposed to Italian rule in founding a National Liberation Movement in 1942. Another resistance group, the National Union, was formed by republican liberals. The Communists, led by a former schoolteacher Enver Hoxha, quickly gained the upper hand in the National Liberation Movement, and rather than fight the Italians began to concentrate on defeating the National Union. The fall of Mussolini briefly united the Albanian resistance groups, however, and for a few weeks they combined to gain control of most of the country. When the Germans replied by taking control of the country to prevent an Allied invasion through Albania, they acted skillfully, setting up a government sympathetic to the National Union and allowing Albania to declare itself neutral. The National Liberation Movement then declared open war on the National Union.

In 1944, the aid and example of the Yugoslav partisan movement brought about the triumph of Hoxha's National Liberation Movement. Their National Liberation Army, Anti-Fascist Council of National Liberation, and Provisional Government were all modeled on Tito's, and their tactics were coordinated with those of the Communists in Yugoslavia, Greece, and Bulgaria by Tito's representative. As the Germans pulled back throughout 1944, the National Liberation Army harassed them and attacked the forces of the National Union. One by one the tribal chieftains were driven out of the north. By November 1944, the Provisional Government was in control of the whole of Albania, and the communization of the country was assured.

The Rise of Greek Communism. For a time during the war it appeared that Greece would follow the pattern of Yugoslavia and Albania. The prewar government in Greece, headed since 1936 by the authoritarian General Metaxas, had set up a police state and ruthlessly removed the vestiges of Greek democratic thought, even to the purging of the Greek classics. Since the recently restored king, George II, had acquiesced in the establishment of the dictatorship to forestall a suspected Communist coup and had persuaded the army to keep Metaxas in power, reform forces determined to end the monarchy as well as the dictatorship. When Italy invaded in October 1940, the Greeks set aside their internal divisions momentarily and united to drive the Italians out. They could do little to stop the German invasion that followed, however; and in May 1941, the king and his government fled.

By the summer of 1942 the first resistance groups had been organized by the Communist party of Greece, which since its foundation in 1918 had been making considerable progress among the intellectual classes, the Greeks expelled from Turkey in the early 1920's, and the factory workers. It had already set up an underground organization during the Metaxas regime, and found it easy to set up the National Liberation Front (EAM) in September 1941 as a union of left-wing parties welcoming all classes into a resistance movement. The next year it formed in the mountains a guerrilla army known as ELAS, the National Popular Liberation Army. Slowly bringing together many independent bands of guerrillas, ELAS numbered some 20,000 disciplined soldiers by the end of 1943, whose political subordination to the aims of the Communist party was assured by the presence at all levels of command of an EAM political representative. The principal rival to EAM/ELAS was the resistance army of Napoleon Zervas, an ex-soldier, republican, and adventurer, who formed in the northwestern mountains a small guerrilla army known as the Greek Republican Liberation League, which maintained a shadowy allegiance to a group of republican politicians in Athens. Isolated from the main population centers and weakened by the lack of appealing political creed, Zervas was never a match for EAM/ELAS, which from 1943 on began eliminating its rivals among the resistance organizations, by force where necessary.

British Intervention in the Greek Civil War. In October 1943, the Communist-dominated ELAS mounted a major campaign against the forces of Zervas, whose destruction was prevented only by last-minute arms delivery by the British. From this point on, British intervention was to be decisive in preventing the takeover of Greece by EAM/ELAS. Churchill was determined to prevent as much of the Balkans as possible from falling into Communist control. At the very least, he intended to hold on to Greece. His policy was to support the monarchy and the government-in-exile, which had been remodeled to exclude former supporters of Metaxas; and, from 1943, British support was withdrawn from ELAS and concentrated on Zervas' forces. The Communists then changed tactics, pressing for greater representation in the government that would be set up at the liberation. Mutinies in the Greek Army and Navy units that were collaborating with the Allies in the Mediterranean, although suppressed in part by British troops, put pressure on the king to remodel the government-in-exile. In May 1944, representatives of all the political parties and the remaining resistance groups agreed to set up a Government of National Unity under George Papandreou, a brilliant orator who headed a tiny splinter party of his own and was convinced of his own mission to restore Greece's national unity. In August EAM representatives joined the government, and in September both guerrilla armies agreed to place their forces under Allied command. The British landed only a few units of commandos and left the main task of liberating Greece to the guerrillas. On October 18, 1944, the Papandreou government returned to Athens. By the beginning of Novmber, the last Germans had withdrawn.

The Battle of Athens. After a few days of national rejoicing and fraternity, the divisions within the country again became exacerbated. The Papandreou government was faced with almost complete economic breakdown—dislocation of transport and industry, a worthless currency, food shortage, habits of sabotage. Its right- and left-wing members split over bureaucratic appointments, punishment of collaborators, organization of a police force, and particularly on the disarming of the guerrillas. Open fighting began in Athens after the British commander, General Scobie, ordered the guerrilla forces, but not the Royalist Third Brigade, to lay down their arms. The EAM ministers resigned from the cabinet on December 2 in protest; ELAS forces in Athens and Pireus were mobilized; and thousands of supporters were called in from all over Greece for a vast demonstration on Sunday, December 3 in Constitution Square, to be followed the next day by a general strike. On the Sunday morning, the police fired on the crowds, killing about twenty demonstrators. A hysterical crowd of about 60,000 then gathered in the Square until they were dispersed, peacefully, by a company of British paratroopers. ELAS troops began to besiege police stations throughout Athens and to execute their defenders when they were not relieved in time by British troops. A general strike on the Monday paralyzed the city, and Papandreou decided to resign so that a government more satisfactory to EAM could be formed. When, however, Churchill demanded that he should remain in office, he agreed to do so. The same day,

General Scobie forced a showdown with the EAM by ordering all ELAS units to withdraw from Athens and Pireus within three days.

ELAS disregarded Scobie's orders and on December 6 launched an attack on the main government buildings of Athens, which was repulsed. A new attack on Zervas' forces was successful in ousting them from the mainland of Greece which, with the exception of Athens and a couple of small coastal areas, was completely in the hands of ELAS by the end of December. The Battle of Athens was nonetheless to decide the future of Greece. British troops were reinforced by two divisions flown in from Italy, and the principal ELAS assault on the night of December 15–16 was driven back after heavy fighting. Churchill and his foreign minister, Anthony Eden, flew into Athens for a conference with all Greek political leaders on December 25–26, which failed to produce any results. Before leaving, Churchill ordered a full-scale attack on the ELAS forces, which began on December 27 and broke the ELAS hold in Athens and the Pireus within three days. An armistice came into force on January 15, 1945, followed on February 12 by the Varkiza Agreement, by which ELAS was disarmed, elections and a plebiscite on the future of the monarchy held within a year, an amnesty granted, and the Communist party and EAM recognized as legal organizations. Even before the armistice, the king had agreed that Archbishop Damaskinos be appointed regent, and Papandreou had been replaced as premier by General Plastiras, a moderate republican. The Varkiza Agreement ended the first stage of the Greek civil war. British intervention had undoubtedly prevented the establishment of the Communist-dominated regime in Greece. Unfortunately, the governments of the next two years were so reactionary that the revulsion from the methods of ELAS, which had involved summary trials, taking of hostages, and even torture, was partially effaced, and the civil war had to be fought over again.

GERMAN OCCUPATION IN CZECHOSLOVAKIA AND POLAND

Exploitation of Czechoslovakia. In Czechoslovakia, the sufferings inflicted by Nazi rule made the Munich Agreement appear to the Czech people more than ever as a betrayal by the Western powers, leaving a legacy of distrust that was to play its part in postwar developments. Although the German Protectorate of Bohemia-Moravia retained a Czech government and administration, it was subordinated at all levels to

German officials, notably the Reich Protector who from 1939 to 1941 was the former German Foreign Minister von Neurath. The task of the Nazi administration, Hitler decided, was assimilation of the Czechs, by "absorption" of about half the Czech nation by the Germans and "elimination" of the other half, particularly the "racially Mongoloid" and the intellectuals. A small riot by Prague university students in November 1939 was made the excuse for closing all Czech universities permanently, and large numbers of students, professors, professional men, and even shopkeepers were deported or sent to concentration camps. The terror became worse after the invasion of Russia, when Reinhard Heydrich, the Gestapo chief for all occupied Europe, was made protector. After eight months of sadistic repression, Heydrich was murdered by a bomb thrown at his car; in reprisal, the Germans imposed a state of emergency and executed thousands. In two villages suspected of helping the assassins, Lidice and Lezaky, the entire male population was killed, and the women and children were deported. Czech hatred for all Germans was to be vented in the great expulsion of 1945, when about two and a half million Germans were driven out of Czechoslovakia. The Protectorate was also exploited economically. About 348,000 Czechs were sent to Germany as forced laborers; and the usual process of expropriation of production of both agriculture and industry lowered living standards to the starvation level.

In Slovakia, conditions were more tolerable, as the Nazis were prepared to show the rewards earned by willing collaboration. The German troops stayed within the military zones assigned to them, and the rest of Slovakia was governed by the clerical party of Father Tiso. Slovak nationalism was encouraged by admission to the Tripartite Pact as an independent country; economic development was furthered by German road building and capital investment in mining and chemicals; and before 1944 there was relatively less repression of Jews. But the enlistment of half the adult population either as laborers in Germany or as soldiers on the Russian front led to growing dislike of the German alliance; and in 1943 the Slovaks, like the other East European satellites, began to consider how they could pull out of the war without incurring German vengeance. The German occupation of Hungary in March 1944, however, ensured Tiso's loyalty, and it was ostensibly to support him against widespread partisan activity that the German Army occupied Slovakia at the end of August 1944. For the next six months,

Slovakia bore the brunt of savage fighting between the Germans and the Russian Army, aided by the partisans, and it was only in January that Slovakia was cleared of the Germans.

Soviet Support of President Beneš. Czechoslovakia seemed more fortunate than the other East European countries, however, having in President Beneš a leader who was acceptable to both the Russians and the West and who proved able, in 1943–44, to appeal to the Slovaks as well as the Czechs. Beneš had formed a Czechoslovak National Committee in Paris in October 1939, to create an autonomous Czech Army that would fight with Britain and France, and in 1940–41, the Committee, under the presidency of Beneš, was recognized by France, Britain, the United States, and Soviet Russia as the legal government of Czechoslovakia. In 1942, both the British government and the Free French informed the Czech government-in-exile that they no longer recognized the Munich Agreement and that Czechoslovakia's postwar boundaries would therefore be those of 1918 and not of 1938. Beneš' great achievement of the war years seemed to be his courtship of the Russians. A long-time democrat, he also admired Russia; and, on a visit to Moscow in December 1943, he was able to persuade Stalin to sign a Czech-Soviet Treaty of Alliance with his government, in which the two countries promised to aid each other in the present war against Germany and to refrain from interference in each others' internal affairs. The next year, the Russians agreed to hand over to representatives of the Beneš government administration of the territories liberated by the Soviet forces. Stalin granted no official position to the Czech Communist leaders Gottwald and Nejedly, who were in exile in Moscow. Even the Communist-led uprising in Slovakia in August–October 1944, during which a "Free Slovakia" was proclaimed in the central mountains, received little aid from the Russians. Nevertheless, the success of the Communist coup d'état of 1948 was assured by the advances that the Communists made during the war and liberation. Communist leadership of the resistance movements had given them much national popularity and had enabled them to gain control of large parts of the local government as the territory was liberated. Communists entrenched themselves in the trade-union movement. And, when Beneš set up a provisional government at Košice in Slovakia in March 1945, he included seven Communists and gave them the vitally important Ministry of the Interior. No immediate test of strength threatened, however. At the end of the war, the American Army as well as the Russian was established on Czech territory, and Beneš seemed on the way to proving that Czechoslovakia could be the bridge between East and West in the postwar world.

Nazi Rule in Poland. It was in Poland that the worst horrors of Nazi rule were perpetrated. Western Poland was annexed to Germany, and there a policy of Germanization was begun, under the direction of the SS chief Himmler. Jews and Polish intellectuals were deported for extermination. Those of German origin were enrolled on a Racial Register, and many were enrolled in the German armies. Thousands of other Poles were used as forced laborers in Germany, and an attempt was made to settle Germans both on the land and in administrative and industrial jobs. Whereas the industrial and agricultural resources of the annexed territories were developed to the full, those of the rump area of Poland, known as the Government-General, were, according to Goering, to be transferred to Germany when not "absolutely essential for the maintenance at a low level of the bare existence of the inhabitants." The ultimate intention was to make the area completely agricultural, a source of the slave labor for which the Nazis regarded the Slavs as suited. A million and a half Poles were working in Germany by 1944. Unwanted people from all German-occupied Europe, particularly Jews, were sent in cattle trucks to the General-Government where ghettos, Jewish towns, labor and extermination camps were prepared to receive them. So great was the exploitation that, by 1941, most of the population was at starvation level.

The Polish Resistance. The Poles were not willing to endure this treatment without resistance; and within a few months of their defeat they had created an underground movement of extraordinary complexity and size, extending over both Russian and German-held Poland, and including all the apparatus of a state—with a parliament, government ministries, and an army. There were even underground schools and official examinations, government bonds that were to be repaid after liberation, and many underground newspapers. This secret state maintained allegiance to the Polish government-in-exile, which had been purged of the prewar authoritarian politicians. The opposition parties of prewar Poland—the National Democrats, the Socialists, the Peasants, and the Christian Democrats—were all represented and maintained their armed underground groups in Poland. There seemed, therefore, to be a clear guarantee that after liberation Poland would have a democratic government dedicated to the welfare of the peasants and workers, even though many of the professional soldiers in the underground army undoubtedly approved of the old regime and would have liked to restore it. The underground engaged in sabotage, espionage, and even in open battles with the Germans; and they replied to reprisals by murdering prominent German officials, including the military commander of Warsaw.

Soviet Policy toward Poland. The Polish underground had attacked the Russians as well as the Germans until 1941, but, with the German invasion of Russia, the Soviet government agreed to the formation of a Polish army of prisoners released by the Russians, which was to be under Polish command but to operate with the Red Army. Quarrels developed, however, and in July 1942 the Russian government agreed that the whole Polish force should be sent to join the British in the Middle East. Other disagreements followed. The Polish Communist party was re-founded in 1942 as the Polish Workers' party, and joined with a left-wing Socialist group in founding a People's Army, which was soon in friction with the Home Army. In 1943, the Germans announced the discovery of a mass grave of thousands of Polish officers in Katyn Forest near Smolensk, each shot in the head by, the Germans alleged, the Russian secret police in August 1940 while they were Russian prisoners. The Russians replied two days later that the Germans had committed the murders in 1941. The leader of the Home Army, Bor Komorowski, reported to the government in London that the murders had been carried out in April 1940 by the Russians. The Polish government-in-exile made public its acceptance of this view; and, on April 26, the Soviet government announced that, since the London Poles had "sunk so low as to enter the path of accord with the Hitlerite Government," they were breaking off relations with them. The Russian action was clearly due to their dissatisfaction with the government-in-exile in London as a suitable postwar government. It had refused to recognize Russia's annexation of eastern Poland in September 1939; opponents of Russia were numerous in both the government and the leadership of the Home Army; and in the People's Army and the Polish Communists the Soviet government had their own candidates for control of Poland.

The Warsaw Uprising. When the Red Army crossed the prewar boundary of Poland in January 1944, it reincorporated into Russia the area annexed from Poland in September 1939; and when in July 1944 it moved into territory recognized to be Polish, it handed its administration over to a Polish Committee of National Liberation, formed in Moscow in July by a union of the Polish Communists and left-wing Socialists. Behind the Russian lines, units of the Home Army were given the choice of joining a Communist-dominated Polish force within the Red Army, or of disbanding. These developments perturbed the leaders of the Home Army in Warsaw, who had hoped to be able to organize a national insurrection in support of Western rather than Russian troops. As the Red Army approached the Vistula, Bor Komorowski ordered the underground to drive the Germans out of Warsaw, in the hope of seizing control of the city a few hours before the Russians arrived. At first, all went according to plan. On August 1–2, the Home Army seized two-thirds of Warsaw; the whole population of the city helped the 35,000 soldiers of the underground and set up hospitals, canteens, and communications. But the Germans counterattacked with dive bombers, tanks, and artillery, using five divisions including the SS Death's Head Division. The Poles were split into four separate areas, whose contact was made through the city sewers. Small amounts of supplies were dropped by British planes from Italy; but the Red Army, faced with strong German defensive positions on the western side of the river, halted its offensive on August 4. In mid-September, the Red Army captured Praga on the right bank of the river, but did not attempt to capture Warsaw itself. The Home Army bore the brunt of the German counterattack for sixty-three days, during which Warsaw was systematically reduced to rubble. After the loss of 15,000 killed, Bor Komorowski surrendered. By then, any influence the Home Army might have exerted on the future political regime in Poland had been destroyed. It has been suggested that Stalin deliberately allowed the Germans to destroy the strongly anti-Communist Home Army. Although it is true that he refused to allow British and American planes to use Soviet-held airfields in supplying the Warsaw Poles, it is certain that German resistance was very strong along the fortified line of the Vistula, that Russian troops were being diverted to Rumania after the coup d'état of August 23, and that Warsaw was not finally captured by the Red Army until January 17, 1945. Bor's action, though understandable, was premature, and its effects were lasting.

The Russians installed the Polish Committee of National Liberation as the temporary government of Poland in Lublin on August 15, 1944. The most Mikolajczyk, premier of the London government-in-exile, could persuade Stalin to offer was the formation of a new cabinet in which three quarters of the seats would go to members of the Lublin Committee. Mikolajczyk resigned in November in despair; in December the Lublin Committee declared itself the Provisional Government of Poland. Neither the London Poles nor their supporters in Poland itself possessed any further influence on the course of events. The last efforts to prevent the communization of Poland would only be made by the British and American governments.

Thus, throughout most of Eastern Europe, the Nazi occupation prepared the way for the establishment of Communist control.

THE JAPANESE OCCUPATION IN EAST ASIA

In the six months following their attack on Pearl Harbor, the Japanese brought under their control in east Asia over a million and a half square miles of territory and 140 million people. Their four years of supremacy were to exercise an enormous influence on the future development of this region.

Effects of Japanese Rule. The first and most lasting effect of the Japanese conquest was to destroy the prestige of the white man. For the first time, an Asian power had inflicted military defeat upon the apparently invincible armies of the colonial powers. The Filipinos had seen Mac-Arthur flee to the safety of Australia, leaving his troops to be rounded up; the Malayans saw the British surprised by a land-based attack on their supposedly impregnable fortress of Singapore, and the greatest British battleships, the "Repulse" and the "Prince of Wales," sunk by Japanese bombers; throughout east Asia Japanese soldiers inflicted public humiliations on the white prisoners of war. Moreover, Japanese propaganda reminded the "liberated" inhabitants of the colonial areas of the racism of their former masters—the American treatment of the Negro, the British attitude to the Indians, the Dutch exploitation of the East Indies. The languages of the colonial powers were replaced by Japanese, which was taught in all schools and universities as a second language; the Japanese even attempted to persuade the peoples of their empire that they had religious ties with Japan, whether they were Buddhist, Moslem, or Christian.

Where the colonial powers had exploited, the Japanese claimed that they would follow a policy of economic cooperation, on the principle of Asia for the Asiatics. The economic development of the Japanese empire was, in theory, to benefit all its parts, through the policies of the Greater East Asia Ministry. The vast natural resources of the region were to be developed on a sound economic plan. Those areas suited to industrialization, especially Manchuria, northern China and Korea, were to receive large investments of capital. Production of the oil of the East Indies and Burma, the rubber of Malaya, and the cotton of the Philippines would be expanded. The countries of the Greater East Asia Co-Prosperity Sphere, it was announced on November 5, 1943, would "through mutual cooperation ensure the stability of their region and construct an order of common prosperity and well-being based on justice," unlike the British and Americans who "especially in East Asia indulged in insatiable aggression and exploitation and sought to satisfy their inordinate ambition of enslaving the entire region."

Finally, the Japanese claimed to offer self-government to the peoples of east Asia. In the Philippines, they set up an "independent" republic in September 1943, under which many well-to-do industrialists and landowners made fortunes by trading with the Japanese. In Burma, the Japanese were at first welcomed as liberators from British rule; and Burmese guerrillas, under Aung San and Ne Win who had been trained in Japan for leadership of an independence army, aided the Japanese invasion. In August 1943, Burma was given its "independence." In the Dutch East Indies, the Japanese created an Indonesian Central Advisory Council under the chairmanship of Sukarno. In 1944, independence was promised; in March 1945, an Independence Preparatory Committee was set up. However, Sukarno finally declared Indonesia independent on August 17, two days after the Japanese surrender, an independence that was to last for six weeks only. In Malaya, the Japanese set up consultative native councils and attempted to turn the Malays against the Chinese. But it was only in 1945, when their defeat was certain, that they promised independence to Malaya. At the same time, the Japanese took over Indochina from the Vichy French and ordered the Emperor Bao Dai to declare Vietnam independent. Bao Dai's example was followed by the king of Cambodia and the king of Laos in March 1945.

The Japanese thus found a minority of nationalists who were willing to collaborate with them; and, even among those who did not, the expulsion of the colonial powers and the promise of independence opened an exciting vista of better things in the postwar world. The reality of Japanese rule quickly disillusioned many who had at first welcomed them. The resources of the Japanese empire were exploited for the war effort. Disruption of trade with Europe and the United States brought economic depression. Bombing by the Allied air forces caused widespread destruction. And the Japanese Army behaved with little regard for co-prosperity propaganda.

Japanese Occupation of Britain's Colonies. Resistance movements opposed equally to Japanese rule and to the return of the colonial powers developed throughout east Asia, giving the Communists an ideal opportunity to expand their influence and to prepare for the final seizure of power. In the British colonies, the Communists and the Nationalists worked together for the overthrow of the Japanese. In Burma, Aung San had been quickly disillusioned with Japanese rule and had linked his People's Freedom League with the Communist organization in the Anti-Fascist People's Freedom League in 1944. This League's guerrillas aided the British in 1945; and they were in a strong position to press for independence when the war ended. In Malaya, the resistance movement was strongest among the Chinese section of the population; the resistance was led by the Communists, who used the weapons supplied them by the British to set up their own control over large numbers of villages and even for a brief period in August 1945 exercised control over Singapore itself. The resistance was not widespread, however, and when the British returned in September 1945 they had little difficulty in restoring their control. In Hong Kong, the British were welcomed back after the harshness of Japanese exploitation. The colony's business community was well aware that its prosperity depended upon it remaining part of the British Empire, and very few demands were made for independence, return to China, or even for political autonomy.

Japanese Influence on India. India, which was not occupied by the Japanese, was deeply influenced by Japan's successes. The Japanese made a deliberate attempt to win the support of Indians living in the conquered territories, especially in Singapore and Malaya, where they created an Indian Independence League and an Indian National Army. For a time in 1942, there was a possibility that the Indian National Army would invade India, but the army's leader quarreled with the Japanese, and the plan collapsed. In India itself, however, the precarious position of Britain seemed to offer an ideal opportunity for pressing independence demands. Both Hindu and Moslem leaders objected that Britain had made India a belligerent without consulting the Indian people; and Gandhi led nonviolent demonstrations against participation in the war. When in 1942 the British asked Indian assent to a plan for granting Dominion status at the end of the war, it seemed only too obvious that Britain's desperate situation was the motive for these concessions; almost all Indian groups rejected the proposals. No solution could be found in wartime to the overwhelmingly difficult problems of the relations of Hindu and Moslem, of the future of the princely states, or of the transition machinery for transfer of sovereignty. With sabotage common to the army's communications with the Assam front, where the Japanese threatened an invasion of India itself in 1944, the British resorted to force, political opponents like Gandhi were jailed, and two million Indians were mobilized in the armed forces. The problem was only postponed, however; and as communal violence flared, a peaceful solution to the Hindu-Moslem problem seemed further away than ever.

Opening of Independence Struggles in French Indochina. In French Indochina, the Japanese left most of the work of government in the hands of the Vichy administrators until March 1945. Although the region was under Japanese military control, exploitation was light, and no famines or epidemics occurred. When the Japanese overthrew the French in March 1945, Communist guerrilla forces, known as the Viet Minh, were able to gain control of northern Vietnam. On August 7, Ho Chi Minh was chosen president of a Vietnamese People's Liberation Committee, which was supported by most Vietnamese nationalists; and on September 2, he declared Vietnam independent of France. Neither the British, who had entered southern Vietnam to receive the surrender of the Japanese forces there, nor the French recognized this action; and the Viet Minh forces were compelled to renew guerrilla warfare in the countryside. For the French, the choice was clear—they had to win Ho Chi Minh over by negotiation or destroy the Viet Minh forces.

In Cambodia and Laos, the two French-protected kingdoms in Indochina, the Japanese also expelled the French in March 1945. In September the French abducted the puppet premier of Cambodia installed by the Japanese, and to counter the appeal of his followers, who had begun to wage war in alliance with the Viet Minh, they granted the beginnings of self-government. Laos, which had been declared independent on

September 1, 1945, by the guerrilla forces of the Free Lao, was reconquered in the following spring. The king was restored, and a pro-French government was imposed.

Indonesian Independence Movement. In the Dutch East Indies, Indonesian nationalists under Sukarno had declared their country independent on August 17, 1945, and when the Dutch sought to return six weeks later they found a functioning Indonesian administration, many of whose members had gained governmental experience under the Japanese. The Sukarno government was supported by the former underground troops of both the nationalists and the Communists. The actual reconquest on behalf of the Dutch was begun by British, Indian, and Australian troops, and even Japanese soldiers were used for keeping order. After three months of harsh fighting, most of Java and Sumatra was still held by the Sukarno forces. For the Dutch as for the French in Indochina, colonial rule could only be restored by reconquest.

Strengthening of Chinese Communists. In China, the most important development of the war years was the strengthening of the position of the Communists, although the Japanese did make an attempt to appease Chinese nationalism by abolishing most of the "concessions" of the European powers, including the International Settlement at Shanghai. After withdrawing to Chungking, the Kuomintang forces under Chiang Kai-shek made almost no attempt to drive out the Japanese, but were content to wait for their ultimate defeat by the Allied powers. The Communists were the only Chinese resistance, and they were able to expand their control throughout the countryside of north and east China, set up an administration, collect taxes, reduce rents, and organize a militia. As a result, they won the cooperation of the peasantry, and indeed made many fervent for social revolution. In Chungking, however, the Kuomintang was internally divided, and corruption spread from the highest ranks to the lowest. Exactions from the civilian population, especially of food supplies, alienated many of the peasantry, who rightly suspected that there was little prospect of land reform under the Kuomintang. Thus, the truce between the Kuomintang and the Communists was virtually ignored, and both sides were aware that the end of the war would bring a final struggle for power between them. Chiang expected, before the atomic bomb was dropped, that the American Army would invade along the coast of east China and would aid his restoration in the southeast, in the rich lower valley of the Yangtze. The sudden surrender of the Japanese changed the situation, however; and Chiang used the position of command in the China Zone given him by the Allied High Command to demand that American planes fly the Kuomintang forces into the cities of the north, including Peking and Tientsin. His forces were thereby able to seize control of the cities in the very heart of Communist-controlled territory. Moreover, when the Red Army invaded Manchuria in August 1945, Stalin concluded a pact with the Kuomintang, in which he promised it military supplies and the withdrawal of Russian troops from Manchuria within three months. Instead of handing over the rich industrial region to the Chinese Communists, the Russians stripped it of its industrial machinery and then handed back the cities to the Kuomintang armies. The gift of Manchuria would probably have assured the immediate victory of the Communists. They were nevertheless so powerful that a full-scale civil war was inevitable. It began in 1946.

Thus, during the six brief years of the Second World War, not only Europe, but every region of the globe was transformed. The struggle that began as an effort to assure the territorial integrity of an authoritarian Poland made possible the communization of Eastern Europe and of China, the collapse of the colonial empires in east Asia, and the reduction of every country of Western Europe to the rank of a second-rate, or in most cases of a third-rate, power.

Chapter Four THE DEFEAT OF
THE AXIS POWERS,
1943-1945

AFTER January 1943 the forces of the United Nations were almost without exception successful. To those unaware of the disputes among the Allied leaders, the military strategy for the defeat of the Axis powers seemed of impeccable logic. Britain and the United States attacked from the west in a two-pronged offensive—the southern attack through Sicily and southern Italy in 1943 and southern France in 1944, the northern attack through Normandy in June 1944. The Russians drove from the east along their whole front, striking from the Ukraine and White Russia into Poland, Rumania, Bulgaria, Yugoslavia, Hungary, Czechoslovakia, and Austria, and from Leningrad into the Baltic states. Eventually, the Anglo-American armies and the Russian armies met in April 1945 at Torgau on the Elbe River. With Germany defeated, a full-scale attack was launched against Japan. The general public was somewhat startled after the war to find that this strategy had been adopted only after long and vigorous quarrels between Stalin and the Western leaders, between the British and the American governments, and even between the American commander-in-chief in Europe and his British subordinate. Postwar critics have claimed that Presidents Roosevelt and Truman failed to realize that after 1943 they were engaged in a struggle with the Russians for control of Eastern Europe, as well as with the Germans, and that they permitted their military experts to dictate a strategy of "head-on assault against the enemy's strongest rampart" totally divorced from political considerations. Churchill, these critics argue, believed that the war could be equally effectively won by first mounting an indirect assault—exploitation of the weakness of Italy, a blow at the soft underbelly of the Axis through the Balkans—thus giving the West a foothold in Eastern Europe. Even in 1945, it is argued, Eisenhower frustrated Montgomery's desire to drive a deep wedge across northern Germany to seize Berlin before the Russians, and

Truman obtusely denied Churchill's demand that he refuse to withdraw American troops from the Russian zone of occupation without demanding a *quid pro quo* in the opening rounds of the Cold War. Perhaps the gravest criticism of all is that leveled at Roosevelt for his Far Eastern agreement with Stalin at Yalta. The critics, mostly American in this case, have argued that by opening Manchuria to the Russians, Roosevelt made possible the communization of China.

These arguments are of enormous importance in consideration of the last three years of the Second World War. The future development of Europe and Asia was dictated as much by the diplomatic decisions taken in the vitally important series of international conferences of the three Allied powers as by the flow of military events. It was becoming increasingly obvious that the method by which victory was won would exercise greater influence on the future than the fact of victory.

FROM THE INVASION OF ITALY TO THE TEHERAN CONFERENCE

Throughout the spring of 1943, the Allies continued to battle stubborn German forces in Tunisia; and only in May was the last Axis army in North Africa, a force of 160,000 men, captured. This long delay, combined with enormous losses of shipping to submarine attacks in the Atlantic in the winter and spring of 1942–43, made it impossible for the Anglo-American invasion of France to be mounted in 1943. At the TRIDENT conference in Washington in May, the Combined Chiefs of Staff recommended that the cross-Channel invasion should be scheduled for May 1, 1944, that the major offensive in Europe in 1943 should be directed against Italy, and that additional forces should be assigned to the advance across the Central Pacific against the Japanese-held Marshall and Caroline Islands. Stalin was informed of the decision in June, and he replied with a series of bitter accusations of lack of faith, in which he belittled the importance of the Italian campaign and reminded his Allies that they were leaving Russia to bear the brunt of German strength for another year. His bitterness was justified, since there were then 185 German and Italian divisions on the Russian front.

Allied Invasion of Sicily. The invasion of Sicily began on July 10, almost 3,000 ships being used to land 160,000 men at three points of the southern coast of the island. A week's bombardment from sea and air had weakened the defenders, and the Italian forces proved only too eager to surrender. To most Sicilians the Allies were liberators, and it was only two German divisions aided by reinforcements from the mainland that prolonged the resistance for a month. Even when their defeat was obvious, the Germans carried out a skillful evacuation of the major part of their troops across the Straits of Messina; but at the end of the campaign the Germans and Italians had lost 167,000 men to Allied losses of 31,000.

The taking of Sicily posed again the question of Anglo-American strategy. The ease of the Sicilian operation convinced Eisenhower that the next attack should be on the Italian mainland; but lack of landing craft made it impossible for him to do more than cross the narrow Straits of Messina on August 17. A seaborne attack on Naples, in accordance with Churchill's demand that the Allies "strike at the knee" instead of "crawling up the leg like a harvest bug," was put off until September 9, by which time the enemy forces were immensely strengthened. When the Italian armistice was announced on September 8, German forces established themselves well south of Rome, along the Garigliano River, with the natural fortress of Monte Cassino as the kingpin of the system.

Churchill's Pressure for a Balkan Invasion. In the interval between the fall of Mussolini and the Italian armistice, Churchill, Roosevelt, and their political and military staffs met again to concert views on future strategy. This conference, called QUADRANT, held at the Château Frontenac in Quebec City, August 17–24, again confirmed the cross-Channel invasion date of May 1, 1944, and gave preparations for this operation, OVERLORD, priority in all planning. Operations on a smaller scale were authorized for the Pacific, northern Burma, and Italy. Before Churchill left the United States for home, however, news arrived of the Italian surrender; and, in a memorandum he presented to President Roosevelt and his advisers, he raised for the first time the possibility that the Dalmatian ports of Yugoslavia might be opened to the Allies by agreement with the partisans and the Italian troops there, and that Allied forces might move "north and northeastward from the Dalmatian ports." Bulgaria, Rumania, and Hungary might well follow Italy's example, he surmised. A month later, he urged the President to support the British attempt to seize the Aegean islands, especially Rhodes, in the hope that all Germany's allies in the Balkans would defect: "Should we not be short-sighted to ignore the possibility of a similar and even greater landslide [than Italy's] . . . ? This may yield results measureless in their consequence"—nothing less than the establishment of British and American troops throughout the Balkans before the arrival of the Russians. No disagreement with the American Chiefs of Staff made Churchill so resentful as their refusal to grant the small reinforcements needed for the taking of Rhodes. "The American Staff had enforced their view," he wrote later, "the price had now to be paid by the British." The British troops that had established themselves on the small Aegean islands of Cos and Leros, as a preparation for the opening of the Aegean, were defeated in September and November, and the Germans were thus able to secure their southeastern front.

Foreign Ministers' Conference in Moscow, 1943. When the American, British, and Russian foreign ministers met in Moscow from October 19 to November 3, 1943, Eden found that the Russians were exclusively interested in the cross-Channel invasion of France and were not sympathetic to British military involvement in the Balkans. Stalin's suggestion that Turkey might be brought into the war helped preserve Churchill's hopes, however, and he determined to fight for his plan at the coming conference in Teheran of the Big Three. Secretary of State Hull's desire that the great powers should bind themselves to observe moral principles in their international conduct after the war was satisfied by the signature of the "Declaration of the Four Nations on General Security," by which the American, British, Russian, and Chinese governments recognized "the necessity of establishing at the earliest practicable date a general international organization, based on the principle of the sovereign equality of all peace-loving states, and open to membership by all such states, large and small, for the maintenance of international peace and security." This declaration was the first assurance of the foundation of the United Nations Organization after the war. At Eden's suggestion, the three powers agreed to set up the European Advisory Commission, whose task would be to formulate the principles for the German surrender and for the subsequent occupation of Germany.

Teheran Conference. A month later Stalin, Roosevelt, and Churchill met in the Iranian capital of Teheran. For the first three days, Churchill struggled for adoption of a campaign in the eastern Mediterranean. He wanted an amphibious landing on the Italian coast for the capture of Rome, the taking of the Dodecanese and the Aegean Islands in connection with Turkey's entry into the war, and aid to the Yugoslav and

Albanian partisans; and he seized with great enthusiasm upon a suggestion of Roosevelt that Anglo-American forces might cross the Adriatic to the Istrian Peninsula of Yugoslavia, from where they could strike through the Ljubljana Gap at Vienna. Stalin, however, now dismissed the idea that Turkey might be brought into the war and pressed the British and Americans to prove that they seriously intended to invade France in 1944, by telling him the date and the name of the commander, and by agreeing to mount a concurrent invasion of southern France. Stalin's coldness and evident distrust, which prevented Roosevelt from achieving the personal closeness he had hoped for, were dissipated on November 30 when the British and Americans informed him that they had agreed to invade northern France on May 1, 1944, to mount an invasion of southern France, and to appoint a supreme commander shortly. According to Stalin's biographer, Isaac Deutscher, "this was a moment of Stalin's supreme triumph. Perhaps only he and Churchill were aware of its implications. Europe had now been militarily divided into two; and behind the military division there loomed the social and political cleavage. Against a vastly different social background, an old dream of Russian diplomacy—the dream of bringing the Balkans under Russian influence—was coming true."

The other decisions of the conference were more tentative. The British agreed that the Russo-Polish border should be the Curzon Line of 1920, thus giving Russia all its gains of 1939–41, and that the western border of Poland should be the Oder River; but Roosevelt took no part in this discussion. Consideration of the possibility of partitioning Germany was turned over to the European Advisory Commission. Stalin made a verbal promise to join in the war against Japan after the defeat of Germany and also undertook to mount an offensive against the Germans to coordinate with the OVERLORD invasion of France. Roosevelt told Stalin that he was pressing for the grant of self-government after the war to the colonial peoples of the Far East and that he wanted the four major powers, including China, to act after the war as the "Four Policemen" guaranteeing world security. None of these conversations, except those on OVERLORD, were conclusive; the main significance of Teheran was that it had finally been determined that the Russian and the Anglo-American armies would meet along a North-South line somewhere in the center of Europe. Ten years later, General de Gaulle summed up, in his *Memoirs,* the relative significance of the three great wartime conferences—Teheran, Yalta, and Potsdam—and found that Teheran was the most important. "I certainly regretted not being present at Teheran," he wrote. "I would indeed have defended the equilibrium of the old continent, there, while there was still time. Later I was irritated not to be able to take part in Yalta, because there still remained some chance of preventing the iron curtain from cutting Europe in two. . . . What could I have done at Potsdam?"

Preparations for Cross-Channel Invasion. Preparations for OVERLORD were hastened by the appointment of General Eisenhower as supreme commander, with British General Bernard Montgomery as commander of the land forces during the assault period. Together, they decided that the initial landings must be effected by five divisions rather than the three originally planned for. Two artificial "Mulberry" harbors, each the size of Dover harbor, were constructed in England ready to be towed across the Channel, to make possible the rapid buildup of troops and equipment that would be needed to meet the German counterattack. To provide covering fire to the moment when the troops hit the beaches, mortars and rockets were mounted on small boats; tanks were invented that could float, carry bridges, and clear mine fields. An army of a million and a half men was assembled in England, and a huge fleet of landing craft and warships spread through all the harbors of southern England. The aim was to land 176,000 men and 20,000 vehicles in the first two days of the assault and to increase the size of the armies ashore to thirty divisions within thirty-five days.

The coming invasion of his "Fortress Europe" did not perturb Hitler greatly. Along the two thousand miles of coast he had erected the massive concrete walls and gun emplacements of the "Atlantic Wall"; sixty divisions, eleven of them armored, were stationed in the West under the over-all command of General von Rundstedt; the northern army group, under Rommel, had covered the beaches with a hideous array of mines and jagged steel spikes and concrete cones; along the Pas de Calais new secret weapons, the jet-propelled flying bombs or V-1's, were ready to be hurled at London; and, under the brilliant direction of Albert Speer, German war production was increasing in spite of the Allied bombing raids. In the summer of 1944, Hitler believed, the Russian front would be stabilized, the Allies would be blocked along the Gustav Line in Italy, and the cross-Channel invasion would be thrown back at the Atlantic Wall.

Allied Advances in Russia and Italy. There was little sign of a halt in the momentum of the Russian attack, however. After the victory of Stalingrad, in January 1943, the Russians had advanced along the whole front. The siege of Leningrad was raised. In the spring of 1943 a final German offensive at Kursk was hurled back with heavy losses; and on July 12, the Red Army began a sweep along the whole front that resulted in the taking of Kharkov, Orel, Taganrog, Smolensk, and Kiev. At the time of the Teheran Conference, the Russians were beyond the Dnieper; and, in new attacks launched in mid-January 1944, the northern armies reached the edge of the Baltic states, and the southern armies recaptured Odessa, cleared most of the Crimea, and penetrated deep into prewar Poland. In April, the spring thaw brought a brief respite, while Stalin prepared his promised June offensive that would accompany the OVERLORD landings. In Italy the German front could not be held. The American Fifth Army, which had been landed on the Salerno beaches on September 9, 1943, in an attempt to outflank the Germans holding Naples, had finally made contact with the Eighth Army advancing from the south on September 14, and Naples had fallen on October 1. The Gustav Line, centered on the monastery of Monte Cassino, had been assaulted with great losses from January to March 1944, and was broken in May. An Allied landing had been made on the beaches of Anzio near Rome in January 1944, and six divisions landed there were finally able to break out to aid in the capture of Rome on June 4.

FROM NORMANDY TO THE RHINE

D-Day. The Germans were badly mistaken in their forecast of the date and place of the invasion. Rundstedt and Rommel were both convinced that the main attack would be at the Pas de Calais where the Channel was only twenty-one miles wide, and the Allies skillfully encouraged this belief by massing dummy ships near Dover, simulating troop movements, and mounting air attacks. Hitler's intuition told him that the landings would be in Normandy, but he believed there would also be an attack along the Pas-de-Calais that would require him to keep back a large share of his armor. German weather reports were so bad on June 5 that Rommel went to visit his wife in Germany, confident that the invasion was two weeks away. Eisenhower, courageously taking advantage of the promise of a brief calming in the rough seas of the

Channel, ordered the invasion to begin on June 6—D-Day. During the night three airborne divisions were parachuted to the base of the Cotentin Peninsula, to seize bridgeheads on the Orne and to prevent enemy reinforcements moving toward Cherbourg. The shore batteries were pounded from the air and the sea, until at 6:30 A.M. the first waves of troops stormed ashore. Only the American VI Corps at Omaha Beach met strong resistance, and by the evening 130,000 men were ashore. Within a week, the Allies held a fifty-mile stretch of coast to a depth of twelve miles with an army of 326,000 men.

The Liberation of France. The Allied plan was for the British forces under Montgomery to take the brunt of the major German offensive at Caen, while the Americans under General Omar Bradley were to break out at St.-Lô, cut off Cherbourg, and wheel in a huge circle toward the Seine. The Germans, forbidden by Hitler to retreat for regrouping, fought savagely to hold Montgomery's forces at Caen, but the Americans broke out on June 17, captured Cherbourg on June 25, and by the end of June were on the edge of Brittany. Throughout July, the Allied buildup increased, and when Montgomery launched a major offensive on July 18 there were already thirty Allied divisions, half American, half British and Canadian, in France. At the beginning of August, however, Hitler ignored the advice of his generals and ordered a counteroffensive against the vital communication center of Avranches. As his generals had predicted, the Allies were able to annihilate some eight German divisions caught in the Falaise pocket; and the United States Third Army of General George Patton was able to speed toward the Seine. Orléans and Chartres were taken on August 17, and Mantes on the Seine was captured on August 19. Eisenhower had wished to avoid a battle for Paris by encircling the city, but on August 19 French resistance forces rose spontaneously, covering Paris with barricades. The Parisians fought with old rifles and knives, and some 3,000 were killed before the French Second Armored Division of General Leclerc completed the liberation of the city on August 25. The German commander, General von Choltitz, who had ignored Hitler's orders to burn the city to the ground, surrendered to Leclerc in the afternoon. In the early evening, General de Gaulle, whose authority in France had been brought home to the British and American governments by the unquestioning obedience he had received in the liberated areas and by the services

ALLIED VICTORY IN THE WEST, 1943–1945

rendered by the resistance, set up his headquarters in the Ministry of War.

Meanwhile, the landing craft from Normandy had been transferred to the Mediterranean, and on August 15 a new invasion was launched from Italy on the southern coast of France. The main strength consisted of seven divisions of the French First Army, formed in 1943 by fusion of de Gaulle's Free French forces with the North African Army and three American divisions. Opposition was light, and the Germans were soon in rapid retreat up the valley of the Rhône. Toulon and Marseille were taken in August, and Lyon fell on September 3. On September 11, these forces joined up with the OVERLORD forces moving east from Normandy, establishing a continuous front from the Channel to the Mediterranean. The Germans by then had lost 400,000 men, 1,300 tanks, and vast amounts of equipment, and seemed on the point of collapse. The abortive attempt on Hitler's life on July 20 had indicated the existence of strong internal opposition. Rundstedt had been fired for opposing the war, and Rommel had been ordered to commit suicide for his share in the July 20 plot. By mid-September, Allied forces had reached the borders of Germany itself at several places in mid-September, and Montgomery's forces had liberated most of Belgium and Luxembourg.

Battle of the Bulge. The war, however, was far from over. An ambitious effort to seize a bridgehead on the lower Rhine at Arnhem with two British and one American airborne division failed against strong German opposition. Montgomery's ambition for a swift thrust on the Ruhr that would end the war within three months had been foiled, and the Allied armies advanced little during the winter months along most of the front, occupying themselves with strengthening their communications and equipment for a major offensive across the Rhine as soon as the weather improved. Hitler, however, ordered Rundstedt, who had been restored to command in the West, to throw two newly equipped Panzer armies through the Ardennes Forest, as in 1940, to seize Antwerp. The American forces were taken completely by surprise, and the German forces advanced fifty miles before American reinforcements and air attacks in the clear weather after Christmas forced Hitler reluctantly to agree to a withdrawal. In the Battle of the Bulge, however, the German casualties were 120,000, almost double the American losses. In this desperate offensive, Hitler had thrown away the

FROM STALINGRAD TO BERLIN, 1943–1945

last concentration of armor and air power that Germany could muster in the West. The opportunity was at hand for Eisenhower's forces to reach the final German defenses, the old Siegfried Line, now renamed the West Wall.

Soviet Summer Offensive, 1944. During the six months when the Anglo-American forces were advancing from the Normandy beaches to the Rhine, the Russian Army mounted one of its greatest offensives of the war. On June 10, the northern armies attacked the Mannerheim Line and broke through into Finland, which sought an armistice on August 25. On June 23, the Russians resumed their attack in White Russia, where they broke the Fatherland Line, captured Vitebsk and Gomel in June, and Minsk on July 6. By the end of July they had reached the Niemen River, an advance of 250 miles that took them through the areas annexed in 1939 and into the heart of Poland. South of the Pripet Marshes, the Red Army broke the German front, and by the end of July reached the Vistula. At the beginning of August, when

Marshal Rokossovsky's forces were within a few miles of Warsaw, the Polish Home Army rose in rebellion; but the Germans had withdrawn to carefully constructed defensive positions on the west bank of the Vistula. The Polish uprising was crushed at the end of September, and the Germans held desperately on to Warsaw until January 17, 1945. At this point, the Russians halted their armies between the Baltic and the Carpathian Mountains, and in August they concentrated their attack on the weakly held line between the Black Sea and the Carpathians. The political rather than the military gains of this advance were enormous; for the Red Army established itself in Rumania between August 23 and September 5, in Bulgaria from September 5 to 9, and in eastern Yugoslavia and southern Hungary in October. By December, the Russians were in the suburbs of Budapest, where, as in Warsaw, the Germans were preparing for a last major stand. Finally, in September and October, the German armies holding the Baltic states were defeated, and Estonia, Latvia, and Lithuania were again incorporated in the Soviet Union.

Thus, at the end of 1944, German forces had been driven back to the inner fortress whose principal defenses were the West Wall along the Rhine, and the citadels of Warsaw and Budapest in the east. The advances both in the west and east since the Teheran Conference in November 1943 had raised many political questions on the fate of the countries liberated or defeated by Anglo-American or the Russian armies; and throughout 1944 there was much diplomatic activity that culminated in the Yalta Conference of February 1945. It was beginning to be clear, however, that the advance of the armies was already settling many political questions.

THE DIPLOMATIC FRONT:
FROM TEHERAN TO YALTA

American, Russian, and British Postwar Goals. Throughout 1944 there was a hiatus in American policy-making. Roosevelt, his confidant Harry Hopkins, and Secretary of State Hull were all ill for large parts of the time. The State Department was completely divorced from the making of military strategy, for Hull was determined that no suspicion of political ambition should disturb the thinking of the military. Roosevelt's desire to postpone making any plans for countries not yet occupied was strengthened by the approach of the 1944 presidential election; and he openly told Stalin and others that he could not afford to alienate such voting blocs as the Polish-Americans or Latvian-Americans. In this case he preferred silence to acquiescence in Stalin's aims. Roosevelt, indeed, seemed more inclined to press the British and the French to give up their colonial empires; the only postwar aim he pressed on Stalin was the establishment after the war of a more effective international organization to replace the League of Nations.

Stalin was most concerned about Russian security. He never wavered in his determination to reincorporate in Russia the Baltic states and the territories taken from Poland and Rumania, whose inhabitants he claimed were related to the nationalities of the Soviet Union—especially those of Poland who were White Russian or Ukrainian and whose incorporation in Russia was essential to scotch the resurgence of White Russian or Ukrainian independence movements. In the line of states from the Baltic to the Black Sea he wanted friendly governments, and had trained in Moscow a series of faithful Communists who could be installed in power—Dimitrov in Bulgaria, Gheorghiu-Dej in Rumania, and Bierut in Poland. In Yugoslavia and Albania, he could profit from the indigenous Communist leaders, Tito and Hoxha; and in Czechoslovakia he seemed prepared to accept Beneš as a suitable candidate. Yet his wish for continuing collaboration with the Western powers appeared genuine. Russia's reconstruction would take years to accomplish and might be aided by a large American loan; and he was inclined to accept American wishes for a United Nations Organization and British wishes for the delineation of spheres of influence, while doing his utmost to prevent British or American influence from being exerted in the areas where the Red Army was advancing. Since it had been decided at Teheran to give the Red Army a free hand in the military operations in Eastern Europe, the one remaining hope for the British and Americans to influence the fate of those countries was at the conference table.

For Churchill, hope of an amicable relationship with Russia in the postwar years was dying fast, killed above all by the impossibility of getting Stalin to work with the Polish government-in-exile in London. Throughout 1944, therefore, Churchill attempted to approach Stalin as one Old World statesman to another. He accepted Russia's demands where he believed Russian security was at stake and recognized Russia's frontiers as those of June 1941. He sought to find compromise governments for the East European countries that woud be both democratic and friendly to Russia, seeing in President Beneš of Czechoslovakia the model. And when aims clearly clashed, he proposed to Stalin a division of Eastern Europe into British and Russian spheres of interest. In this way, he hoped to keep Communist advances in Eastern Europe to the minimum, since he had already failed in 1943 to get British and American armies into the Balkans and the Danube Valley ahead of the Russians. Outside Europe, he was determined on a return to the status quo, to restore British, French, and Dutch colonial dominion, in spite of Roosevelt's desire for the liquidation of all colonial empires.

In May, Churchill had openly asked the British cabinet, "Are we going to acquiesce in the Communisation of the Balkans and perhaps of Italy?" and he proposed to the Russians that they should regard Rumanian affairs "as mainly their concern," while the British would do the same for Greece. Roosevelt was noncommittal, and the decision was postponed until Churchill's visit to Moscow in October. There, Churchill reduced the matter to figures. Russia was to have 90 per cent "of the say" in Rumania, 75 per cent in Bulgaria, 50 per cent in Hungary and Yugoslavia, and Britain would have 90 per cent of the say in Greece. Stalin made a large check mark on the agreement with a blue pencil. This extraordinary agreement, while mathematically unworkable, did imply that Russia would leave the British a free hand in Greece; and Stalin scrupulously deserted the Greek Communists, accepting even the British military intervention of December without a protest. The British for their part defended Russia's right to influence the governments in Rumania, Bulgaria, and Hungary.

German and Polish Problems. Two major questions remained for settlement between the Russians and the Western powers—the treatment of Germany and the future of Poland. Since its formation in October 1943, the European Advisory Commission had been working on a plan for the postwar division of Germany into three zones of occupation. A British proposal giving the Russians a zone lying roughly between the Elbe and the Oder rivers, the Americans the southwestern region, and the British themselves the northwestern region, including the Ruhr and the Channel ports, was accepted by the Russians in February 1944. At the time, this appeared to the British and Americans as abnegation on the Russian part, as it was generally thought that at the end of the war the Red Army might well have reached the Rhine. The

Americans refused to take the southwestern zone, however; and a wag remarked that the Russians were being given the agriculture, the British the industry, and the Americans the scenery. But the most telling factor was Roosevelt's unwillingness to be dependent upon French transportation for the redeployment of American troops to the Pacific war, since he suspected there might well be revolution in liberated France.

The question of zones and the whole problem of policy to be applied in occupied Germany were discussed by Churchill and Roosevelt at their second Quebec Conference on September 13–16, 1944. By then, de Gaulle was bringing order to France, and Roosevelt agreed to take the southwestern zone, to which would be added the ports of Bremen and Bremerhaven. When Secretary of the Treasury Henry Morgenthau, a close friend and neighbor of Roosevelt's, was summoned to discuss the British desire for postwar credits, he suggested that between the defeat of Germany and the defeat of Japan, the British should receive $3.5 billion in Lend-Lease aid and a nonmilitary credit of $3 billion. He also suggested what became known as the Morgenthau Plan for the postwar treatment of Germany—that German industry should be dismantled and the mines flooded, France be given the Saar and Poland Silesia, and the pastoral demilitarized rump be divided into two states, each organized on a federal basis. Churchill and Roosevelt initialed the plan; but within a few weeks, on the vehement protests of their cabinets, both repudiated it. Nevertheless, details were leaked to the press, and Nazi propaganda made great play of the fate reserved for the German people once unconditional surrender had been enforced. It is doubtful whether the revelation of the existence of the plan stiffened German resistance. It is certain that features of it were incorporated into the first instructions given to the American military government and that the plan as a whole appealed to many European nations, especially the French, who had been suffering from German occupation. Roosevelt, who disliked "making detailed plans for a country we do not yet occupy," reacted to public displeasure at this plan by refusing to make any policy for occupied Germany; the American members of the European Advisory Commission found themselves unable to participate in policy-making; and detailed instructions to the occupying forces were drawn up, not in the State Department, but in the War Department. The official handbook for the American military government, JCS 1067, was very close to the thinking of Henry Morgenthau.

Meanwhile, the chances of persuading Stalin to come to terms with the London Poles were growing slimmer. Relations with the Mikolajczyk government had been broken off by the Russians in April 1943; and, in the hope of getting Stalin to come to an understanding with the London Poles, Churchill summoned Mikolajczyk to Moscow during his visit of October 1944. Although Stalin was willing to allow the London Poles a few seats in a future Polish government, he was not willing to modify his demands for annexation of Poland as far as the Curzon Line. After Mikolajczyk's refusal, Stalin made no further effort to deal with the London Poles. On January 5, 1945, he recognized the Communist-dominated Committee of National Liberation in Lublin as the Provisional Government of Poland.

Thus, by the end of 1944, a large number of questions were crying for a solution by agreement of the Big Three. Policy to be applied in Germany had to be determined; the relation of the London Poles and the Lublin Committee required definition; the status of France had to be decided, since General de Gaulle was pressing for a French zone of occupation in Germany and for an invitation to participate in all conferences concerning Europe; and President Roosevelt, assured by his military advisers that the coming invasion of Japan would cost a million American casualties, was anxious to gain a precise Russian commitment to aid in the defeat of the Japanese. Since Stalin refused to lose contact with the battlefront by leaving Russia, Roosevelt and Churchill finally agreed reluctantly that they would meet with Stalin at the Black Sea resort of Yalta in the Crimea, in February 1945.

The Yalta Conference. The British and American Chiefs of Staff held a preliminary meeting at Malta on January 31–February 3. The British were reviving two of their favorite plans—to defeat Germany by a single overwhelming thrust through north Germany, under Montgomery's command, rather than by the pincer movement around the Ruhr desired by Eisenhower and Bradley; and to establish Allied troops in Austria and Yugoslavia by a seaborne landing on the Istrian Peninsula followed by a drive through the Ljubljana Gap. Montgomery's personal squabble with Bradley and Patton after the Battle of the Bulge added to American dislike for the British proposal, and after a heated argument the British were forced to give in on both matters.

Accommodations at Yalta for the delegations who accompanied the heads of state were sumptuous. From the Yusupov Palace, Stalin carried on the detailed direction of the Red Army's advance into Eastern Europe. Roosevelt was lodged in the luxurious Livadia Palace, where all the main sessions were held. The British were somewhat isolated five miles away in the palace of a Tsarist ambassador to the British Court. After driving across the devastated Crimea, the British and Americans found that no comfort had been spared—food, wine, flowers, servants. It was evident that the Russians were going to enormous pains to be genial. What Stalin hoped to achieve at Yalta was above all the security of the Soviet Union—by crippling Germany and creating friendly states on its borders in Eastern Europe, and by maintenance of the solidarity of the Big Three who were, he remarked, a "very exclusive club, restricted to a membership of nations with five million soldiers." He was prepared to join the war against Japan, but part of his price was the Pacific territories that Russia had lost in 1905 at the end of the Russo-Japanese War; and he was determined to aid the economic reconstruction of Russia with vast German reparations and, if possible, with an American loan.

In private discussions with Stalin on February 8 and 10, Roosevelt settled the question of Russian intervention in the Japanese war, which was to take place in Manchuria "two or three months after Germany has surrendered." Russia's reward was to be the return of southern Sakhalin, the cession of the Japanese Kurile Islands, recognition of the status quo (i.e., the communization) in Outer Mongolia, the internationalization of the Manchurian port of Dairen, the grant to Russia of a lease on Port Arthur, and joint administration by the Russians and the Chinese of the Chinese-Eastern Railroad and the South Manchurian Railroad. Although Churchill took no part in the negotiation, he signed the final agreement. Four years later, after the victory of the Chinese Communists, this agreement was subjected to blistering attack in the United States. It was held that Roosevelt had invited Russia to participate in the Japanese war unnecessarily, since even without the atomic bomb the American forces could easily have defeated the Japanese; that the agreement smacked of old-style imperialism and ignored the moral principles of the Atlantic Charter; and above all that Russian influence in the Manchurian ports and railroads was used to further the military success of the Chinese Communists. Yet at the time Roosevelt was elated at his success, which seemed to promise a substantial lightening of American casualties in the Japanese campaign for little more than restoration to Russia of rights and territories it had possessed in Tsarist days.

Stalin proved almost equally willing to satisfy Roosevelt on the formation of the United Nations Organization. Plans had been drawn up at the Dumbarton Oaks Conference on August 21–October 9, 1944; but on certain crucial points there had been disagreement between the Russians and the Americans. Although both were in agreement that there should be a General Assembly in which each nation would have one vote, the Russians had demanded that each of the sixteen Republics constituting the Soviet Union should have a seat. At Yalta, Stalin was appeased by the grant of seats to the Ukraine and White Russia besides the Soviet Union's seat; and he even agreed that the United States might have three seats, if it wished. He accepted the American formula for voting procedure in the Security Council, by which permanent members could not use their veto power to prevent the Council attempting to solve by peaceful methods disputes to which they themselves were a party; and he agreed that the founding session of the organization should begin in San Francisco on April 25. In the Far East and the United Nations Organization agreements, Roosevelt felt he had achieved his primary goals at Yalta.

Churchill's main efforts were directed to the French and Polish questions. He fought vigorously for grant of a zone of occupation in Germany to France, since "the French had had long experience in occupying Germany and they would not be lenient." Roosevelt's statement, in reply to an apparently casual question from Stalin, that American troops would not be kept in Europe longer than two years, clinched the argument, and it was agreed that the French would be given a zone of occupation formed from territory originally lying in the British and American zones. This decision restored France to great-power status. Except for the Potsdam Conference, they would henceforth enjoy a position of equality with the Big Three in all diplomatic conferences. The question of Poland's eastern frontier was quickly settled, the Curzon Line being taken as the approximate boundary. Poland was to be compensated by taking part of East Prussia and by extending its boundaries to the Oder; all Germans living in that area were to be expelled. Roosevelt and Churchill would not accept Stalin's demand that the frontier line should follow the western rather than the eastern Neisse to its junction with the Oder, since that would have greatly extended Poland's German annexations. In the final communiqué, therefore, the statesmen temporized, agreeing only that "Poland must receive substantial accessions of territory in the north and west" and "that the final delimitation of the western frontier of Poland should thereafter await the Peace Conference." Thus was created the problem of the Oder-Neisse territories, which the Red Army handed over to Poland without more ado, from which six million Germans were expelled, and whose cession has not been recognized by any West German government.

At first, Roosevelt and Churchill attempted to persuade Stalin to permit the formation of an entirely new government in Poland, in which the Communists would occupy a minor role; but the most Stalin would accept was the broadening of the Provisional Government to include "democratic leaders from Poland itself and from Poles abroad" and to create a commission of representatives of the three powers to supervise the formation of this government. Roosevelt consoled himself with the thought that this situation, which clearly favored the Polish Communists, was to last only until "the holding of free and unfettered elections as soon as possible on the basis of universal suffrage and secret ballot." With Poland in the hands of the Red Army, the agreement was, Roosevelt remarked privately, "the best I can do for Poland at this time."

Having gained his goal in Poland, Stalin agreed to the issuing of a Declaration on Liberated Europe, by which the three powers pledged to aid the liberated and former satellite countries of Europe to re-establish order, hold free elections, and carry out emergency relief. The declaration appeared to give the British and Americans the right to intervene in Eastern Europe, but since such intervention could come about only by agreement of all three powers, the document remained little more than a heady statement of principle.

Finally, the Big Three attempted to formulate a policy for occupied Germany. They at once accepted the draft of Germany's instrument of unconditional surrender submitted by the European Advisory Commission, and its proposals for zonal boundaries, joint occupation of Berlin, and administration by an Allied Control Council consisting of the Allied commanders-in-chief in Germany. Nazism and German militarism were to be eradicated. The possibility of dismembering Germany was to be discussed by a special commission. On reparations, Stalin was categorical—Germany should pay $20 billion of reparations in kind, and Russia should take half. Both Roosevelt and Churchill thought this too high a figure, although they did not dispute the fact that Russia's sufferings justified their claim to half the reparations. Once again, a commission of experts was given the task of making detailed recommendations. Thus, the German question received surprisingly summary treatment and had to be considered again in detail at the Potsdam Conference in July.

The conference broke up on February 11. Roosevelt carried out a triumphant progress through the Mediterranean, receiving King Farouk of Egypt, Emperor Haile Selassie of Ethiopia, and King Ibn Saud of Saudi Arabia on board the cruiser "Quincy." He was snubbed only by de Gaulle, who refused a summons to fly to Algiers. Roosevelt, though invigorated by what he regarded as the success of the conference, was a sick man; six weeks later he was dead. Churchill, vigorous as ever, took a quick trip to the battlefield of the Light Brigade at Balaklava, spoke to the crowds in Constitution Square at Athens, met Ibn Saud, and was back in the House of Commons on February 27, where he declared optimistically that "the Crimea Conference leaves the Allies more closely united than before." Stalin too was apparently well pleased, for *Izvestia* called the conference "the greatest political event of current times." Events in Eastern Europe were soon to show that Stalin's confidence was better founded than that of his Allies.

THE END OF THE EUROPEAN WAR: FEBRUARY–MAY 1945

Allied Victories, February–May 1945. At the end of 1944, Hitler still had seven million men in his armies, giving him a total of 260 divisions, twice the number he had in May 1940. Along the Rhine in the west, the Vistula in the east, and the Danube in the south, strong defensive positions were ready. New weapons were in use, or near completion—the V-2's, or long-range rockets, were being launched at London and Antwerp from the western Netherlands, some 1,300 in all falling on southern England, where 9,000 people were killed or wounded; an extremely fast electro U-boat had been invented, although its production was hampered by Allied bombing. But optimism was hardly justified. The 260 divisions were widely scattered, and Hitler refused to allow withdrawals of the large forces in Norway, Denmark, and Latvia. Many of the soldiers were old men or young boys with no military training; the last raw materials and military supplies were about to run out; and the Russians enjoyed a superiority of six to one on their front. Hitler himself was in total physical decline, dependent upon the injections of a quack doctor; his body trembled, his voice was barely recognizable, and "there was an indescribable flickering glow in his eyes, creating a fearsome and wholly unnatural effect." He was fanatically determined that all Germany should perish with him and gave orders that everything was to be destroyed before the invading armies and that all obstructing the policy were to be hanged or shot. "Those who remain after the battle," he told Speer, "are of little value; for the good have fallen."

The Russians, who had been inactive along the whole Eastern front from the Baltic to the Carpathians since August 1944, while advancing on Budapest from the south, launched their last major offensive on January 12, 1945. Four army groups struck simultaneously. Konev broke across the upper Vistula and took Cracow. Zhukov occupied Warsaw on January 17. Rokossovsky crossed the Narev River and isolated Danzig, while Cherniakovsky cut off Königsberg. Danzig was finally taken on March 30, and Königsberg on April 9. Konev's drive soon took him into German Silesia, the major remaining source of coal, and Bunzlau fell on February 15. Zhukov continued with little opposition and reached the Oder on February 10, some fifty miles from Berlin. In Hungary, the drive on Budapest by the armies of Malinovsky and Tolbukhin had begun in November 1944; it was only in February 1945 that the city fell. On March 3, Hitler mounted a last desperate counterattack similar in strategy to that of the Ardennes offensive of December, using the same SS Panzer Army to spearhead a drive past Lake Balaton toward the Danube. The tanks ran out of gasoline, and the attack was soon broken. Together, Tolbukhin and Malinovsky advanced into Austria and by April 13 were in occupation of Vienna Thus, at the beginning of April, the Red Army had occupied or liberated all the great capitals of Eastern Europe—Bucharest, Sofia, Belgrade, Budapest, Warsaw, and Vienna. Only Berlin and Prague remained in German hands, and they seemed relatively easy prizes.

In the west, Eisenhower began the attack on the Rhine in March. Montgomery's British and Canadian forces in the north met harsh opposition and were delayed by flooding when the Germans smashed open the Roer dams. In the center, American forces under General Bradley soon captured the whole Rhine Valley between Düsseldorf and

Koblenz, and the Ninth Armored Division advanced so rapidly that it took the railway bridge at Remagen while it was still usable. This gift of a bridge enabled Bradley to establish four divisions on the right bank of the Rhine. In the south, the French First Army of Marshal de Lattre de Tassigny wheeled through the Rhenish Palatinate, crossed the Rhine in small boats with heavy losses, and after taking Karlsruhe, drove through the Black Forest to take Stuttgart on April 21. Bradley then took the Ruhr in a gigantic pincer movement, and on April 18, 325,000 German troops surrendered. The encirclement of the Ruhr left central Germany open to attack, and Bradley's army continued eastward, reaching the Elbe on April 11. Eisenhower's forces were thus almost as close to Berlin and Prague as the Russians, and German resistance in the west had collapsed while a last desperate defense had been improvised in the east. On March 28, however, Eisenhower announced that he considered Berlin no longer significant as a military objective. He intended to prevent the formation of an Alpine redoubt by the remaining German forces by concentrating his main forces on a drive toward Leipzig and Dresden, which would make contact with the Red Army and would split Germany in two; and he informed Stalin of this strategy at the same time as Roosevelt and Churchill. Churchill reacted vehemently. On April 1 he suggested to Roosevelt that both on military and political grounds the Western forces should be the first to enter Berlin; and on April 30 he begged President Truman to allow the American armies to take Prague. For Churchill, the transformation of the political situation in Eastern Europe that was taking place behind the line of the Red Army had finally ended the need for disguising the ideological struggle with the Russians.

Soviet Intervention in Rumania. In Rumania, where King Michael's coup d'état of August 23, 1944, had opened the country to the Russians, the coalition government of General Sănătescu composed largely of regular army officers had found itself under strong pressure from the Communists and their allies in the National Democratic Front to increase their representation in the government and to purge the bureaucracy. In November, Sănătescu re-formed his government with civilians, giving most of the ministries to the traditional political parties, particularly to Maniu's Peasant party, but permitting the National Democratic Front a larger representation. A new government formed in December under General Rădescu embarked upon a needed purge; but

Rădescu found himself under attack from the Communist party for taking the Ministry of the Interior himself. When the Rumanian Communist leaders, Gheorghiu-Dej and Ana Pauker returned from a visit to Moscow in January 1945, they apparently had instructions to embark upon an all-out attack on the Rădescu government. After a battle between Communists and Peasant party followers at the Malaxa steel works and the attempted suppression of a mass Communist demonstration in Constitution Square, the Soviet government intervened directly. Russian troops disarmed the Rumanian forces in Bucharest; and on February 27, the Soviet Deputy Foreign Minister Vishinsky ordered King Michael to ask the National Democratic Front to form a government. After temporizing briefly, Michael appointed Dr. Petru Groza of the Ploughmen's Front as premier, the Communists taking the Ministries of the Interior and Justice and thus gaining virtual control of the police and the law courts. Vishinsky's intervention came barely a fortnight after the Big Three had accepted the Declaration on Liberated Europe at Yalta, in which they pledged themselves not to take unilateral action in countries they controlled; and Roosevelt and Churchill were both deeply disturbed at this proof of Russian intentions. Churchill, however, felt bound by the spheres-of-influence agreement he had made with Stalin in October 1944, especially as Stalin had observed his part of the bargain with regard to Greece; and the American government made no significant effort to influence the Rumanian situation until the war was over. Groza sought to strengthen his position by decreeing a popular land reform in March and by embarking on a thorough purge of all government officials.

Communist Advances in Bulgaria. In Bulgaria, communization, though less peremptory, was equally advanced. The Fatherland Front government, which had seized power in September 1944 included with the Communists, the Agrarian Union, the *Zveno,* the Social Democrats, and Independents. The Communists, as in Rumania, however, held the Ministries of the Interior and of Justice. In a vicious, and probably popular, purge of the leaders of the old regime, over 2,000 people were executed, including the three regents and twenty-two ministers, and 3,500 were sentenced to long prison terms. Among those imprisoned was the pro-Western Muraviev and several other democratic leaders who had opposed the prewar dictatorship. Another pro-Western leader, Dr. G. M. Dimitrov, who was attempting to build up his peasant party, the

Agrarian Union, to the point where it could challenge the Communists, was accused of rousing defeatism in the Bulgarian Army, and in January he was forced to resign his position as general secretary. His successor, Nikola Petkov, was also at odds with the Communists, and in May Communist sympathizers packed the party's convention and forced Petkov's resignation. The Social Democratic party was similarly split. With the Communists in control of the police and most of the provincial and village administration, the traditional political parties found themselves paralyzed.

Supremacy of Tito in Yugoslavia and Hoxha in Albania. In Yugoslavia and Albania, the triumph of communism was assured even before the entry of the Red Army. The failure of Mihailović to win what he regarded as a civil war against Tito's partisans left the Communists the heirs to political power; and it was only under strong pressure that Tito had admitted representatives of the London government-in-exile into his cabinet of March 1945. Tito admitted later that he never intended these unwanted members of his cabinet to have any say in policy: "We could not during the period of joint government make any concessions to those elements in the Government who actually represented the interests of the overthrown monarchy, the bourgeoisie and their patron abroad, international reaction." None of the prewar parties found it possible to organize meetings or revive their organizations. "I am not against parties in principle," said Tito, "but to create parties just for the sake of parties—that is something for which at present we have no time." The secret police was active in punishing former "collaborators," a term that was widely interpreted to permit action against possible opponents of the new regime. Although the Red Army had left Yugoslavia in March 1945, large numbers of military advisers remained; the Yugoslav Army was trained, dressed, and equipped in the Soviet manner; and on April 11, 1945, a Soviet-Yugoslav Treaty of Friendship and Mutual Assistance was signed. The Western powers were then unaware of the tensions already building up between Tito and the Soviet leaders and of the resentment the Russian military and technical advisers were arousing.

In Albania, the situation was similar. A Democratic Front, dominated by the Communists and led by Enver Hoxha, took power when the Germans were expelled. Opposition leaders, who were either tribal chiefs or individual landowners owing to the nonexistence of political parties before the war, were either driven into exile or executed. In August 1945, the large landholdings were distributed among the peasantry, and the Hoxha government at once won popularity and destroyed the economic power of their opponents. Communization was therefore certain, but it was hard for the Western governments in this case to summon up much enthusiasm for the dispossessed classes.

Coalition Government in Hungary and Czechoslovakia. In Hungary, the Red Army brought with it a series of Moscow-trained Hungarian Communists, some of whom were survivors of the Béla Kun revolution of 1919 and others exiles of the interwar years. They collaborated effectively with the Social Democratic and Smallholder parties, even helping them reorganize; and in the government of General Miklos, formed in December 1944, they were satisfied to take only the Ministries of Agriculture and Trade and to install a fellow traveler as minister of the interior. Infiltration of the police, of the local administration, and of the trade unions was rapid, however, and the presence of Marshal Voroshilov as chairman of the Allied Control Council and the control of all instruments of propaganda by the Red Army were signs of the pressure that might yet be exerted if the political situation did not evolve according to plan.

In the spring of 1945, however, the Russians seemed to be observing the terms of the Yalta Declaration on Liberated Europe in Hungary, while in Czechoslovakia, an apparently model relationship was established in the restoration of the government of President Beneš first at Košice in March and then in Prague in May 1945. The new premier, Zdenek Fierlinger, was a left-wing Social Democrat who had been Czech ambassador in Moscow during the war; Jan Masaryk, son of the founder and first president of the Czech state, was foreign minister; and the Communists took the Ministries of the Interior, Agriculture, Education, and Information. Administration of the liberated areas was handed over to the Beneš government by the Red Army; and it appeared that a workable compromise had in this one instance at least been reached.

Further Communist Gains in Poland. Beneš' satisfaction with his achievement was partly due to his awareness of events in Poland. The Commission of Ambassadors in Moscow, which had been designated at Yalta as a body to supervise the broadening of the Warsaw government to include other representative Poles, met many times between February and April, with little success in determining which Poles should be invited to meet representatives of the Warsaw government, who particularly objected to dealing with Mikolajczyk. In Poland itself, the Communist party was rapidly establishing its control over the police and the regular army and was installing its sympathizers in many of the other political parties. In one of the most glaring examples of direct Russian intervention, sixteen leaders of the Polish underground and of the prewar political parties were informed by the Red Army that they would be flown to Moscow to take part in the talks on governmental reorganization. On arrival they were taken to Lubianka Prison and, in June, were tried for crimes against the Red Army and sentenced to long prison terms. The Russian government strengthened even further the impression that it was blocking any attempt to change the Warsaw government's composition by demanding that it be represented at the San Francisco Conference and by signing with it a Treaty of Friendship, Mutual Assistance and Postwar Collaboration on April 21, 1945.

Anglo-American Reaction. Thus, through large parts of Eastern Europe, the triumph of communism seemed to be either achieved or near; and Churchill, therefore, for the last two months of the war, made desperate attempts to persuade the Americans to establish Allied forces as far east as possible and in particular in Berlin and Prague. The Polish dispute had convinced the British prime minister that the Western nations must have bargaining power if they were to exert any influence on Russian policy in Eastern Europe. Although Roosevelt had joined Churchill in protesting to Stalin at the situation in Poland and had taken as a deep affront Stalin's suggestion that the Western powers were negotiating a separate peace with German emissaries in Switzerland, on the very day of his death he cabled Churchill that he wished to "minimize the general Soviet problem as much as possible, because these problems, in one form or another, seem to arise every day, and most of them straighten out." Roosevelt's sudden collapse, at the time of his greatest triumph, thrust the enormous responsibilities of the American presidency in the untried hands of Harry Truman who, as vice-president, had been given almost no share in the formulation of policy and little access even to government documents. He could get little help from the State Department, which had not been consulted on the planning of military strategy; and so Truman quite naturally attempted to follow the policy, and keep the promises, of Roosevelt. He accepted the military advice of Eisenhower and of the American Joint Chiefs of Staff, who wanted to halt the Allied advance eastward at the Elbe in Germany and at Pilsen in western Czechoslovakia, since the taking of Berlin for what were regarded as prestige purposes might cost 100,000 casualties and the advance on Prague might endanger the reduction of the suspected Alpine redoubt.

Germany Defeated. Throughout April the American First and Third Armies advanced to take Leipzig, while to the south the American Seventh and the French First Armies took south Germany and advanced into western Austria. In the north, the British Second Army swept across the plains between the Weser and the Elbe, taking Bremen, Hamburg, and Lübeck and swinging north to liberate Denmark. The Canadian First Army cut off the German forces in the western Netherlands, but rather than inflict upon the Dutch the further horror of a final campaign, a truce was concluded with the German Reich Commissioner Seyss-Inquart, by which the Allies halted their advance and the Germans permitted relief supplies to be distributed among the Dutch. The forces of Marshal Zhukov launched their attack across the Oder on a two-hundred-mile front on April 16, and within nine days they had surrounded Berlin. In Italy, Alexander's troops broke across the Apennine barrier in mid-April, quickly capturing Bologna, Padua, Verona, and Milan, with the aid of the Italian partisans. Mussolini was caught by a group of Italian partisans as, dressed in a German helmet and greatcoat, he was attempting to flee to the Swiss border; he was shot and delivered to Milan to be displayed, strung upside down, to a jeering mob. The remaining German forces in Italy surrendered unconditionally on April 29.

In Berlin, Hitler spent the last days of the *Götterdämmerung* he had brought upon Germany in his offices in the Reich Chancellery and in the concrete air-raid shelter in the garden. Turning for hope to the example of Frederick the Great, he had Goebbels read to him, from Carlyle's biography, of how the sudden death of the Tsarina Elizabeth in 1762 had saved "Old Fritz" at the darkest hour of his fortunes. The death of Roosevelt seemed a reassurance that fate was still on the Prussian side. Ten days later, the first Russian shells landed in the garden of the Chancellery, and it became obvious to Hitler that the end had come. His most trusted followers began to desert him. Goering proposed that he should take over "total leadership" of the Reich on April 23, in Hitler's place; and, in a final outburst of fury, Hitler ordered him dismissed from all his posts and arrested. On April 28, the news came to Berlin that Himmler had attempted to negotiate peace terms through the Swedish Count Bernadotte. This final blow persuaded Hitler to end his life. On April 29, he married his mistress Eva Braun, in the early hours of the morning, and dictated his will and his political testament. At half past three in the afternoon of April 30, he shot himself through the mouth. His body, and that of Eva Braun who had taken poison, were burned in the garden outside, while Russian patrols were barely a mile away. On May 1, Goebbels poisoned his six children and shot himself and his wife; the next day, the Russians occupied the Reich Chancellery.

Admiral Doenitz, whom Hitler had appointed his successor, continued the fighting on the Eastern front in order to permit as many troops as possible to surrender to the British and Americans. Piecemeal surrenders throughout the West followed. On May 4, Admiral von Friedeburg appeared at Montgomery's headquarters at Lüneburg Heath and unconditionally surrendered the German forces in Denmark, northwestern Germany, and the Netherlands. On May 6, Friedeburg and General Jodl went to Eisenhower's headquarters at Rheims where, after playing for time, they signed the general instrument for the unconditional surrender of all German forces on all fronts. Fighting stopped at midnight on May 8. To satisfy the Russians, a second ceremony was held in the early hours of May 9 in Berlin, at which Field-Marshal Keitel signed for Germany, Marshal Zhukov for the Russians, General Spaatz for the United States, General de Lattre de Tassigny for France, and Air Chief Marshal Tedder as Eisenhower's deputy. Two days later, the Red Army entered Prague. Ten of the capital cities of prewar Europe were then in Russian hands.

THE FIRST THREE MONTHS
OF PEACE IN EUROPE:
FROM RHEIMS TO POTSDAM

In the ten weeks between the German surrender and the opening of the last wartime conference of the Big Three at Potsdam on July 17, the façade of Allied unity began to collapse. Throughout Europe—in Germany and Austria, in Poland, and in the Balkans—the Western powers found themselves at odds with the Russians. It was clear that the power of Nazi Germany had been the only force uniting such disparate Allies.

Allied Disputes over Eastern Europe. In the East European countries, the rapid process of communization continued. In Rumania and Bulgaria, the prewar parties were under such constant harassment that the British and American representatives on the Allied Control Commissions in Bucharest and Sofia pressed their governments to raise the issue with the Soviet government, particularly since they found their protests ignored or roughly rejected by their Russian colleagues. Tito had become an open enemy of the West. His troops had been sent to seize Trieste and the whole Istrian Peninsula, even though Anglo-American forces were assigned this task; and for a few weeks in May there was danger of fighting between the two armies in the streets of Trieste. Lacking Soviet support for such action, Tito was forced, on June 9, to agree to withdraw his forces from the city of Trieste, which was to be left under Anglo-American military administration until the Italian peace treaty was drawn up. Meanwhile, at home Tito so restricted the powers of the government members forced on him by the West that they soon resigned in protest. In Czechoslovakia and Hungary, where the Communists held the Ministries of Agriculture, the redistribution of landholdings as a result of the expropriation of the great landowners and of the expulsion of the Germans was being used to create popular support for the Communist party and to create in the Czech Sudetenland, which had been largely German in population, a Communist stronghold. In June, the cession to Russia by Czechoslovakia of Sub-Carpathian Ruthenia, whose population was Ukrainian-speaking, gave Russia a common boundary with Hungary, further emphasizing its permanent involvement with the affairs of Eastern Europe. But as ever the Polish question caused the most heated dispute. In April, the Red Army handed over to Polish administration all German territory to the east of the line of the west Neisse and the Oder rivers, including Danzig. The American government protested that no such action had been authorized at Yalta and demanded that German territory remain under Soviet occupation. The dispute over membership in a reorganized Polish government was finally eased by the admission of Mikolajczyk as a deputy premier in the new cabinet formed on June 23; but the former Warsaw government retained sixteen out of the twenty-one cabinet seats, including the Ministry of the Interior. Nevertheless, the British and American governments accepted the formation of this government with relief and gave it official recognition on July 5.

Foundation of UNO. Settlement of the Polish government question enabled the San Francisco Conference on the United Nations Organization (April 25–June 26, 1945) to conclude its work. For two months, the delegates of forty-six governments, which had declared war on the Axis powers before March 1, 1945, worked to prepare a "charter for a general international organization for the maintenance of international peace and security." Many wrangles exacerbated relations between the delegations, from minor disputes over the chairmanship to major quarrels over the trusteeship for dependent territories and the extent of the veto power of permanent members of the Security Council. The Charter was finally accepted unanimously in ceremonies on June 26, in the San Francisco Opera House; during the next four months it was ratified by the governments of fifty-one nations; and on October 24, the United Nations Organization officially came into being.

Establishment of German and Austrian Occupation Zones. Meanwhile, amid the devastation of Germany and Austria, the Allied powers were grappling with the enormous problems of occupation. At the time of the German capitulation on May 8, Anglo-American forces had reached one hundred and twenty miles into the Russian zone over a four-hundred-mile front and were in possession of such great cities as Leipzig, Erfurt, and Magdeburg. In Austria, however, where the occupation zones had been delimited in March, the Russian armies were in occupation of areas of the proposed British and American zones, and on April 29 had established in Vienna a Provisional Government of Social Democrats and Communists, under the Social Democrat Karl Renner. Whereas it had been agreed in the European Advisory Commission that the central administration of Germany should be carried out by the four commanders-in-chief meeting in an Allied Control Council, and that each of the occupying powers should administer a sector of Berlin, no such arrangements had been made for Austria.

Churchill believed the coming weeks would be of enormous significance to the future of Europe. On May 12, he telegraphed to President Truman his famous warning that the Russians had drawn an "iron curtain" down upon their front and that the West must negotiate a settlement with them before reducing the size of its armies and before withdrawing from the Russian zone of occupation. Truman himself was deeply perturbed at Russian actions in Eastern Europe and at the difficulty of getting an agreement on joint occupation of Vienna.

Nevertheless, he was not willing to risk the loss of Russian good will that would follow from delay in returning to the zones agreed upon by Roosevelt, and he felt that such action would prevent the establishment of the Allied Control Council in Berlin and agreement by the commanders on access routes to Berlin. On July 1, therefore, American and British troops withdrew from the Russian zone, and at the same time the French took over occupation of two triangles of German territory cut from the British and American zones. The Russians responded to this enormously important gesture by agreeing, on July 4, to establishment of a four-power Control Council for Austria and to the division of Vienna into four sectors of occupation.

The Potsdam Conference. When Stalin, Truman, and Churchill (who after his defeat in the British elections was replaced on July 28 by Attlee) met in Potsdam on July 17 for the last, longest, and least useful of the wartime meetings of the Big Three, the occupation machinery in Germany and Austria was already functioning. The policy to be applied by the occupying powers still remained to be formulated, however; and preparations had to be made for concluding a peace settlement for Germany, Austria, Italy, Rumania, Bulgaria, Hungary, and Finland. Disagreements over Russian policy in Eastern Europe required resolution. And final plans had to be concerted for the defeat of Japan.

President Truman and his newly appointed secretary of state, James F. Byrnes, were at once elated at Stalin's acceptance of the formation of a Council of Foreign Ministers of Russia, the United States, Britain, and France. The Council, which was to meet at regular intervals, was assigned the task of preparing the peace treaties with the former enemy states. Allied policy in occupied Germany was laid down in two parts—political and economic principles. There was little difficulty in agreeing to the destruction of all instruments of the Nazi Party's tyranny, to Germany's disarmament and demilitarization, and to "the eventual reconstruction of German political life on a democratic basis," especially through decentralization. Economic principles could only be drawn up, however, when the Allies had decided what reparations should be taken from Germany. For Stalin, one of the main purposes of the conference was to induce his Allies to agree that reparations should be set at $20 billion, of which Russia was to receive half. Both Britain and the United States were adamant against naming a figure at all at Potsdam; and an extraordinary compromise was reached by which "industrial capital equipment unnecessary for the German peace economy" would be made available for reparations. Russia was not only to take such equipment from its own zone but was to be entitled to 10 per cent of that taken from the Western zones free of payment and an additional 15 per cent in return for food and raw materials from the Soviet zone. The Control Council was handed the task of determining what would constitute the desirable level and character of the "German peace economy." Other economic decisions were more easily arrived at. German war potential was to be eliminated; German cartels and trusts were to be broken up; and uniform economic policies for the four zones were to be enforced, using German administrative machinery to the greatest possible extent. It later became clear that the Big Three had made a mistake in not inviting General de Gaulle to participate in the conference, because the French declared that they had no intention of applying in their zone those sections of the Potsdam decisions with which they disagreed. Since they objected to treating Germany as a single economic unit and to "equitable distribution of essential commodities between the different zones," they vetoed the efforts of the Allied Control Council to create interzonal trade unions, political parties, and even a central railroad administration.

Both the British and Americans continued to object to the establishment of the new German-Polish border along the Oder and western Neisse rivers on the grounds that Poland could not absorb so much territory and that a huge flood of German refugees could not be received in the occupation zones. Stalin replied that the Germans had already fled, leaving the land to the Poles, and that in any case it was better to make difficulties for Germans rather than for Poles. The Western powers were forced to accept a face-saving formula by which they agreed that "the final delimitation of the Western frontier of Poland should await a peace settlement" and that in the meantime, the German territories to the east of the Oder and western Neisse rivers should be "under the administration of the Polish state," except for the city of Königsberg and the adjacent area of East Prussia, which would be taken by Russia. Thus, Poland acquired control of 38,660 square miles of German territory which was, however, part of the zone originally assigned to Russia. Had this area not been handed to Poland, the Russian zone of occupation and hence the East German Republic would have almost doubled in size, and would have approached the area of West Germany.

German Refugees. The expected flight of German refugees from the Oder-Neisse territories reminded the statesmen that they were witnessing the reversal of one of the greatest and longest of history's migrations, that of the Germans toward the east. For the past eight hundred years Hanseatic merchants, Teutonic knights, Baltic barons, Prussian *Junkers,* and land-hungry peasants in their millions had migrated across the East European plains to establish themselves from Riga on the Baltic to Klausenburg in Transylvania. In the summer of 1944, between 8 and 9 million Germans lived in East Prussia and the Oder-Neisse territories, 2 million in Poland, 3 million in Czechoslovakia, 470,000 in Rumania, 430,000 in Hungary, and 400,000 in Yugoslavia. As the German armies were forced back, the Poles, Rumanians, Hungarians, Czechs, and Yugoslavs had begun to drive these Germans back to Germany from which their ancestors had come centuries before. For Stalin, these expulsions were no more than justice for the sufferings meted out by the Germans over the centuries; and the British and Americans could only recognize that "the transfer to Germany of German populations, or elements thereof, remaining in Poland, Czechoslovakia and Hungary, will have to be undertaken," and express the pious but unattainable wish that "any transfers that take place should be effected in an orderly and humane manner."

Only one meeting was held between the British, American, and Russian military staffs to discuss coordination of their efforts against Japan; and three almost independent campaigns were agreed upon, with the Russians moving against Manchuria, the Americans against the Japanese home islands, and the British against Malaya and Singapore. On July 16, however, Secretary of War Stimson received a telegram from Alamogordo, New Mexico, stating: "Operated on this morning . . . results seem satisfactory and already exceed expectations." The explosion of the first atomic bomb had been successful, and the weapon would be ready for use against Japan in early August. The British government had already agreed to use of the bomb before the test explosion; and, after informing Stalin of the existence of "a new weapon of unusual destructive force," Churchill and Truman, with Chiang Kai-shek's acquiescence, issued a warning to Japan that "the prodigious land, sea and air forces of the United States, the British Empire, and China . . . are poised to strike the final blows upon Japan" and called upon the Japanese to surrender. Even then, however, the Combined Chiefs of Staff pessimistically envisioned that the Japanese war would last another eighteen months. It was to be over within three weeks.

THE DEFEAT OF JAPAN

American Campaigns in the Pacific. The bulk of the fighting against Japan was undertaken by the United States; but the American government never swerved from its determination that the principal forces of the United States should be used for the defeat of Germany. As a result, the American commanders in the Pacific developed a style of attack that involved heavy use of ships and planes but as little use of manpower as possible. Japan was peculiarly vulnerable to maritime attack, since the highly industrialized home islands and occupied China were dependent for raw materials upon the outlying regions of the Co-Prosperity Sphere. Carrier-borne planes and submarines destroyed almost nine million tons of the Japanese Merchant Marine, and in the few pitched battles like those of the Coral Sea, Midway, and Leyte Gulf, the major part of the Japanese Navy was destroyed or forced to flee into harbor. While the Japanese were doing little to replace their losses, American shipyards made up the losses of Pearl Harbor within a year.

Naval and air superiority alone, however, could not displace the Japanese from their empire, nor bring about the unconditional surrender required after the Casablanca Conference. The taking of Guadalcanal and southern New Guinea at the beginning of 1943 had blocked the Japanese advance toward Australia and Fiji. American strategy was now to break the Japanese inner defense line, which stretched in the south from the Solomon Islands across New Guinea to the Philippines, and in the east along the parallel island chains of the Gilberts and Marshalls and the Carolines and Marianas. General MacArthur and Admiral Halsey launched the southern attack in July, isolated the great fortress of Rabaul, and for the next twelve months "leapfrogged" along the New Guinea coast, taking western New Guinea in September 1944.

Between November 1943 and February 1944, American forces established themselves on the Gilbert and Marshall Islands. After the great naval victory in the Battle of the Philippine Sea in June, the Caroline and Mariana Islands were taken. These terrible battles, fought

THE DEFEAT OF JAPAN, 1943–1945

for possession of small coral atolls, were now seen to be strategically justified; for the capture of the Marianas brought American air bases to within 1,500 miles of the Japanese home islands and thus enabled the new B-29 Superfortresses to begin bombing the heart of Japan as well as the next great fortress on their island-hopping advance, Iwo Jima.

MacArthur mounted the assault of the Philippines on October 20, 1944, two months ahead of schedule, with landings on Leyte in the central Philippines. The successful landings were followed by the greatest sea battle of the Pacific war, Leyte Gulf. Japanese losses in the three-day battle were heavy, and the American fleet won complete command of the seas around the Philippine Islands. Ashore the 250,000 American troops found the going hard against heavily reinforced Japanese under General Yamashita, one of the most experienced of the Japanese commanders. Leyte was not finally captured until the end of December; but almost immediately an invasion of the main Philippine island of Luzon was launched, Manila was taken on February 23, 1945, and in March and April most of the remaining islands were invaded.

Meanwhile, the advance toward Japan itself from the Marianas had continued with the capture of Iwo Jima, a tiny, heavily fortified atoll only 775 miles from Japan. From this island fighter planes could accompany the long-distance bombers. The Japanese put up perhaps the most fanatic resistance of the whole war in a month of fighting (February 23–March 14, 1945), inflicting 27,000 casualties upon the invaders. From the Philippines, at the same time, amphibious landings were made on Okinawa in the Ryukyus, an island the Japanese considered an integral part of the home country. Kamikaze pilots diving planes loaded with over a ton of high explosives sank thirty-three ships, and heavy losses were required before the entrenched Japanese troops could be driven from the southern tip of the island. The American losses were over 1,000 planes and 12,000 men, but the Japanese probably lost more than 3,000 planes and 100,000 men.

By May 1945, Japanese forces had also been defeated in the "forgotten front" of Burma. Throughout 1943, 50,000 British and American guerrilla forces under Brigadier General Orde Wingate and General Frank Merrill had operated behind Japanese lines, cutting railroads and harrying troop movements, in conditions of incredible hardship. In November, after months of slow advance across tortuous mountains, hampered by dense jungles, monsoon rains and tropical disease, British-Indian forces under Lieutenant-General Slim and American troops under General Wingate joined hands. Mandalay, the key to central Burma, fell on March 20, and Rangoon was taken by attack from sea and land on May 3. The British had thus recovered the first of their colonial possessions; and they began to prepare for the subsequent invasion of Malaya.

Alternative Ways to End the Japanese War. That operation was not to be needed, however, for Japan surrendered before it could be launched. Throughout the spring of 1945, the American Air Force had launched daily raids on all parts of Japan. Many influential leaders of the American Air Force felt that Japan could be driven to surrender by air power alone, especially after the night attack on Tokyo on March 9 when incendiary bombs destroyed fifteen square miles of the city's heart.

Nevertheless, plans were drawn up for the invasion of the home islands, where a well-equipped army of a million men was expected to inflict between half a million and a million casualties upon the invading American armies. The initial strike was to be upon the island of Kyushu in November 1945, followed by landings on the industrialized plains around Tokyo in March 1946. The surrender of Japan was not expected until eighteen months after the surrender of Germany, and this calculation assumed that Soviet armies would engage the Japanese forces in Manchuria, whose strength had been greatly overestimated. Two other alternatives remained: to offer peace on terms that the Japanese could accept, including the promise that the Emperor Hirohito, whom the Japanese considered divine, would not be dethroned, or to strike a blow of such overwhelming destruction that the Japanese would feel compelled to give up the struggle. After the explosion of the atomic bomb at Alamogordo, an attempt was made in the Potsdam Declaration of July 26 to combine the last two alternatives. Japan was threatened with "inevitable and complete destruction," but was told that "we do not intend that the Japanese shall be enslaved as a race nor destroyed as a nation." No mention was made of the emperor, nor of the atomic bomb.

The Atomic Bomb. The Japanese government and military did not believe that the Declaration was hinting at the existence of a terrible new weapon. Premier Suzuki declared that he would "kill the Declaration with silence," and most military leaders pressed him to reject it outright. President Truman thereupon ordered the first of the two atomic bombs that were ready to be dropped on Hiroshima, after millions of leaflets had been scattered over twenty-one Japanese cities warning them of coming air bombardment. At 9:15 A.M. on August 6 a single B-29, called the "Enola Gay," loosed the first atomic bomb from a high altitude over Hiroshima. It exploded as planned just before hitting the ground, widening the area of destruction. Over 70,000 people were killed, and thousands more were injured or affected by radiation. Only then did the American government announce that the weapon had been an atomic bomb: "The force from which the sun draws its power has been loosed against those who brought war to the Far East." On August 8, the Soviet Union declared war on Japan and began the invasion of Manchuria. Even at so desperate a moment, the military members of the Japanese Supreme War Direction Council, who personally had little to expect from peace except imprisonment or execution as war criminals, refused the Allied terms; and the explosion of the second atomic bomb over Nagasaki, which killed 36,000 people, did not change their opinions. The emperor himself finally intervened at two o'clock on the morning of August 10; two hours later the Allies were informed that the Japanese would accept the Potsdam Declaration if the prerogatives of the emperor were guaranteed. They replied that "from the moment of surrender the authority of the Emperor and the Japanese government to rule the state shall be subject to the Supreme Commander of the Allied Powers. . . ." On August 14, the Japanese accepted the terms and ordered their armies to cease fire. The first American forces reached Japan on August 28 and were unopposed; General MacArthur, as supreme commander, with representatives of the major Allied powers, accepted the Imperial Proclamation of Unconditional Surrender on board the U.S.S. "Missouri" in Tokyo Bay.

Japanese Surrender. The Allies at once asserted their control over the different regions of the Japanese empire. Japan and the Pacific islands were placed firmly under American control, and efforts by its Allies to gain a share in supervising the occupation were brusquely rejected. MacArthur, in one of his first proclamations, did, however, divide Korea along the 38th parallel into Russian and American zones of occupation. The Russian armies annexed southern Sakhalin and the Kuriles, the territory Stalin had been promised by Roosevelt at Yalta, and proceeded to strip Manchuria of its industrial equipment. Chiang Kai-shek's forces, airlifted by American planes, took control of the main cities of northern China, but found themselves opposed in the countryside by well-entrenched Communist forces; and the civil war began again in full fury. Chinese forces also moved into Indochina to take the surrender of Japanese forces north of the 16th parallel. The British took possession of their colonies as rapidly as possible. The British Pacific Fleet occupied Hong Kong on August 30, to forestall Chiang Kai-shek's avowed intention of restoring it to China. Japanese forces in Malaya and Singapore surrendered to Lord Mountbatten on September 12, while Australian forces took the colonies in Borneo in August. It fell to the British also to move into French Indochina south of the 16th parallel, although they were replaced by French forces from September on, and to accept the surrender of Japanese forces in Indonesia on behalf of the Dutch. The colonial masters returned to find, however, that the wartime advances of nationalism and communism had completely changed their once-docile subjects and that the remaining days of colonialism in Asia would be bloody but few.

Results of War. The Second World War had brought changes whose scope was still unsuspected by the crowds that danced euphorically through the night in Trafalgar Square or the Place de la Concorde in celebration of "Victory-Europe" and "Victory-Japan." Yet the forces that would dominate postwar Europe were already evident. (1) An Iron Curtain had descended across Europe, behind which communization was proceeding with ruthless efficiency. The small states of Eastern Europe, whose economic weakness, political instability, and social conflicts had invited the intervention of their greater neighbors were to see their societies transformed in accordance with the dictates of an authoritarian ideology. (2) To the west of the Iron Curtain, the nation-states were painfully weakened by human and economic losses of enormous proportions. Unable to restore their economic well-being by their own efforts, they would be dependent for aid on a scale hitherto unknown upon the good will of the United States of America. (3) This dependence, moreover, underlined the fact that the world would henceforth be dominated by continent-states, like the Soviet Union and the United States, against whose vast human and economic resources no single European state could pit itself. (4) Since, however, the continent-states were divided by apparently irreconcilable ideological differences, the European states would be compelled to join the camp of one or other of the giants. They would find themselves the most minor of partners in a conflict of titans. (5) Overseas, too, the European states would be too weak to hang on to their colonial possessions, in spite of great sacrifices of men and material. Against the tide of nationalism, combined at times with communism, they were powerless. (6) The lesson for the West European states was already clear to the more farsighted of their leaders. Only by transforming itself into a continent-state by the integration of the individual nation-states could Europe achieve its full economic potential and stand again independent among the great world powers. For Europe, however, the process of self-education in the realities of the postwar world would be long and painful.

Chapter Five　　　　THE OPENING
OF THE COLD WAR,
1945-1953

IN December 1943, in the communiqué issued after the Teheran Conference, Roosevelt, Churchill, and Stalin had optimistically assured the peoples of the world of their "determination that our nations shall work together in war and in the peace that will follow. . . . We are sure that our concord will win an enduring peace." Bitterly disillusioned at the shattering of these promises, the European nations found themselves, in the immediate postwar years, forced to take sides in an ideological struggle between liberal democracy and communism that constantly threatened to erupt into open war. At the same time, however, they were slowly coming to realize that no European nation would again play more than a minor role in the exercise of world power. Economically and politically, the age of European hegemony had been decisively terminated by the Second World War. Even their power to control the millions of ill-fed, ill-educated people in their colonial domain had withered. For Europe the end of the war brought only the chilling realization that the titanic struggle had inflicted upon them greater problems even than those they had hoped to settle when they embarked upon the adventure six years before.

THE DIMINISHED STATUS OF EUROPE

Wartime Destruction in Europe. The destruction inflicted during the Second World War dwarfed that of the First. Twice as many men were mobilized, and almost twice as many—17 million—were killed in battle. Civilian dead numbered at least another eighteen million. Millions were permanently disabled. Population losses were greatest in Russia, which admitted that seven million Russian citizens had died during the war, but probably had lost 15–21 million. Germany had lost over 6 million, France 500,000, Britain 400,000, about the same number as American losses. Although the scourge of bombings, land battles, famine, and disease had not spared women nor children nor the very old, as in the First World War it was again the generations of young men in their twenties and thirties that suffered the greatest losses. Throughout Europe the loss of intellect and labor was to be grievously felt in the years of reconstruction.

The survivors were surrounded by the ruins of a great civilization. Both the economic and the cultural creations of hundreds of years had been laid in shambles. Transportation, the target of untold bombing raids, had been paralyzed. Every bridge over the Rhine had been destroyed and was lying in the river bed, blocking shipping; and the situation was similar on almost every great river of Europe. Only the tiny Ponte Vecchio still crossed the Arno in Florence; temporary military bridges provided the only crossing of the Seine below Paris; retreating Nazi troops had dynamited even local bridges in Germany itself, except where local officials like the mayor of Stuttgart had had the courage to countermand Hitler's orders. The highly developed canal system of Western Europe was virtually unusable. In France, 316 miles out of 5,976 were in operation. In Germany, half the railroad track was out of use; in Greece and Yugoslavia, two thirds. The rolling stock was either damaged or worn out. Telephone and electricity wires were down. Water-supply and sanitation systems were impaired. Industrial plants had suffered enormously. Those that had survived the bombing had received little capital investment during the war years. Machinery was aged and in need of replacement. Raw materials, especially coal, were in very short supply. Industrial production in such widely separated countries as France, Poland, and Greece had slumped to one-fifth of the prewar figure. Agriculture was equally affected. Herds had been slaughtered to supply war needs; fertilizer and pesticide production had been slight; seeds were lacking; the forests of the occupied countries had been heavily felled for German needs. Following a scorched-earth policy both the Russians and the Germans had laid waste large sections of the Ukraine and the Crimea. A bad drought in 1945 helped lower the European grain harvest to half that of 1939. At the end of the war it was estimated that 100 million Europeans were near starvation.

The bombing of Germany, like the V-1 and V-2 attacks on England, had been directed at the civilian population as well as at military and industrial targets, while destruction of homes had also been heavy in the expansion and contraction of the German empire. Excluding Germany and Russia, 2 million homes in Europe were completely destroyed and another 3 million damaged. In Germany over 2 million houses were destroyed and 4 million damaged; and it was estimated that in the cities of over 100,000 population, 89 per cent of the buildings were wholly or partly destroyed. In Russia, 25 million people were homeless. What had disappeared was the irreplaceable heritage of at least a thousand years of European civilization. The more fortunate cities mourned isolated monuments—London had lost among much else its Guildhall and many of the Wren city churches that rose after the Great Fire of 1666; the cathedral of Rouen was damaged but reparable; Amsterdam had lost a few old homes. But many of Europe's most beautiful cities were no more than ruins—the Rotterdam of Erasmus, including the philosopher's birthplace, disappeared in the German air attack of May 14, 1940; the great Baroque city of Dresden went up in flames to American fire bombs; Warsaw, Budapest, and Belgrade, fortified as final barriers to invasion of Germany itself, were in rubble when the Red Army took them. Perhaps most tragic of all was the destruction of superb old towns of little military value by the American Air Force in the closing two months of the war when valid military targets were difficult to find. In April 1945, the lovely episcopal city of Würzburg lost its Romanesque cathedral and most of its Baroque and Rococo streets and palaces, in a raid lasting twenty minutes.

Other effects of the war were less visible but equally significant. To pay for the war Europe had drawn upon the accumulated capital reserves of several generations and had accepted internal and foreign debt of tremendous proportions. Britain was perhaps the most outstanding example of this attrition. Five billion dollars worth of its investments overseas, particularly in North and South America, had been sold; its national debt had risen to $100 billion; foreign debt totaled $12 billion. In all, Britain had lost one quarter of its prewar wealth, approximately the same as Russia.

Population Displacements. To disrupt the process of recovery even further, Europe was enduring the greatest displacements of population in all its history. At war's end, 11 million prisoners of war, forced laborers, and deportees required repatriation to their home countries from all parts of Hitler's Europe; but, through the work of the Allied occupying forces and of the United Nations Relief and Rehabilitation Administration, most were sent home within three months. There was still, however, a tragic residue of 650,000 displaced persons, over half of whom were Poles, who refused to be repatriated for fear of the treatment they would receive on returning. For them, a program of resettlement had to be devised. The most significant population displacement involved the permanent resettlement of 15 million Germans and East Europeans. Hitler had already moved out most Germans living in the Polish territories and the Baltic states ceded to Russia at the Secret Additional Protocol of August 1939. In 1944–45, between 3 and 4 million Poles were driven from this area by the Russians to be resettled in the Oder-Neisse territories that Poland would acquire from Germany. From these territories and from the Russian section of East Prussia, over 6 million Germans were driven west of the Oder-Neisse line. The Potsdam Conference had sanctioned the expulsion of the German populations of Czechoslovakia, Hungary, and Yugoslavia; and over 3 million Germans were driven from these countries. After a more or less brief stay in the Russian zone, however, many continued west. By 1961, the West German government estimated that 13 million of its citizens were refugees or children of refugees. In a sense, this population movement solved many of the national minority problems that had plagued the peacemakers at Paris in 1919. In Poland, non-Polish elements composed 4 per cent of the population compared with 25 per cent before the war. Czechoslovakia no longer had the irritation of Sudeten German nationalism. The inclusion of all Ukrainians inside Soviet Russia ended the possibility of nationalistic agitation from outside its borders. But the human suffering in the move was incalculable, while a new irredentism, that of the *Heimatvertriebene,* those driven from their homeland, exacerbated the German problem and made any understanding between the West and Russia appear to sanction the loss of the Oder-Neisse territories. Finally, mention should be made of the Jewish refugees, mostly the survivors of the Nazi death camps, who feared to remain in Germany, Austria, and Poland. About one million Jews, excluding those in Russia, had survived the Nazi scourge, but of these only 20,000 were German and 80,000 Polish. The majority of the Central European Jews sought refuge in the three Western zones of Germany preparatory to moving whenever possible to Palestine. The British, who held the mandate in Palestine, at first halted immigration almost completely but agreed in 1946 to allow the resettlement of 100,000 Jews at a rate of 2,000 a month. In spite of the efforts of

Haganah, the Jewish underground organization, to smuggle in illegal immigrants, only about 60,000 European Jews managed to settle in Palestine between 1945 and 1948. In the first eighteen months after Israel gained its independence, however, another 20,000 followed. By 1951, the mass migration of Central European Jews was virtually complete. Israel had accepted 400,000 European Jews, and other countries 165,000. Thus, in the generation following Hitler's seizure of power Europe lost, by extermination or migration, over 7 million Jews.

Age of the Continent-State. What most emphasized the diminished significance of Europe was, however, the appearance on the world scene of two great continent-states, Soviet Russia and the United States. The population of each was almost three times that of the largest European state. Each could with ease put armies of 5 million men in the field. Each possessed virtually unlimited resources within its own frontiers of basic raw materials—coal, iron ore, oil, natural gas, copper, lead, zinc, manganese, potash, and sulphur. The United States, with only 10 per cent of its population on the land, produced huge agricultural surpluses. Russia, except for occasional times of shortage, was agriculturally self-sufficient. In products of industrial importance, like timber, cotton, and flax, both had ample resources. In both countries, the technological revolution was well advanced; and both were far ahead of European countries in the numbers of scientists and engineers being trained in their colleges. Perhaps most important of all, both countries were unified states. In Russia, with 16 per cent of the world's land surface and in the United States with 5.8 per cent, the movement of goods, labor, and investment capital was unhindered by internal barriers. In the age of continent-states, Europe was still divided into twenty-nine political units whose boundaries cut across natural economic units like coal fields, river valleys, and even cities. In 1945, however, European unification was still regarded by most European leaders as a radical and impractical chimera of a few idealists in the resistance movements. Each European country attempted to rebuild its strength with little reference to its neighbors. It took two years before the European powers realized the full extent of their decline. By then they were in the midst of an ideological battle between the United States and Soviet Russia, in which their weakness compelled them to line up under the banner of either liberal democracy or communism.

THE END OF THE GRAND ALLIANCE, 1945–47

Stalin's Postwar Goals. Even those European statesmen who had been aware of the quarrels among the Big Three were astounded at the suddenness with which, in 1945, Soviet leaders declared to the Russian people that the next enemy after fascism was capitalism. "Our country remains the one socialist state in the world," Mikhail Kalinin, the titular head of state, reminded a group of party workers. "Only the most concrete, most immediate danger which threatened us from Hitler's Germany, has disappeared." The continuing sacrifices that reconstruction would demand were to be justified in part by depicting the Western powers, especially the United States and Britain, as predators determined to destroy the Russian state. But, far more important, Stalin now revived the doctrine of world Communist revolution that he had denied during the generation in which he preached "socialism in one country." The expansion of communism beyond Russia imposed several goals. First, Russia itself must continue its enormous industrial growth, in order to be the base of the world Communist movement. The achievement of the 1920's and 1930's had been proven in the defeat of Nazi Germany. The task now, in Molotov's words, was "to overtake and surpass economically the most developed capitalist countries of Europe and the United States of America." Second, the East European countries in the Russian orbit must be communized, and their economies integrated into the Russian system. According to Stalin's biographer Isaac Deutscher, Stalin "now replaced his socialism in one country by something that might be termed 'socialism in one zone.' " On the edges of the Russian orbit, in such countries as Greece, Turkey, and Iran, a probe would be made to find "soft spots" where Russian hegemony could be exercised. Third, among the vast populations of the underdeveloped continents of Asia and Africa, local Communist movements would be supported with material and financial aid in their efforts to overthrow non-Communist rulers, and nationalist movements, especially where Communist-influenced, would be helped in their effort to expel their colonial rulers. Finally, in the capitalist countries, especially France and Italy, the Communist parties were to strengthen their hold on the proletariat, but were not to attempt to seize power by direct assault. Rather they were to increase the popularity derived from their share in

the resistance movements by loyal collaboration in the work of reconstruction, and even participation in non-Communist governments. This
policy, Stalin admitted later, was forced on him: "The reason why there
is now no Communist government in Paris is because in the circumstances of 1945 the Soviet Army was not able to reach French soil."
Until 1947, the Soviet government accepted the possibility of a "competitive coexistence" with the West; but Stalin made no secret of his aim
to replace "capitalist encirclement" of the Communist camp with "socialist encirclement" of the capitalist states.

American Desire for Normalcy. The American government and
people found great difficulty in adjusting to this pressure from the Soviet
Union. Roosevelt had been in constant friction with Churchill over what
he believed to be the British desire to split the world into spheres of
influence, not only because he saw that as a cause of future war, but
because such a division would demand continuing American commitment of military and economic resources to the support of its own
sphere. Roosevelt was certain that the American people would not
accept such a responsibility; and he convinced the Russian government
that American troops would remain at most two years in Europe after
the war, that Western Europe would have great difficulty in winning
American economic aid, that America would give its blessing to the
liberation of the colonial possessions of its European allies, and that
American responsibility for world affairs would be largely turned over to
the United Nations Organization. Truman at first seemed to continue
this basic policy. Responding to the American desire for "normalcy," he
hurried the demobilization of the vast American armies in Europe,
which fell from 3.5 million in 1945 to 400,000 in 1946. Wartime
controls over the economy were rapidly removed. Lend-Lease was
canceled on the day of Japan's surrender. All the obligations toward
Russia contracted during the war were scrupulously observed. American
troops withdrew from the Soviet zone of occupation on July 1; factories
in the American zone of occupation were dismantled and shipped to
Russia; the terms of the Far Eastern agreement between Roosevelt and
Stalin at Yalta were implemented; and a serious attempt was made to
cooperate in the Control Councils in Germany and Austria. Even in
Eastern Europe, the American government accepted face-saving com-
promises that enabled it to sanction Russia's position of predominance.
On receiving guarantees that free elections would be held, it recognized

the provisional governments of Austria and Hungary in October and November 1945; and, when in December the Russians offered to create a three-power Commission for Rumania and to broaden the Bulgarian government, the United States government promised that recognition would be forthcoming. Even the Russian demand for a share in supervising the occupation of Japan was met by creation of a Far Eastern Commission of eleven nations with interests in the Pacific area by an Allied Council for Japan, although these bodies had little effect in controlling Commander-in-Chief Douglas MacArthur.

The Satellite Peace Treaties. The main aim of James F. Byrnes, Truman's secretary of state from June 1945 to January 1947, was to complete the peace settlement with Germany and its allies. He was unable to make any progress toward drawing up treaties for Germany and Austria, but he did succeed in negotiating the settlement for the Axis satellites—Finland, Italy, Rumania, Bulgaria, and Hungary. It had been decided at Potsdam that the foreign ministers of Russia, the United States, Britain, China, and France would meet in London to formulate the peace settlements and for regular discussion of other matters of common interest. The first meeting of the Council of Foreign Ministers, from September 11 to October 2, 1945, ended in deadlock, and an informal bargaining session in Moscow in December was necessary before compromise was reached on the procedure for calling a peace conference. The second meeting of the Council of Foreign Ministers, in Paris from April 25 to May 15 and from June 15 to July 12, succeeded in drafting the main sections of the five treaties, although there was considerable argument over Russia's demands for trusteeship of an Italian colony in the Mediterranean and over Yugoslavia's demands on Trieste. Twenty-one nations attended a peace conference in Paris from July 29 to October 15, 1946, and many amendments, mostly on minor matters, were incorporated in the treaties. After a final month of heated argument at the third meeting of the Council of Foreign Ministers in New York from November 4 to December 11, 1946, the treaties were finally accepted, and came into force on February 10, 1947.

The treaty with Italy was most satisfactory to the United States and Britain. Italy was to pay the relatively small sum of $360 million in reparations, of which Russia was to receive $100 million. Only minor changes were made in its European frontiers. France took four small strips of Alpine territory. Yugoslavia received most of the peninsula of

Venezia Giulia, but the port of Trieste, whose population was largely Italian, was made into a Free Territory guaranteed by the Security Council. (In 1954, Trieste itself was handed to Italy, and Yugoslavia gained the hinterland.) The South Tirol, which had been annexed by Italy in 1919, was left in Italian hands, thus perpetuating an irredentist problem when extreme groups among the 260,000 Austrians of that region began to use terrorism to assert their claim to autonomy. Italy's colonies were left under British military rule for a year. Libya became an independent kingdom in 1951, and Eritrea became an autonomous province of Ethiopia in 1951. Somaliland, which was returned to Italian trusteeship in 1950, became independent in 1960. The treaty with Finland recognized Russian annexation of the Arctic port of Petsamo and of a continuous strip of territory from the Arctic to the Gulf of Finland, including most of Karelia. Russia also received a long-term lease on a naval base at Porkkala, on the Gulf of Finland, which it gave up in 1955. All Finnish reparations—$300 million—went to Russia. Rumania recognized Russian annexation of Bessarabia and the northern Bukovina and Bulgaria's annexation of the southern Dobrudja, but it regained northern Transylvania from Hungary. Like Finland, it was to pay $300 million in reparations to Russia. Bulgaria came off more lightly, paying only $70 million in reparations to Russia. Hungary gave up Bratislava to Czechoslovakia and paid $200 million in reparations to Russia. Russia thus gained considerably from the treaties. It received $900 million worth of reparations; signature of the treaties brought an end to the Allied Control Commissions in Rumania, Bulgaria, Hungary, and Finland; Allied troops were to be withdrawn from Italy, but Soviet troops could continue to pass through Rumania and Hungary en route to the Soviet zone of Austria and across Poland en route to Germany.

Shortly after the conclusion of the peace treaties, Byrnes was pressured into resigning as secretary of state. He was replaced by General George C. Marshall, an open exponent of the doctrine of "containment" of Soviet expansionism. But Byrnes's policy of "patience with firmness" had already been eroded months before his resignation. Throughout 1946, American suspicions of Soviet intentions grew. Soviet attempts to create an autonomous, Communist-dominated state in Azerbaijan, the northern province of Iran, were criticized by the American representatives at the first meeting of the United Nations Organization; and the American government was agreeably surprised when Soviet troops were withdrawn from Iran on May 6, 1946. The United States government backed Turkey in its refusal to give Russia a share in garrisoning the Dardanelles or to return the provinces of Kars and Ardahan it had acquired in 1918. In Germany, the American military government lost patience with Russian refusal to supply surplus food from its zone to the more industrialized Western zones or to make accounting for dismantling in its zone; in May 1946, in the first deliberate break with the Potsdam Agreement, the deputy commander-in-chief, General Clay, announced that no further shipments of surplus industrial equipment would be made to the Russians.

Churchill's "Iron Curtain" Speech. Public debate in the United States over Soviet policy was precipitated by Winston Churchill's famous speech at Fulton, Missouri, on March 5, 1946, in which he called for the continuance of military cooperation between the United States and the British Commonwealth, because "there is nothing [the Russians] admire so much as strength, and there is nothing for which they have less respect than for weakness, especially military weakness." Firmness was necessary, Churchill warned, since "from Stettin in the Baltic to Trieste in the Adriatic an iron curtain has descended across the Continent. . . . The Communist parties, which were very small in all these eastern states of Europe, have been raised to pre-eminence and power far beyond their numbers and are seeking everywhere to obtain totalitarian control. . . . This is certainly not the liberated Europe we fought to build up." Many American liberals took issue with Churchill; and the secretary of commerce, Henry Wallace, declared that, since Russia was going to socialize Eastern Europe whatever the United States did, toughness toward Russia would simply let "British balance-of-power manipulations determine whether and when the United States gets into war." Truman, however, had personally decided that neither the appeasement proposed by Wallace nor the piecemeal obstruction of Byrnes were sufficient to meet the Soviet challenge. With the appointment of General Marshall as secretary of state in January 1947, he openly accepted the doctrine being advocated by George F. Kennan, head of the Planning Division of the State Department, "long-term, patient, but firm and vigilant containment."

European Suspicions of American Policy. This evolution in American policy was not wholly pleasing to the states of Western Europe. Although few had been sanguine enough to expect the persistence of the supposedly warm collaboration of the wartime alliance, most were prepared to accept a spheres-of-interest agreement that would leave the Soviet Union a free hand in Eastern Europe and thus satisfy the understandable Russian desire for security. Fear of Germany was so strong that no objection was raised to the extension of Poland's borders to the Oder-Neisse line, and the idea of transforming Western Germany into an ally against Russia was violently rejected. In France and Italy, the Communist parties, supported by a quarter of the electorate, were collaborating in the work of reconstruction and did not seem to cherish immediate ambitions of seizing power. Throughout Europe, the democratic Socialist parties were strong and were in power in Britain and the Scandinavian countries. The Socialists believed that they would be able to work with Russia more easily than the conservative parties in their countries and that any division of Europe between a capitalist and a Communist camp could only strengthen the forces of reaction at home. Moreover, in the immediate postwar period Europe was indulging in a bout of anti-Americanism that was increased rather than diminished by awareness of American contribution to the common victory. Europeans were envious of American prosperity and resentful of American power, particularly as Americans were felt to be too inexperienced to be trusted with world leadership. The most outspoken critic of America's predominance was the French premier, Charles de Gaulle, who raged at the Big Three's cavalier disposal of the future of the continental European states without even a pretense of consultation. In October 1945 he suggested that Europe's alternative to alignment with America in a conflict with Russia was its own unification: "To persuade the states bordering on the Rhine, the Alps, and the Pyrenees to join together on the political, economic and strategic planes. To make this organization one of the three planetary powers, and, should it one day be necessary, the arbiter between the Soviet and Anglo-Saxon camps." Other European nations also resented American interference. The Dutch and the Portuguese objected to American criticism of their colonial policy, and the British were infuriated at American objections to their attempts to keep Jewish refugees out of Palestine. Western Europe had to be convinced that Soviet Russia had become a danger to its own security and that American leadership was reliable before it would agree to unite in an economic and military grouping with the United States.

The British Loan. Ironically enough, it was the Labour government of

Britain that was to thrust the United States into a position of leadership and that was then to gather the states of Europe together in the American camp. The defeat of the Conservatives in July 1945 removed Churchill in the middle of the Potsdam Conference at the very moment, he noted later, when he was preparing for a showdown and even a "public break" with Stalin over the Polish frontier question. Ernest Bevin, the Socialist foreign secretary from July 1945 to March 1951, at first shared the American hope of making the Grand Alliance endure into the peace. He had declared before the election that "Left would be able to speak with Left"; and he went to Moscow to offer Stalin an extension of the Anglo-Soviet alliance of 1942 from twenty to fifty years. But Stalin was unreceptive; and Bevin was soon opposing Russian ambitions in Azerbaijan, Turkey, and Germany with a bluntness that won him censure from the left wing of his own party. Throughout 1945 and 1946, Britain became the principal opponent of Russia and the main target of its propaganda. Britain, however, was on the point of economic collapse at the end of the war; and a delegation under Lord Keynes was dispatched to Washington in September–December 1945 to ask the American government to shore up the British economy with a vast loan that would be, the British hoped, little different from a direct gift. The decision to grant Britain a loan of $3.75 billion at low interest rate was contested in Congress for seven months on the grounds that the United States could not afford to make such vast loans in peacetime and that the loan was committing the United States to support Britain in its opposition to Russia. By July 1946, when the House of Representatives ratified the loan, American opinion toward Russia had hardened so greatly that passage was assured by presenting the bill as a means of strengthening Britain in the struggle with communism. In the same month, the British agreed to unite their zone of occupation in Germany with the American zone; as a result, the United States found itself sharing the financial responsibility for the reconstruction of the Ruhr. Finally, in February 1947, British economic weakness compelled it to give up its support of Greece, which had cost $528 million in three years, and of Turkey, which had cost $360 million in nine years. The decision was dramatically presented to President Truman on February 27, with the warning that British aid would stop abruptly in five weeks time. This decision compelled Truman to act immediately, or allow Greece and Turkey to fall behind the Iron Curtain.

THE TRUMAN DOCTRINE
AND THE MARSHALL PLAN

Between 1947 and 1949 the United States moved decisively to counter Russian influence in Europe. The Truman Doctrine of March 12, 1947 laid down the principle that the United States would "support free peoples who are resisting attempted subjugation by armed minorities or by outside pressure." The Marshall Plan proposed on June 5, 1947 restored the economic prosperity of Western Europe. The North Atlantic Treaty of April 4, 1949 linked the United States and Canada in a powerful defensive alliance with the countries of Western Europe.

Precarious Situation of Greece and Turkey. The British note of February 27 gave President Truman the opportunity for which he had been waiting for a year to state in dramatic form the determination of the United States to call a halt to Communist expansion. In Greece, the two years since the Varkiza Agreement of February 1945 had seen a revival of Communist strength. The central government in Athens had been unable to deal with the country's terrible economic problems, like unemployment and inflation, or with growing terrorism of both right-wing and left-wing groups. The Communist party harassed the government and its numerous British advisory missions with a series of strikes throughout the country, and the Communist complaint against the presence of British troops was carried to the United Nations by Soviet Russia. To meet these complaints, the Greek government called upon Allied countries to send observers to the elections of March 31, 1946. The Russians refused, but British, American, and French teams of an Allied Mission to Observe the Greek Elections declared that the results, which gave a majority to the Populist party of former Premier Papandreou, were reasonably fair. The Communists had refused to participate, however, and made great play of the fact that only 49 per cent of the electorate voted. The new premier, Constantine Tsaldaris, at once organized a plebiscite on whether the monarchy should be restored. As a result of a campaign in which a vote against the monarchy was represented as a vote for the Communist party, on September 1, 1946, 69 per cent of the voters called for the return of King George II. Growing guerrilla activity in northern Greece undoubtedly influenced the result. Aided with weapons and advisers by Yugoslavia, Albania, and Bulgaria, the Communist forces had begun a full-scale war in the hope of gaining complete control of a section of northern Greece where they could establish a rival government. The Greeks appealed to the United Nations on December 3, 1946, against this interference in their internal affairs by their neighbors; and a United Nations Committee of Investigation, which reported eighteen months later, upheld the Greek charges. The British decision to withdraw from Greece left the American government with the alternatives of taking over Britain's responsibilities or of permitting a Communist victory.

Soviet determination to gain access to the eastern Mediterranean had already been seen in its demand for the Dodecanese Islands and Tripolitania, and in its request to Turkey that it be permitted to share in the garrisoning of the Dardanelles. To meet Soviet pressure, Turkey had mobilized an army of 650,000 men, the financial burden of which was crippling the country's already weak economy, and increasing the social discontent of the underprivileged masses of the country. This opportunity for Communist influence was increased by the corruption and inefficiency of President Inönü's People's party, which had monopolized power since the revolution of Kemal Ataturk in 1920. Although a new Democratic party had been permitted to contest the elections of 1946, it received only a few seats, and its leaders declared that the election results had been falsified. Thus, as in Greece, American aid to Turkey might well be construed as support for a repressive and anachronistic privileged class whose principal merit was to block Russia's outlet from the Black Sea.

The Truman Doctrine. President Truman attempted to meet these criticisms by describing the great economic weakness of Greece and Turkey, whose social problems could be met only by rapid modernization with the aid of American capital and advisers. "The seeds of totalitarian regimes are nurtured by misery and want," he declared. "They spread and grow in the evil soil of poverty and strife. They reach their full growth when the hope of a people for a better life has died. We must keep that hope alive." But the crux of his message was that the United States would "help free peoples to maintain their institutions and their national integrity against aggressive movements that seek to impose upon them totalitarian regimes," as was occurring, he said, in Poland, Rumania, and Bulgaria. Congress would be asked to appropriate $400 million in economic aid and military supplies up to June 30, 1948 and to authorize the sending of civilian and military missions. This doctrine, which implied the duty and self-interest of the United States in interfering anywhere in the world to prevent the spread of communism, was at once fiercely attacked in the United States; but the aid bill passed both the Senate and House of Representatives by large margins and was signed into law on May 22, 1947.

American aid brought a rapid improvement in the Greek government's military effort against the guerrillas. With better weapons, training, and morale, the Greek Army embarked on a series of offensives to clear areas in which the rebels were strong and was occasionally able to bring large Communist forces to battle in conditions favorable to the regular forces. The government position was strengthened by a wise policy of amnesties, by the appointment of the Second World War hero, General Papagos, as commander of the army, and by the determined leadership of King Paul, who succeeded his brother George II on April 12, 1947. By the end of 1949, the Communists had been decisively defeated. By then, Greece had received $648 million under the Truman program, of which $529 million had been spent on military expenses. Turkey used the $100 million it received for the support of its army and thus was able to free other funds for much-needed internal expenditures. The American military mission in Turkey increased rapidly in size, to number over 14,000, and military aid over the next thirteen years amounted to $2 billion.

Council of Foreign Ministers, Moscow, 1947. Truman's speech, coming two days after the opening of the fourth session of the Council of Foreign Ministers in Moscow (March 10–April 24, 1947), undoubtedly weakened chances for agreement on a German peace settlement. Russian suspicions of American intentions in Europe redoubled, and Russia's determination to maintain its hold on eastern Germany while gaining a leverage in western Germany was strengthened. Complete deadlock was reached in the Moscow negotiations. The British and Americans refused to accept Molotov's demand that Russia receive $10 billion worth of reparations or that reparations be taken from current German production. They dropped their proposal for the internationalization of the Ruhr when Molotov demanded that Russia have an equal share in the Ruhr's supervision, refused to recognize the Oder-Neisse line as anything more than a provisional administrative boundary until final agreement at a peace settlement, and demanded a decentralization of German government rather than the unitary state

proposed by the Russians. The only agreement reached was the abolition of the state of Prussia. Although Stalin and Bevin both declared
that the conference had progressed by bringing disagreements into the
open, Marshall was less patient. The deteriorating economic situation in
Germany and, indeed, in all the other countries of Europe, seemed to
him to require immediate action; and he was not prepared to wait for
agreement with the Russians before making his next move.

The Offer of Marshall Aid. On returning from Moscow, Marshall
began to emphasize in his speeches the significance for the United States
of the economic plight of Europe, which not only opened the way for
communism but was preventing Europeans from buying what they
needed from American industry and agriculture. Even $5 billion in
loans and grants was proving ineffective in restoring Europe's capacity
to produce and thus its ability to pay its own way. At the Harvard
Commencement on June 5, 1947, Marshall offered Europe aid on a
scale never before considered possible. The extent of destruction in
Europe had been correctly estimated, he pointed out, but "it has become
obvious during recent months that this visible destruction was probably
less serious than the dislocation of the entire fabric of the European
economy. . . . The truth of the matter is that Europe's requirements
for the next three or four years of foreign food and other essential
products—principally from America—are so much greater than her
present ability to pay that she must have substantial additional help or
face economic, social, and political deterioration of a very grave
character. . . . Any assistance that this Government may render in the
future should be a cure rather than a mere palliative. Any government
that is willing to assist in the task of recovery will find full co-operation,
I am sure, on the part of the United States Government. . . . The role
of this country should consist of friendly aid in the drafting of a
European program and of later support of such a program so far as it
may be practical for us to do so. The program should be a joint one,
agreed to by a number of, if not all, European nations."

European Reaction to Marshall's Offer. To British Foreign Secretary
Bevin, the Marshall speech was like a "lifeline to sinking men." It was,
he told the House of Commons, "one of the greatest speeches in world
history"; and, since Marshall explicitly included Russia and the countries
of Eastern Europe in his offer, it might "throw a bridge to link east and
west." French Foreign Minister Bidault was equally enthusiastic; on

June 19, he and Bevin invited the Soviet government to send Foreign Minister Molotov to discuss the Marshall speech. The inclusion of Russia in Marshall's offer undoubtedly reassured many Europeans who feared that acceptance of American economic aid implied alignment in an anti-Soviet bloc, yet it was doubtful whether the American Congress would have sanctioned aiding the economies of Communist nations. The Soviet government, however, was not willing to tolerate coordination of its economic planning with that of the capitalist countries of Europe, to provide detailed information on its economy, or to allow American supervision of its use of the aid funds. Molotov came to Paris with a large group of technical experts, but after a week of discussions (June 27–July 2, 1947) he denounced the plan for unwarrantable interference in the affairs of sovereign nations. Bevin and Bidault thereupon invited every country of Europe, except Russia and Spain (whose government was still considered beyond the pale), to a conference in Paris on July 12. The discipline exercised by Russia over its satellites was re-emphasized when Poland, Czechoslovakia, Hungary, Rumania, Bulgaria, Yugoslavia, and Albania turned down the invitation. Nor did neutral Finland risk Russian displeasure by attending. The conference assigned a Committee of European Economic Co-operation the task of reporting on what aid Europe would need during the coming four years to achieve its productive potential. This committee worked with extraordinary speed and on September 22 presented the American government with an outline recovery program and a request for American aid, particularly in food and raw materials, valued at $19 billion. The purpose of American aid was to provide Europe with the necessities of life, making it possible for Europe to devote its major effort to the work of reconstruction.

The Marshall Plan. Meanwhile, deep study was being made in the United States of the implications of such a program of foreign aid. A committee under Secretary of the Interior Julius A. Krug reported that the American economy could easily carry the burden of even so expensive a program as Marshall Aid. The Committee on Foreign Aid, under Secretary of Commerce W. Averell Harriman, warned that if the European countries "by democratic means do not attain an improvement in their affairs, they may be driven to turn in the opposite direction. . . . [Communism] wins by default when misery and chaos are great enough." Europe's requirements in American aid, the committee estimated, would be between $12 and $17 billion over the four-year period. So vast were these sums that the Marshall Plan came under criticism from both the right and the left within the United States. Republican critics, led by Senator Taft, thought it would lead to inflation and socialization of the American economy. Progressive critics, led by Henry Wallace, argued that the plan would precipitate the division of Europe, making a new war inevitable. The terribly severe winter of 1946–47 in Europe, following a summer of drought, provided the greatest proof of the urgency of the plan, however, and Truman went before Congress in November 1947 to ask for interim aid of $597 million to stave off economic collapse in France, Italy, and Austria. Debate continued in Congress for four months, but finally on April 2, 1948, Congress appropriated $6.8 billion for the first fifteen months of the plan and agreed to make three annual grants later.

The plan, known as the European Recovery Program, was to be administered from the American side by the Economic Cooperation Administration under Paul G. Hoffman, while the sixteen European countries participating created the Organisation for European Economic Co-operation with permanent headquarters in Paris. The division of the aid among the European countries was made by OEEC, which presented its comprehensive request for aid to the ECA. Most of the aid was given in the form of direct grants, but the firms receiving American goods were required to pay for them in their own national currency. This currency was placed in a "counterpart fund," which with American consent, could be used by the national government to bolster up the home economy. French counterpart funds, for example, were used for capital investment in the country's major industries laid down in the Monnet Plan. In all, during the four years of the Marshall Plan's operation, the European countries received $13.15 billion. Britain received the largest share of the aid, $3.176 billion; France received $2.706 billion; Italy $1.474 billion. At the opposite end of the scale were Portugal, with $50 million, the Free Territory of Trieste with $32 million, and Iceland with $29 million.

The results of the plan were generally good. Industrial production rose to 35 per cent and agricultural production to 10 per cent above the prewar level. The gross national product in real value increased by 25 per cent during the four years of the plan, putting it at 15 per cent above prewar. Trade among the OEEC countries increased 70 per cent. In most countries inflation was checked, confidence in the currency restored, and unemployment was greatly reduced. Certain individual industries, such as steel and chemicals, showed enormous gains in productivity because they were singled out for large-scale investment and for technological improvement. The political results were also notable. The American government and Congress, and indeed the American people, became accustomed to the responsibility of sharing American wealth with the rest of the world and were encouraged to do so by the success of this first major venture in foreign aid. Large numbers of Americans, whether Marshall Plan administrators, businessmen, or even Congressmen, became personally acquainted with their European counterparts, and developed a feeling of kinship with Europeans that was to provide a firm foundation for the development of the ideal of an Atlantic Community. Europeans, for their part, found that acceptance of American aid did not imply subservience to American leadership in their own affairs. They also grew accustomed to working together in the day-to-day administration of economic affairs and to coordinating national policies for the common good. But OEEC did not bring about the economic integration of Europe, as Marshall and Hoffman had hoped. Tariffs were barely reduced. No provision was made for the free movement of capital or labor across national boundaries, nor for the harmonization of investment policy to avoid duplication and harmful competition. Within OEEC, a division became apparent between those countries that were satisfied that the Marshall Plan had not endangered their national economic autonomy and those that were disappointed at the failure of OEEC to further European economic integration. Belgium, the Netherlands, and Luxembourg had already shown their willingness to integrate by forming the customs union of Benelux in January 1948. France and Italy had unsuccessfully attempted to form a similar union in March 1949. It was from the disappointed administrators of the Marshall Plan that the firmest proponents of European economic integration were to come—Paul-Henri Spaak, Robert Marjolin, Jean Monnet, Franz Blücher, and Attilio Cattani. For them, OEEC was no more than a beginning.

THE CAMPS FORMED:
FROM THE COMINFORM TO NATO

Foundation of the Cominform. The world had been divided into two camps by the Marshall Plan, Stalin's heir-apparent A.A. Zhdanov told the representatives of the European Communist parties meeting in Poland on September 22–23, 1947. The United States had taken the lead of the "imperialist" and "capitalist" countries, and it was the duty of the "democratic" countries to unite in their own defense. The nine Communist parties represented at the Conference (Soviet Russia, Yugoslavia, Poland, Czechoslovakia, Hungary, Rumania, Bulgaria, France, and Italy) thereupon agreed to form a Communist Information Bureau, or Cominform, which would coordinate the policies of Communist parties throughout the world, and from its headquarters in Belgrade issue an information and newsletter. The real purpose of the foundation of the Cominform was soon apparent. From September to December 1947, the French and Italian Communists launched a vast series of strikes that were openly described as protests against the Marshall Plan. Swift governmental action, coupled with the economic distress of the harsh winter, forced the strikers back to work, however, and the willingness of the Communist leaders to inflict misery on the working classes for political ends disillusioned many of their followers.

Conflict over Germany. At the London meeting of the Council of Foreign Ministers (November 25–December 15, 1947), Soviet Foreign Minister Molotov bitterly attacked the Western powers for imperialism and bad faith. Once again, no progress was made toward a German or Austrian peace settlement, as no agreement could be reached over Russian demands for $10 billion in reparations, over the frontiers with Poland, or over the creation of a central German government. The three Western powers took this conference to imply definitive failure to reach agreement with the Russians on the German question, and they at once began the process that was to culminate in the unification of their zones of occupation into an independent West German state. Between February and June 1948, British, French, and American delegations met in London with representatives of Belgium, the Netherlands, and Luxembourg, to determine the future of the three Western zones of Germany. On June 7, the conference announced that it had decided that the Germans of the three Western zones should be permitted to create a democratic, federal government for West Germany, and to empower a constituent assembly to write a constitution. The occupying powers would retain mainly the right of supervision, through a three-member Allied High Commission, although German disarmament would be ensured by a Military Security Board and distribution of Ruhr coal by an International Authority for the Ruhr. West Germany would be eligible for Marshall Aid immediately. On June 20, 1948, currency reform was carried out in the three Western zones. On July 1, 1948, the three Western commanders-in-chief invited the elected German governments in their zones to organize the drafting of a constitution for West Germany. This constitution, known as the Basic Law, was approved by the commanders-in-chief and ratified by the Germans in May 1949. The German Federal Republic came into being on September 21, 1949.

Germany thus became the setting for an open trial of strength between Soviet Russia and the Western powers. On March 20, 1948, the Russian commander-in-chief, General Sokolovsky, walked out of the Allied Control Council, after declaring that the Western powers had broken the Potsdam Agreement and "by their actions these three delegations once again confirm that the Control Council virtually no longer exists as the supreme body of authority in Germany." Ten days later, the Soviet occupation authorities imposed a blockade on road and rail traffic crossing from the Western zones through the Soviet zone to West Berlin. By August, all traffic into West Berlin by land and water was blocked. The reply of the Western powers was to supply West Berlin, with its population of two and a half million, by air. By 1949, 8,000 tons of supplies were being flown in daily by the British and American Air Forces, while a counterblockade on goods moving through the Western zones to the Soviet zone was producing hardship on the Germans there. On May 12, 1949, the Russians admitted failure and declared that the roads, railroads, and canals, which had been officially "closed for repairs" for a year, were ready for reopening to traffic from the West. For the moment, Russian ambitions in Germany had been checked, and West Germany was a potentially powerful acquisition for the Western bloc. But the price to be paid was the definitive division of Germany into two states, with the consequent danger that the issue of German reunification could precipitate a crisis between the two blocs. The maintenance of West Berlin in Allied hands as a result of the success of the Berlin airlift was an even more pressing source of tension. As an escape route for refugees from the Soviet zone it presented a major obstacle to the successful communization of East Germany. As a Western outpost one hundred miles behind the Iron Curtain, it was the first place in which a renewed Soviet offensive against the Western powers would be directed.

Effects of Communist Coup in Czechoslovakia. The most impressive example of Communist aims was, however, the successful coup d'état in Czechoslovakia in February 1948. The two statesmen, President Beneš and Foreign Minister Jan Masaryk, whose return to power in 1945 had symbolized the possibility of the coexistence of democracy and communism in Eastern Europe, both disappeared from the international scene. By the end of 1948, Czechoslovakia was one of the most disciplined of Soviet satellites. The reaction in Western Europe to the Communist seizure of Czechoslovakia was immediate. Finally convinced of the reality of the Soviet danger, the West European democracies decided to create a permanent military alliance for their own defense.

The Treaties of Dunkirk and Brussels. The lead had been taken by Ernest Bevin in January 1947, when he had proposed to the French premier, Léon Blum, the conclusion of a treaty of alliance and mutual assistance between their two countries, directed explicitly against German aggression. On March 4, 1947, the treaty was signed at Dunkirk. On January 22, 1948, Bevin told the House of Commons that "Britain cannnot stand outside Europe and regard her problems as quite separate from those of her European neighbors." Russia's refusal to accept Marshall Aid and the failure of the conferences of the Council of Foreign Ministers "point to the conclusion that the free countries of west Europe must draw closely together. . . . I believe that the time is ripe for the consolidation of Western Europe." The supporters of European unification were disappointed in Bevin's proposals, however, for he firmly opposed any renunciation of national sovereignty and the creation of any form of supranational European government. He proposed only the extension of the Dunkirk Treaty to include the Benelux countries and, eventually, Italy. The Belgian premier and foreign minister, Paul-Henri Spaak, at once welcomed Bevin's initiative, even though it would imply Belgian renunciation of its century-old policy of neutrality. For Spaak, the experience of the Second World War had shown that Belgium could no longer attempt to stand alone, politically, economically, or militarily. He wished for the strongest possible integration of Western Europe, and he felt above all that British participation was necessary to make such unification a success. With the support of the Dutch and Luxembourg governments, he was able to persuade the British and the French to broaden the proposed military agreement to include economic, social, and cultural collaboration. The treaty was signed at Brussels on March 17, 1948. The five signatory powers bound themselves for fifty years to work together in raising the standard of living of their peoples, "to lead their peoples towards a better understanding of the principles which form the basis of their common civilization," and to give military aid if any of the five should be the object of an armed attack in Europe. A consultative council of the foreign ministers of the five powers was to meet every three months, and it was later decided to create a committee of the five defense ministers and a permanent military committee in London. Although the basis of a Land, Air, and Naval Command was created, the idea of integrating the military forces of the five countries into one common force was not even considered. Fully aware that he was disappointing those who hoped that the Brussels Treaty would provide the nucleus for a United States of Europe, Bevin justified his functional approach as that of a down-to-earth Englishman who genuinely believed that the final result would be a "practical organism in Europe in which we should cease to be English or French or other nationality, and would be Europeans, with an organization that would carry out a European policy."

The Atlantic Pact. In spite of all Bevin's professions of Europeanism, the American alliance appeared to him even more precious; and the natural extension of the Western European Union created by the Brussels Treaty was, in his view, to an Atlantic Community embracing the United States and Canada, linked through the British Commonwealth with Asia and Africa and through the Pan-American Union with South America. The United States government had welcomed the signature of the Brussels Treaty, although it was clear that the military strength of its five members could be bolstered only by American aid. On the day of the treaty's signing, President Truman told a joint session of Congress that "the determination of the free countries of Europe to protect themselves will be matched by an equal determination on our part to help them to do so." On June 11, 1948, Republican Senator Vandenberg, chairman of the Foreign Relations Committee, persuaded the Senate to pass a resolution in favor of giving military aid to members of a collective-security pact when it would contribute to the security of the United States and of sending American forces to aid a peace-loving nation under attack. With bipartisan support, Truman was able to begin discussions with the Brussels Treaty powers during the summer. By October, they had agreed to join the United States and Canada in a "defensive pact for the North Atlantic." In December, Denmark, Iceland,

Italy, Norway, and Portugal were invited to participate in the pact. The treaty was signed on April 4, 1949 in Washington.

The North Atlantic Treaty, or Atlantic Pact, was a short but telling document. The twelve signatory nations agreed that "an armed attack against one or more of them in Europe or North America shall be considered an attack against them all and consequently they [agreed] that, if such an armed attack occurs, each of them in exercise of the right of individual or collective self-defense recognized by Article 51 of the Charter of the United Nations, will assist the Party or Parties so attacked by taking forthwith, individually and in concert with the other Parties, such action as it deems necessary, including the use of armed force, to restore and maintain the security of the North Atlantic area." An attack in the North Atlantic area was defined as an "armed attack on the territory of any of the Parties in Europe or North America, on the Algerian Departments of France, on the occupation forces of any Party in Europe, on the islands under the jurisdiction of any Party in the North Atlantic area north of the Tropic of Cancer or on the vessels or aircraft in this area of any of the Parties." In this way most of the colonies of the European powers were deliberately excluded from the American military guarantee. The treaty was to be of indefinite duration, but any member could withdraw after twenty years by giving one year's notice. The Atlantic Pact was ratified by the Senate on July 21, 1949 and signed by President Truman on July 25. On the same day, Truman submitted to Congress the necessary corollary to the pact, a Mutual Defense Assistance Program providing $1.45 billion during the coming two years to the Atlantic Pact powers and other countries the President himself would designate. The final bill, which, after many amendments, appropriated $1.314 billion for the NATO powers, Greece, Turkey, Iran, Korea, and the Philippines, became law on October 28, 1949. On July 26, 1950, $1.222 billion was appropriated for the second year of the Mutual Defense Assistance Program.

European Reactions to the Atlantic Pact. In Europe, suspicion that the Marshall Plan was a first step to military alignment with the United States against Russia was now confirmed, and the Atlantic Pact was attacked not only by the Communist parties and left-wing Socialists but by all would-be neutralists who did not wish to have to choose between Russia and the United States. In Britain, Bevin was strongly supported by the Conservative party, but was attacked by the left wing of his own party. In France, the right-wing parties united with the Communists in opposition to the pact on the grounds that it could lead to the rearmament of Germany, while the neutralist case was argued in the influential *Le Monde* by such eminent scholars as the philosopher Etienne Gilson. The Italian government was subjected to great pressure from the Communist party and from the left wing of the Socialists; demonstrations against the pact were organized throughout the country; and the Soviet government warned Premier De Gasperi that the pact contravened the Italian peace treaty. Norway and Denmark, which were also warned by the Soviet government not to join the pact, were reassured by the agreement that no foreign bases would be set up on their soil in peacetime, a concession that Portugal also demanded. In every member country in Europe, however, the pact was ratified by large majorities. Fear of the overwhelming land forces of the Soviet Union, suspicion of the tactics of Russia in Eastern Europe and of the Communist parties at home, the conviction of the need for a legal commitment by the United States to defend Europe at the Iron Curtain itself, and a belief that peace would be secured by a balance of power—all these considerations determined the European countries to become members in a military alliance dominated by the United States.

Between 1947 and 1949, the policy of "containment" appeared to have been successful in Europe. After the coup in Czechoslovakia, communism made no further gains in Europe, and indeed with the expulsion of Yugoslavia from the Communist camp in June 1948, the unity of Eastern Europe seemed threatened. The Communist parties of France and Italy were never again to be as strong as during the thwarted strikes of September–December 1947. Marshall Aid was restoring Western Europe's prosperity and its conviction in the value of its own political and social system. The Atlantic Pact gave it an increasing feeling of security. War in Korea, however, was soon to disturb that self-confidence and to remind Europeans that events in Asia were moving rapidly to the disadvantage of the West.

DECOLONIZATION IN ASIA, 1945–49

The economic and military reinforcement of Western Europe through the Marshall Plan and the Atlantic Pact brought about a stalemate in the relations of the Western powers and Soviet Russia in Europe that lasted until the death of Stalin on March 5, 1953. In Asia, however, the

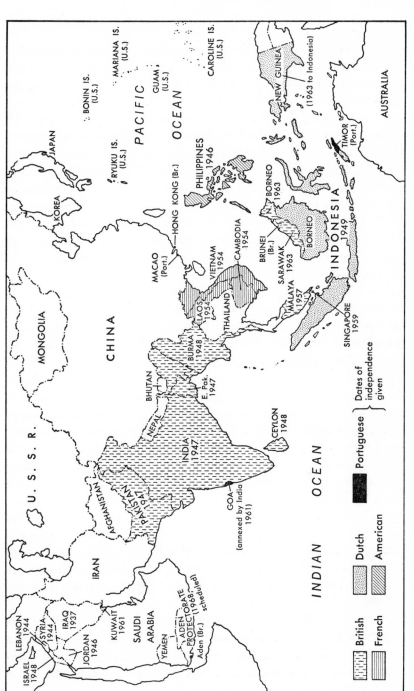

LIQUIDATION OF COLONIAL EMPIRES IN ASIA

U. S. S. R.

MONGOLIA

CHINA

JAPAN

KOREA

IRAN

AFGHANISTAN

LEBANON
1944

SYRIA
1944

IRAQ
1937

ISRAEL
1948

JORDAN
1946

KUWAIT
1961

SAUDI
ARABIA

YEMEN

ADEN
PROTECTORATE
Aden (Br.)

(1968-
scheduled)

PAKISTAN

NEPAL

BHUTAN

INDIA
1947

E. Pak.
1947

BURMA
1948

LAOS
1954

THAILAND

VIETNAM
1954

CAMBODIA
1954

MACAO
(Port.)

HONG KONG (Br.)

RYUKU IS.
(U.S.)

BONIN IS.
(U.S.)

MARIANA IS.
(U.S.)

GUAM
(U.S.)

CAROLINE IS.
(U.S.)

PACIFIC   OCEAN

PHILIPPINES
1946

GOA
(annexed by India
1961)

CEYLON
1948

INDIAN   OCEAN

N. BORNEO
1963

BRUNEI
(Br.)

SARAWAK
1963

MALAYA
1957

SINGAPORE
1959

BORNEO

INDONESIA
1949

TIMOR
(Port.)

NEW GUINEA

(1963 to Indonesia)

AUSTRALIA

British

French

Dutch

American

Portuguese

Dates of
independence
given

advances of nationalism and communism brought home to the United States and its European allies that Stalin's plan for bringing the under-developed regions of the world under communism before mounting the final attack on the capitalist countries was making great progress.

American Policy in Asia. Both the American and British governments attempted to make a difficult distinction in Asia between nationalism, to which they were selectively sympathetic and communism, which they would oppose by force. Truman at first shared Roosevelt's distrust of colonialism, and the American government antagonized the British by criticizing their hold on Malaya and Hong Kong, the Dutch by opposing in the United Nations their attempted suppression of Indonesian nationalism, and the French by suggesting international trusteeship of Indochina. After carrying out a program of relief and reconstruction, the United States fulfilled the promise of 1934 by giving the Philippines their independence July 4, 1946. Over half a billion dollars was paid to the Philippines to cover war damage to public and private property; and the Philippine Trade Act of April 1946 allowed free trade between the two countries for eight years. American defense interests in the Pacific were, however, safeguarded by an agreement in March 1947 permitting the United States the use of military and naval bases on the Philippine Islands for ninety-nine years, and American economic interests were served by preferential treatment of American capital in exploitation of Philippine natural resources. The greatest source of unrest, however, was the peasants' poverty and their hatred of the landlord classes who had retained their favored position throughout the American occupation. These grievances were to be exploited by the Communist guerrillas, the Huks, who had taken to the mountains at the time of the return of MacArthur's armies. Truman made no pretense of granting independence to the strategic defense outposts that the United States still held in the Pacific—Guam, Midway, Wake, and Samoa; and in April 1947, the United States was granted by the United Nations the right to administer the former mandated islands of Japan, including Okinawa and the Bonin Islands, as a Trust Territory. In Japan, General MacArthur carried out a highly successful occupation, in which he attempted to prepare the way for democracy by land reform, cartel busting, a purge of the civil service, demilitarization, war-crimes trials, and adoption of a democratic constitution. In 1951, a peace treaty with Japan was signed in San Francisco by most of the Western powers. Russia, although present at the conference, would not accept the treaty; no representative of China was invited; India declared that its neutrality would not permit it to participate. The treaty restored Japan's independence, made permanent the loss of its overseas territories as carried out at the armistice, and promised reparations by negotiation with individual claimants. Concurrently with the peace treaty, the United States signed a security pact, which gave it the right to station forces in Japan for an indefinite period and to use those forces to safeguard the security of the Far East or the internal security of Japan against insurrections instigated by a foreign power. Moreover, the Japanese government agreed to ask American consent before granting military bases in Japan to a third power. Thus, the United States was able to pose as the opponent of colonialism while maintaining in the Pacific a defense perimeter based on Alaska, Japan, the Trust Territories, its Pacific islands, and the Philippines.

Colonial Policy of the British Labour Government. The British Labour party had long been on record as desiring the liquidation of the British colonial empire, which was coming to be regarded not only as morally indefensible but as an economic and military liability. In 1945, Britain's empire included three major areas of Asia—the Middle East, where it held mandates in Transjordan and Palestine; the Indian subcontinent and the island of Ceylon; and Southeast Asia, where its holdings comprised Burma, Malaya, Singapore, Hong Kong, North Borneo, Sarawak, and Brunei. The mandates in the Middle East were quickly ended. Transjordan became an independent kingdom in January 1946; and in May 1948, British troops were withdrawn from Palestine, the resulting war between Jews and Arabs culminating in the creation of the state of Israel. Nevertheless, Britain remained deeply involved in the Middle East. Its oil supplies were drawn from the Anglo-Iranian Oil Company and the protected sheikdoms of Kuwait, Bahrein, and Muscat on the Persian Gulf. The Protectorate of Aden and the military base of the Suez Canal Zone, and control of the canal itself through the Suez Canal Company, were retained to safeguard the sea route to Asia.

Independence of India, Pakistan, and Ceylon. The Labour government moved quickly to grant India and Ceylon their independence. Unable to get the Moslem League and the Hindu Congress party to come to an agreement on India's future, Attlee finally decided to force the Indians to a compromise, by announcing in February 1947 that Britain would withdraw its forces in June 1948. When the new viceroy, Lord Mount-batten, surveyed the growing communal riots between Moslems and Hindus, he advanced the transfer of sovereignty to August 15, 1947. The Indian Independence Act passed the British Parliament in July 1947. Two separate states were created. India, with a population of 380 million, was to be a largely Hindu state. Pakistan, divided into two regions seven hundred miles apart—West Pakistan at the Indus mouth and East Pakistan in Bengal—was a Moslem state with a population of only 80 million. At the time of partition, terrible bloodshed occurred when some ten million Hindus and Moslems attempted to move, or were forcibly driven, to the state of their own religion. In all, probably more than a million died during the disorders, a frightful side effect of the haste with which the British withdrew. Ten million Hindus remained in Pakistan and forty million Moslems in India. Both India and Pakistan claimed the state of Kashmir, whose ruler was Hindu and whose population was largely Moslem. Fighting for control of Kashmir was stopped in January 1949 by the United Nations, and Kashmir was left divided along the cease-fire line. Ceylon was also given independence as a self-governing Dominion on February 4, 1948. Britain retained the use of military bases on the island and of the port of Trincomalee, and for a number of years Ceylon's economy remained closely tied to Britain's through British ownership of rubber and tea plantations and Britain's importation of the greater part of Ceylon's exports.

Communism did not make great advances in India, Pakistan, or Ceylon. Individual Communists had joined the Congress party until forced out in the fall of 1945, and Communists were thought to have infiltrated the Indian Navy. The party, however, collaborated with the Congress until 1948, when strikes and riots led to its outlawing in large parts of the country. Only in the southern province of Kerala did the Communists manage to gain control of the government, but after two years they were ousted by the central government in 1959. The Indian government, under Prime Minister Jawaharlal Nehru, followed a policy of neutralism in the Cold War, but aided the remaining colonial peoples in seeking independence. Within India's own territory, the French were persuaded to give up their four colonial enclaves in 1954, and the Portuguese were driven from Goa by force in December 1961. Neutral-ist, anticolonial India was to exert growing influence as more Asian and African nations gained their independence. The Western powers would be compelled to readjust their foreign policy to accommodate this new factor. Unlike India, Pakistan at first sided openly with the Western powers, putting great importance on its Commonwealth membership and joining in 1954 in the anti-Communist military alliance of the Bagdad Pact. Russia's support of Afghanistan's antagonistic policy toward Pakistan in 1955 and of India's claims on Kashmir also helped strengthen Pakistan's commitment to the West. Throughout Pakistan's first decade, independence seemed to have created a reliable ally of the West in south Asia. Ceylon, fearing like Pakistan the unrest of its Hindu minority and the ambitions of its neighbor, India, at first clung closely to the British alliance, but the election of 1956 brought to power S. W. R. D. Bandaranaike, a neutralist who made overtures to Peking and forced the British to give up their defense bases in Ceylon. He was thus able to accept substantial economic aid from Russia and China as well as from the Western powers.

Independent Burma. Of Britain's holdings in Southeast Asia, Burma was the first to gain its independence. Although it underestimated the Burmese desire for immediate independence and the strength of Aung San's party, the Anti-Fascist People's Freedom League, the Labour government eventually promised independence on the same terms as India. Before it was achieved on January 4, 1948, the country, which had been ravaged by the war, suffered further from riots, banditry, communal strife between the Burmans and the minority group of the Karens, and the assassination of Aung San and five of his party's leaders by discontented rivals. Rival Communist guerrilla bands, known respectively as the Red Flags and the White Flags, organized insurrections against the central government of Aung San's successor, U Nu. The central government fought back with military force and a series of political and economic reforms, including the establishment of an autonomous Karen state. By 1950, most of the country had been brought back under control; and the Burmese government, which had chosen not to become a member of the Commonwealth, was able to hold to a policy of coexistence in the Cold War, while accepting loans from Britain and the United States in 1950 and concluding trade agreements with Soviet Russia and Communist China in 1955. Nevertheless, when the Burmese Army seized power in 1962, under General Ne Win, its leaders felt it necessary to refuse all foreign aid in order to affirm Burma's determination not to become a member of either bloc.

Communist Insurrection in Malaya. Britain's economic stake in Malaya, the world's largest producer of rubber and tin and the main dollar-earner of the sterling area, was far greater than in Burma; and the grant of independence to India and Ceylon increased the significance of Singapore as Britain's most powerful military and naval base on the sea route from Europe to Australia and Hong Kong. Even during the Japanese occupation, nationalism had been fomented largely by the Chinese section of the population and had made little advance among the Malays and the Indians. The British were welcomed back by most of the country's inhabitants, and even the Communist guerrilla leader Ch'in P'eng went to London to receive a decoration—ironically enough, the Order of the British Empire. To salve the grievances of Singapore, whose population was largely Chinese, the city was detached from the rest of Malaya in April 1946 and was later given its own legislative council. The Malayan peninsula was organized as the Federation of Malaya, in 1948, as a method of preserving the supremacy of the Malays and the rights of the sultans. Eventual grant of self-government was promised. At this point, the Malayan Communists attempted to seize Malaya by force. Ch'in P'eng reappeared at the head of his old army, soon renamed the Malayan Races' Liberation Army. Using terrorism against the owners and managers of the rubber plantations and tin mines and then against the villagers, the Communist guerrillas attempted to gain control of several "liberated areas" from which to conquer the rest of the country. Most of the guerrillas were Chinese, and their support came from Chinese villagers, while the Malays tried not to become involved in the battle on either side. The British fought back with increased army and air forces against the 10,000 Communist terrorists. The Chinese villagers were regrouped in "New Villages," behind barbed wire, to protect them and to prevent them from aiding the guerrillas.

Independence for British Colonies in Southeast Asia. The most important reason for the failure of the Communists was, however, the increase in self-government that the British carried through from 1950 on, which enabled the leader of the United Malay National Organization, Tunku Abdul Rahman, in alliance with a conservative Malayan Chinese Association, to become prime minister in 1955. The Malayan Federation became independent within the Commonwealth on August 31, 1957. Three years later, the Communist rebellion was officially declared to be over. The new state accepted financial aid from Britain and the United States, and, although refusing to join in a military alliance, definitely favored the Western bloc in the Cold War. The city of Singapore, which Britain had developed enormously as a military base in the postwar years, lagged behind the mainland in moving toward independence. After two years of rule by the British governor (1946–48), the share of local population in administration and legislation was slowly increased. In 1955, a new constitution permitted elections for a Legislative Council; and in 1959, Singapore also became an independent member of the Commonwealth. The three British colonies in Borneo—North Borneo, Brunei, and Sarawak—made little progress toward self-government or independence until the 1960's. Brunei was under British military administration from 1945 to 1946 and was thereafter governed by an absolute sultan. Sarawak, which had been the personal fief of one British family since 1841, became a Crown Colony in 1946, but did not receive partial autonomy until 1957. North Borneo was given a constitution in 1950, but not until 1963 were members of the Legislative Council chosen by direct election. In 1961, the Malayan premier, Tunku Abdul Rahman, proposed to the British government that the Federation of Malaya, the state of Singapore, and the three British colonies of North Borneo, Sarawak, and Brunei, should unite in a federation called Malaysia. In this way, he hoped, Singapore would be prevented from falling into Communist hands, the percentage of Malays would be higher than in Malaya alone, and a viable trading unit would be formed around the port of Singapore. The federation was created on September 16, 1963, after the British government had sampled opinion in its colonies on Borneo. At the last minute the sultan of Brunei refused to participate, however, and Singapore withdrew from the federation in 1965.

Independence Struggles of the Dutch East Indies. Britain was thus able to maintain its hold on its colonies in Southeast Asia, with the exception of Burma, throughout the postwar decade when its balance-of-payments crisis could be most eased by the dollar earnings of those territories. The Dutch and the French were not so fortunate, nor, when they were ejected, did they leave a reservoir of good will such as the British were able to draw upon in India, Ceylon, and Malaysia. The Netherlands East Indies, or Indonesia, had declared its independence on August 17, 1945, in the hiatus between the defeat of the Japanese and the arrival of the Allies. Since the Dutch, who were themselves liberated only three months earlier, had almost no military forces, the surrender of Japanese forces on Indonesia was made to a small force of British and Australian troops who began to arrive at the end of September. They found themselves in a very difficult position; for the Indonesian Republic, with Sukarno as president, was already administering the country. It had 100,000 troops armed with Japanese weapons, was holding the Dutch civilians and prisoners of war in internment camps, and was determined to prevent the restoration of Dutch colonial rule. The Dutch promised a partnership with the Netherlands in which the Indonesians would have freedom in their internal affairs; but, with 25 to 30 per cent of all Dutch capital invested in Indonesia, which had a prewar Dutch population of 230,000, the Netherlands government was determined not to be ousted. The British, faced with growing disorder throughout the country, decided to use force to restore control on behalf of the Dutch. They first seized the principal coastal cities, using both British and Indian troops. Dutch soldiers began to arrive in 1946, and the British finally withdrew on November 30, 1946. The Dutch attempted to enforce their control by so-called police actions; but, unable to break Sukarno's control on Java and Sumatra, they agreed to the foundation of a federal state of Indonesia and of a Netherlands-Indonesia Union under the Dutch monarchy. Both sides soon broke the detailed provisions of the agreements, however.

The situation fitted perfectly into Communist plans, drawn up in Calcutta in February 1948, for a coordinated offensive throughout Asia. The Communist party of Indonesia had grown significantly in membership, especially among trade unionists, and had its own terrorist underground. In September it attempted to seize control of Indonesia by force. The moment was well chosen because many Indonesians were becoming disheartened at the continuing economic distress and at the failure of the Republic to achieve a settlement with the Dutch. President Sukarno reacted vigorously. The Communist center of Madiun was captured by the regular army. Many leading Communists were arrested and shot. Tan Malaka, a charismatic, independent-minded Communist agitator who had been released from jail in September, thereupon formed his own Communist movement, but he too was defeated by the army in April 1949 and was executed. The Communists had again failed, as in the Philippines, by opposing not colonialism but nationalism.

While occupied with the Communist insurrection, Sukarno was rebuffing Dutch attempts to bring the Republic into an Indonesian federation. Two months after he had put down the Communist coup, he was himself captured by the Dutch. In their second "police action," the Dutch seemed almost totally successful. Dutch paratroops and land forces took most of the major towns of Java and Sumatra within a few days. They had, however, affronted the United Nations by ignoring its cease-fire order and had lost the sympathy of most of the world. Criticism came not only from Soviet Russia and the neutralist countries like India and Burma but also from the United States and especially from Australia. This pressure, as well as the continuing guerrilla resistance, brought the Dutch to the conference table again. Sukarno was released. After four months of negotiations at The Hague, agreement was finally reached on the transfer of sovereignty in Indonesia from the Dutch to a United States of Indonesia and on the establishment of a Netherlands-Indonesia Union. On December 27, 1949, Indonesia became a sovereign state. It lost little time in jettisoning the unwanted clauses of the agreement. The power of the Republican government of President Sukarno was confirmed by replacing the federal system with a centralized government, and replacing the name of United States of Indonesia with Republic of Indonesia. Dislike of the Dutch was so great that the Netherlands-Indonesia Union was never implemented. Dutch economic interests received no special safeguards. The number of Dutch in the Republic was reduced to 10,000 by 1960. On August 10, 1954, the Indonesian government formally ended the union with the Netherlands. The Dutch had done much to develop Indonesia's economy, especially in production of rubber, tin, oil, and palm oil. But the Indonesian people had received too few of the benefits of this exploitation of the rich natural resources of the country. The Dutch had made little effort to educate the Indonesians or to prepare them for self-government. For five years after the war, they had used their armies in the attempt to put down a popularly supported Indonesian government. The new Indonesian state, which with a population of 73 million in 1953, was by far the most significant country in Southeast Asia, began life with a profound hatred of the colonial powers and indeed of the West in general. It was quickly to become the most left-leaning of the neutralist countries.

French Colonial Policy. The French, like the Dutch, were opposed to both nationalism and communism in their colony of Indochina. France's official policy toward its colonial empire before the Second World War had been "assimilation," by which the colonial peoples were made good Frenchmen through acquaintance with French civilization. In practice, the system had implied centralized rule from Paris through French administrators in the colonies, while the educational policy had produced only a small native elite. A new approach had been promised by General de Gaulle in his Brazzaville speech of January 1944, in which he envisaged the creation of a French Union of autonomous states in close association with France. As actually formed by the Constitution of 1946, the French Union was a disappointment. The Assembly of the French Union, in which France had the same number of members as the rest of its territories combined, had little power or prestige. In all the colonies, electoral machinery was created to give French inhabitants predominance over native inhabitants, and little preparation was made for the promised political independence. In the most backward areas France controlled, as in French Equatorial Africa and French West Africa, or the smaller island possessions, like Reunion, the Society Islands, or Miquelon, there was little agitation against this imposed inferiority. In Algeria, Tunisia, and Morocco there was unrest, which quickly culminated in demands for outright independence. In Asia, France's hold was even more precarious. British and Free French forces had invaded the mandated territories of Syria and Lebanon in 1941, after their governors had recognized the Vichy government. Although the Free French themselves set up independent republics there in 1941, French troop reinforcements were moved into Beirut in May 1945, while the future French rights in the area were being negotiated. After Damascus had been bombarded for three days (May 29–31, 1945) by French troops, Churchill ordered British troops to intervene. Both the French and British were unwanted, however, and after Syria and Lebanon had appealed to the United Nations, all foreign troops were withdrawn in 1946. The French thereby lost all hold on the Middle East, and their military intervention incurred lasting hostility of the Arab states. The French gave up their last four trading stations in India in 1954. In Indochina, however, France had a large economic stake, which it was unwilling to give up.

War in French Indochina. When the troops of General Leclerc finally reached Saigon on October 3, 1945, they found the situation extremely unfavorable to the restoration of French control. Indochina had twice been declared independent—by the Japanese puppet emperor, Bao Dai in March, and by Ho Chi Minh on September 2. The Viet Minh forces were strongly entrenched throughout the country, and their nationalist propaganada had won them widespread support both in the country and among other powers, including, it seemed, at least part of the American government. In the north, the Chinese were disarming Frenchmen, and they permitted Ho to conduct elections for a National Assembly in January 1946. The new Assembly chose Ho as president, and he thereupon set up a new government, including not only the Viet Minh but two other nationalist groups. In the south, however, the British pulled out their troops in October 1945, and the French high commissioner at once began military operations to bring the southern part of Vietnam under French control. To deal with Ho, the French first attempted compromise, signing an agreement with him on March 6, 1946, by which the Republic of Vietnam was recognized as "a free State with its own government, parliament, army and finances, which is part of the Indochinese Federation and of the French Union." The French were trying to offer Ho Chi Minh what the Dutch had offered Sukarno, recognition of his authority in the section of the country he actually controlled simultaneously with creation of states under amenable leaders in the other parts of the country. Realizing his own weakness, Ho continued to discuss the settlement with the French at Dalat and then at Fontainebleau. He also permitted French troops to move into Hanoi, his capital, as laid down in the March Agreement. He refused to recognize that the rich state of Cochin China, the southern portion of Vietnam that included Saigon and the Mekong River delta, was not a part of the Republic of Vietnam, however, even though the French declared Cochin China an independent state within the Indochinese Federation in June 1946. In November, after a minor quarrel over customs collection, the French suddenly bombarded the port of Haiphong, killing thousands of Vietnamese. In retaliation, two hundred French people in Hanoi were killed or wounded on December 19, the day when Vietnamese Army Commander Giap launched a major offensive against the French troops in Tonkin. In this first battle of the Indochinese war, the French were successful, driving Giap's forces back to the Chinese border without difficulty.

The French then turned to the "Bao Dai solution," persuading the ex-emperor who had abdicated in August 1945, to return to the throne and to appoint an anti-Viet Minh government. On Bao Dai's insistence, they recognized the unity and independence of the country, in 1948. On December 30, 1949, France officially renounced its sovereignty over Vietnam and recognized Bao Dai as head of state. In the north, however, Giap had embarked upon "revolutionary war," using skillful nationalist propaganda, political indoctrination, and terrorism to win control of the villages of Tonkin, reducing French control to the major cities. Ho Chi Minh kept in existence his own government of the Republic of Vietnam, and upon the French renunciation of sovereignty, he declared that his was the only sovereign government of the country. While the United States, Britain, and most Western countries recognized the Bao Dai regime, Russia and the Communist world recognized Ho Chi Minh's. The stage was thus set for France's long and unsuccessful war with the Viet Minh.

Meanwhile, in the neighboring protectorates of Cambodia and Laos, the French had acted with a combination of force and concession. The Cambodian premier installed by the Japanese was kidnapped by French and British troops in September 1945, but Cambodia was placated by the grant of a modicum of self-government in January 1946. On November 8, 1949, full independence within the French Union was granted, and Prince Sihanouk became an independent head of state. In Laos, independence from the French had been declared, under Chinese Nationalist patronage, by Prince Pethsarat. The French drove Pethsarat out in the spring of 1946 and restored the king. Thereupon an important section of Pethsarat's government joined cause with the Viet Minh, and with their followers, the Pathet Lao, took to the jungles. On July 19, 1949, the French recognized the independence of Laos within the French Union. At this point the Asian situation was transformed by the victory of the Communists in China in 1949 and by the military involvement of the United States in Korea in 1950.

COMMUNIST VICTORY IN CHINA

Triumph of the Chinese Communists. Deeply involved in their difficult tasks of reconstruction, with the Communist threat in Europe, and with colonial problems, the European powers could merely watch passively while the fate of China was settled. Britain held on to Hong Kong but refused to become involved in the affairs of the mainland. Russia withdrew its troops from Manchuria in April 1946 and approved efforts to bring the Chinese Communists into a coalition government with the Kuomintang. The only power that could intervene in strength was the United States. The position of the Truman administration was that, since Chiang Kai-shek was the legal government of China, he should be restored to control of the formerly Japanese-held areas of north China and that his troops should continue to receive American equipment and training. Since, however, the Chinese Communists were clearly in control of large areas of rural China, they should be brought into a coalition government, which would, moreover, be rendered more genuinely liberal by inclusion of members of the Democratic League, a weak group composed of university intellectuals.

To bring about this compromise settlement, Truman sent General Marshall to China in November 1945, to pressure Chiang into a settlement with the Communists and, if necessary, to threaten the suspension of American aid. For a time, it seemed that Marshall might succeed. Hostilities between the Communists and the Kuomintang were stopped in January 1946, and a Committee of Three, including one American, one Communist, and one Kuomintang representative, was set up. Fighting flared up in Manchuria, however, as the Communist and Kuomintang forces fought for control of the rich province after the Russian withdrawal. Marshall left China in January 1947, disgusted with the venality of the Kuomintang regime, and for the next year American aid was drastically curtailed. During that time, Chiang embarked on a last, disastrous attempt to destroy the Communist forces. His armies were larger and better equipped than those of the Communists, but his tactics were unwise. He overextended his communications and supply lines by attempting to bring both Manchuria and north China under his control at the same time. The Communists were thus able to destroy the railroads, to attack isolated groups of Kuomintang forces, to maintain their control over the peasantry, and to confine Chiang's hold to a few of the larger cities. In the disorder of war, corruption within the Kuomintang became monumental, whereas the Communists skillfully required a puritanical morality in their soldiers. As the hold of reactionary groups, like the so-called C. C. Clique, became more blatant in the Kuomintang, more and more of the liberal-minded groups began to turn to the Communists. Even American economic assistance of $275 million authorized in 1948 failed to stop the economic collapse that had begun the previous year, with the disruption of internal and external trade, the failure of the currency, and the virtual cessation of the supply of food to the cities. As the Kuomintang visibly weakened, Communist military campaigns became more ambitious. In 1947, Chiang's attempt to conquer the province of Shantung, the vitally important link between Peking and Nanking, was defeated, and his armies in Manchuria were besieged in the main cities. By mid-1948, the Communists were ready for the final blows against the Kuomintang. Equal in armaments and greater in numbers, they were able to meet Chiang's best forces in open battle. In September and October, they took most of north China and, easily foiling Chiang's last desperate attempt to relieve his forces trapped in Manchuria, swept into Mukden in October. By December 1948, in a powerful southern attack, the Communists reached the banks of the Yangtze River. After ineffectual negotiations with opponents of Chiang in the Kuomintang, Peking was taken in January, after a six-week siege of the inner, walled city.

Chiang resigned from the presidency on the day before Peking's surrender, and his successor engaged in three months of negotiations with the Communists for the establishment of a coalition government. In April, however, the new president fled to Canton, and the Communist armies crossed the Yangtze, capturing Nanking in April, Shanghai in May, and Canton itself in October. The northwest provinces were taken in August and September, and by the end of the year most of the principal Kuomintang leaders and those forces that could escape had taken refuge in the island of Formosa. On October 1, 1949, the victorious Communists announced the formation of the People's Republic of China.

Significance for Europe of Communization of China. The European governments at once recognized that the Communist victory in China had changed the balance of power in the world, but they were uncertain of the immediate consequences for them. China was obviously a major power that had the potential to rival Russia and the United States. Covering one-thirteenth of the world's land surface and with one-fourth of the world's population—470 million in 1946, 646 million in 1957, 700 million in 1963—it possessed rich deposits of coal, iron ore, and oil. In Manchuria, the Japanese had developed an efficient iron and steel industry. It had a highly educated intellectual class, a hard-working, disciplined peasantry, an enthusiastic urban proletariat, and a determined group of leaders devoted to the communization of Chinese society and to the advancement of communism to the rest of the world. The strength of those leaders was increased by the fact that the Chinese people did not expect them to govern democratically. As the Australian Sinologist C. P. Fitzgerald has explained, "The Chinese people looked now for a government which could govern, which knew its mind, had power and purpose, a theory and a practice which fitted together—in fact for a modern version of the government under which they had lived for so many centuries." Power was vested in the hands of a small group of men in key positions in the army, the government, and the Communist party, especially in Chairman of the Central People's Government Council Mao Tse-tung and Premier Chou En-lai, who governed by what they called a "democratic dictatorship."

The policies of the new regime were deeply disturbing to the West European powers. The totalitarian control exercised by the Communist party was undisguised. In the process of land redistribution begun in 1950, probably more than a million people were killed. Many millions were sent to labor camps. Intellectuals were forced to give positive aid to the party program, and suspect groups were put to labor that would help remold their way of thinking. Foreign priests and missonaries were persecuted, and the lands of Buddhist and Taoist monasteries were confiscated. Yet the new regime undoubtedly succeeded in harnessing the frustrated idealism of much of China's youth and in mobilizing the peasantry and city workers in support of the regime. New educational opportunities, the disappearance of the landlord class, the restoration of internal commerce, and a moderate economic revival appeared in the early years of the regime to have won the regime "the backing and active support of very large numbers, probably the big majority, of the peasant, educated and professional classes."

Eastern Europe and Red China. The Communist countries of Eastern Europe at once welcomed this giant to their camp. The Soviet Union's aid to the Chinese Communists in the civil war had been slight—Japanese armaments in Manchuria had been allowed to fall into Communist hands, Chiang's forces had been denied the use of Port Arthur in their Manchurian campaign, and American Lend-Lease equipment may even have been passed on. Stalin had advised Mao Tse-tung to accept a coalition government under Chiang in 1945 and had suggested he continue guerrilla war rather than attempt to win final victory in 1948; in both cases his advice had been ignored. Nevertheless, the Soviet press declared that the Communist victory in China was a triumph for the world Communist movement; the Soviet Union gave formal recognition to the Chinese People's Republic and broke relations with Nationalist Chinese government on Formosa on October 2. Mao himself declared on July 1, 1949, "Internationally, we belong to the side of the anti-imperialist front, headed by the Soviet Union." In December, he began a two-month-long visit to Moscow and on February 15, 1950 signed a Sino-Soviet Treaty of Friendship, Alliance and Mutual Assistance, ostensibly directed against future Japanese aggression. The Soviet Union promised to return to China the concessions it had won in the secret Yalta Agreement: Port Arthur, Dairen, and the Manchurian Railroad; China was to receive a credit of $300 million; and a military alliance was concluded. Two months later it was agreed that China would receive arms, machinery, and technical advice from Russia in return for the supply of raw materials. Finally, four joint Sino-Soviet companies were set up to exploit the resources of Sinkiang and Manchuria. Although China did not become a member of the Cominform, it thus appeared that the Soviet Union had gained an important, devoted supporter in the Cold War. The Communist countries of Eastern Europe quickly followed the Soviet lead in recognizing the new regime and in establishing trade relations. India led the neutralist countries in recognizing the Communist government, and was quickly followed by Pakistan and Ceylon.

Western Europe and Red China. Of the West European powers, Britain was especially concerned about the intentions of the Chinese Communists with respect to Hong Kong. The Chinese, however, made no attempt to seize Hong Kong, whose New Territories on the mainland would return to them legally when the British lease expired in 1998 and which offered commercial and financial advantages to China. The British recognized the People's Republic on January 6, 1950, and most of the West European countries, which had long despaired of Chiang Kai-shek's regime, followed suit. France, however, did not do so, as the Chinese had recognized Ho Chi Minh's government as the legal government of Vietnam in January 1950 and had provided bases and advisers for the Viet Minh forces in southern China. The United States government, which Mao had branded as the leader of the imperialists, seemed prepared in 1949 to rid itself of Chiang and to allow the Chinese Communists to take Formosa. In 1950, after ill-treatment of American diplomats in China, the conclusion of the Sino-Soviet Treaty, and especially after the invasion of South Korea, support for Chiang Kai-shek was increased, the Seventh Fleet was ordered to prevent an attack on Formosa, and a policy of nonrecognition of the Chinese Communist government was adopted. From that point, the United States took upon itself the enormous task of blocking Chinese expansion in Asia.

THE KOREAN WAR

Korea Divided. On June 25, 1950, sixteen divisions of North Korean troops crossed the 38th parallel into South Korea. This invasion was, however, of Russian rather than Chinese inspiration. Russian troops had occupied North Korea until the end of 1948 and had converted the country into a Communist satellite on the East European pattern. A Communist-dominated Democratic Front under a resistance leader Kim Il Sung had been allowed to set up a "Democratic People's Republic" in August 1948, which was given Soviet economic and military aid and recognized as the legal government of Korea. The United States retaliated in the South by encouraging the creation of the Republic of Korea under the presidency of Dr. Syngman Rhee, a veteran Korean politician who had been in exile in the United States. This government was recognized by the United Nations as the legitimate government of Korea. United States troops were withdrawn in June 1949, and American economic assistance on a large scale was granted to Rhee's government. South Korea, however, was plagued by inflation, unemployment, Communist guerrilla bands, and the authoritarian methods of Rhee. After Secretary of State Acheson's declaration of January 1950 that South Korea would have to take care of its own defense, North Korea increased its army from four to sixteen divisions and, undoubtedly with Stalin's approval, prepared for the easy overthrow of Syngman Rhee's Republic.

American Intervention. The government was taken completely by surprise; but on June 27 President Truman ordered American air and naval forces to aid South Korea, and three days later sent American ground troops into action. The United Nations Security Council, in the absence of the Russian delegate, branded North Korea as an aggressor, called for military assistance to South Korea, and invited Truman to appoint a commander for these forces. The next day, General MacArthur was chosen to head the United Nations forces. For a month, the North Koreans were completely successful, driving the South Korean and United Nations forces back into the southeastern tip of the peninsula around Pusan. MacArthur counterattacked in September with a brilliant amphibious operation at Inchon, the port of Seoul, the South Korean capital, and by the end of September the North Koreans had been pushed back beyond the 38th parallel. In October, most of North Korea was taken, including the capital, Pyongyang, and United Nations forces approached the Chinese border in Manchuria. Authorized by the United Nations to reunite North and South Korea, MacArthur attempted to envelop the remaining North Korean forces by a gigantic pincer movement, in which his forces were to drive up the east and west coasts of Korea and meet at the Chinese border along the Yalu River. He was forestalled, however, by Chinese entry into the war on October 14. About 200,000 Chinese troops, including the experienced Fourth Field Army, which had been preparing to invade Formosa, struck at the two separated wings of MacArthur's forces and drove them back precipitately across the snow-covered mountains into South Korea. Only in January 1951 was the Chinese attack halted by the strongly reinforced Eighth Army of General Matthew Ridgway. MacArthur, whose plan for defeating the Chinese invasion involved bombing the Yalu bridges and Manchuria and permitting Chiang Kai-shek's troops on Formosa to invade the mainland, had been categorically ordered to keep the fighting inside Korea; but, after he had, without authorization, invited the Chinese commander-in-chief to negotiate peace, he was dismissed on April 11, and was replaced by Ridgway. By June, the United Nations forces had pushed the Chinese back to the 38th parallel; and both sides agreed to a Soviet suggestion that cease-fire and armistice talks begin at once. The negotiations at Kaesong and Panmunjom dragged on until June 1953, often interrupted by new outbreaks of fighting. In face of United Nations' refusal to repatriate forcibly the 70,000 prisoners in their hands, the Communists finally agreed to allow each prisoner to choose whether to return to Communist rule or not. Only one in four returned to the North.

The effects of the Korean War were hard to estimate. The United States had for the first time shown its willingness to use military force to stop Communist expansion; it had lost over 33,000 men in doing so. The American forces had been supported by Britain and by Canada, Australia, and New Zealand. Symbolic forces of one infantry batallion each had come from Belgium, the Netherlands, France, and Greece; Turkey had sent an infantry brigade; and Luxembourg had provided a small force. Only two African countries participated—Ethiopia and the Union of South Africa, and one South American—Colombia. In Asia, the Philippines and Thailand each sent an infantry batallion. Chiang's aid was refused. But the West had learned a sobering lesson, too. The Chinese Communist armies, with their apparently inexhaustible supply of manpower, were a major military force that would be used if an attempt was made to win back an area that had once fallen under Communist control. Limited war was to remain an ever-present possibility for which new preparation of men, material, and strategy had to be made.

THE DIVISION OF VIETNAM

French Defeat in Indochina. While the Korean truce negotiations continued, the Communist forces were completing their victory over the French in Vietnam. Supplied with Chinese equipment and military advice, the Viet Minh forces of Vo Nguyen Giap slipped into the jungles south of the Chinese border, and in September and October 1950 captured the whole line of French forts along the Chinese border. The French thereupon demanded American aid because "of the international character of the conflict begun by the Viet Minh, which threatens the future of Southeast Asia." President Truman at once increased the aid he had promised at the time of the Korean invasion, and during the next four years the total of American aid reached $4.2 billion. Neither American material and money, nor the efforts of successive commanders, like the dashing Marshal de Lattre de Tassigny or the colorless General Henri Navarre, nor the loss of 91,000 men could stop the growing Viet Minh predominance in battle. By 1954, the Communist forces were in control of the countryside of North Vietnam. Giap had a regular army of more than 60,000 men, as well as innumerable part-time guerrillas recruited from the peasantry. Navarre determined to meet the Communist challenge in the North by fortification of the base of Dien Bien Phu, on the Laotian border. Giap's greatest triumph was the massing of four divisions and heavy artillery, which had been dragged manually through the jungles, with which he besieged and finally overwhelmed the French garrison on May 6, 1954. As a result of this stunning defeat, the French government was overthrown, and the new premier, Pierre Mendès-France was chosen for the specific purpose of making peace by negotiation.

The Geneva Conference on Indochina. The Geneva Conference of April 26–July 21, 1954, attended by delegations from Soviet Russia, Communist China, the Viet Minh, Vietnam, Cambodia, Laos, Britain, the United States, and France gave Mendès-France the opportunity to relieve France of its burdens in Indochina. With victory in their hands, the Communist powers seemed prepared to ease the retreat for France. The Chinese premier, Chou En-lai, dropped the demand that the Communist forces in Laos and Cambodia be recognized as the legal governments. Vietnam itself was to be partitioned along the 17th parallel, and not at the 14th, as the Viet Minh had desired. Vietnamese civilians were to be given a year in which they could decide whether to live in the North or the South, while the French were allowed 305 days for the evacuation of their troops and equipment from North Vietnam. The French agreed to give independence within the French Union to South Vietnam, Laos, and Cambodia. All foreign troops, including guerrillas, were to be withdrawn from Cambodia, but the Communist Pathet Lao was allowed to retain control of the two northern provinces of Laos. The "Final Declaration of the Conference," which was not signed, noted that the division of Vietnam along the 17th parallel was a temporary demarcation line and that elections would be held in Vietnam by 1956, presumably to permit the reunification of the country. The American government disassociated itself from the declaration, as did the new cabinet in South Vietnam, headed since June by Ngo Dinh Diem, a tough-minded Catholic politician who had spent the last four years in exile in the United States. In October, the United States government decided to back the Diem regime directly; American military advisers began to replace the French; and, within two years, the United States had assumed complete responsibility for maintenance of the independence of South Vietnam. The French gave up their richest colony with relief.

The death of Stalin on March 5, 1953 marked the end of the first phase of the Cold War. (1) In the ten years since the Battle of Stalingrad, communism had made enormous gains. The advance of the Red Army to the center of Europe had enabled Communist governments to take power in seven European countries and in eastern Germany, while the three Baltic states had been incorporated into Soviet Russia. In Asia, Russia had regained the territories it had lost to Japan in 1905. The whole of mainland China and Korea north of the 38th parallel (and, a year later Vietnam north of the 17th parallel) were in Communist hands. By 1953, 800 million people lived under Communist rule. (2) The Western democracies, however, had reacted to the Communist challenge with speed and effectiveness. Accepting both the political leadership and the economic and military aid of the United States, the West European powers had succeeded in rebuilding their economic base and in restoring their prosperity. After a period of hurried disarmament, they had formed defensive military alliances that culminated in the North Atlantic Pact and had begun to renew their military strength. (3) To the surprise of many diehard colonialists, the shedding of the burden of maintaining colonial rule against the will of the native inhabitants had proved both a psychological and an economic blessing, and only one newly independent country, North Vietnam, had become Communist. Whereas a few of the new states like the Philippines sided openly with the West in the Cold War, most of them attempted to introduce a moderating element in world politics by proclaiming policies of neutralism in foreign relations and of nationalism at home. Thus in 1953 the Western powers, the Communists, and the neutralists could all see reasons for self-congratulation.

Chapter Six DIVIDED EUROPE, 1945-1953

THE opening years of the Cold War were, for Europe, a period of political and economic reconstruction, which was to bring profound changes in almost every part of the Continent. Soviet Russia, while successfully rebuilding its productive base, relapsed into Stalinist autocracy. Eastern Europe was forcibly subjected to the rule of native Communists who accepted political and economic subordination of their own countries to Soviet Russia, a domination so intolerable that Yugoslavia risked direct conflict with the whole Eastern bloc to regain its national autonomy. Occupied Germany was first remolded according to the diverse conceptions of the four occupying powers and was then divided into two semi-independent states, which joined opposite camps in the Cold War. Britain and the Scandinavian countries sought to renovate their societies by a policy of democratic socialism. In France, Italy, and the Benelux countries, the Socialists joined with the Christian Democrats and, at times, with the Communists in carrying out a moderate reform program. Only in neutral Switzerland and in authoritarian Spain and Portugal were few fundamental changes brought about.

STALIN'S LAST YEARS

The ambitious foreign policy of Soviet Russia during the first seven years after the war was extremely costly to the Russian people. To enforce Communist rule in Eastern Europe, to foment revolution in Asia, and to challenge directly the immensely prosperous United States and its West European allies, Russia had to maintain armed forces of four million men, reconstruct its heavy industry and expand its military technology, especially in atomic research, at the expense of consumer goods, and refuse the economic aid of the capitalist countries. Yet Stalin had no hesitation, and apparently little difficulty, in demanding of his exhausted people yet another supreme effort of work and self-sacrifice in order to rival and eventually overcome the ideology of the West.

Wartime Destruction. In 1945, only the most efficient autocracy would have dared demand such effort from a country so devastated. Between 7 and 15 million civilians and some 6 million soldiers had died. Taking into account both deaths and shortage of births, it was calculated that Russia's population would have been 45 million larger by 1950, had there been no war. Twenty-five million were homeless. Over 30 per cent of Russia's farm animals had been killed, and 30 per cent of its tractors had been destroyed. Transportation in the western part of the country was paralyzed by destruction of 40,000 miles of railroad track, 15,000 locomotives, and over 400,000 railroad cars. Factories that had employed 4 million workers were out of action. Probably a quarter of Russia's prewar wealth had been lost. Those who had survived the grueling four years of war were physically exhausted, undernourished, and longing for respite. Nevertheless, on August 19, 1945, the government leaders ordered the drawing up of a fourth Five-Year Plan that would once again give top priority to the construction of heavy industry, particularly in the Urals and Siberia, and to military preparation, especially in atomic research and guided-missile development.

The Plan for National Reconstruction. The Plan for National Reconstruction was announced on March 15, 1946. By 1950, steel production was to reach 25.4 million tons. To increase the electricity supply and to extend irrigation, great power stations were to be built on the Volga and the Dnieper. The system of water transportation was to be extended with construction of the Turkmenian Canal in Central Asia and of the Volga-Don Canal, which completed the link of the Baltic, White, Black, and Caspian seas. The shift of the center of Russian production to the Urals and beyond was to continue. Agricultural production was to be increased by production of tractors and other agricultural machinery, by greater use of motor power, irrigation, soil conservation, and by the planting of vast forest belts for shelter on the steppes of the south. While A. A. Andreyev, the head of the Council for Collective Farm Affairs, undoubtedly helped raise production by enforcing labor requirements on collective farms and by permitting the use of small labor groups, often based on families, within the collective farms, progress was hampered by a terrible drought in 1946, which made impossible the immediate end of bread rationing, and by shortage of workers and transportation. Food shortages in 1949 provided an excuse for Nikita Khrushchev, then chairman of the Council of Ministers in the Ukraine, to attack Andreyev's policies and to demand larger work groups, amalgamation of collective farms, and the transformation of the conditions of peasant life by erection of "farm-cities" (*agrogoroda*) in which the farm workers would enjoy the amenities of city life. After Khrushchev moved to Moscow in 1949 as a secretary of the Central Committee of the Communist party, the amalgamation of collective farms proceeded rapidly, their number falling from 254,000 in 1950 to less than 100,000 in 1952. Agricultural production still failed to meet the assigned level, however, and the food supply in the cities remained extremely poor.

Disciplining of Soviet Life. To force this program to success, harsh discipline was introduced. The black market was severely curtailed by the currency reform of December 1947, by which one new ruble was issued for ten old rubles, a measure that effectively restored the value of current wages. Absenteeism was punished. Turnover in jobs was discouraged by renewed use of labor books, a kind of workers' passport. A vast pool of captive labor was created from German prisoners of war, minority nationalities, and political suspects. The intellectuals were cowed by the *Zhdanovschina,* a campaign against those expressing admiration for the West inaugurated by Stalin's chief aide, Andrei Zhdanov. From 1946 to 1948, Zhdanov lashed out at poets, playwrights, philosophers, economists, and musicians who failed in their duty to subordinate their work to the needs of the Soviet state. The leading Soviet economist, Eugene Varga, was criticized for failing to predict an imminent collapse of the American economy. The great composer, Dmitry Shostakovich, was accused of "homeless cosmopolitanism." The climax was reached in 1948 when Russian biologists were ordered to accept Trofim Lysenko's contention that acquired characteristics could be inherited. A more ludicrous side to the repression of free inquiry was the chauvinistic campaign to show that Russians were responsible for most of the discoveries and inventions of the past century, including the electric light bulb, the radio, the steam engine, and penicillin. Stalin himself gave a new ideological twist to this nationalism when, in criticizing the linguistic theories of the previously accepted authority, Nicholas Marr, he declared that language was independent of economic and social conditions and that the future would see, not the appearance of a "language of socialism," but the triumph of one superior language, Russian. The Russian state, Stalin added, would not wither away with the triumph of communism, but would continue to play a major role in influencing political and economic development.

Stalinist Autocracy. The state machinery was, moreover, to remain the preserve of the Communist party. All possible rivals to the party were brought under control. The influence of the army officer corps was drastically reduced. Marshal Zhukov, defender of Moscow and victor of Berlin, disappeared from public view. Soldiers who had done service in Europe and who had presumably become disaffected as a result were transferred to service in Asia. The party itself, increased in size to over six million by 1947, was urged to undertake political indoctrination of the rest of the population, especially of those areas that had recently been annexed in the West. The work of party members was supplemented by the ubiquitous activity of Lavrenti Beria's secret police, renamed the MVD in 1945, while Stalin preserved total obedience among the highest ranks of the party by arbitrary executions like that of the brilliant young chairman of the State Planning Commission, Nicholas Voznesensky. The party hierarchy was deeply shaken by this evidence that Stalin was again, as in the 1930's, turning against his closest aides. Zhdanov had died in mysterious circumstances in 1948; his supporters were liquidated in 1949 in the so-called Leningrad case; in January 1953, a group of Kremlin doctors, many of them Jewish, were charged with poisoning Zhdanov and other leading Soviet officials and with preparing to poison many army commanders. This "doctors' plot" appeared to be the excuse for a new terror in which Stalin, growing increasingly sadistic in his old age, would strike wildly at those who hoped to succeed him. For several years there had clearly been a competition for the position of Stalin's heir, and when, at the Nineteenth Party Congress in 1952, the main report was given, not by Stalin as was customary, but by Georgi Malenkov, the choice seemed to have been made.

Nineteenth Party Congress. The Nineteenth Party Congress, the first to be held since 1939, proved to be a landmark in other ways. The need to allay the growing discontent throughout the Russian population was clear. There was deep dissatisfaction among both peasants and workers at the failure of living standards to rise. The lowering of liquor prices led to outbreaks of violence officially labeled "hooliganism." The peasants were engaged in passive resistance. A coordinated series of strikes broke out in labor camps throughout the country. The Congress promised greater discipline and self-criticism within the party. The Central Committee's two executive bodies, the Politburo and the Orgburo, which were feared both abroad and in Russia, were abolished and replaced by a twenty-five member Presidium, and the party dropped the name Bolshevik from its official title. Power was to be wielded by the Party Secretaries, now ten in number. A slight relaxation in the contest with the West was promised, following Stalin's statement that the revolutionary flood of the years 1939 to 1952 might now be followed by an "ebb" in which the Soviet Union would consolidate its gains. Malenkov, with his close ties with the class of governmental and industrial administrators might well be expected to pass on some of the benefits of Soviet industrial expansion to the consumer.

On March 1, 1953, Stalin suffered a stroke that affected his brain and paralyzed his right side. He died on the evening of March 5 and was buried on March 9 in Lenin's mausoleum in Red Square in a ceremony attended by the highest Communist officials from all over the world— from China's Chou En-lai to Italy's Togliatti. Stalin's death had incalculable effects upon the development of world communism. In the Soviet Union, it led to a temporary period of collective leadership, slightly better living standards, and relaxation of pressure on the East European satellites and in the Cold War with the West. It made possible a rapprochement with the heretic Yugoslav regime, but led the Chinese Communists to challenge the Russian leadership of the Communist movement. The removal of Stalin's dictatorship led to a demand for intellectual independence and ushered in the "Thaw," that brief period of "mid-winter spring."

THE ESTABLISHMENT OF COMMUNIST RULE IN EASTERN EUROPE, 1945–47

The Process of Communization. The evolution of Eastern Europe in the last years of Stalin's life was almost entirely shaped by the Soviet government. Neither the peoples of that region nor the Western powers were able to prevent the establishment and consolidation of Communist control that had begun behind the Iron Curtain that the Red Army had triumphantly established across Europe from the Baltic to the Adriatic. Between 1945 and 1947 the Communist parties gained complete control of the governments of Poland, Rumania, Bulgaria, Hungary, Yugoslavia, and Albania, and in February 1948 of Czechoslovakia. Between 1948 and 1953 Communist rule was consolidated by destruction of possible opposition, political or religious, by large-scale social and economic reform, and by such rigid enforcement of ideological uniformity that Yugoslavia chose the heresy of Titoism rather than conform.

The establishment of Communist rule between 1945 and 1947 went through three stages, according to Hugh Seton-Watson, in a pattern repeated with minor variations throughout Eastern Europe. The first step was the formation of a "genuine coalition," in which the Communists joined with several of the democratic parties in adopting a program of social reforms, especially of land redistribution, a purge of Fascists, and maintenance of political freedom. During this period, however, the Communists prepared for their future seizure of power by taking of the Ministry of Information, the Ministry of the Interior, and often the Ministry of War, thus gaining control of the means of propaganda, the police and local administration, and the army. The second stage was the "bogus coalition," in which a few hand-picked members of other parties were permitted to share in the government. The popular Peasant and moderate parties were forced into opposition; their political activity was almost entirely circumscribed; and their leaders were in danger of their lives. The final stage was the "monolithic" regime, in which the government was in the hands of a Communist-dominated "Front," created by fusion of left-wing Social Democrats and other reliable groups with the Communist party. Opposition was crushed; one list of candidates picked by the government was presented to the voter in elections; and the organization of all aspects of national life was controlled by the governmental hierarchy.

Transformation of Poland. Poland virtually missed the first stage. The coalition government formed on June 23, 1945 under American and British pressure was far from genuine. Although the Peasant party leader Stanislaus Mikolajczyk was deputy premier and minister of agriculture, all the "levers of power" were in the hands of the Communists or their allies, who controlled the police, the regular army, and the administration of the Oder-Neisse territories annexed from Germany, which proved an important source of patronage. Mikolajczyk attempted to behave as though normal conditions of political freedom existed. He formed a new Polish Peasant party, which he believed was supported by the majority of Poles, and he refused to join the government bloc or to agree that only one list of candidates should be presented at the coming elections. Throughout 1946, his party was under constant harassment from the secret police, official propaganda, and blatant terrorism, and little political campaigning could be done. A first trial of strength between the Polish Peasant party and the Communists occurred on July 28, 1946, when the Poles were asked in a referendum whether they approved abolition of the Upper House, or Senate, the new regime's economic reforms, and the annexation of the Oder-Neisse territories. Mikolajczyk told his supporters to vote against abolition of the Senate as a symbol of their opposition to the new regime, and when the official results showed 68 per cent in favor of abolition, he claimed that the government had falsified the results. The parliamentary elections of January 19, 1947 were preceded by an increase in violence against the Polish Peasant party. Two show trials were instigated to prove that Mikolajczyk was a Germanophile traitor who supported underground activity against the government. New peasant and labor parties were created to split his supporters. His party's candidates were arrested, a million people were disqualified from voting, and the voting districts were redrawn to favor the Communist-dominated Oder-Neisse territories. The Communists also attempted to appeal to the voters by concluding an electoral alliance with the left-wing Socialists, by emphasizing the patriotic origins of the Workers' party in the resistance to Germany, and by capitalizing on the popularity of Wladislaw Gomulka, the party's secretary-general. The results announced by the government gave the government bloc 394 seats and the Peasant party only 28, although Mikolajczyk claimed that his party had received 74 per cent of the vote. Thousands of arrests and many executions for espionage or treason followed the elections, local party offices were closed down, and Mikolajczyk, fearful for his own life, fled from Poland in October. In February 1948 the Polish Peasant party, after purging, was admitted to the government bloc; and, in December 1948, after a year of internal manipulations within the Polish Socialist party, it too was admitted to the bloc. The Polish regime was then in the monolithic stage.

During these years Poland underwent major social and economic changes. With the loss of the eastern territories to Russia and the acquisition of the Oder-Neisse territories, Poland had changed its ethnic and economic character. Its racial minorities had been reduced from a prewar figure of 9 million to only 500,000; its Catholic population had increased from 75 to 98 per cent, although many were not practicing Catholics. Economically, the boundary changes were of great value. The

German lands annexed included the great ports of Stettin and Danzig, the Silesian coal fields and industrial complex, and rich and empty farmlands on which almost 5 million Poles were settled by 1948. Destruction in Poland was estimated at more than $18 billion, however, and economic restoration was urgent. The receipt of emergency aid from the United Nations Relief and Rehabilitation Administration valued at $500,-000 helped the Poles through the worst postwar months; and between 1947 and 1949 a Three-Year Plan helped bring industrial production up to the prewar level. Particular emphasis was laid upon the coexistence in Poland of private industry with state and cooperative enterprises, although the nationalization laws of 1944–46 brought all German plants, the mines, and the power, communications, armaments, sugar, flour, and textile industries, and any factory employing more than fifty persons, under state ownership. By 1948, the private sector operated only 6 per cent of Polish industry. Land reform was extremely popular. More than 6 million hectares [1] were redistributed, usually in small farms; and, partly owing to Gomulka's opposition, collectivization was not adopted, even on a voluntary basis, until 1948. Thus, a social revolution was carried out in Poland by expropriation of large- and medium-sized landowners and factory owners; but the emphasis on Polish nationalism against Germany, the postponement of collectivization, and Gomulka's opposition to the creation of the Cominform in September 1947 indicated that at least some Polish Communists believed that there might be a national road to communism. They were soon to be the object of a Stalinist purge.

The Monolithic Regime in Rumania. Rumania had known genuine coalition government between August 1944, when King Michael overthrew the Antonescu regime, and March 1945, when he was compelled by Soviet Deputy Foreign Minister Vyshinsky to accept a Democratic Front government under Dr. Petru Groza, in which the Communists held the Ministries of the Interior and Justice. Groza attempted to strengthen the position of his government by introducing a far-reaching land reform and a purge of the government and local administration, while the Soviet government aided him by returning northern Transylvania from Hungary, and by giving his government legal recognition in August. The British and American governments refused to do so. Encouraged by their firmness, King Michael retired to his mountain palace

---

[1] One hectare = 2.47 acres.

at Sinaia in the Carpathians and the opposition parties, led by the Peasant party of Iuliu Maniu, demonstrated in Bucharest in November in favor of the king and of the Western powers. Pressured by the British and American foreign ministers at the Moscow Conference in December 1945 to broaden Groza's government, the Soviet foreign minister agreed that Groza should admit a representative of the National Peasant party and of the Liberal party. Although this had no practical effect on governmental policy in Rumania, the British and American governments both recognized the new regime in February 1946. That year both the National Peasant and Liberal parties were broken by intimidation, propaganda, and repression of their political activity; and, in the parliamentary elections held in November 19, 1946, the government bloc was officially awarded 348 seats to 32 for the National Peasant party and 3 for the Liberals. The following year, the National Peasant party was banned, and Maniu, seventy-four years old, was condemned to solitary confinement for life. In November 1947, the left-wing Socialists merged with the Communists in a United Workers' party. King Michael, who had been decorated by Stalin in 1944, was ordered to abdicate in November 1947, but was permitted to leave the country safely. After new elections in March 1948, Rumania became a People's Republic. The new government of the renamed People's Democratic Front included such veteran Communists as Ana Pauker as foreign minister and Gheorghiu-Dej as minister of national economy, a clear indication that the monolithic stage had been reached.

Dimitrov's Bulgaria. In Bulgaria, the Fatherland Front government formed in September 1944 was a genuine coalition of four left-wing parties, but it did not last long. When opposition to Communist tactics appeared within two member parties of the Fatherland Front, the Agrarian Union and the Social Democratic party, both were forcibly seized by Communist sympathizers. Anti-Communist leaders of the Agrarian Union were compelled to resign. The leader of the right-wing Socialists was arrested and imprisoned for five years; the left-wing Socialists were obliged to accept a leader picked by the Communists. The third member party of the Fatherland Front, the *Zveno,* was subjugated in 1946. By midsummer, over a third of the party's leaders were in prison or concentration camps. Elections held in November 1945 and October 1946 were run in an atmosphere of terrorism, and the results were rigged. In both cases the Fatherland Front won three quarters of the seats in parliament. In September 1946, King Simeon went into exile after 96 per cent of the electorate voted for abolition of the monarchy.

Personal power akin to Stalin's was exercised for the next three years by the new premier, Georgi Dimitrov. Dimitrov had first come to international notice when he was tried by the Nazis in 1933 for complicity in the burning of the Reichstag. After defending himself vigorously, he had been released, and took refuge in Russia where he became a Soviet citizen and eventually a member of the Supreme Soviet and secretary-general of the Comintern. Throughout the war, he broadcast to Bulgaria from Russia. He returned home in November 1945, a thoroughly reliable instrument of Stalin's wishes, resumed Bulgarian citizenship, and organized the taming of the parties allied with the Communists. Once premier, he mercilessly used arbitrary arrests, torture, and show trials against all possible opposition. In August 1947 the former Agrarian Union Secretary Petkov was found guilty of treason by a panel of three Communist judges and, despite protests from the British and American governments, was hanged. Ironically, his father, a Liberal premier, had been murdered in 1906, and his brother, an Agrarian, in 1924. The remaining leader of opposition within the Socialist party, Lulchev, was condemned to fifteen years in prison, and in 1948 the Socialist party was merged with the Communist party. Dimitrov's personal rule continued until July 1949 when he died during a visit to Moscow for medical reasons. His body was embalmed and placed in a mausoleum similar to Lenin's in the main square of Sofia, Bulgaria.

Delayed Victory in Hungary. In Hungary, the Communists started at a slight disadvantage, owing to universal dislike for the Russians, to the presence of British and American troops in nearby Austria and Czechoslovakia, to the survival of the traditional cadres in the army and bureaucracy, and especially to the great popularity of the Smallholder party. Even the memories of the Béla Kun failure in 1919 reminded the Communist leaders to move cautiously. A vast program of land reform introduced by the coalition government of General Miklos led to the seizure of more than 7 million acres which were redistributed among 600,000 people, and, although controlled by the Communist minister of agriculture, Imre Nagy, the land reform increased the popularity of the Smallholder party at least as much as that of the Communist party. Free elections held in the municipalities in October 1945 gave the Smallholders 51 per cent of the vote, and in national elections in November they won three-fifths of the seats in parliament. When Hungary became a republic in January 1946, Smallholder leader Zoltán Tildy became its first president, and a new government was formed under another Smallholder, Ferenc Nagy. He bowed to Communist insistence that the Ministry of the Interior be given to Imre Nagy.

The following two years saw the destruction of all the parties opposed to Communist hegemony. The police, the bureaucracy, and the trade unions were brought under Communist influence. In 1946, several members of the Smallholder party were arrested, confessed to committing treason, and implicated the party's secretary-general, Béla Kovács. On February 25, 1947, Kovács went voluntarily to the police to answer questions, but the following day he was taken away by Soviet occupation forces and died in their captivity. In May, Premier Ferenc Nagy was ordered to return from a Swiss vacation to answer treason charges. He refused to return and was replaced as premier by a supporter of the Communists, Lajos Dinnyes. Tildy himself was compelled to resign the présidency in August 1948. The weaker opposition parties were soon cowed, and compliant leaders were put in office. In the elections of August 1947, the Communists and their allies got 60 per cent of the vote; more opposition leaders fled from the country; and in June 1948 the Communist party merged with what remained of the Socialists. Communist domination was proved in the new elections of May 1949, when the government list received 95.6 per cent of the vote.

Elimination of Opposition in Yugoslavia and Albania. In Yugoslavia and Albania, the Communist party was entrenched in power from the time when the German armies were expelled. Tito's cabinet of March 1945, which included several politicians from the prewar parties, was already bogus. These politicians found themselves unable to organize meetings or even to suggest alternative courses of action to those adopted by the government bloc. Šubašić resigned as foreign minister in September. When elections were held in November 1945, the government list of candidates was approved by a 96 per cent vote, according to government figures. Tito at once construed this vote to mean that King Peter should be ousted, and Yugoslavia became a People's Republic on November 29, 1945. In 1946, General Mihailović was found guilty of collaborating with the Germans and was shot. Professor Jovanović, a Serbian Agrarian leader who had offered some mild criticism, was expelled from his university chair and from his party, and in 1947 was

found guilty of treason. During these years Tito was undoubtedly popular with the mass of the Yugoslav people. To the glamor of his partisan
leadership was added the appeal of expropriation of most large- and
medium-sized industries and land reform based largely on seizure of
property of Germans and of the churches. National pride was sated by
Tito's obvious ambition to exercise hegemony in the Balkans, by his territorial demands on Italy, Austria, Greece, and Bulgaria, and by his
determination to industrialize Yugoslavia even against Soviet advice.
When he quarreled with Stalin in May 1948, Tito knew that internally,
at least, he was unassailable. In Albania, the Communist leader Enver
Hoxha had destroyed the political opposition in the civil war of 1944.
Elections were held in December 1945. No opposition candidates were
permitted. The government block received 93 per cent of the vote. The
new assembly declared Albania a republic, and King Zog went into comfortable exile in Egypt. The few remaining leaders who seemed capable
of opposition were arrested and tried for spying in 1946, and as a result
most of the Western countries, including the United States and Britain,
broke diplomatic relations with Hoxha's government. Of all the East
European countries, Yugoslavia and Albania seemed the most convinced opponents of the Western democracies.

The Czech Modus Vivendi. Czechoslovakia, on the other hand, at
first succeeded in maintaining good relations with both sides in the Cold
War. The genuine coalition, which lasted from March 1945 to February
1948, included members of six prewar parties. With Beneš as president
and Jan Masaryk as foreign minister, the Western powers felt that Czech
democracy was secure. The Communists, however, controlled the police
through their minister of the interior, the radio through the minister of
information, and the schools through the minister of education. Property
confiscated from the almost three million Germans who were expelled
from the border areas permitted the Communist minister of agriculture
to build up a solid geographical base of support, just as the Polish Communists were doing in the Oder-Neisse territories. The Soviet forces permitted the local Communists to take control of regional administration
in most of the country, before they were withdrawn in December 1945.
When free elections were held in May 1946, the Communist party received the largest vote (38 per cent), and the Communist leader Klement Gottwald became premier. Debate in parliament remained free,
however; the non-Communist parties were able to conduct political ac-

tivity relatively unmolested; and the law courts enforced impartial justice. In June 1947, however, the Czechoslovak government officially accepted the invitation of the British and French governments to attend
the Paris conference of those European states that wished to receive
Marshall Aid. But on July 4–8 Premier Gottwald and Foreign Minister
Masaryk, during a visit to Moscow, were informed by Stalin that acceptance of Marshall Aid was incompatible with the Soviet-Czech Treaty,
and somewhat ignominiously they announced their withdrawal from the
conference. Stalin's decision that the East European countries should
not participate in the Marshall Plan marked the beginning of a crack-
down in Eastern Europe that lasted until Stalin's death in 1953.

CONSOLIDATION OF COMMUNIST UNIFORMITY IN EASTERN EUROPE, 1947–53

Communist Coup d'État in Czechoslovakia. The first country to feel
the increased pressure was Czechoslovakia, where the Communists had
clearly received instructions to put an end to the independence of the
allied parties. After several months of crisis, the non-Communist members of the government decided in February 1948 to challenge the Communists openly. When the Communist minister of the interior replaced
eight Prague police chiefs with his own nominees, a majority of Gottwald's cabinet ordered him to reinstate them. When he was supported by
the premier, all the non-Communist ministers except the Social Democrats resigned en masse, apparently in the hope that President Beneš
would dismiss Gottwald. Their tactics proved disastrous. Guided by
Soviet Deputy Foreign Minister V. A. Zorin, who had opportunely arrived two days earlier, the Communists called armed bands of factory
workers into the city where they occupied non-Communist party headquarters and demonstrated in the streets. On February 24, a general
strike was proclaimed and Communist Action Committees aided by
workers' militia seized public offices, including the telephone and
telegraph, throughout the country. Old and sick, President Beneš decided not to risk calling upon the army and thus precipitating civil war
and possible Soviet armed intervention. On February 25, he agreed to
the formation of a new government in which all key positions were held
by Communists, with the exception of the Foreign Ministry where Jan
Masaryk courageously attempted to carry on. On March 10, however,

he was found with a broken spine in the courtyard of his Ministry. Beneš resigned on June 6 and died in September. Gottwald became president in his place, and a fellow traveler, Antonin Zápotocki, became premier. The elections held on schedule in May gave the government list an 89.3 per cent vote. From being the most independent of the satellite states, Czechoslovakia suddenly had become the most obedient.

Yugoslavia's Defection. Stalin's decision four months later to bring about the subordination of the Yugoslav Communists, however, had the effect of converting the most orthodox of his adherents into a heretic. Tension had existed between Yugoslavia and the Soviet Union since the end of the war. The Yugoslavs resented the arrogance of Soviet officers assigned to advise the Yugoslav Army. The Soviet-Yugoslav joint-stock companies set up in 1947 were regarded as a form of Russian exploitation of the Yugoslav economy, the first two companies set up giving the Russians control of all Yugoslavia's air transport and of Danube shipping. The Soviet experts had shown contempt for Yugoslav industrialization plans; and Soviet agents had unsuccessfully attempted to gain control of the secret police. The Russians too had their grievances. The Yugoslav Communists ignored Soviet advice and considered their national interest before that of the Communist bloc. Tito apparently had plans for hegemony over the Balkans, where he already had a satellite in Albania. Above all, Tito asserted his equality with Stalin, by resisting Soviet efforts to form spy networks in Yugoslavia, by ignoring the complaints of the Soviet ambassador, and by objecting to the trade relations the Soviet government was attempting to impose upon him. Although Stalin asserted that Tito had failed to eliminate the kulaks, was too slow in collectivization, and was too kindly to the bourgeoisie, these complaints were less relevant to Yugoslavia than to the other East European states. Tito represented an independent power within the Soviet bloc, and for that reason he had to be cowed.

On March 18, 1948, the Soviet government withdrew its military and economic advisers from Yugoslavia. On March 20, Tito expressed concern that the Soviet government should find cause for complaint. The Soviet reply added further details, objecting especially to criticism of Russia and to Yugoslav secrecy on economic matters, but transforming the quarrel by accusing the Yugoslav leadership of incorrect doctrine, of lacking feeling for the class struggle, and of falling into Menshevik heresy. Again, the Yugoslavs expressed surprise and regret. On May 4, the Soviet note attacked Tito and his Vice-Premier Kardelj personally: "Comrades Tito and Kardelj, it seems, do not understand that this method of groundless denial of facts and documents can never be convincing but merely laughable." On June 28, 1948, the Cominform expelled Yugoslavia from membership, and castigated its leaders: They had "pursued an incorrect line on the main questions of home and foreign policy. . . . An undignified policy of defaming Soviet military experts and discrediting the Soviet Union has been carried out in Yugoslavia. . . . The leaders of the Communist Party of Yugoslavia have taken a stand unworthy of Communists, and have begun to identify the foreign policy of the Soviet Union with the foreign policy of the imperialist powers. . . . Instead of honestly accepting this [Soviet] criticism and taking the Bolshevik path of correcting these mistakes, the leaders of the Communist Party of Yugoslavia, suffering from boundless ambition, arrogance and conceit met this criticism with belligerence and hostility. . . . In view of all this, the Central Committee of the Communist Party of Yugoslavia has placed itself and the Yugoslavia Party outside the family of the fraternal Communist Parties, outside the united Communist front and consequently outside the ranks of the Information Bureau." "Healthy elements, loyal to Marxism-Leninism" inside the Yugoslav Communist party were invited to remove Tito and his supporters. Stalin evidently believed that this denunciation would be enough to bring about Tito's ouster. When the Yugoslav party and people rallied in Tito's support, Stalin directed a wild propaganda barrage against him. When rumors were spread that the Russians were fomenting internal revolution, Tito purged the army and police. Economic boycott followed. By the end of 1949, Yugoslavia's trade with Russia and the East European satellites had almost come to a halt, and shortages of all kinds were reducing the already low living standards. Once again, Stalin's policy backfired. Tito turned to the West, without giving up his claims to be a good Communist, thereby presenting the especially dangerous example of an alternative, national road to communism. In 1949, he ended his aid to the Greek Communists and returned Greek prisoners, made overtures to Italy, and sought to improve relations with Britain and the United States. A loan of $20 million from the Export-Import Bank was followed by the grant of surplus American food when drought reduced the Yugoslav harvest. In November 1950, President Truman persuaded Congress to allot $38 million for emergency food shipments to Yugoslavia. By 1955, Tito had received $500 million in American aid, as well as large credits from Britain. Internally, he further outraged Stalin by adopting the very policies of which he had been accused in 1948. Collectivization was halted, industrial control was decentralized, and some freedom of the market was introduced.

The Pattern of Communist Uniformity. The failure to cow Tito only persuaded Stalin to increase the demand for uniformity in the remaining satellites. The new pattern, according to Zbigniew K. Brzezinski, stressed four characteristics: the political supremacy of the Communist party; intensification of the class struggle to purge not only known class enemies but dangerous elements within the party; socialization of agriculture; and rapid industrialization. The whole program was to be based upon Stalin's supposedly successful transformation of Russia in the 1930's.

The domination of the Communist party had been realized in all the East European countries by 1948, with the destruction of the leading peasant parties, the splitting of the Socialist parties, and the incorporation of the docile rumps of the former parties with the Communist party into national fronts. The power of the Communist party was felt in every side of life. New curricula were introduced in the schools and universities; artists were expected to follow the Russian forms of Socialist Realism; huge "gingerbread" buildings, like the Printing Trades Building in Bucharest and the party headquarters in Sofia reflected the taste of Stalin's Moscow University. Concentration camps in large numbers provided labor for large-scale public works. Everywhere the secret police came to exercise terror, not only over the population in general, but also over party members.

The most immediate task for the secret police was to weed out possible Titoists, usually among those who had spent the war years in the resistance at home rather than in Moscow. The most obvious suspect was the Polish party secretary, Wladislaw Gomulka, who had opposed the formation of the Cominform in September 1947 and had at the time expressed doubts about Poland's need for collectivization of agriculture. He emphasized his deviationism in June 1948 by suggesting that Poland might embark on an individually Polish Communist line. Gomulka, however, was opposed by the majority of the Polish Communist leaders, led by President Bierut. On being censured, he recanted slightly, but lost the vice-premiership in January 1949 and his membership in the Central Committee in November. In July 1951 he was jailed without a trial and remained imprisoned until December 1954. No show trials followed, but 370,000 members were expelled from the Communist party. In Albania, the vice-premier and minister of the interior, Koçi Xoxe, who was suspected of having had too close ties with Yugoslavia, was arrested in November 1948. At his trial six months later, he confessed to treasonable plotting with the Yugoslavs and was executed. The Hungarian minister of the interior, Laszlo Rajk, was arrested in June 1949. He later confessed to being a spy for Admiral Horthy, the Gestapo, the United States, and Tito, and was hanged. The Bulgarian vice-premier, Traicho Kostov, and ten associates were arrested for anti-Russian activities in June 1949. Kostov repudiated his confession at his trial in December, thereby causing something of a sensation, but was found guilty and hanged. In Czechoslovakia, the foreign minister, Vladimir Clementis, and the former secretary-general of the Communist party, Rudolf Slansky, were tried in November 1952, in a trial notable for its anti-Semitism, and were hanged in December. Huge purges of the Communist leadership accompanied these trials, reaching its height in Czechoslovakia where more than half of the Central Committee was purged. By 1953, the remaining East European leaders were rivaling each other in their subservience to Stalin's wishes.

The purge trials were accompanied by an attack upon the Catholic Church in Eastern Europe, which was regarded as the one major obstacle in the Communist party's absolute rule. Tito had provided the example as early as 1946, when Archbishop Stepinac of Zagreb was tried for maintaining relations with the Fascist regime of Pavelić during the war, and was sentenced to sixteen years' imprisonment. Tito won favor in the West by releasing him in 1951. After a long struggle with the Communist regime, Archbishop Wyszynski, primate of the Polish Church, was arrested in 1953, following the imprisonment of a number of his bishops. Archbishop Beran of Prague was interned in March 1951. And, in the most notorious trial of all, Cardinal Joseph Mindszenty, the head of the Church in Hungary, a tough, outspoken opponent of the regime, was accused in February 1949 of trying to restore the monarchy, of illegal currency trafficking, and of plotting with the United States. He was sentenced to life imprisonment. Thus, the power of the Catholic Church was considerably reduced by the persecution of its

(*Top*) Hitler and Mussolini conferring at Hitler's Eastern Front headquarters, August 1941. Left to right, Italian chief Ugo Cavalerro, Mussolini, Hitler, General Wilhelm Keitel (behind Hitler), General Alfred Jodl, and Major Christian. (*Bottom*) Prime Minister Churchill inspecting damage done to the House of Commons by the heavy German air raid over London on May 10, 1941. (*Middle*) The Big Three at Yalta, February 1945 —Prime Minister Winston Churchill, President Franklin D. Roosevelt, and Premier Joseph Stalin. In the rear are Admiral Sir Andrew Cunningham, Admiral Ernest King, Admiral William D. Leahy, and other high ranking Allied officers.

(*Above*) The Allied landing on the French coast, D-Day, June 6, 1944. (*Below*) Parisians scattering for cover as a German sniper fires into the crowd from a building on the Place de la Concorde, August 26, 1944, the day after the liberation of Paris.

(*Above*) Student fighters in Budapest during the Hungarian uprising of 1956. In the background are knocked-out Russian tanks. (*Bottom*) Hungarian refugees in a refugee center near Vienna, Austria, in November 1956, awaiting U.N. arrangements for emigration to other countries. (*Right*) Building the Berlin Wall in 1961. The barbed wire used was enough to encircle the entire globe. "The Wall is our success," said Soviet Premier Khrushchev when he visited East Berlin. It stands as a grim and hideous reminder of the division of the old German capital.

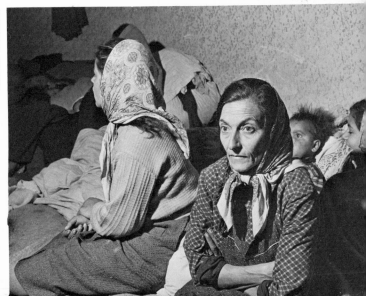

(*Above*) French Premier Charles de Gaulle speaking at Brazzaville, French Equatorial Africa, August 23, 1958, on a tour of French African colonies to outline his new Constitution. (*Below, left*) The Union Jack is hauled down at Uhuru Stadium for the last time as Kenya becomes independent (1964). (*Below, right*) Forward portion of a Swedish supply caravan passing the UN flag at the United Nations Emergency Force Swedish Camp at the Egypt-Israeli demarcation line, March 1957.

(*Above*) A worker of the German Development Service shows Tanzanians in East Africa how to repair a Volkswagen motor. (*Right*) A Renault assembly plant in the Ivory Coast Republic provides industrial employment for native workers. (*Below*) Retreading tires in a factory in Ceylon under the Colombo plan of economic and technical aid from a group of Western nations.

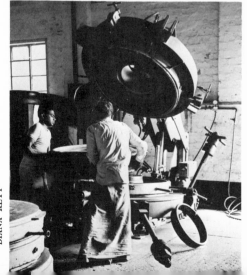

UNITED PRESS INTERNATIONAL

(*Above*) Kuwait University in the oil-rich Arab state of Kuwait (formerly British), which now has the highest per capita income in the world. The great wealth of the country which comes from the oil royalties paid by foreign companies is reflected in the modern buildings which have sprung up almost overnight to replace the shabby village mud huts and in the many trees which have been planted and are well tended, since no trees grow naturally in Kuwait's soil. (*Below*) Moscow's new Kalinin Avenue with its skyscrapers lit up in November 1967 to celebrate the 50th anniversary of the Russian Revolution. The building at the left, with the lighted anniversary figure 50, is the headquarters of Comecon, the Eastern equivalent of the Common Market.

BRUNO BARBEY FOR MAGNUM

World War II destruction and postwar recovery: Two cathedrals, ruined by devastating air raids over their cities, have deliberately been left standing as symbols of the senseless destruction of war, with the modern church edifices rising beside them. (*Top*) The shell of the 14th century Cathedral of St. Michael in Coventry, England, and the new building, connected to the ruins of the old by a canopied arch. The center of this manufacturing town, destroyed in an 11-hour air raid in November 1940, has been rebuilt according to a modern plan. (*Bottom*) The ruined Kaiser Wilhelm Cathedral in Berlin, with the modern campanile at one side of it and the low, octagonal cathedral auditorium on the other side. Light enters the cathedral through 22,000 glass blocks. The new buildings at the left are part of the great Europa shopping center.

(*Above*) France's most powerful nuclear plant at Chinon on the Loire River. (*Below*) Tank "farm" at the Genoa, Italy, terminal of the Central Europe crude oil pipeline, built by Ente Nazionale Idrocarburi (ENI), the Italian government-controlled hydrocarbons agency. Tankers bringing crude oil across the mediterranean from the Middle East dock at Genoa, the oil is transferred to the tank farm for storage, and from there it is conveyed to refineries in Italy, Switzerland, and Germany by a continuous pipeline that runs from Genoa through Switzerland to the terminal at Ingolstadt, Germany. In some places it was necessary to tunnel the line through the Alps. By agreement the pipeline is used by ENI, Esso, Shell, and British Petroleum. The photo shows a new tank under construction in the foreground, and in the background a complex of new apartment houses in Genoa, and the Mediterranean Sea.

leaders, by state control of the education system, and by confiscation of Church lands in the reform programs.

In agriculture, subservience to the Soviet model meant immediate collectivization. Whereas the land-reform programs had wiped out the large landowners, they won peasant support by creation of small- and medium-sized individual holdings. In 1948–49, every East European satellite adopted a collectivization law and began to apply it in 1950. The wealthy peasants, or kulaks, were to be driven out by heavy taxation, increased production deliveries, and, when necessary, by violence. Although efforts to force the peasants to accept common ownership of land and machinery in collective farms provoked great resentment, collectivization was pushed with varying degrees of determination. By 1953, 62 per cent of farmland was collectivized in Bulgaria, 48 per cent in Czechoslovakia, though only 17 per cent in Poland. The object of the long-term industrial-development plans was to copy the Soviet Union's success in turning agrarian States into industrial states. The emphasis in all these plans was the creation of heavy industry, especially steel, engineering, chemical, and power plants; the increase in the size of the industrial proletariat as compared to the peasantry; and the rapid achievement of extremely high production goals. Poland, for example, claimed in three years to have almost doubled its industrial output. Undoubtedly, these countries achieved large increases in production of steel, coal, machinery, chemicals, and hydroelectric power, but there were great weaknesses. The consumer industries were largely slighted; agricultural production trailed well behind; and the creation of similar heavy industries in all these countries indicated that, as in the interwar years, national autarky in economic matters might yet lead to wasteful competition and overproduction. Although the Soviet government claimed to aim at the creation of an integrated economic bloc, in practice the Soviet government concentrated on its own interests in the satellites, from receipt of reparations to profits from the joint-stock companies. When the Council for Mutual Economic Assistance (Comecon) was formed in Moscow in January 1949 to organize the East European states in an Eastern counterpart of the Organization for European Economic Cooperation, it did nothing at first to encourage rational economic development or regional specialization, but rather became Stalin's instrument for conducting the economic boycott of Yugoslavia. During

Stalin's lifetime, the opportunity for creating an East European Common Market was ignored.

When Stalin died in 1953, there was no force in the East European satellites that could challenge either Soviet autocracy or the local Communist hegemony. Social and industrial revolutions of enormous scope had been carried out, and a revolution in agricultural ownership and production was beginning. Yet even in the ranks of convinced Communists there was doubt about the wisdom of Stalin's policies. Onetime heroes in the different national struggles for communism had been tortured and executed. The secret police was taking precedence over the party. Peasant resistance to collectivization had left the workers short of food. Industrialization had done little to raise living standards, which still, eight years after the end of the war, were abysmally low. A potentially dangerous situation existed in the satellites when Stalin's repressive hand was finally lifted.

GERMANY UNDER OCCUPATION, 1945-49

The Soviet and Western spheres of influence, in theory at least, merged in Germany. During the war, Roosevelt, Churchill, and Stalin had agreed that, pending the conclusion of a peace treaty, they would govern Germany jointly, through an Allied Control Council consisting of the commanders-in-chief of the four zones of occupation. The administration of Germany was to be carried out by a four-power Allied *Kommandatura* in Berlin, and by the military governments of the four zones. In fact, common policy was only established for demilitarization, dismantling of surplus industrial equipment, deconcentration of industry, and denazification. In all other matters, the four zones developed their own policies, and the dismemberment of Germany, which had never been accepted in principle, soon became a political reality.

Demilitarization and Dismantling. For the first months of the occupation, while the Allies were busy with the removal of the remnants of the Nazi regime and with the urgent tasks of economic reconstruction, the joint administration continued to function. Disarmament proceeded smoothly. The German soldiers surrendered meekly, and in the British and American zones most of them had been demobilized by 1946. The French were determined to use the labor of their million prisoners, and many Germans did not leave France until 1948. The Russians held be-

GERMANY UNDER OCCUPATION, 1945

Map labels: NORTH SEA, DENMARK, BALTIC SEA, U.S.S.R., BREMEN ENCLAVE (U.S. ZONE), Danzig, SOVIET ZONE, Vistula, NETH., BRITISH ZONE, Elbe, POLAND, Berlin (Joint Occupation), BELG., Rhine R., Cologne, Leipzig, Dresden, Oder, Neisse R., Breslau, Bonn, LUX., FRENCH ZONE, Frankfurt, AMERICAN ZONE, CZECHOSLOVAKIA, SAAR, Strasbourg, FRANCE, ZONE, Munich, Freiburg, AUSTRIA, HUNGARY, SWITZ., ITALY

Legend: Annexed by U. S. S. R. / Annexed by Poland

tween one and three and a half million prisoners and kept many of them in work camps in Russia for more than a decade. Where military equipment and stores remaining could not be assigned as reparations, they were destroyed. Demilitarization also implied the destruction of Germany's war industry. A subcommittee of the Control Council attempted to solve this difficult question by defining the "Level of Industry" that would be permitted in Germany: Germany was to be permitted to produce 5.8 million tons of steel a year; all armaments industry was to be dismantled; industries like chemicals, which were useful for either war or peace production, were to be restricted; and obviously innocuous industries, like textiles, were to be unrestricted. Dismantling was also to provide reparations in kind for twenty of the victorious powers, the United States having waived any claims to reparations. The Soviet Union was never able to persuade its Allies to accept its claim of $10 billion worth of reparations, but it was agreed that Russia should take reparations for itself and Poland from the Soviet zone and that it should receive in addition 25 per cent of the dismantled equipment of the Western zones, paying for three-fifths of that equipment with food shipments. Vast quantities of movable goods and industrial equipment were shipped to Russia in the early months of the occupation, much of it proving unusable. By 1946, the Russians had decided to keep the factories functioning in Germany and to take reparations by seizure of current production. Dismantling in the Western zones continued until 1951. German sources estimated that dismantling reduced the annual national product by $1,347,619,000 (1936 price level), but that the three Western zones accounted for only $314,285,000 of that total. In the Western zones, dismantling probably reduced German productive capacity by 5 per cent, but these losses were replaced with new equipment by Marshall Aid. In the Soviet zone, where dismantling may have reduced capacity up to 45 per cent, no Marshall Aid was received, and industrial revival lagged disastrously as a result. When all reparations, including the confiscation of the German Merchant Marine, the German gold reserves, and German patents are included, total Soviet reparations receipts may have exceeded $8 billion, compared with Western reparations receipts of $517 million. Whereas German patents and gold were of obvious value, much of the equipment dismantled was out of date or too difficult to reassemble, and many of the supposed benefits of dismantling proved illusory.

Deconcentration of Industry. The Potsdam Agreement had also required joint action on the decartelization and deconcentration of German industry. "As soon as possible," it stated, "the German economy should be decentralized to eliminate the excessive present concentration, characterized particularly by cartels, patronal syndicates, trusts, and other forms of monopolies." After deciding to confiscate the property of the great chemical trust, I. G. Farben, and of the Krupp Coal and Steel Company, the Allied Control Council was unable to agree upon a joint law for deconcentration of German industry. The Soviet administration dealt with the problem drastically. By 1946, 40 per cent of Soviet zone industry was nationalized, this figure rising to 62 per cent by 1953. Two hundred firms that had belonged to the German state or the Nazi party were transferred to Russian ownership. The factories under private ownership were maintained under strict controls through production quotas and Communist party supervision. In the Western zones, cartels in restraint of trade were broken up, and an attempt was made to end the power of the six great steel companies that controlled 94 per cent of

German production by dividing them into twenty-four supposedly competing companies. A special effort was made to destroy the family empires of the Krupps and the Thyssens, who were regarded as major supporters of the Nazi war effort; but on emerging from an Allied jail in 1951, Alfried Krupp was able to hang on to most of his industrial empire, which by 1955 had a turnover of $230 million. By 1959, the Thyssen family had regained control of 24 per cent of the Ruhr's crude-steel production. In the Western zones, therefore, deconcentration and decartelization were a complete failure; German experts replied that it was better so, since the program had the aim of breaking up efficient rational productive units essential to German economic revival.

The Nuremberg Trials. The most notable example of joint action was in the trial of major war criminals at Nuremberg between November 1945 and October 1946. The International Military Tribunal consisted of a British, American, French, and Soviet judge and was presided over by the British member Lord Justice Lawrence. It was empowered, by a charter issued by the four occupying powers in London in August 1945, to judge whether the major surviving Nazi leaders and German groups such as the Reich government, the General Staff, and the SS, had committed either crimes against peace, war crimes, or crimes against humanity. Meticulous preparation of documents in evidence was made by Allied investigating teams, and over a million pages of evidence were presented, including the most startling proof of human cruelty ever seen in a law court. On October 1, 1946, Goering, Ribbentrop, Frick, Seyss-Inquart, Streicher, Frank, Kaltenbrunner, Sauckel, Keitel, Jodl, Rosenberg, and Bormann (who was in hiding) were condemned to death by hanging; Hess, Raeder, and Funk were sentenced to life imprisonment, Speer and Schirach to twenty years, Neurath to fifteen, Doenitz to ten; Fritzsche, Schacht, and Papen were acquitted, but were subsequently sentenced in German courts to terms of imprisonment. The Tribunal also proclaimed the "criminal character" of the Nazi Leadership Corps, the SS, the SD, and the Gestapo, but not of the German General Staff. Although all the niceties of judicial procedure were scrupulously observed at the trial, it came under great criticism, not least from Western lawyers, for creating the precedent of "victors' justice." It was pointed out that such categories as "crimes against humanity" or of "aggression" were not recognized by international law; that obedience to orders was not accepted as exoneration, even though disobedience would have brought death to those pleading moral scruples in the Nazi dictatorship; and that condemnation of groups rather than individuals introduced the novel principle of collective guilt. Similar war-crimes trials continued in all four zones, and the isolated cases remaining were taken over after the end of the occupation by the German authorities.

Denazification. The process of denazification had also been ordered by the Potsdam Agreement, which required that "all members of the Nazi party who had been more than nominal participants in its activities and all other persons hostile to Allied purposes shall be removed from public and semi-public office, and from positions of responsibility in important private undertakings." Since one-fifth of the German population had been members of the Nazi party or dependent organizations, the task of identifying the dangerous persons and of running the administration of the country without them was enormous. In 1946, the Allied Control Council attempted to formulate a uniform system for all four zones, by dividing those proven to be implicated in the Nazi regime into five categories—major offenders, offenders, lesser offenders, followers, and persons exonerated. Before then, however, each of the zones had worked out its own system. The Russians made use of the German anti-Fascist committees in their denazification procedure, but emphasized that they regarded the capitalist structure of society as the principal source of Nazism. Since they were transforming the social structure of their zone, they were incidentally eliminating Nazism. They therefore accepted into important offices and into the Communist-dominated Socialist Unity party many ex-Nazis who gave proof of their willingness to work with the new system. By 1948, denazification was complete in the Soviet zone. The military government officers of the three Western zones found themselves overwhelmed in a mass of paperwork as they attempted to classify the millions of Germans according to the answers they gave to the 133 questions on official *Fragebogen,* or questionnaires. Only by making use of reliable Germans of anti-Nazi, or often of religious, background was the process speeded up. By 1949, over three million Germans had been examined in the American zone and two million in the British. The slowness of the procedure and the punishment of those found guilty by monetary fines, often of quite small amounts paid in inflated currency, brought the whole procedure into disrepute, and, many thoughtful Germans felt, put an end to the hope of a moral regeneration in the German people that recognition of their own guilt would have brought about. Where such philosophers as Karl Jaspers or historians like Friedrich Meinecke were calling upon the Germans to recognize the forces in their character and their nation that had produced Nazism, many came to feel that guilt was a category invented by the occupying powers.

Economic Policy in French and Soviet Zones. There were thus common policies for demilitarization, deconcentration, and denazification agreed upon in the Allied Control Council, although their implementation differed from zone to zone. Major differences of opinion existed from the beginning of the occupation upon the economic and political reconstruction of the country. Although the Potsdam Agreement had specified that Germany should be treated as an economic unit, neither the French nor the Russians were willing to allow this to happen. The first vetoes in the Control Council were exercised by the French, to prevent the creation of a centralized German transport agency, centralized trade unions, and free passage of Germans across zonal boundaries. The French intended to exploit their zone economically without interference from the other occupying powers, by recuperation of French goods, dismantling of factories, compulsory delivery of goods from current production, maintenance of their army and military government at German expense, and control of the foreign trade of their zone. Until 1948, they carried out the extraordinary feat of running their zone at a profit. The Russians, while exploiting even more thoroughly than the French, were also determined to destroy the capitalistic structure of the zone's economy. All bank accounts were blocked as a preliminary measure of control over the wealthy. In August 1945, all landholdings in excess of 250 acres were confiscated, without compensation, and the land thus freed was distributed in small holdings of between twelve and fifty acres. The Prussian *Junker* class was wiped out by this move. Control of deserted plants by local Communists, nationalization, and strict governmental control over raw materials, production quotas, prices, and sales destroyed almost as thoroughly the power of the industrialists and even of the less wealthy middle classes. The economic foundations for the communization of the Soviet zone had thus been laid by 1949.

Economic Policy in American and British Zones. The Americans and the British found very quickly that the division of Germany into four airtight compartments was preventing the revival of the German economy and was forcing them to pay vast sums of money to maintain even a minimum standard of living in their zones. The British were appalled that after winning the war they had spent $120 million in 1946 for the Germans in their zone. Deprived of their traditional food supplies from eastern Germany, with trade and communications interrupted by zonal boundaries, and with no common currency policy, the British and American zones stagnated. An agreement merging the two zones economically into a Bizone was signed in December 1946, and five months later a large measure of responsibility for the economy of the Bizone was handed to an Economic Council of Germans that had many of the attributes of a parliament. The Bizonal military government proceeded unilaterally to reduce the number of factories dismantled and to raise the permitted level of industry. The most important, indeed revolutionary, step taken was, however, the harsh currency reform of June 20, 1948, in the three Western zones, which followed by a few days the decision to extend Marshall Aid to them. The German currency was deflated by 93.6 per cent, thus wiping out not only the inflated reichsmark and the black market founded on cigarettes but also the cash savings of the whole people. The day after the reform, shop windows that had been empty for five years suddenly filled with goods that the shopkeepers had refused to sell for the old, valueless currency; overtime became popular because wages again had value; production figures spurted, marking the beginning of the "German economic miracle." The currency reform and receipt of Marshall Aid completed the economic division of Germany into two states.

Establishment of Communist Control in the Soviet Zone. It was, however, in political reconstruction that the Soviet and the three Western zones drew most rapidly apart. In the Soviet zone, during the early months of the occupation, the same parties were allowed to function as in the Western zones, namely the Communist, Social Democratic, Christian Democratic, and Free Democratic parties. As in all the East European countries, however, the Red Army ensured that local administration and police would be in the hands of Communists or trusted collaborators. After 1945, the activity of the Christian Democrats and Free Democrats was strictly curtailed, and Soviet Commander-in-Chief Zhukov personally dismissed the heads of both parties. The Social Democratic party was split between those willing to collaborate with the Communists and those who wished to compete with them for working-class support. The leader of the Berlin Social Democrats, Otto Grotewohl, agreed to work for the fusion of the Socialists with the Communists, which took place on May 1, 1946. The new party, the Socialist Unity party (SED) was given special privileges by the Russians for meetings, newsprint allocation, vacations, and better rations. In local elections in September 1946, the SED was able to take control of the state governments throughout the Soviet zone, although in coalition with the other parties, which were permitted to continue their innocuous existence. A nominated People's Council, representing all political parties of the zone was created in 1948, and in May 1949 its members were selected in proportions determined beforehand. To the chagrin of the occupying authorities, a third of the zone's population dared to vote against the one official list of candidates. On October 5, 1949, this People's Council declared itself to be the parliament of the German Democratic Republic (DDR) and named the Communist Wilhelm Pieck first president, Otto Grotewohl premier, and Walter Ulbricht, the secretary of the SED's Central Committee, vice-premier.

Political and Economic Revival of Western Zones. The Western powers also restored self-government in their zone, beginning in 1946 with the restoration of elected German administration in the rural districts and small towns. In 1947, each province, or *Land,* was allowed to elect its own assembly and state government. In free elections, the Communist party received about 5 per cent of the vote. The Free Democrats, a middle-class party favoring individual liberties and the relaxation of state controls over economic life, received between 6 and 10 per cent of the vote. The main struggle for power lay between the Christian Democrats and the Social Democrats. The Christian-Democratic Union (CDU) had been founded after the war by a group of idealistic Christians, mostly Catholics but with a small Protestant membership, with the aim of transforming the political and economic life of the country. Until 1949, the predominant wing of the party was led by Jakob Kaiser in Berlin and Karl Arnold of Düsseldorf, who demanded a planned economy and government responsibility for widespread welfare programs. After 1949, however, a more liberal wing, led by Konrad Adenauer, the former lord mayor of Cologne, and Professor Ludwig Erhard, opposed state planning, demanded that the government restrict its interference to control of fiscal policy and of imports, and allow the free-market economy to produce prosperity. Erhard, a pudgy, cigar-smoking professor of economics, had first had the opportunity to apply his theories of the *Soziale Marktwirtschaft,* or social market economy, as economics minister in Bavaria and then as head of the Economic Administration of the Bizone, where he daringly swept away all production and delivery quotas and canceled most of the controls exercised by the occupying powers over the economy. This program, combined with the currency reform and Marshall Aid, produced astounding economic progress. Between May 1948 and March 1949, for example, steel production doubled, while over-all industrial output increased from 47 per cent of the 1936 figure to 89 per cent. Adenauer himself, however, was primarily interested in leading the German people to independence. A tough, independent-minded Catholic, he had been dismissed from his position as lord mayor of Cologne by the Nazis in 1933 and by the British, after his reinstatement by the Americans, in 1945. He became chairman of the Christian Democratic party in the British zone and in 1949 of the three Western zones, as a result of his extraordinary presence, his biting ironic oratory, and his mastery of government administration. The Christian Democrats were strong in the French and American zones and formed a close federation with the Christian Social union of Bavaria. In the British zone, the Social Democratic party (SPD) received the large working-class vote of the Ruhr and the port cities, but it suffered greatly because traditionally a large part of its strength had lain in eastern Germany. In Kurt Schumacher, the party had a crusading, intransigent leader. Broken in health after twelve years in Nazi concentration camps, he was a bitter, brilliant spokesman for the working classes, for German unity, and for disarmament. Backed by the quiet efficient organizing ability of Erich Ollenhauer, who had led the party in exile during the Nazi period, Schumacher built up the party to a membership of almost a million by 1947.

Foundation of the West German Federal Republic. The decision to permit the three Western zones to unite as a semi-independent country was taken at the London Conference of February–June 1948. The elected German officials were invited to write a constitution for West Germany and to hold national elections. The new constitution, called the Basic Law, was approved by the provincial assemblies in May 1949. Elections held on August 14 throughout the three Western zones gave the Christian Democrats 139 seats, the Social Democrats 131, the Free Democrats 52, and the Communists 15. After the Free Democrats had agreed to form a governmental coalition with the Christian Democrats,

Konrad Adenauer was named first chancellor of the Federal German Republic and a Free Democrat, Theodor Heuss, was chosen for the largely ceremonial position of president.

The West German government quickly proved itself effective. Installed in the buildings of a teachers' college on the banks of the Rhine in the little university town of Bonn, the Bundestag developed a strong committee system and efficient legislative procedure. The Socialist party acted as a vigorous and often vituperative opposition, taking principally the roles of protector of German reunification and of watchdog of the interests of the working classes. Liveliness of debate was enhanced during the early years by the presence of the Communist party, which was banned in the Federal Republic in 1956, and of various smaller groups, like the Refugees, the Bavarian party and the All-German party, which all failed in 1957 to get the minimum 5 per cent vote required for representation. The executive was in the hands of Chancellor Adenauer's coalition, which attempted, with great electoral success, to follow a policy that would appeal to the German people as a whole. As economic minister, Ludwig Erhard presided over the extraordinary economic boom. The prewar level of production was reached in November 1949. By 1952, production was 46 per cent higher. Almost 16 million tons of steel were being manufactured. The workers were living better. Consumption of meat, eggs, and fruit almost tripled between 1949 and 1952. In 1952, two million radios were produced. The worker responded with long working hours, averaging forty-eight hours a week, and with an increase in productivity per hour of 43 per cent over that of 1949. A powerful trade-union federation, the Deutscher Gewerkschaftsbund, with a membership of six million, safeguarded the workers' interests; social securities benefits accounted for 17 per cent of the national revenue; and workers' committees were set up in 1952 to take a share in the management of their own companies. Given the incentives of a free-market economy, and particularly the favor shown by the government to reinvestment of capital for growth purposes, West German business leaders took a vigorous role in reconstruction, the search for new markets and products, the rationalization of production, and the revival of German foreign trade. Most important of all in giving the prosperity a solid foundation, between 1949 and 1954, West Germany received $1.5 billion in American economic aid, the equivalent of $29 per person, while profiting from the economic boom set off by the Korean War.

Chancellor Adenauer at once put pressure on the Allied High Commission, the three-member board appointed by the occupying powers to supervise his government, to reduce its controls. In 1949, the end of dismantling was promised. In 1951, West Germany was permitted to run its own foreign policy, and Adenauer became his own foreign minister. In May 1952, the Bonn Agreements, signed by Adenauer and the foreign ministers of Britain, France, and the United States, affirmed that West Germany would become an independent state, free of all occupation controls, at the time of the creation of a European army. This decision implied a complete break by the Western powers with the Potsdam Agreement. After the invasion of South Korea, the United States government had proposed to its allies that West Germany be permitted to defend itself against attack from East Germany with an autonomous German army; but the French, fearful of the revival of German armed might, had countered by proposing that the armies of France, Germany, Italy, and Benelux should be merged as a European army in a European Defense Community, which would have a similar structure to the merger of the coal and steel industries of those six countries in a European Coal and Steel Community that had been proposed in May 1950. The Bundestag, which had approved German membership in the Coal and Steel Community in January 1952, finally ratified membership in the European Defense Community in February 1954. West Germany's economy was thus a modified form of capitalism, and its foreign policy was based upon alignment with the United States and on integration with the other West European powers.

Sovietization of East Germany. In East Germany, the process of Sovietization continued rapidly. A governmental bloc, consisting of all the permitted parties, known as the National Front of Democratic Germany, was set up on January 7, 1950. One list of candidates for all levels of government presented to the voters in the elections of October 15, 1950, received a 99.7 per cent vote of approval. Under the possible influence of the new Soviet Ambassador Pushkin, a thorough purge of the party was announced in August 1950. Compliance with the will of the regime was ensured both by the Soviet secret police and by the East Germans' own State Security Service, and by recruitment of military people's police, the *Volkspolizei* or *"Vopos,"* who numbered 110,000 by 1955. Propaganda was continuously and blatantly spread through schools, workshops, neighborhood organizations, radio, and in ubiquitous placards and banners. Two million young people were enrolled in the Free German Youth. As in the other satellites, pressure was exerted against the churches, and it became politically unwise to attend church services.

In 1950, a Five-Year Plan was introduced whose purpose was to double industrial production, with particular emphasis on heavy industry and industrial machinery. By maintenance of a low standard of living and by requiring high production norms, these goals were almost met; but workers' discontent became dangerously high. Far worse, however, were the conditions of life of the 150,000 German workers compelled to work for the Russians in the uranium mines of the Erzgebirge in Saxony, and the possibility of being sent to the mines was a potent threat that the regime could use to ensure discipline among the more fortunate. Socialization of agriculture began in 1952, with emphasis on the creation of cooperative farms like the Russian *kolkhoz* formed particularly from those holding more than 49 acres. Terrible living conditions combined with the lack of individual freedom to bring about a continual flood of refugees to West Germany—142,000 in 1950; 161,000 in 1951; 186,000 in 1952; and 331,000 in 1953. In May 1952, in retaliation for the West German government's agreement to rearm within the proposed European army, the East German government established a "death strip" along the whole five-hundred-mile border between the two German states. First came a strip ten meters wide completely cleared of houses, trees, and shrubbery; the next 500 meters were a "forbidden zone"; finally, for five kilometers there was a security belt, which could only be entered with a special pass. These measures effectively ended the possibility of flight except through West Berlin.

The Problem of West Berlin. The existence of the West Berlin outpost, one hundred miles within East Germany, thereby became the main cause of tension in Germany. The occupation forces of Britain, France, and the United States had taken control of their sectors of Berlin in July 1945; a German administration for the whole city elected on October 20, 1946 took office, with a Social Democrat as lord mayor, but during the Berlin Blockade, in November 1948, a separate city government was set up in the Soviet sector of East Berlin, and the administrative division of the city was completed by the Soviet boycott of the *Kommandatura* at the same time as the Control Council. In the three Western sectors, there were just over 2 million people compared with 1.2 million in the

Soviet sector. West Berlin's communications with West Germany consisted of three air corridors, a canal, a railroad, and three roads. Until 1961, there was quite easy travel between West and East Berlin by the elevated railway and the subway; many East Berliners worked in West Berlin; and West Berliners had no difficulty visiting relatives in the Soviet sector. In spite of rigorous checks on East Germans traveling into East Berlin, from where they could easily escape into West Berlin and, by air, to West Germany, after 1952 most East Germans fled to the West through Berlin. West Berlin itself, however, was a danger to the successful Sovietization of East Germany, as an example of the political practice and economic prosperity of the West. The reconstruction of West Berlin's industry was made possible by favorable tax privileges, by government pressure on West German firms to set up branches in Berlin, and by massive financial aid from West Germany and the Marshall Plan. The Bizone spent $98 million on West Berlin; a special tax and the produce of a two-pfennig stamp on domestic mail in West Germany collected since 1949 brought up to $240 million a year for West Berlin; American aid of over $300 million was received between 1949 and 1952. Although West Berlin's production in 1953 was only 67 per cent that of 1936, and 160,000 were unemployed, the contrast with the harsh conditions in East Berlin was still outstanding; and indeed many foreign observers believed that the West was unwisely provoking conflict with the Soviet Union by creating so indefensible a showplace. The Berlin problem rather than the German problem was to dominate the relations between the Soviet Union and the West for the next decade.

INNER EUROPE: FRANCE, ITALY, AND BENELUX

One of the most significant features of postwar Europe was the move of France, Italy, Belgium, the Netherlands, and Luxembourg (and later West Germany) toward close collaboration, and then toward integration in a supranational community. This progress in the creation of what may eventually become a United States of Europe was largely due to the fact that these countries found themselves in 1945 with essentially similar problems and similar aspirations. They were to realize that only in closer union could these aspirations be satisfied.

Purge of Collaborators. The first problem was the renovation of their constitutional structure in response to the demands of the resistance groups. Collaborators were quickly dealt with. In Luxembourg, the head of the Volksdeutsche Movement and a few of his assistants were executed. About 100,000 were arrested in the Netherlands, and the head of the Dutch Nazi party and his colleagues were shot. In Belgium, however, the purge problem was exacerbated by being linked to the Walloon-Fleming rivalry and to the question of the restoration of Leopold III to the throne. A slight majority of the 300,000 collaborators arrested or put under surveillance were Flemish; Leopold's return to the throne, which was opposed by most Walloons on the ground that he had aided the Germans, was supported by most Flemings. Open conflict was avoided, however, when the government conveniently postponed until 1950 the popular referendum that was to decide Leopold's future. Immediate vengeance was taken by both Italian and French resistance groups in sporadic attacks on suspected collaborators, and many personal scores were settled. Purge courts were soon set up by the central governments, however, and thousands were imprisoned or lost their civic rights. Like denazification, however, the purges failed in their literal purpose of "cleansing" societies supposedly sullied by collaboration. Isolated victims seemed more like hostages than villains, and a general revulsion against the whole process soon set in.

Ineffective Constitutional Renovation. Nor was there much greater success in reforming constitutional practice. Grand Duchess Charlotte was restored in Luxembourg amid popular rejoicing, her modest way of life and unshakable patriotism deeply admired, and the Dutch rallied again to Queen Wilhelmina on her return in May 1945. In Belgium, Italy, and France, however, there was deep dissatisfaction with the prewar form of government. Demands that Belgium's constitution be revised in favor of a federal regime, giving greater autonomy to Wallonia, Flanders, and Brussels, or that the three regions be equally represented in the Senate, were rejected. To avoid increasing Leopold's support, women were not given the vote until 1948. When the referendum was finally held on March 12, 1950, the return of the king was supported by 57.5 per cent of the electorate. On his return to Brussels, rioting broke out throughout Wallonia, and King Leopold decided to abdicate in favor of his son Baudouin, who was crowned in 1951, when he became twenty-one. In that way, the immediate irritant in Walloon-Fleming relations was removed. The Italians rid themselves of their king in a referendum on June 2, 1946. The result was almost as unsatisfactory as the Belgian referendum, however. A month before the referendum, King Victor Emmanuel III had abdicated in favor of his son Umberto, who had proved himself moderately progressive as lieutenant-general since 1944; and the middle classes, the Church, and the south were strongly in favor of his retention, which was demanded by 46 per cent of the electorate. The constituent assembly elected the same day wrote a new constitution that was almost identical with the Albertine Statute that had greatly contributed to weaken the parliamentary democracy of United Italy between 1871 and 1922. The king was replaced by a president; a hundred life-members appointed for their personal distinction were to join the 247 elected members in the Senate, although this practice was not to be continued; and since the premier was responsible to both chambers, Italy was doomed to return to the dismal practice of government by constantly fluctuating party coalition and to frequent cabinet crises. The French swept away the Third Republic in October 1945, by a 96.4 per cent vote. When the Constituent Assembly offered a new constitution, in which power would lie in the hands of a single chamber that would choose the premier, it was opposed by General de Gaulle, the MRP, and all conservatives, and was rejected by a million votes. Six months later, a new draft, far closer to the constitution of the Third Republic, was approved by only 37 per cent of the electorate, 32 per cent of whom did not vote. The Fourth Republic, like the Third, was to have two houses. The premier was to be chosen by the president, but responsible to the lower house. A regime of governmental crisis was assured by the fact that it was made extremely difficult for a premier to dissolve the Assembly whose members thus enjoyed the security of a five-year tenure. Between de Gaulle's resignation in January 1946 and his return to power in June 1958, France had twenty-three premiers. The longest ministry, Guy Mollet's, lasted fifteen months; and the shortest, Henri Queuille's, four days. Thus, the parliamentary hemispheres of continental Europe did not always present a very inspiring example of democratic practice. Debate in France would be paralyzed by the prolonged banging of desk lids; ushers had to form phalanxes in the aisles to prevent Italian deputies from punching each other; Belgian Socialists took to the streets to oppose the majority verdict of a referendum.

The Communist Challenge Mastered. The political scene was not wholly discouraging, however. The Communist parties quickly recognized that they could not seize power by force. Until 1947, Communist strategy was to increase the popularity they had won by their resistance efforts by collaborating loyally with left-center governments in the urgent tasks of economic reconstruction. In Luxembourg, for example, a Communist became minister of health and of repatriation. In Belgium, the extremely difficult work of the Ministries of Reconstruction, Food, Public Works, and Health was undertaken by Communists. After participating in the Bonomi and Parri governments, the Italian Communists joined the Socialists and Christian Democrats in the experiment of *tripartismo,* undertaking the exacting Ministries of Public Works and Transport as well as the more politically rewarding Ministry of Justice. In France, General de Gaulle refused outright to give them the "levers of power" of the Ministries of Foreign Affairs, the Interior, or National Defense, and the French Communists obligingly held Ministries like Health or Industry. Only in the Netherlands was it felt possible to dispense with Communist cooperation. The party's approach quickly paid dividends. In the 1946 elections they received 18.9 per cent of the vote in Italy and 21 per cent in France. Four to five million supporters were to remain faithful to them for the next two decades. The trial of strength between the Soviet Union and the West, marked by the strengthening of Communist hold on Eastern Europe and by the American riposte in formation of the Bizone and proclamation of the Truman Doctrine, broke these rather anomalous alliances. The Communists withdrew from the Belgian government in March 1947, and were forced from the French and Italian governments two months later. Following the formation of the Cominform in September 1947, the French and Italian parties, in accordance with the instruction of Zhdanov, plunged their countries into economic chaos in a series of strikes in the winter of 1947 and again in the summer and fall of 1948. The results were damaging to the Communists themselves. Stern and immediate government action broke the strikes. Many workers were disillusioned at strikes called, not to better their living conditions, but for the political purpose of preventing the acceptance of the gift of American economic aid. Italian Socialist and Catholic workers took the opportunity to follow the French example by founding trade unions of their own. For the next decade, the Communist parties were to be a negative force, incapable of taking power themselves, yet able to make every pro-Western move by the government the occasion for a major test of strength.

Reformist Parties in the Netherlands and Belgium. The most hopeful aspect of the political scene was the appearance of new parties of moderately reformist character. In the Netherlands, a new vigor was imparted to political life by the formation in the resistance of the Popular Dutch Movement, with a moderately Socialist program of social reforms, participation of workers in factory administration, individual freedoms, and colonial evolution. The Movement was transformed in 1946 into the Labor party, which, following the elections of May 17, agreed to form a governmental coalition with the majority Catholic party. This new government nationalized the Bank of the Netherlands and several large industrial enterprises, enacted a social welfare program, and carried through the necessary constitutional amendment to authorize the abortive Netherlands-Indonesian Union. The Catholic-Labor coalition lasted until 1959. More important, however, was the foundation of a series of new Catholic parties, favoring collaboration with other Christian groups, moderate social reform, and closer European cooperation. The Catholic party in Belgium, as proof of its progressive aims and determination to loosen its ties with the Catholic clergy, changed its name in August 1945 to the Christian-Social party. In spite of disagreement over the return of the king, the Christian-Social party collaborated with the Socialists until 1950, in placing indirect state controls over the banks, transport, and the railroads. There was, however, no nationalization, and Belgium remained the most liberal in economics of the West European countries.

De Gasperi's Democrazia Cristiana. It was in Italy and France that the new Catholic parties reaped their greatest successes. When the reform demands of the Italian resistance movement, called the "wind from the north," forced the resignation of the Bonomi government in June 1945, it seemed for a brief period that with the choice of Ferruccio Parri as premier the renovation of Italian society and politics would be entrusted not to the Christian Democratic party but to the Action party, an elite group of intellectuals formed in exile in Paris, which had the support of Communists and Socialists. Parri, however, who was inexperienced in politics, found himself caught between the extreme-left parties and the Christian Democrats and attacked by the reviving conservative forces through a new movement called *Uomo Qualunque* (Average Man). He resigned in November, taking the Action party with him into obscurity. His place was taken by the Christian Democrat Alcide De

Gasperi, an austere, dedicated genius who was slowly to win personal dominance over Italian political life for the next eight years. De Gasperi had represented the city of Trento in the Austrian parliament before 1919, and, after the cession of South Tirol to Italy had become an Italian deputy of the Partito Popolare, the Catholic party. After spending sixteen months in a Fascist jail, he took a librarian's post in the sanctuary of the Vatican City, and there, with several former leaders of the Partito Popolare, he organized the Democrazia Cristiana, or Christian Democracy, in 1943. The new party, while stressing good relations with the Catholic Church and depending heavily upon the aid of the local clergy and of the Catholic Action group, demanded wider social insurance, progressive taxation, land reform, and greater autonomy for the provinces. It thus appealed to a wide variety of classes, from the conservatives who saw it as a bulwark against left-wing revolution to Catholic industrial workers and the poverty-stricken peasantry of the south. In the elections of June 1946, the Christian Democrats received 8 million votes and 207 seats, but De Gasperi was forced to form a coalition with the Communists and Socialists who together had 219 seats.

During the next two years, De Gasperi made the Christian Democrats predominant. The Socialist party was split by the determination of its leader, the brilliant but erratic Pietro Nenni, to follow the lead of the Communists. In January 1947, Giuseppe Saragat led almost half of the Socialist deputies out of the party convention to form a new, democratically minded group known later as the Social Democrats. When the Communists were forced out of the government in May 1947, the Socialists were also excluded, and De Gasperi's new government was frankly conservative. His minister of the interior, Mario Scelba, put down the Communist riots with great efficiency; the country's finance was stabilized by the deflation program of Luigi Einaudi, the minister of the budget; and interim American aid was sent while the Marshall Plan was under debate. The elections of April 18, 1948 gave the Christian Democrats a smashing victory with 48.4 per cent of the vote, a total of 12.7 million ballots. With 304 seats, De Gasperi commanded an absolute majority in the Chamber of Deputies. For five years, supported by Saragat's Social Democrats and two minor parties, De Gasperi enjoyed parliamentary strength unique in Italian politics. By 1953, however, the inherent weaknesses of the party were beginning to appear. The Christian Democratic party's close ties to the Catholic Church perturbed the small lay parties with whom it was allied. Conflict between the party's left wing and its conservatives over social reform stultified many worth-while proposals for fairer distribution of national wealth. A spoils system that filled administrative positions with Christian Democrats annoyed many outsiders. De Gasperi himself became too involved in mediating disputes and satisfying grievances. Above all, the obvious disappearance of the danger of a Communist coup d'état, which had influenced the 1948 elections, weakened his position. Indeed, the fact that it was possible for many to quit the Christian Democrats was proof that they had succeeded in their primary task of avoiding political revolution in Italy. In the elections of June 7, 1953, the Christian Democrats received 10.8 million votes and 216 seats. When De Gasperi attempted to form a one-party government, the galleries of the Chamber of Deputies filled to overflowing like a Roman circus for his overthrow. His defeat, and death a year later, ended the precarious political stability he alone had been able to maintain.

The Game of Politics in France. The Popular Republican Movement (MRP) in France never achieved the pre-eminence of the Democrazia Cristiana, partly because it never united the center and right wings and partly because it did not produce a leader of the political prowess of De Gasperi. Founded in Lyon in 1944 by leading members of the Catholic resistance groups including Georges Bidault and Robert Schuman, it attempted to reconcile Catholics and the working classes with a program of social reform and with a roster of new men unsullied by participation in the workings of the Third Republic. In the three parliamentary elections of 1945–46, the party averaged over 5 million votes. From its advantageous position in the center of the political spectrum, it was able to demand participation in almost every government of the Fourth Republic. Its influence was particularly felt in foreign policy, since except for one month either Bidault or Robert Schuman was foreign minister between 1944 and 1954. The party's reformist program was soon whittled down, however, since it appeared that the majority of its supporters were conservatives who saw in the new Catholic party a barrier against communism and their only refuge until conservatism became again politically respectable. When General de Gaulle founded the Rally of the French People in 1947, the MRP lost half its supporters and was left with barely a seventh of the seats in the Assembly.

The Rally of the French People was de Gaulle's attempt to re-create a great national consensus. In 1944, he had the status of a great national hero and the power to govern as he wished. De Gaulle, however, concentrated on the restoration of France's great-power status, by rebuilding its army to a million men, sharing in the invasion of Germany, and administering a zone of occupation. His government, based largely on a coalition of Communists, Socialists, and MRP, carried through the nationalization of the northern mines, some airplane factories, and the Renault Automobile Company. De Gaulle, however, refused to sanction a harsh deflation proposed by Pierre Mendès-France, his economics minister, who resigned in protest. Inflation ran unchecked, adding to the daily misery. De Gaulle's principal error was his refusal to build a middle-of-the-road party of his own, and he realized too late that the political parties intended to write a constitution that would deny the president the executive powers de Gaulle regarded as essential. De Gaulle compounded his error by resigning suddenly on January 20, 1946. Rather than sweeping him back into power on his own terms, as he had expected, the French people reacted with annoyance and disillusionment; and when de Gaulle called upon them in 1947 to give the Rally an overwhelming majority of the vote, he was joined only by the conservatives. To his bitter disappointment, the Rally received only one-fifth of the vote in the 1951 elections, and he disbanded it in disgust two years later. Thus, neither the MRP nor the RPF became a powerful center party like that De Gasperi briefly presided over in Italy. As a result, coalition government slowly lost its momentum. After de Gaulle's resignation, the Communist-Socialist-MRP coalition continued to govern until May 1947, when the Communists were ousted. The movement to the right continued with the resignation of the Socialists in 1951, and the inclusion in the governments first of the Radicals, then of the Independent Republicans and of the Peasants, and finally in 1953 of the remnant of the Gaullists. Between 1951 and 1954, under Antoine Pinay, Joseph Laniel, and Henri Queuille, a period of "immobilism" was reached, during which the financial situation deteriorated, the French Army in Indochina was defeated by the Viet Minh, and independence movements began in Morocco and Tunisia. The fall of Dien Bien Phu shook the assembly from its lethargy and led to the investiture of the brilliant, vigorous, and much-disliked Mendès-France. The new premier, aided by his promise to resign if he failed to meet any of the deadlines of a self-imposed schedule, brought peace in Indochina, promised autonomy to

Tunisia, approved West Germany's rearmament within NATO, and introduced a program of financial reforms. So dynamic a force proved intolerable to the politicians, and he was overthrown in February at the proposal of a member of his own party. The center-right coalition again took power.

Reconstruction in Benelux. The economic development of the five countries followed a similar pattern. All were faced with reconstruction problems in 1945, although Belgium and Luxembourg found their industry relatively unharmed and were able to return to prewar levels of production quickly. Belgium was particularly aided by control of the rich resources in copper, rubber, and diamonds of the Belgian Congo and by a strict governmental policy of deflation and price controls, and it received only one grant of $14 million from Marshall Aid. The Netherlands, by contrast, had suffered greatly from bombing, flooding, dismantling of factories, and famine. Half its merchant fleet, a vitally important source of foreign currency, was destroyed. Japanese conquest of the Dutch East Indies had enabled an independence movement to gain a base of power from which it would not be dislodged. Transport was quickly restored; the port of Rotterdam was rebuilt; gypsum was spread over the fields that had been flooded with sea water to restore their fertility; and an 80 per cent deflation of the currency was introduced. Marshall Aid of $980 million enabled more basic capital investment to be made, especially in land reclamation. The three countries had agreed in 1944 to form a customs union, called Benelux, which came into being in 1948. The union abolished internal tariff barriers and set up a common tariff on imports from nonmember countries. By creating a wider market for the products of the three countries, the Benelux union provided an important stimulus to their economic development and provided an example that the other countries of Western Europe would emulate, and exceed, in the Common Market of 1958.

Italian Economic Difficulties. The devastation in Italy exceeded that of all West European countries, except Germany, but was localized in the two bands between Naples and Rome and between Florence and Bologna where the Germans had halted the Allied advance. In the great industrial region of the north, the factories were largely undamaged and were able to resume production quickly. Allied occupation proved a benefit by making the United States partly responsible for maintenance of minimum standards of life and security, and by making millions of

Americans aware of Italy's rural and urban poverty. The sympathy of the American government was expressed practically through United Nations Relief and Rehabilitation Agency aid of $485 million, support of a loan of $100 million from the Export-Import Bank, demands for leniency in the Italian peace treaty, and especially through Marshall Aid of $1.5 billion. A brief postwar boom in 1946–47, a successful though harsh deflation of the currency, the lifting of wartime controls, the rise in real wages, and after the receipt of Marshall Aid the rise in productivity in 1952 to 40 per cent above prewar level—all these factors seemed to indicate the successful revival of the Italian economy. Terrible problems remained, however. Rural poverty in the south and the islands of Sardinia and Sicily, as a result of absentee ownership of great estates, lack of irrigation, fertilizer and technical knowledge, and overpopulation required urgent government action. Industry, in the hands of either a few very large or many very small companies, as in France, favored a policy of high prices and stable markets rather than dynamic expansion and competition. With up to two million unemployed, the major concerns of the trade unions was security of employment and increase of the welfare benefits of those employed rather than cooperation in increase of the national product. After years of procrastination, the De Gasperi government finally attempted to deal with the agrarian problem in 1950, by a group of land-reform laws. In all, 1.75 million acres were redistributed, mostly in the south, Sardinia, and Sicily, in lots of about 22 acres, to 109,000 families. At the same time, a start was made in stimulation of the south's agriculture and industry through state investments in dams, aqueducts, roads, and port facilities. At the time of De Gasperi's fall, however, the increasing birth rate was already wiping out the little gains made. A government commission reported that almost a million people were living four or more to a room or in cellars, caves, lean-to huts, or even in the Roman tombs along the Appian Way.

France's Economic Revival. France was fortunate to possess the organizing genius of an economist and administrator like Jean Monnet, who in 1946 was appointed to head France's Planning Commission, the group responsible for drawing up and implementing France's four-year modernization plan. One of the least known and most influential men in postwar Europe, Monnet had been a cognac manufacturing executive, administrator of supplies during both world wars, economics adviser to many foreign governments, and deputy secretary-general of the League of Nations. He attacked the traditional conservatism of French business groups by channeling investment into several growth areas of the economy—coal, transport, electricity, cement, agricultural machinery, and steel—whose dynamism would drag the rest of the economy upward. Since the first three were nationalized industries, they were necessarily responsive to the planning demands of the state. Recovery was aided by several other factors. After falling for more than half a century, the French birth rate rose sharply in 1946 and remained consistently high throughout the postwar years. Marshall Aid of $3.1 billion was received. Occupation of the French zone in Germany enabled the military government to take $257 million worth of goods as restitution, the equipment of 106 factories as reparations, and occupation costs of $737 million. Moreover, between 1948 and 1960, the rich coal-and-steel complex of the Saar was fused economically with France, giving the French control of the Saar coal supplies during the postwar penury of fuel. Even the German economic revival aided French industry by stimulating French business to adopt a more progressive attitude to economic competition and to seek to stimulate growth in the static sections of the economy. Wider markets, availability of chemical fertilizers and farm machinery, and the flight of labor from the farm into industry encouraged the mechanization of French farming which increased rapidly in productivity. By the end of the first Four-Year Plan, in 1950, industrial production was 23 per cent above the prewar level and the following year exceeded it by 41 per cent. After 1952, it became increasingly evident that France was experiencing an economic boom comparable to the more publicized miracle in West Germany. The French economy seemed sufficiently sound for the government to propose, in May 1950, the formation of the European Coal and Steel Community, within which the French coal and steel industries would compete, naked of tariff protection, with the giants of the Ruhr.

Thus, by 1953, the period of political and economic reconstruction was over in France, Italy, and the Benelux countries. They could now turn to long-term problems, solutions of which were dependent on their recognition of the inability of the small nation-state to maintain either political independence or economic prosperity in the age of continent-states.

SOCIALIST EUROPE:
BRITAIN AND SCANDINAVIA

Britain's Problems. At war's end, victorious Britain was badly in need of renovation. The cost of the war had been enormous—300,000 soldiers and 60,000 civilians killed, one-third of the merchant fleet sunk, half a million houses ruined, a quarter of capital investments overseas sold, and one-tenth of the national wealth at home destroyed. More significant, however, was the legacy of 150 years of social injustice that had accompanied the Industrial Revolution. Millions of British workers still lived in antiquated slums, like the East End of London or the Potteries of the Midlands or the Rhondda Valley of south Wales. For the mass of the people, medical care was insufficient and beyond their means; schools were old and overcrowded; unemployment was a bitterly remembered specter. Labor unions smarted with memories of the failure of the general strike of 1926. Twice in the interwar years, in 1924 and 1929, the working classes had seen Socialist governments unable to govern without Conservative support. The elections of 1935 had given the Conservatives an extraordinary majority of 387 Members of Parliament to Labour's 154; and, as a result of the decision to prolong the life of this parliament throughout the war, the same dispiriting group held on to their seats for ten years. Churchill had been forced onto the Conservative majority in May 1940 by Labour's refusal to join a National Government under Neville Chamberlain; and throughout the war years the Labour cabinet members continued to polish their party's image by their loyal service under Churchill. Clement Attlee as deputy prime minister, Ernest Bevin as minister of labor and national service, and Herbert Morrison as minister of supply became figures as familiar to the public as the more aristocratic countenances of Lord Halifax or Anthony Eden. Nevertheless, when the decision was taken on May 23, 1945 to hold elections on July 5, without waiting for the end of war with Japan, most observers expected Churchill's personal popularity to bring the Conservatives back to power with a small majority.

Labour's Victory. The war, however, had not effaced the bitterness of the working classes at what they regarded as Conservative disregard for their sufferings during the interwar years. The idealism stimulated in the fight against Nazi wickedness provoked soldier and civilian alike to demand that injustice at home be remedied also. To them, the Labour party offered a carefully thought-out program of economic and social reform, promising in their manifesto, *Let us face the future,* both the nationalization of several key industries and construction of a welfare state. The Conservatives were content to advise the electors to vote for Churchill—"Let him finish the job"—but Churchill in an unusual lapse of political judgment, furnished the Labour leaders with evidence that he would make a partisan peacetime leader, by tastelessly declaring that "socialism is inseparably interwoven with totalitarianism" and would involve "some sort of Gestapo." The results, announced twenty days after the election to enable the soldiers' votes to be flown to England, gave the Labour party 393 seats, to 215 for the Conservatives and their supporters, 11 for the Liberals, and 2 for the Communists. Attlee, who had returned with Churchill from the Potsdam Conference for the election results, formed his cabinet within forty-eight hours, and went back to Potsdam with his new foreign secretary, Ernest Bevin. The cabinet was an amalgam of the two wings of British socialism. The Labour unions were represented by Bevin, a tough, dedicated Socialist, who had fought his way upward from parentless farm laborer, dish washer, and van driver to be secretary of Britain's largest union, the Transport and General Workers' Union; Herbert Morrison, son of a policeman and a housemaid, who helped win the London Labour party control of the capital; and Aneurin Bevan, the most dynamic and controversial of the Labour leaders, a Welsh coal miner. In contrast with them, Clement Attlee and Stafford Cripps, the ascetic president of the Board of Trade, were the sons of well-to-do London lawyers, graduates of exclusive boarding schools and Oxford and London universities, who had turned to socialism from moral and religious commitment. British socialism was thus far more than the instrument of one class and was able with some justice to claim to be bridging rather than widening class divisions.

Nationalization. The promises of the election manifesto were quickly kept. The Bank of England was nationalized in March 1946, although the measure was largely a change in name, since the government had already exercised supervisory control. Both miners and mineowners were in agreement that the coal industry should be nationalized, since private owners had given up any effort to make the capital investment necessary for working the difficult coal seams left after 150 years of mining. Following the impeccable example of the administration of the British Broadcasting Corporation, the Coal Industry Nationalization Act of July 1946 appointed a National Coal Board as an autonomous public corporation to manage the mines; mineowners were paid compensation of about $750 million. While government investment helped increase productivity, the change did not achieve the harmony between worker and employer that had been expected. Far from feeling himself a part owner of the mine in which he worked, the miner saw the Coal Board as a new and more distant employer, against whom future strikes would have to be directed. Absenteeism and rapid turnover of workers remained a problem, and for a while it was necessary to allow young men to work in the mines in place of their term of military service. In the first four years after nationalization, production advanced only 10 per cent, but after 1950 increased investment began to produce better results. Other measures of nationalization roused lethargic opposition and little enthusiasm. Civil aviation and overseas telephone and telegraph communications were nationalized in 1946, electricity, the railroads, road transport and the canals in 1947, and gas in 1948. When the Labour government turned in 1949 to the nationalization of the iron-and-steel industry, which unlike most of the industries previously nationalized was neither a public utility nor a money-loser, the Conservatives mounted a campaign of obstruction, especially by threatening to use the power of the House of Lords to delay the bill for two years. To meet this challenge, the Labour government forced through Parliament a reform bill, reducing the veto power of the House of Lords to one year. Although the Steel Nationalization Bill passed the Commons in May 1949, the Lords were still able to delay enactment by proposing innumerable amendments; and a compromise was reached between the two parties by which the bill was to become law in 1950 but was not to be enforced until after the general election. In 1950, after Labour had been returned to power by a small majority, the steel industry was nationalized, but the Conservatives made good in 1953 their threat to denationalize steel when they returned to power.

The Welfare State. Labour's welfare measures made a much greater impact than nationalization on the life of the average citizen. A blueprint for this program had been drawn up during the war by a Liberal, Lord Beveridge, to eliminate "want, ignorance, squalor and disease" and to guarantee to every citizen a "national minimum" standard of

living. A comprehensive scheme of national insurance for old-age, unemployment, and health benefits and a government plan for compensation for industrial injuries were introduced in 1946; and the National
Assistance Act of 1948 guaranteed a weekly payment to those lacking
minimal food and shelter. Two Housing Acts in 1946 and 1949 encouraged the building of municipal low-cost housing. But the most contested
and most far-reaching of all the welfare schemes was the National
Health Service Act of 1946, which provided medical and dental care to
every citizen (and indeed to many foreign visitors) regardless of ability
to pay. After many skirmishes between the British Medical Association
and Minister of Health Aneurin Bevan, it was determined that patients
would be free to choose and to change their doctor, that doctors could
choose between remuneration based solely on the number of patients
enrolled with them or based upon an annual salary plus an allowance for
the number of patients, and that doctors would be permitted to devote
part of their time to fee-paying patients. By 1949, 95 per cent of the
population, or forty million people, had enrolled in the scheme, and 90
per cent of the doctors and 95 per cent of the dentists had joined. Since
the average British citizen had consistently avoided medical or dental
treatment that he could not afford in the past, the first years of the
scheme proved far more expensive than the government had expected.
Three million pairs of glasses had been issued free and two million people had received dental care by 1949, and there were long waiting lists
for hospital beds. Once the enormous backlog of previously untreated
illness had been made up, however, the system began to function with
astonishing success. Doctors found that their salaries compared favor-
ably with those of other professional groups, like teachers or lawyers,
and many found satisfaction in being able to prescribe the drugs or
hospital treatment relevant to each case without regard to the patient's
financial capacity. The average Briton, treated by the same doctors in
the same surgeries and hospitals as before, found enormous relief in the
knowledge that serious prolonged illness would no longer endanger his
life's savings, while inhabitants of slum districts whose inability to pay
medical fees had discouraged doctors from establishing practices there
were at last well served. Finally, the Labour government attempted to
make educational opportunity equal to all. The wartime coalition government had passed the Education Act of 1944, creating a Ministry of
Education, providing for the raising of the school-leaving age after the

war, and making primary and secondary education free of charge. Emergency measures were taken by the Labour government to train teachers and to provide temporary classrooms. School-leaving age was raised to fifteen in 1947. Free lunches and milk were provided in all state schools. Scholarships dependent upon parents' income were made available to all students who received entrance to a university, and almost two-thirds of the operating expenses of the universities were paid by the government. Although less than 3 per cent of the population was able to attend the university, it was true that entrance was dependent upon ability rather than means.

Economic Shortcomings. While the Labour government was carrying out the costly program of nationalization and welfare, it was faced with continual economic difficulties. British capital losses at home and abroad were so great that exports would have to exceed the prewar level by 50 per cent in order for Britain to enjoy its prewar income. The Labour government deliberately enforced a policy of austerity, which Churchill characterized as "Strength through misery." Prices of many goods were controlled; rationing of food and clothing continued; foreign travel was discouraged by restriction of the amounts of currency that could be spent abroad to as little as 25 pounds a year; high taxation was used to redistribute the national income, although it also discouraged initiative; high purchase taxes and excise duties discouraged the sale of luxury goods or goods of foreign manufacture. Aided by an American loan of $3.75 billion in 1946 and a further $3.6 billion in Marshall Aid, British exports slowly rose from 45 per cent of the prewar level in 1945, to 99.3 per cent in 1946, 108.7 per cent in 1947, 136.3 per cent in 1948, and 150 per cent in the first half of 1949. Fuel shortages in the bitter winter of 1946–47 caused the temporary unemployment of almost five million men, a quarter of the work force, and led to even firmer austerity measures, including cuts in the food ration. The onset of a mild American depression in 1949, which cut British exports to the dollar area, forced the devaluation of the pound from 4.02 to 2.80 to the dollar and imposition of a cut in expenditure on social services and food subsidies.

The Swing to the Conservatives. The Labour party thus entered the campaign for the general election of February 23, 1950 at a considerable disadvantage. It had already achieved its aims in social welfare. Nationalization had failed to stimulate much popular enthusiasm. Austerity, though equally shared, made everyday life rather grim. Although there was only a 3 per cent shift in votes between Labour and Conservative parties, the former's absolute majority was reduced from over 150 to 6. The new government was plagued by revolts within its own left wing, by the sickness of Cripps, Bevin (who died in April 1951), and Attlee, and by the expenses of rearmament following the beginning of the Korean War in June 1950. Aneurin Bevan and Harold Wilson both resigned from the cabinet in April 1951, when the government decided to impose charges for supply of dentures and glasses under the National Health Service. Dispirited and divided, the Labour party made a poor showing in new elections on October 25, 1951. A further 1 per cent of the electorate went over to the Conservatives, giving them 321 seats to Labour's 295, even though the Labour party actually polled 231,000 more votes than the Conservatives. At seventy-six years of age, Winston Churchill became prime minister for the last time.

The six years of Labour government had brought profound changes to Britain. The coexistence of nationalized and private industry, in proportions of roughly one to four, was accepted. The structure of the welfare state, with benefits from cradle to grave, was firmly shaped. The greater part of the responsibilities of empire had been laid aside, with the grant of independence to Transjordan and Palestine, India, Pakistan, Ceylon, and Burma, and preparations were being made for the independence of the African colonies. A new orientation had been given to British policy by alignment with the West European nations and the United States in the Marshall Plan, the Brussels Treaty, and the North Atlantic Treaty Alliance. To a large extent, Britain was gracefully accepting the novelty of having become a second-class power.

Scandinavian Socialism between the Wars. The Scandinavian nations had not nourished ideas of grandeur since the seventeenth century; and they had shown considerable skill in adapting their societies to the imperatives of the twentieth century. Their populations were small: In 1946 Denmark had 4 million people; Norway, 3 million; and Sweden, 6.6 million. Arable land area was low, and population density was high. All three countries had faced their economic problems by intensive exploitation of their natural resources. Electricity was produced from water power in Norway and Sweden, whose forested mountain slopes produced high-quality timber in great demand for Europe's postwar reconstruction. Diversification of industrial base had taken place during the interwar years, so that machinery, chemicals, and automobiles became important export items; foreign currency was earned by such "invisible exports" as the Norwegian freighter fleet. As a result of the growing industrialization, well-organized trade unions became strong after 1919 and aided the Social Democratic parties in taking power—in Sweden in 1920, in Denmark in 1924, and in Norway in 1928. Although the Social Democrats never captured a majority of the votes, the opposition was divided into four main parties—Conservatives, Agrarians, Liberals, and Communists—and the Social Democrats could usually count upon the cooperation of the Agrarian groups. By 1939, a form of moderate socialism was accepted throughout Scandinavia. Public ownership of utilities like railroads, gas and electricity, ports, and hospitals had been enforced even before the First World War. Cooperatives of both consumers and producers, particularly of farmers, became strong at the end of the nineteenth century, and during the interwar years expanded greatly to include, for example, 90 per cent of all Danish farmers and some 12 per cent of Swedish retail trade. The Social Democratic governments used state controls over investment, taxation, and subsidies to direct economic development toward planned goals, especially toward full employment, and toward greatly expanded state welfare services covering sickness, industrial accidents, and old age.

Sweden's Postwar Prosperity. Neutrality during the war left Sweden prosperous and in a good position to profit by supplying the reconstruction needs of the ravaged countries of Europe. Premier Per Albin Hanssen remodeled his wartime coalition cabinet in July 1945 on a purely Socialist basis, but on his death the next year his successor Tage Erlander invited the Agrarians to join his government. The elections of 1948 gave the coalition an absolute majority. In spite of a break with the Agrarians in 1957 over a more expensive compulsory pension scheme, the Socialists were returned to power at each successive election, and Erlander remained as premier for two decades. An agrarian reform law was passed in 1947; welfare benefits were increased by vote of higher family allowances and pensions in 1948, a compulsory health insurance scheme in 1955, and a controversial pension scheme in 1959. In the immediate postwar prosperity, the Swedish government enforced rationing at home to be able to give humanitarian aid to thousands of Norwegian and Finnish children and to the 300,000 refugees on its soil. Facing economic difficulties by 1947 as a result of inflation at home and the slow recovery of its trading partners in Europe, Sweden was forced to take emergency measures, which included blocking of salaries, rationing of tea and coffee, and immigration of large numbers of Italian workers. Marshall Aid, trade with both the Western and the Soviet blocs, and the establishment of free movement of labor among the Scandinavian countries as a result of the formation of a Nordic Council in 1952, helped pull the economy out of its recession. Rising prices, industrial lockouts and strikes, and the deterioration of overseas trade brought a further crisis in 1956, which was again surmounted by strict economy measures. Discontent in Sweden, however, was the result of high expectations, for its living standard remained among the highest in Europe; the Swedes had more automobiles, radios, and telephones per thousand of the population than any country in Europe.

Danish Socialism. The Social Democrats were in power in Denmark, except for the periods 1945–47 and 1950–53 when the Agrarian party, supported by the Conservatives, took control of the government. The Socialists, who had been in power for sixteen years, had called for a "peaceful revolution" in the election campaign of October 1945, but their strength had been sapped by the Communists, who won 12.5 per cent of the vote. Denmark's vulnerability to any fall in the market for its agricultural produce, notably in Britain and West Germany, was emphasized in economic troubles of 1947, while in the growing tensions of the Cold War, the Danish people clearly sided with the West. In the elections of 1947, following the death of King Christian X, the Socialists were returned to power, and Communist representation was cut by half. The Socialist governments continued to widen the welfare activities of the state, but found themselves constantly struggling to balance the foreign-trade budget by means of restrictions on imports and restraint on salaries that reduced their popularity with the working classes. Nationwide strikes in 1956 and 1961 were met by compulsory mediation and finally by increased salaries for industrial workers and subsidies for the farmers. To meet its economic problems, Denmark accepted Marshall Aid, unsuccessfully sought a Nordic customs union on industrial products, and joined the European Free Trade Association (EFTA) in 1959. Seeing that neutrality had been no defense in 1940, the Danish government joined the North Atlantic Treaty Organization in 1949, and after the invasion of South Korea increased its army to 50,000 men. Like the Swedes, the Danes continued to enjoy one of the highest standards of living in Europe. With a consumption of 3,430 calories per head each day, they were the best-fed people in the world!

The Revival of Norway. The Norwegians had to cope with far greater reconstruction problems than their neighbors. Inflation was quickly combated by withdrawing from circulation the currency issued by the Germans. Food from the United States and Sweden was of major help in the early postwar period. Agreements signed between employers and unions, planning by a Council of Economic Coordination, and the workers' willingness to put in additional hours aided immediate economic revival. The Socialist government nationalized only those industries created by the Germans and the Bank of Norway, while purchasing shares in other industries. Investment was promoted in the merchant and fishing fleets, in forestry, and especially in hydroelectric power and aluminum. With occasional balance-of-payments difficulties, Norway's economic progress was steady, with a growth rate of just under 4 per cent. Like Denmark, Norway sought its security by membership in NATO, after rejecting a Swedish proposal for establishment of a Nordic defense union; and it joined EFTA in 1960. Thus, the three Scandinavian countries continued to present the world with a model of civilized cooperative living. Their value to world diplomacy was recognized by the choice of Norway's Trygve Lie and Sweden's Dag Hammarskjöld as first and second secretary-general of the United Nations, and of Sweden's Count Bernadotte as UN mediator in the Arab-Israeli dispute.

Chapter Seven

CRISES AND
READJUSTMENT,
1953-1960

BETWEEN 1949 and 1954, the Far East had been the center of world tension. With the defeat of the Communist guerrillas in Malaya and the Philippines, the signature of the Korean armistice, and the division of Vietnam, a temporary peace returned to that troubled area. The focus of crisis shifted to the Middle East, where the forces of resurgent Arab nationalism clashed with the colonialism of Western Europe, and to Central Europe, where two satellite nations challenged the imperial control of Soviet communism. These conflicts, which culminated in the concurrent Suez invasion and Hungarian uprising of October–November 1956, did not disturb the temporary truce in the Cold War that had been observed by Russia and the United States since the ending of the Berlin Blockade in 1949. In November 1958, however, Soviet Premier Khrushchev precipitated a second Berlin crisis, which reached its climax and perhaps its solution with the erection of the Berlin Wall on August 13, 1961. Both the Suez and Hungarian crises further emphasized the inability of the individual European states to act alone either directly against, or even contrary to, the wishes of one or both of the continent-states; and realization of their impotence when acting individually impelled the states of Western Europe to restore their significance not only by coordinating but by integrating their economic and political activity.

CRISIS IN THE MIDDLE EAST: SUEZ

Establishment of European Hegemony of the Arab World. In the hundred years following Mohammed's death in 632, the Arabs surged from their homeland in the Arabian Peninsula to conquer North Africa and Spain, Syria, Persia, and Central Asia as far as the Indus River; and later Moslem conquests included the islands of Indonesia, the upper valley of the Nile and central Africa beyond the Sahara. During the next eight hundred years, in spite of the fall of several great dynasties, Arab rule was only overthrown in Spain, for a temporary period in parts of the Holy Land by the Crusaders, and in Central Asia by the Mongols. Between the fourteenth and sixteenth centuries, the Ottoman Turks expanded their empire to include most of the Arab world, accepted the Moslem religion, and built upon the Arabs' cultural achievements. The European powers profited from the growing weakness of the Turks throughout the nineteenth century to take possession of those parts of the Arab world that were economically or strategically attractive to them. The French took Algeria in 1829–47 and made protectorates of Tunisia in 1881 and of Morocco in 1912. The British, who were principally concerned with safeguarding the sea routes to India and the Far East, took the port of Aden, which controls the mouth of the Red Sea, as early as 1802, and soon established protectorates over the sheikdoms, like Muscat and Oman, along the southern and eastern shores of the Arabian Peninsula. The completion of the Suez Canal in 1869, by a French company financed largely by France and Turkey, turned British attention to Egypt, where Turkish sovereignty over the pasha had been purely nominal since Napoleon's invasion in 1798. After buying a controlling interest in the Suez Canal Company in 1875, the British found an excuse for bombarding Alexandria and occupying Egypt in 1882. They thus assured themselves control of the sea route to India through the fortified ports of Gibraltar, Malta, Cyprus, Suez, and Aden. In 1911, the Italians seized the Turkish provinces of Tripoli and Benghazi, thereby completing European hold of the North African coast. Within these areas, European domination produced, before the First World War, a ferment among the Arab military leaders and intellectuals who desired the overthrow of European control, modernization of Moslem society, and national independence.

The Arab Revolt that broke out in 1916 against Turkish control of the Arab lands in Asia, was led by Hussein, the Grand Sharif of Mecca and head of the Hashemite family who claimed descent from Mohammed. The military campaigns were directed by his third son, Feisal, who entered Damascus in triumph on October 3, 1918, in the expectation of uniting in an independent state all the Arab lands of the Near East and the Arabian Peninsula. In accordance with a secret agreement of 1916, however, the French were permitted to rule Syria and Lebanon as mandated territories under the League of Nations, while the British took as mandates Iraq, where Feisal was installed as king; Transjordan, which provided a throne for his brother Abdullah; and Palestine, where a Jewish "national home" was to be created. Hussein, the father of the two new kings, was driven from Mecca by a rival Arabian sheik, Ibn Saud, who, after gaining control of most of the peninsula by 1932, renamed his kingdom Saudi Arabia. The Arab world was thus "Balkanized," divided into a series of small, jealous states, which in 1919 had only two positive aims in common—the end of foreign domination and opposition to the establishment of a Jewish national home in Palestine.

French Unpopularity in Syria and Lebanon. During the interwar years, nationalism in the Arab world expressed itself in the desire of each of the small states for independence. The French mandate in Syria was particularly unpopular. Feisal was expelled from Damascus by force in 1920; the Druse minority was antagonized into bloody rebellion; Damascus was shelled in 1926 to end a nationalist uprising; and Léon Blum's attempt to end the mandate in 1936 was not ratified by the French parliament. In Lebanon, where 52 per cent of the population was Christian, the French forfeited their initial popularity by adopting an anticlerical policy, restricting civil freedom, and giving French business a strangle hold on large areas of the Lebanese economy.

British Control in Iraq, Transjordan, Palestine, and Egypt. The British were little more successful in their mandates. A popular revolt in Iraq in 1920 cost thousands of lives. Continuing nationalist agitation, the skillful pliability of Feisal, and the grant of military bases and economic concessions, persuaded Britain to sign a treaty in 1930 giving Iraq its independence. But the British remained unpopular because of their persistent economic influence, their policy on Palestine, and the success of Nazi propagandists. Transjordan, comprising the lands east of the Jordan River, was handed to Abdullah in 1921, and he was supported in power with British financial assistance of from half a million to a million dollars annually and by the efficient, British-led Arab Legion. Extreme nationalists opposed both the British and Abdullah, who was accused of leniency toward the Jews and of subserviency to Britain. The thorniest problem was Palestine. In 1919, the Arabs outnumbered the Jews ten to one and were willing to envisage a small continuing Jewish influx. In the Balfour Declaration of 1917, however, the British announced they "viewed with favour the establishment in Palestine of a national home for the Jewish people." Immigration, particularly after the Nazis took power in Germany, rose sharply, and by 1939 there were 445,000 Jews, just under half the Arab population. The Arabs used violence against both the Jews and the British to stop the Jewish immigration. The British, after unsuccessfully offering to partition the country into Jewish and Arab states, finally in 1939 attempted to win the favor of the Arabs, by promising independence in ten years and the end of Jewish immigration in five, unless the Arabs agreed to its continuance. Since the Arabs demanded immediate independence, the British incurred the hatred of both sides.

In Egypt, the British failed to win favor by their unilateral declaration of independence in 1922, since they retained control of Egyptian foreign affairs and defense, and the majority nationalist party, the Wafd, continued to agitate for complete independence. Shortly after the accession of the country's second king, Farouk I, in 1936, the British government felt compelled by Italian advances in Ethiopia to agree to end its military occupation of Egypt. In return, the British were allowed a larger military base in the Suez Canal zone for the twenty-year life of the treaty. Thus, at the outbreak of the Second World War, independence movements were powerful in Syria and Lebanon, while semi-independent Arab states were in existence in Iraq, Egypt, and the Arabian Peninsula. European interest in the Arab countries was still dictated primarily by strategic considerations, and economic interests were largely in the more traditional products like cotton, tropical foodstuffs, and small quantities of raw materials like phosphates.

European Interests in Arab Oil. After the Second World War, three factors assumed revolutionary importance in shaping the evolution of the Arab world—oil, Pan-Arab nationalism, and social revolution. Oil was discovered in southern Iran before the First World War, and the concession was taken over by the Anglo-Iranian Oil Company. Between the wars, oil deposits in Iraq were tapped by a joint partnership of British, American, Dutch, and French capital, and oil pipelines were laid from the oil fields of Kirkuk in Iraq to Haifa in Palestine, and to Tripoli in Lebanon. Other deposits were discovered along the Persian Gulf, largely by American companies, but at the outbreak of war, those wells had been little exploited. In 1939, the Middle East was still the infant of the oil-producing regions of the world, accounting for only 16 million tons. After the war, the great demand for sources of power,

Europe's dollar shortage, and the determination of American companies to exploit low-cost Arabian oil caused a vast boom in oil production in the Middle East. In Saudi Arabia, large deposits of oil, struck in 1938, were developed by the Arabian American Oil Company (Aramco); and an enormously long pipeline was constructed from the oil fields on the Persian Gulf to Sidon in Lebanon, between 1948 and 1950. Production rose from 165,000 barrels daily in 1946 to half a million in 1950 and to over a million in 1955. The American companies paid the highest oil royalties in the area, 50 per cent of profits, and by 1955 Ibn Saud was receiving more than $250 million annually. Even more important deposits were discovered in the small British-protected sheikdom of Kuwait by the Kuwait Oil Company, which was owned jointly by British Petroleum and the Gulf Oil Company, but managed largely by the British. By 1954, this country of 200,000 people was the largest oil producer in the Middle East, with annual output of 47.7 million tons, and receipts in royalties of over $250 million; and during the following five years, production increased 50 per cent. Other sources were also tapped in the island-sheikdom of Bahrein, and in nearby Qatar, both of which were under British protection. In 1954, they produced 6 million tons of oil. Meanwhile, the older fields in Iraq continued to expand production. In Iraq, the holding was held jointly by British, Dutch, French, and American concerns, who increased production between 1947 and 1954 from 4.5 million tons to 30.66.

Conflict over Nationalization of Anglo-Iranian Oil Co. In the first six years after the war, however, the major oil supplies came from the fields of the Anglo-Iranian Oil Company, in which the British government held a majority interest. As a result, when the Iranian government of Dr. Mohammed Mossadeq announced, on April 29, 1951 the nationalization of the Anglo-Iranian Oil Company, the British government was one of the parties to the dispute. Mossadeq succeeded in inflaming his countrymen against the British and turned down not only the British government's attempt to refer the matter to the International Court of Justice but also several offers of better royalties. The company abandoned its installations at Abadan in October, and production ceased. The Iranian economy was unable to stand the economic strain of the loss of royalties and the cost of supporting the thousands of workers left jobless. Mossadeq attempted to ride out the storm by taking the power to govern by personal decree in July 1952; and on August 13, 1953, he

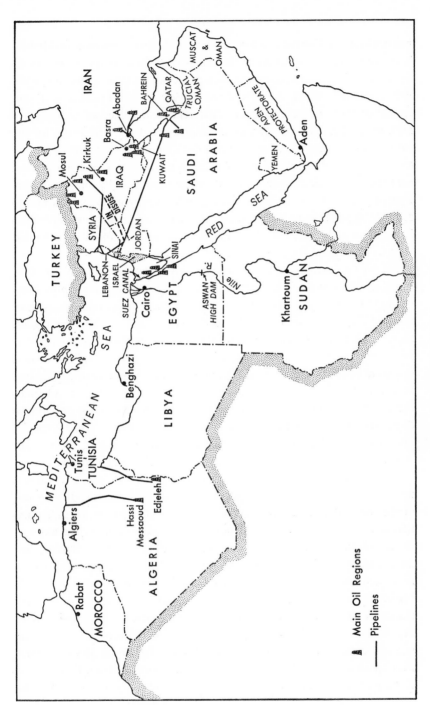

THE ARAB WORLD, 1956

Main Oil Regions
Pipelines

usurped the shah's constitutional rights by dissolving parliament himself. The shah thereupon dismissed him and fled the country when rioting broke out, but returned in triumph a few days later when the army gained control of Teheran. Mossadeq himself was arrested and sentenced to three years' solitary confinement; and a face-saving compromise agreement was signed with an international oil consortium for the formation of a new National Iranian Oil Company. The Anglo-Iranian Company took 40 per cent of the holdings in the new company and was compensated both by the Iranian government and by the American, French, and Dutch companies sharing in the new company. Iran was to receive 50 per cent of the profits of the new company. New discoveries in 1956 brought Iranian oil production above that of Iraq, exceeded only by Saudi Arabia and Kuwait.

Oil thus gave the Western powers a vital economic stake in the Arab world in addition to their strategic concern with the area as the gateway to Asia. Whereas in 1938 the area was producing only one-twentieth of the world's oil, by 1948 it produced one-eighth and in 1960 one-fourth. Since almost none was consumed in the area, the total production was available for export to the industrial countries whose use of oil as a source of power began to rival that of coal. Vast amounts of capital had been invested in the area by a small number of very large private companies, mostly American, British and French. The enormous importance of steady oil supplies to their economies and, at times, direct financial involvement in the oil companies, gave the governments of these countries a direct interest in the political stability of the Arab world.

Rise of Arab Nationalism. That stability, which for so long was based upon Western support for the princely regimes that controlled every oil-producing state, was, however, disturbed by the forces of Arab nationalism and by the demands for political and economic liberation of the depressed masses. During the war and after, Arab nationalists had three demands—the ouster of the foreigner, the prevention of a Jewish national home in Palestine, and the union of the Arab world. When a pro-Nazi uprising in Iraq in April 1941 overthrew the regent and endangered British troop movements through Basra to the Libyan front, the British seized control of the whole country; in June, in cooperation with the Free French, they occupied Syria and Lebanon; and in August, in cooperation with the Russians, they took control of Iran. By a display of military force in the streets of Cairo in February 1942, they compelled King Farouk to appoint the pro-British Nahas Pasha as premier. In the French colonies in North Africa, the unwillingness of the French to do more than widen the electorate caused a strengthening of movements for national independence, led by Habib Bourguiba in Tunisia, Ferhat Abbas in Algeria, and the Sultan Sidi Mohammed ben-Yusef in Morocco. Once the Nazi danger was ended, the British attempted to work in cooperation with the nationalist forces to maintain their position. The independence of Syria and Lebanon, recognized in principle by the French since 1943, became a reality when British and French troops were finally evacuated in 1946. The British government hoped the new republics would align themselves with Iraq which was favored by the British as a force to unite the Arab countries of the Fertile Crescent.[1] In strong man Nuri es-Said Pasha, who was the power behind each of the twenty-one Iraqi cabinets between 1943 and the revolution of 1958, the British found a fairly constant ally. In neighboring Transjordan, which was run as the personal fief of Abdullah, their influence and financing were still welcome; and in 1947 Transjordan signed a treaty of friendship and brotherhood with Iraq. Syria and Lebanon, however, were reluctant to move into the orbit of Iraq, particularly when its pre-eminence was being challenged by Egypt.

Israeli Victory in the Palestine War. Egypt now took the lead, first of Pan-Arab nationalism and then of Arab social revolution. On October 8, 1944, Farouk dismissed Nahas Pasha. His successor was assassinated the day he declared war on Germany. Riots in February 1946 brought the ouster of yet another premier for insufficient toughness in negotiating a new treaty with Britain. Even when an agreement was finally initialed in 1947, by which Britain would evacuate its troops from Egypt by 1949, the refusal of Britain to recognize the Sudan as part of Egypt prevented the treaty's ratification. Egyptian feelings were therefore already inflamed against Britain when affairs in Palestine came to a crisis. Unable to stand the further financial strain, or even the moral dilemma, of remaining in Palestine against the wishes of both Jews and Arabs, the British government attempted unsuccessfully to win American cooperation in finding a solution; then, in February 1947, it handed the problem to the United Nations, which sanctioned a partition plan for the creation of a Jewish and an Arab state. Although the Arabs rejected partition,

[1] Fertile Crescent refers to the countries of the Tigris-Euphrates Valley and of the shores of the Eastern Mediterranean.

the British withdrew their troops, as they had promised, on May 15, 1948. Fighting was already widespread within the country. When David Ben-Gurion proclaimed the foundation of the state of Israel on May 14, the Arab states found at last a force to unite them, in their enmity of the new state. The instrument for their united action was the Arab League, founded in Cairo on March 22, 1945 by Iraq, Syria, Lebanon, Trans-jordan, Saudi Arabia, and Egypt, for "the strengthening of the relations between the member states and the co-ordination of their policies." The League was to be the platform for the ideas of Arab unity that had been effectively spread from Geneva during the interwar years by the great apostle of Pan-Arabism, Chekib Arslan, author of the extremely influential book, *The Arab Nation*. The forces of the League entered Palestine on May 15, the major successes being won by Transjordan's Arab Legion. But the desperate and united forces of the Jewish army were rapidly able to push back the divided and badly equipped Arab forces. The Lebanese and Syrians made only a token show of force. The Arab Legion did not enter territory assigned to Israel under the UN partition plan. The Egyptians were ignominiously pushed back out of the Negev. Between February and April 1949, armistice agreements were signed under United Nations auspices. With the help of funds raised all over the world, and especially in the United States, private American investment, and German reparations payments, Israel succeeded in surviving the Arab League's economic blockade. Hatred of Israel was, however, maintained at fever pitch by the refusal of the Arab states to attempt to resettle the 900,000 Arab refugees from Israel, who remained in refugee camps around Israel's borders, meagerly fed with relief supplies from the United Nations Relief for Palestine Refugees.

Military Revolution in Egypt. The failure in the Palestine war transformed the Pan-Arab movement into a political and social revolution. The leaders of the new movement were Arab officers who blamed the defeats in the war upon the governments and the anachronistic social systems of their own countries. The Syrian government was overthrown in March 1949; and a group of army officers began a moderate reform program and established a relatively efficient state bureaucracy. In Egypt, the Moslem Brotherhood, a fanatic Moslem sect that demanded the purification of Islamic society, agitated for the end of Western influences. Farouk, immensely wealthy in the midst of growing economic distress, sought to maintain his power by pandering to the anti-British passions of the mob. In October 1951, his obedient parliament declared him "King of Egypt and the Sudan" and abrogated the Anglo-Egyptian Treaty of 1936. Guerrilla warfare broke out around the British bases in the Suez Canal Zone, and the British replied with force, on one occasion storming the police barracks at Ismailia. After six months of disorders, a group of young army officers led by Major General Mohammed Naguib seized power on the night of July 22–23, 1952, and promised a far-reaching renovation of Egyptian society. In September, all estates of over 200 acres were confiscated; in 1953, all of the political parties were dissolved and were replaced by a single mass movement, the National Liberation Rally; corruption trials were staged to punish the officials of the old regime. In 1954, Naguib was pushed aside by Colonel Gamal Abdel Nasser, the most powerful member of the Revolutionary Command Council, the instrument by which the army had run the new regime.

British Evacuation of Suez Canal Zone. The British Government at first welcomed the new Egyptian government, and negotiations advanced rapidly on the twin issues of the Sudan and the evacuation of the Suez Canal zone. In February 1953, the two governments agreed to end their "condominium" in the Sudan, which had been established in 1899; for an interim period of three years, the Sudan was to be self-governing, after which it was to decide by plebiscite whether or not to unite with Egypt. (By 1956, Sudanese fears of Egyptian predominance had become so great that the premier, formerly a strong supporter of union with Egypt, declared the Sudan independent.) After stormy months of negotiation, a Suez Canal Zone Treaty was finally signed between the two states on October 19, 1954. Britain agreed to withdraw its troops from the Suez Canal zone base by June 18, 1956; the British would be permitted to reactivate the base in the case of an attack on one of the members of the Arab League or on Turkey. The United States government, which had been pressing Nasser to conclude this agreement, rewarded him with a $40 million loan for economic development and agreed to consider plans for the construction of a high dam at Aswan on the Upper Nile.

Nasser's Ambitions. Although Nasser was attacked for concluding the treaty by the Moslem Brotherhood, the Communists, and Egyptian nationalists, and was even the object of an assassination attempt, he had clearly carried out a great coup by peacefully ousting the British. For the next two years, he concentrated on the military and economic strengthening of Egypt. Failing to persuade the American government to supply him with military equipment he turned to the Soviet Union, which in September 1955, agreed to send him jet fighters, tanks, submarines, artillery, and small arms, without making any political preconditions. This move, called by one Middle East expert "a single stroke of astounding political genius," was a well-timed Soviet attempt to move into the place that Britain was vacating; its success seemed certain because, while pressing the Arabs to side with the West in its conflict with the Soviet Union, the Western powers would not side with the Arabs in their conflict with Israel. The one anti-Communist military alliance which any Arab state had been persuaded to join, the Bagdad Pact, comprising by October 1955 Britain, Turkey, Iran, Pakistan, and Iraq, proved to be a liability to the West. It branded the Iraqi premier, Nuri es-Said, as a tool of the West and destroyed his standing at home, but it also appeared to Nasser to be an attempt by the Western powers to make Iraq rather than Egypt the arbiter of the Arab world.

Nasser redoubled his efforts to take the lead of Arab nationalism. In the Palestinian refugees in Jordan, who as a result of Abdullah's annexation of the territories west of the Jordan outnumbered the Bedouins who were loyal to the Hashemite dynasty, Nasser had a passionate body of supporters. One of them had carried out the assassination of Abdullah in 1951, and refugee pressure on his successor Hussein sufficed to prevent him from joining the Bagdad Pact. In Syria, the increasing strength of the left-wing Baath Socialist party gave Nasser leverage on the government. Above all, Egypt's role in the continuing border clashes with Israel and in denying Israeli ships and cargoes the use of the Suez Canal made Egypt the principal hope of destroying the Jewish state. An essential element of the coming tragedy was the growing conviction of Western leaders, notably the British, that Nasser's undisguised aim of hegemony of the Arab world could be halted not by appeasement but by force alone.

Independence Movements in French North Africa. Nasser's ambitions in the Fertile Crescent had embroiled him with the British; his determination to aid independence movements in Arab countries of North Africa also embittered his relations with the French. Halfhearted attempts to satisfy nationalist aspirations of the Moslem populations of Tunisia, Algeria, and Morocco by moderate reform programs were unsuccessful. In Tunisia, in spite of the exile of Habib Bourguiba, the leader of the main independence movement Neo-Destour, nationalist organization became strong in the trade-union movement, and Neo-Destour increased rapidly in size and confidence. The attempt of MRP Premier Robert Schuman to grant autonomy in 1950 was blocked by French settlers and their supporters in the French parliament. Violence continued throughout 1952–53, the French administration jailing thousands of suspected nationalists and terrorists of the French colonists' group, the Red Hand, murdering many others. In July 1954, however, Premier Mendès-France freed Bourguiba, and himself flew to Tunis to promise internal autonomy, which was granted a year later. In March 1956, Tunisia's rights to control its own foreign policy and to maintain its own defense were recognized, although France retained the right to station troops in Tunisia and to operate the Bizerta naval base. In Morocco, the French attempted to break the strength of the nationalist movement, which had formed around the Sultan Sidi Mohammed ben-Yusef and in the Istiqlal party, by turning the Berber tribesmen against the Arabs. Their instrument was el-Glaoui, the pasha of Marrakesh who, with the support of the French Resident-General Juin and of the extremely wealthy and influential French colonists, demanded the deposing of the sultan. After nationalist riots in 1952 and 1953, the French government banned the Communist and Istiqlal parties and deported the sultan to Madagascar. Violence and terrorism increased, since the French had succeeded in uniting all factions of Moroccans against them. When even el-Glaoui demanded the return of the sultan, the French were forced to reverse themselves; in November, he was recognized as the lawful sovereign of Morocco; in March 1956, Morocco was given the internal autonomy, and in May, its full sovereignty.

Nasser's part in aiding Tunisian and Moroccan independence was restricted largely to financial and propaganda support. His aid to the rebellion in Algeria was more open and more significant. The French had turned down Ferhat Abbas' demand in the Algerian Manifesto of 1943 for internal autonomy, and when Victory-day rejoicings on May 8, 1945 turned into anti-French riots, they had used tanks and fighter planes to subdue the mobs, killing as many as 50,000 Moslems. Attempted conciliation through the Algerian Statute of 1947, which aimed at giving Moslem Algerians greater political representation, produced such overwhelming support for Messali Hadj, an outspoken supporter of

Pan-Arabism, that most of the concessions were quickly withdrawn; and Algeria seemed to have been pacified. A small terrorist offshoot of Hadj's organization, known as the Special Organization and headed by Ahmed Ben Bella, was, however, encouraged by the Egyptian government to enlist in Cairo Algerians trained in guerrilla warfare; and, in 1954, this group, calling itself the National Liberation Front (FLN) ordered a revolutionary insurrection throughout Algeria in November. With Egyptian arms and money, and by ruthless terrorism, the FLN gained control of the Algerian independence movement. The French, faced with the loss of Tunisia and Morocco, were determined not to be pushed out of Algeria, especially as they were transferring many battle-hardened troops from Indochina. Whereas there were only 200,000 European settlers in Tunisia and 300,000 in Morocco, there were a million in Algeria. In more than a century of colonization, these settlers had modernized the Algerian economy, building roads, railroads, ports, factories, schools, universities, and hospitals, as well as creating a thriving agriculture. This economic stake was greatly increased by the discovery of vast oil and natural-gas deposits in the Sahara Desert where systematic exploration had begun in 1953. The French government increased the number of troops in Algeria to almost 500,000. Gunboats patrolled the coast to intercept arms shipped in from Egypt. Most important of all, by 1956 the French government had decided that a direct blow to bring down Nasser would aid them in crushing the rebellion in Algeria.

Nationalization of the Suez Canal Company. The one hope of winning Nasser's friendship for the West seemed to be by supporting his ambitious schemes for the economic development of Egypt. With population increasing by half a million a year, Egypt's most urgent need was for land reclamation by irrigation. The construction of the high dam on the Nile at Aswan appeared to be the key to Egypt's problems because it would irrigate two million acres and increase arable land by 30 per cent; at the same time, it would produce hydroelectric power in vast quantity at low price and thereby make possible industrialization in the Upper Nile. The work was estimated to cost $1.4 billion and to take ten years. In spite of Nasser's arms deal with Russia, the American and British governments agreed in 1955 to put up $56 million and $14 million, respectively, while the International Bank for Reconstruction would provide $200 million, on its normal condition of technical control of the project and supervision of the Egyptian budget during the period of the loan. Nasser did not moderate his criticism of the Western powers, however, and, apparently in the hope of getting better terms from the West, he made it known that Russia had offered to finance the Aswan Dam on liberal terms with no strings attached. In the United States, criticism of the Aswan Dam loan was voiced by supporters of Israel, by Southern cotton growers fearing new Egyptian competition, and by Congressmen determined to pare American foreign-aid commitments. On July 19, 1956, the State Department informed the Egyptian ambassador that the offer had been canceled; and shortly afterward, both the British government and the International Bank also withdrew their loan offers. The Russians did not at once make good their supposed promise to finance the dam; and Nasser, faced with enormous loss of support at home, sought a dramatic step to strike back at the West and to regain his prestige. On July 26, 1956, he nationalized the Suez Canal Company, announcing that canal revenue would finance the building of the dam.

European Reactions. The shares of the Suez Canal Company were largely owned by Britain and France. Annual revenues were $100 million, but profits were only $31 million. Since 1949, Egypt had been receiving a bare $2 million each year, although under Nasser's pressuring, the Company agreed in 1956 to invest $60 million in Egyptian development projects. The concession originally granted the Company was due to expire in 1968, at which time the Company was to pass into Egyptian hands. By nationalizing the Company, Nasser could claim that he was merely taking possession twelve years ahead of schedule. The operation of the canal was governed by the Suez Canal Convention of 1888, which guaranteed freedom of passage to the ships of all nations in peace or war, except where dangerous to Egyptian security, a clause that Egypt had invoked to block the canal to Israeli shipping. The British government felt itself directly challenged by Nasser in several ways. The Suez Canal Company's property and operations, in which the British government was a major shareholder, had been seized, and compensation seemed uncertain. A threat was posed to the use of the canal by British shipping, which accounted for one third of the 14,666 ships using the canal in 1955, and to British oil supplies, half of which passed through the canal; for the Egyptians were regarded as incapable of running the canal efficiently, of providing skilled pilots, and of making the necessary capital investments in the future to widen the canal for bigger oil tankers. Above all, Nasser was distrusted, in British Prime Minister Eden's words, as a "megalomaniac dictator" with leanings toward the Communist world, who could not be trusted to observe the 1888 Convention. "No arrangements for the future of this great international waterway," Eden told the House of Commons, "could be acceptable to Her Majesty's Government which would leave it in the unfettered control of a single power which could, as recent events have shown, exploit it purely for purposes of national policy." Aware that the withdrawal of British troops from the Suez Canal zone on July 19 had given Nasser the courage to nationalize the canal, the British government determined on July 27 to use force if necessary "to keep the canal international." The French were equally willing to take strong action, in part because of their holdings in the Suez Canal Company, but principally because they saw in the canal issue an excuse for dislodging Nasser from power and thereby ending his aid to the Algerian rebellion. The Israeli government, disturbed by Egypt's receipt of Soviet arms, and by the constant border raids from Egyptian irregulars from the Gaza Strip, saw in the canal crisis an opportunity of waging a preventive war against Egypt with the aid of the British and the French.

Immediate military action was not taken, however, because the British were not prepared for such a large operation by air and sea, and because the American government urged negotiation. The British and French therefore pressed on with preparations for military seizure of the Suez Canal, calling up reservists, massing paratroopers on Cyprus, and gathering an invasion fleet at Malta. At the same time, negotiation was attempted. A conference of twenty-four maritime nations met in London on August 16–23 and decided to propose to Nasser the management of the canal by an international body representing the states using the canal. When Nasser turned down this idea, American Secretary of State Dulles attempted another delaying tactic by proposing formation of a Suez Canal Users' Association, which would provide its own pilots, pay for the upkeep of the canal, and give Egypt a fee for its use. When Nasser rejected this proposal also, Britain and France took their grievance to the Security Council, which elaborated six "principles" that Egypt should respect in running the canal, only to have them vetoed by the Soviet representative. To the British, French, and Israelis delay appeared to be bringing a worsening of their position in the Middle East. Nasser's success in seizing and in operating the canal had immensely bolstered his prestige not only at home but in Syria, where the pro-Egyptian Baath Socialist party had taken office in June, and in Jordan, where the British commander of the Arab Legion had been ejected and elections had produced a victory for pro-Nasser parties. From mid-September, border raids on Israel had been stepped up, and there was evidence that Egypt was stockpiling Soviet equipment in Sinai in preparation for a full-scale invasion of Israel.

British-French-Israeli Invasion of Egypt. Although the diplomatic archives will be closed for many years and when opened may not contain the relevant documents, it is now suspected that the British, French, and Israelis concerted their plans for the invasion of Egypt at secret meetings on the outskirts of Paris, in late October, which were attended by Israeli Premier Ben-Gurion, British Foreign Secretary Lloyd, and French Premier Mollet and Foreign Minister Pineau. On the morning of October 29, the Israeli Army invaded Egypt across the Sinai Peninsula. On October 30, the British and French governments issued an extraordinary ultimatum to both Egypt and Israel, ordering them to pull their troops back ten miles on either side of the Suez Canal, although the Israelis had not yet reached that point, and to permit British and French troops temporarily to seize the canal. Nasser informed the British ambassador that Egypt would fight: "The last time we let you British in, you stayed seventy years." President Eisenhower was not informed of the ultimatum in advance and was furious to learn of it first on the ticker tape. That day, the American ambassador to the United Nations demanded that Israeli forces withdraw from Egyptian soil immediately, but the resolution was vetoed by the British and French. For a week, British and French planes bombed Egyptian airfields, radio stations, and railroads; paratroops from Cyprus captured Port Said on November 5; and the huge invasion fleet, which had been slowly steaming from Malta, finally put ashore 22,000 troops the next day. By then, the Israelis were in control of the whole of the Sinai Peninsula, where they had without difficulty defeated the Egyptian Army and captured vast stockpiles of military equipment. The Egyptians replied with sporadic street fighting and by sinking blockships at both ends of the canal. Syria cut the oil pipelines from Iraq to the Mediterranean; but no military aid to Egypt was proffered by the other Arab countries. The British and French, however, were under extreme international pressure to agree to a cease-fire. On November 2, the UN General Assembly had demanded an immediate cease-fire by a vote of 64 to 5, only Australia and New Zealand standing with the British, French, and Israelis. Canadian Premier Lester Pearson had provided a face-saving solution by proposing the formation of a UN peace-keeping force for the canal area. President Eisenhower, who was seeking re-election on November 6, was pressuring all sides to stop the fighting. At 11:30 P.M. on November 5, Soviet Premier Marshal Bulganin sent an ultimatum to the three powers, threatening the use of force, including rockets, if they did not cease their aggression. Finally, a run on the British pound was threatening the whole British economy. The cease-fire was therefore ordered at 5 P.M. on November 6.

Strengthening of Nasser. For two years after the Suez invasion, Nasser's fortunes were on the rise. The British and French forces left Egypt in December, and Israel was finally compelled to give up Sinai in January and the Gaza Strip in March 1957. The canal was cleared by a United Nations force under an American general, and by May 1957 all the maritime nations, except France, were paying tolls to Egypt. Jordan renounced its alliance with Britain, refused further financial aid, and joined an Arab solidarity pact with Egypt, Syria, and Saudi Arabia. On February 1, 1958, Nasser's dream of heading a Pan-Arab state seemed to have advanced greatly when the Baath government of Syria agreed to the formation of the United Arab Republic by the merger of Egypt and Syria. The domination of Egypt in the new state was assured by choice of Nasser as president, and by grant to Egyptians of three-fourths of the seats in the parliament. Soon afterward, the Imam of Yemen fused his state with the United Arab Republic in a somewhat vaguely defined federal union. Finally, on July 14, 1958, the Iraqi military, strongly influenced by the example of Nasser, seized power in Bagdad, while a mob murdered, in unspeakably brutal manner, the crown prince, the former regent, and Nuri es-Said, the power behind the throne, and shortly afterward young King Feisal II himself. The wave of social revolution thus seemed to have broken on the most firmly entrenched and pro-Western of the Arab states, and at the same time to have removed from the scene Nasser's great rival for Arab leadership, Nuri al-Said.

The Eisenhower Doctrine. In spite of its attitude in the Suez crisis, the American government was not willing to see the Middle East fall into the grasp of an Egypt tied so closely to Soviet military and economic aid. On January 5, 1957, the President proposed to Congress the "Eisenhower Doctrine"; the United States would oppose, by force if necessary, Communist aggression against any Middle Eastern country, and would distribute between $400 and $500 million over a two-year period to countries accepting the Doctrine. The first adherent was the reactionary King Saud of Saudi Arabia, who was feted in the United States and who responded by guaranteeing the position of the American oil companies and the maintenance of the American air base at Dhahran. In May 1957, King Hussein of Jordan forced the resignation of the pro-Nasser government, and, with the aid of Saudi forces and the presence of the American Sixth Fleet off Beirut, foiled a plot to overthrow him; and in February 1958, Hussein joined with his cousin Feisal of Iraq in counter-ing the formation of the United Arab Republic by declaring the fusion of Jordan and Iraq into the "Arab Union." The real test of the Eisen-hower Doctrine, however, occurred at the time of the Iraq revolution, when President Chamoun of Lebanon and King Hussein of Jordan appealed for help to prevent their overthrow by internal revolution. British paratroops were at once flown to Jordan, and a strong American task force was sent to Lebanon. This intervention, while successful in its immediate objective, was probably harmful in the long run. Liberal regimes like Chamoun's in Lebanon were branded as being too pro-Western; the return of British paratroops only two years after the Suez invasion was an affront to Arab nationalism.

The Arab World after 1958. After 1958, both Russia and the West-ern powers became reticent about too open an involvement in the affairs of the Arab world, since they learned, as Elizabeth Monroe has pointed out, that "in countries torn by internal dissension, foreign powers that try to meddle incur as many liabilities as assets." Both the United States and Russia continued to pour foreign aid into the area. Whereas after the Suez crisis the United States supplied Egypt with over $1 billion in aid, mostly in surplus food, the Soviet Union agreed in October 1958 to guarantee 30 per cent of the $1 billion cost of financing the Aswan High Dam, a far more dramatic stroke in popularizing the benefits of Soviet friendship. The French remained preoccupied with bringing an end to the Algerian war, which was finally achieved, by the grant of indepen-dence, in July 1962. As a result of far-sighted statesmanship on General de Gaulle's part, France retained some influence in its former North African colonies by generous grants of economic aid. Britain after 1958 attempted to restrict its efforts to maintaining its client-states

along the Arabian coast and Persian Gulf and by crushing an independence movement in the colony of Aden. Meanwhile, Pan-Arabism made
little progress. In a quick coup in 1961, Syria broke away from the
United Arab Republic; the Baath party returned to power in Syria in a
coup d'état in March 1963, but did not seek to re-create the union with
Egypt. After the 1958 revolution in Iraq, General Kassim disappointed
Nasser by jailing his supporters and by competing for Arab leadership;
Kassim, however, was executed after a coup d'état in January 1963,
which brought pro-Nasser forces under Abdel Salam Arif to power.
Plans to form a new United Arab Republic of Egypt, Syria, and Iraq
have made little progress, but Israel's plan to divert the waters of the
Jordan River to the Negev Desert did promote a revived interest in the
Arab League whose members met in Cairo in January 1964 to devise
countermeasures, including a unified military command and a plan for
Arab diversion and use of Jordan River waters. The ouster of King Saud
of Saudi Arabia in favor of his brother Feisal in 1966 weakened Nasser's
position, however, by giving the conservative forces in the Arab world
a more persuasive leader; and Feisal challenged Nasser openly by continuing the Saudi support of the royalist forces in Yemen that were
waging a guerrilla war against the Nasser-backed regime of President
Sallal.

Third Arab-Israeli War. For a brief period in 1967, it appeared that
a war for the destruction of Israel would unite the Arab world. In
May, following increased border conflicts of Israel with Syria and Jordan, Nasser called for the withdrawal of the UN peace-keeping force
from Egyptian soil, closed the Gulf of Aqaba to Israeli shipping, and
received pledges of support from eleven Arab nations. In five days
(June 5–10), however, Israel totally defeated the armies of Egypt, Jordan, and Syria, and took possession of the Sinai Peninsula, the right
bank of the Jordan River including the Jordan section of Jerusalem, and
the Syrian Highlands overlooking northeastern Israel.

This Arab defeat had major repercussions in Europe. Egypt's closure
of the Suez Canal forced a re-routing of all Suez-bound shipping especially oil tankers, around South Africa, increasing the cost of Europe's
fuel supplies; Arab countries placed an embargo on the shipping of their
crude oil to Britain and to the United States, in retaliation for their
supposed favoring of Israel in the war; Russia, after attempting unsuccessfully to gain UN condemnation of Israel, began to replace the

lost military equipment of Egypt and Syria and moved part of its Black Sea fleet into Egyptian ports. In Western Europe, where General de Gaulle was the only government leader to take an anti-Israeli stand, the war emphasized once more the political impotence of a divided Europe and the vast difficulty of attaining any form of political consensus among the European nations.

CRISIS IN CENTRAL EUROPE: EAST BERLIN, POZNAN, BUDAPEST

While the Soviet Union was attempting to profit from the anti-Western bias of Arab nationalism and social revolution to establish its own influence in an area that for eighty years had been a Western preserve, it found its apparently secure hegemony in Eastern Europe challenged by forces that the death of Stalin had stimulated.

The East Berlin Uprising. Within twenty-four hours of Stalin's death on March 5, 1953, his posts as premier and first secretary of the Communist party were taken by Georgi Malenkov; and the Soviet Union embarked upon a "New Course" at home and abroad. (See Chapter Eight.) The urgent need of a change of policy toward Eastern Europe was dramatically demonstrated at the beginning of June, when unrest among the industrial workers in Czechoslovakia broke into open riots, during which the city hall of Pilsen (Plzeň) was seized. On June 16, after the East German government had raised work norms, and thereby cut wages, workers demonstrated in the streets of East Berlin, and shouted down ministers who tried to speak to them. The next day, during a general strike, government buildings were set on fire, and Russian tanks attacked. Rioting spread to most of the major cities of East Germany. The Russians quickly regained control of East Berlin by sending in three armored divisions, while in the other cities the workers withdrew behind barricades in their factories. Calm was restored when the East German government promised lower work norms, more consumer goods, cheaper travel, and higher pensions, and admitted that it had moved too fast in industrialization. Living conditions did improve during the next year as prices were reduced, reparations to Russia ended, and Russian-managed factories were handed to East German control; and tension was temporarily relieved.

The "New Course" in Eastern Europe. The East Berlin uprising apparently encouraged the Soviet leaders to press the satellite governments to adopt the New Course, at least in economic matters. The most important change took place in Hungary, where the extremely unpopular Rákosi was replaced as premier by Imre Nagy on July 4. Nagy gave higher priority to consumer and light industries, abolished internment camps, released many political prisoners, and even permitted dissolution of collective farms by vote of a majority of the members. In a short while, Nagy became popular with the mass of the people, but was opposed by the majority of the party leaders, particularly Rákosi who had remained first party secretary. In Rumania, Bulgaria, and Czechoslovakia, a similar attempt was made to alleviate economic tensions by lowering quotas, increasing wages, and slowing down the rate of industrial growth, while posts in party and state were more widely spread to create the impression of a collective leadership. In Czechoslovakia in particular the reforms were successful, and the rise in living standards, following the destruction of potential opposition in the Stalinist period, made the Czechs the most docile of the satellites. In Poland, at first only the slightest alleviation of living conditions was introduced; and the crushing of opposition continued with the arrest of Cardinal Wyszynski in September 1953. Dissatisfaction within the party itself forced the leaders unwillingly to adopt a more liberal attitude from December 1954 on. The power of the secret police was curbed; former Vice-Premier Gomulka was released; two hundred clubs sprang up in which political issues were debated; and an attack was made on the stereotyped forms of Socialist Realism in art. Perhaps the most dramatic policy change was symbolized by the visit of Soviet First Party Secretary Khrushchev to Marshal Tito at Belgrade on May 27–June 2, 1955. The permitted growth of diversity among the satellites made possible a reconciliation with the former heretic, Tito, whose determination to find a national road to socialism had brought about his condemnation by the Cominform in 1948. In spite of the opposition of old-time Stalinists, Khrushchev publicly recognized that the national form of socialist development was "exclusively the concern of the peoples of the respective countries." Three months later, a Soviet-Yugoslav economic assistance pact was concluded. Tito had thus outlasted Stalin's attempt to crush him, and his return to the Communist camp on his own terms was a significant lesson to the other states of Eastern Europe.

Khrushchev, however, who had forced out Malenkov from the premiership in February 1955, was not prepared to accept all aspects of

Malenkov's New Course in the East European satellites. Nagy, a Malenkov protégé, was replaced as Hungarian premier by Rákosi, who upheld the Khrushchev program of continuing industrialization and farm collectivization. On May 14, 1955, the Soviet Union and the East European Communist states signed the Warsaw Pact, as an immediate answer to the admission of West Germany to NATO. The pact legalized the stationing of Soviet troops throughout the satellites, provided for their joint defense under a Soviet commander, and instituted machinery for coordination of foreign policy. After 1954, the Council of Economic Mutual Assistance was revived, to promote specialization and rationalization of industrial development in Eastern Europe and thereby further the economic integration of the Soviet bloc. Nevertheless, at the Twentieth Party Congress in February 1956, Khrushchev again emphasized the possibility of achieving communism by different methods, and by his outright denunciation of Stalin, the ruthless imposer of uniformity, and of Stalinism as a system of repression, he gave the lead to forces in Eastern Europe demanding the overthrow of their own Stalinist regimes. In April, the Stalinist party leader, Chervenkov, was dismissed from the Bulgarian Central Committee. Traicho Kostov, who had been executed in the purge of 1949, was rehabilitated. The Czech government released two prominent "Titoists" and publicly apologized to Tito for the anti-Yugoslav accusations in the Czech purge trials. It was in Poland and Hungary, however, where economic dissatisfaction with the regimes was at its height, that "de-Stalinization" took revolutionary form.

Poznan Riots and the Triumph of Gomulka. In Poland, oppressive labor conditions resulted in a strike by factory workers in Poznan on June 27, during an international trade fair attended by many Western businessmen. In spite of this audience, the army was sent to break up a mass demonstration of factory workers and other Poznan citizens on June 28. Up to a hundred demonstrators were killed, and hundreds were arrested. Although attributing the rioting to "imperialistic agents," the government agreed to raise workers' living standards, and sentences on the rioters were light. In spite of the arrival in mid-July of Marshals Bulganin and Zhukov, the Polish Communists continued their self-criticism. Gomulka was readmitted to the party in August; and on October 19, he was invited to attend a meeting of the Politburo, which obviously intended to ask him to head a new government. To forestall this step, Khrushchev flew to Warsaw, bringing with him former Foreign

Minister Molotov, and at the same time Soviet troops began to move toward Warsaw. A Polish delegation, including Gomulka, apparently met Khrushchev at the airport and told him that if the Soviet troops were not withdrawn the Polish Army would be ordered to resist them and that the whole country would rise in revolt. The next day, after the departure of Khrushchev's party for Moscow, Gomulka was appointed head of a new Polish government and first party secretary. Faced with a government that was clearly popular, genuinely Communist, and desirous of better relations with Russia, Khrushchev determined to accept the Gomulka appointment. Soviet troops were withdrawn to their barracks; the Russian Marshal Rokossovski, who had headed the Polish Army since the end of the war, returned to Russia, and, when Gomulka visited Moscow in November, Khrushchev accepted the domestic policy of the new regime. Gomulka had thus achieved, without challenging the Soviet Union by force, the opportunity to carry out domestic reforms, and had done so by maintaining the power of the Communist party within Poland and by accepting Poland's international obligations as a member of the Soviet camp.

The Hungarian Uprising. In Hungary, the ouster of Nagy in April 1955 had infuriated both the Communist party members and the intellectuals who had welcomed his attempt to create a Hungarian brand of communism; and Rákosi, once back in power, introduced all the most unpopular features of Stalinism—pressure to collectivize farming, arrests of kulaks, party purges, and police terrorism. Nagy himself was expelled from the party in November. Slight concessions followed Khrushchev's denunciation of Stalin at the Twentieth Party Congress; and Rákosi himself was dismissed. Discontent remained strong, however, and events in Poland persuaded the Hungarians that they too could win acceptance of their right to national communism.

The victory of Gomulka in his confrontation with Khrushchev was hailed by the Hungarian intellectuals and workers, and on October 23 a demonstration was organized by the students of Budapest in favor of the Poles. They were joined by large numbers of disgruntled workers in front of the parliament building, where Nagy appeared briefly to ask them to disperse quietly. That evening, Party Secretary Gerö made plain in a radio speech that, although he had just returned from Belgrade, he did not intend to become a Hungarian Tito. The crowds became angry; and one group toppled the monstrous statue of Stalin in the city park.

When the students demanded that a petition, which included the evacuation of Soviet troops from Hungary, should be broadcast, the secret police fired on them, killing several. Meeting in panic, the Central Committee declared the formation of a new government, with Nagy as premier, and called upon Soviet troops to intervene. Soviet tanks at once began to patrol the streets of Budapest, and, when the crowds failed to disperse, several tank commanders fired into them. The uprising then spread to the rest of the country, and revolutionary workers' councils were set up. Soviet Deputy Premier Mikoyan hurried to Budapest on October 25, and, presumably on his instructions, Gerö was replaced as first party secretary by János Kádár; and Nagy, who had been under semiarrest at Communist party headquarters, was permitted to announce that negotiations were beginning for the withdrawal of Soviet forces from Hungary. The next day, Nagy reorganized the government to include non-Communists like the Smallholder Béla Kovács, and declared that Soviet troops would withdraw to their bases after restoration of order. A cease-fire was proclaimed in Budapest on October 28, and the Soviet tanks withdrew. In other parts of the country, where many secret police had been murdered by the crowds, the Soviet troops promised the local revolutionary councils that they would not intervene.

Soviet Suppression. The Hungarians seemed to have achieved an easy victory, and Nagy found himself under pressure to go further in dismantling the Communist hold on Hungary. The one-party system was abolished, and former political parties like the Social Democrats and the Smallholders were reorganized. A special Revolutionary Military Council was set up to control the army. Most important of all, on October 31 Nagy informed the Russians that Hungary intended to withdraw from the Warsaw Pact and adopt a policy of neutrality. The Soviet Union was not prepared to allow Hungary to withdraw from the Communist camp, for its defection would undoubtedly serve as an example to the other satellites. Soviet troops began to cross the border into Hungary on the evening of October 31. On November 1, Hungary withdrew from the Warsaw Pact and asked the UN secretary-general to place on the agenda discussion of Hungary's status. On November 2, Soviet troops surrounded all airfields in central and eastern Hungary and took control of the railroads. On November 3, Soviet troops reached the Austro-Hungarian border. In the early morning hours of November 4, the

Soviet forces suddenly attacked Hungarian troops in Budapest and succeeded in gaining control of the major buildings, in spite of widespread and desperate resistance from the civilian population of the city. On the same day János Kádár, who had been posing as a firm Nagy supporter, was named premier at the Headquarters of the Soviet Army, Nagy fled to asylum in the Yugoslav Embassy, and within a week the Soviet troops were in control of the country. The Hungarians replied with a general strike, during which 200,000 fled across the border into Austria, through harsh winter weather. Nagy himself was arrested by the Russians when leaving the Yugoslav Embassy on a safe-conduct pass issued by Kádár, and was deported to Rumania. In 1958 the Hungarian government announced that he had been executed.

The Soviet decision to use force to overthrow the Nagy government was undoubtedly due partly to unwillingness to tolerate the military defeat inflicted on Russian troops in Budapest on October 23–24 and partly to Nagy's unwise timing in withdrawing from the Warsaw Pact on November 1. But the advocates of intervention within the Soviet government were clearly strengthened by the Franco-British attack on Suez on November 1–6, which disrupted the Western alliance, guaranteed that the Western powers would not come to the aid of Hungary, and diverted world attention from the brutality of Soviet repression to attempted revival of Western colonialism. The Soviet action caused great misgivings among Communists throughout much of the world. Even in Russia student protests were voiced. The United Nations General Assembly called upon Russia to withdraw its troops. The Poles, who had recognized the Nagy government, openly declared their sympathy. Tito, under great pressure at home, declared that, although he approved the intervention of November 4 because it saved communism, the first Soviet intervention of October 23 was a disastrous mistake. Nevertheless, the repression in Hungary had surprisingly little effect in Asia and Africa, and in Eastern Europe it served as a reminder that popular revolution would be forcibly suppressed and would not be supported by the United States.

Changes in Soviet Policy. After the Polish and Hungarian crises, the Soviet government was compelled to review the basis of its policy toward the satellites. The first decision was to remove the most evident sources of discontent, namely the extra-territorial status of Soviet troops and the exploitation of the satellites' economies. One after another, the leaders of East Europe were summoned to Moscow in the early months of 1957, and all were granted greater control over the movement of Soviet troops in their territories, more advantageous trade terms, and large loans amounting to the equivalent of $1 billion. Secondly, the economic integration of Eastern Europe through the Council for Mutual Economic Assistance was speeded up. At its eighth session, held in Warsaw in June 1957, the specialized commissions were authorized to draw up plans for specialization, standardization, and integration for the coming fifteen years. A multilateral payments scheme was to eliminate balance-of-payments difficulties among members. The following January, at a conference in Moscow attended by heads of governments, a comprehensive plan of cooperation was drawn up, and the tasks of member countries were outlined. The ultimate object of the planning was to tie the economies of the East European countries more closely to Russia, as the source of their principal raw materials and as a market for their industrial goods, and to make them dependent upon each other by division of production among them. Rumania, for example, was assigned the role of grain and oil producer; East Germany was to manufacture precision instruments and electrical equipment; Poland, chemicals and ships; and Czechoslovakia, automobiles. Finally, an attempt was made to reach ideological uniformity. The leading role of the Soviet Union in the Socialist camp was warmly espoused by the East Germans, the Czechs, and the Bulgarians, and to a lesser degree by the Kádár regime in Hungary. The most reticent was Poland's Gomulka, who seemed determined in 1957 to justify Poland's right to find its national road to socialism. To reimpose unity, Khrushchev, who had defeated the threat to his own position of the "anti-party group" in June 1957, called the leaders of all the Communist parties in the world to a gigantic celebration of the Fortieth Anniversary of the Bolshevik Revolution, to be held in Moscow in November 1957. Although Gomulka attempted to turn the condemnation of the meeting against "dogmatists" who were unable to apply Marxism-Leninism to fresh situations, the conference chose rather to anathematize the "revisionists" whose reformist ideas offended the fundamental dogma of the party. In this condemnation, which clearly included both Gomulka and Tito, the Russians were strongly supported by the Chinese delegation. The conference ended with a twelve-party declaration referring to the "invincible camp of socialist countries headed by the Soviet Union." Finally, at the Twenty-First Party Congress in Moscow in February 1959, the right of the Soviet Union to leadership was justified by the enormous economic advances envisaged in the Seven-Year Plan. By 1959, therefore, the Soviet Union appeared to have re-established the domination that the events of 1956 had endangered.

THE CONTINUING EAST-WEST CRISIS: WEST BERLIN

While the Soviet Union was attempting to establish its influence in the Middle East and maintain its hold in Eastern Europe, its relations with the United States and Western Europe remained in a stalemate. Between 1953 and 1956 there was even a relaxation of tensions between the two blocs, and wary but inconclusive negotiations were conducted on the principal questions at issue between them. In 1958, however, Soviet Premier Khrushchev abruptly precipitated a second Berlin crisis, which brought the threat of armed conflict near for the following three years.

Mutual Deterrence. In November 1952, General Dwight D. Eisenhower was elected the first Republican President of the United States in twenty years. During the election campaign, he had severely criticized the Democrats' policy of "containment"; and his future secretary of state, John Foster Dulles, had called for a rollback of communism, "a psychological and political offensive" in which the United States would make it known that "it wants and expects liberation to occur." The new administration, however, pledged itself to reduce expenditures, and in December 1953, a new look in America's military policy was announced. Instead of maintaining large ground forces ready for limited wars like that in Korea, the United States would concentrate on the deterrent power of its atomic weapons delivered by the planes of the Strategic Air Command. The threat of "massive retaliation" was to prevent any further expansion of Communist control. In practice, the new military strategy made intervention on behalf of an uprising in a Communist satellite impossible unless the United States was willing to attack Moscow or Peking directly. A state of "mutual deterrence" came to exist with the announcement in 1949 that the USSR had the atomic bomb, in 1953 that it had exploded a hydrogen bomb, and in 1957 that it had placed Sputnik I, the first man-made satellite, in orbit, and thus possessed rockets capable of striking directly at the United States.

After the death of Stalin, the new Soviet leaders at once sought to establish better relations with the West. Following an air collision over the Soviet zone between a British and Soviet aircraft, they proposed a three-power conference on air safety in Germany. At the United Nations, they withdrew their objections to the appointment of Dag Hammarskjöld as secretary-general. Turkey was informed that the Soviet Union was giving up its territorial claims against her. Soviet pressure played an obvious role in bringing the Panmunjom armistice talks in Korea to a successful conclusion. The West European powers responded elatedly to this evidence that the Stalin era was over. On April 20, 1953, Winston Churchill called for talks "at the highest level," behind closed doors, at which the most outstanding problems might be resolved. Although the Soviet suppression of the East Berlin uprising somewhat dampened these hopes, the three Western foreign ministers decided in July to invite the Soviet Union to such a meeting, where the German and Austrian peace treaties could once again be discussed. After five and a half months and the exchange of thirteen notes, it was finally agreed that a conference of foreign ministers would be held in Berlin on January 25, 1954; and to concert their policies, President Eisenhower, Prime Minister Churchill, and Premier Laniel met in Bermuda early in December.

Berlin Foreign Ministers' Conference, 1954. The Berlin Conference (January 25–February 18, 1954) proved a great disappointment. The Western powers proposed that free elections should be held throughout Germany; that the elected assembly should draft a constitution and choose an All-German government; and that this government should negotiate a peace settlement with the occupying powers. Molotov refused to consider free elections, which was hardly surprising so soon after the East German uprising, and proposed instead the formation of a government representing both East and West Germany, which would conduct the elections, negotiate a peace treaty, and maintain German neutrality. The Western powers refused to permit any recognition of the Communist regime of East Germany, and would not agree to the eventual neutralization of Germany. No progress was made toward an Austrian treaty. Molotov refused to consider withdrawing Soviet troops from Austria before conclusion of a German peace settlement, whereas the Western powers proposed the recognition of Austria immediately as a sovereign state and the withdrawal of occupation troops. Finally, the Western powers rejected Molotov's suggestion that they should conclude a European security pact and agree to the withdrawal of most of the occupation forces from Germany within six months. Perhaps the most concrete result of the Berlin Conference was the Soviet announcement on the last day that they were willing to take part in a conference on Korea and Indochina with France, Britain, the United States, the Chinese Communists, the Viet Minh, and representatives of the states of Indochina; and at this conference (April 26–July 20, 1954), the Soviet government undoubtedly pressed the Viet Minh to accept partition along the 17th parallel, in spite of their military victory over the French.

The Rearming of West Germany. After emphasizing once more its refusal to abandon the Communist regime in East Germany, the Soviet Union continued its attempts to block the American plan to rearm West Germany. The constitution of a West German army had first been proposed by Secretary of State Dean Acheson in September 1950, after the early American defeats in Korea. The French government, unwilling to accept the reconstitution of an autonomous German army but unable to oppose American determination to rearm Germans, hit upon the idea of creating a "European army," an integrated army in which the military forces of France, West Germany, Italy, Belgium, the Netherlands, and Luxembourg, would be merged. The treaty creating this European Defense Community (EDC) was signed in Bonn on May 26, 1952; but the treaty was soundly defeated in the French parliament on August 30, 1954. To their surprise and chagrin, the French deputies who had opposed the treaty to prevent the rearmament of Germany, found themselves faced a month later with a proposal for the constitution of a West German army within a West European Union whose only merit was the membership of Great Britain. As a result of the Paris Agreements, which were ratified by the French in December, the occupation of West Germany was to end, and West Germany was to create an army of half a million men and become a member of NATO. The Soviet Union, which had mustered Communist opposition to the EDC treaty and the Paris Agreements in France and Italy and had deluged the Western powers with objections and threats, made a last compromise offer on January 15, 1955, by offering to hold free elections throughout Germany under international supervision on the basis of the electoral laws of East and West Germany. The West paid little attention to this offer, and the Paris Agreements went into force on May 5, 1955. The same month, in retaliation, the East European powers formed the Warsaw Pact.

End of the Allied Occupation of Austria. In spite of the increased animosity that the rearming of Germany had aroused, the Soviet government made a gesture of genuine conciliation in February 1955, by offering to consider the possibility of a separate peace treaty with Austria. Like Germany, Austria had been divided in 1945 into four zones of occupation; Vienna, which like Berlin was in the center of the Soviet zone, was divided into four sectors, but the inner town was made into an international zone. Although Austria was treated officially not as an occupied but as a liberated country and was allowed to set up its own government under the former Social Democratic Chancellor Karl Renner as early as April 1945, a strict denazification policy was applied. Although no reparations were demanded, the Soviet military government interpreted very widely its right to take possession of German assets in the Soviet zone. Food remained short for several years after the end of the war, and relief supplies from UNRRA were a principal sustenance for many of the city-dwellers. The occupation regime continued to function far more smoothly than in Germany, however. Elections held on November 25, 1945 resulted in the reappearance of the two major parties of the interwar years, the People's party representing the Catholic countryside and the Social Democratic party representing the cities, especially Vienna. The Communists received only 5 per cent of the vote. The three-party coalition formed by Renner continued in office, with Leopold Figl of the People's party as chancellor. Currency reform carried out in all four zones in 1947 helped restore the economic stability of the country, and Austria was included with the independent nations of Europe in Marshall's offer of aid in 1947. By 1954, Austria had received $726 million in Marshall Aid, a per capita total one-third higher than that of any other participant. Figl was replaced as chancellor in 1953 by Julius Raab, another member of the People's party. After preliminary conversations between the Austrian ambassador and the Soviet government, Raab was invited to Moscow on April 11–16, 1955, and told the cheering news that an Austrian State Treaty could soon be concluded. The Soviet government was willing to withdraw its troops, accept a settlement of $150 million in goods for its right to German assets, and return control of the oil refineries of eastern Austria. In return, Austria was asked to guarantee its neutrality and to ban foreign bases on its soil. The three Western foreign ministers met with the Soviet foreign minister and representatives of the Austrian government in Vienna and signed the

Austrian State Treaty on May 15. Within three months, occupation forces were completely withdrawn. The motives of the new Russian government, dominated after Malenkov's ouster on February 8 by Khrushchev, were probably to win the support of Yugoslavia, to establish the principle of neutralizing countries lying between the two blocs, and thus to raise again the prospect of preventing German rearmament by neutralizing the two Germanies. Before leaving Vienna, the four foreign ministers announced that they had reached agreement on the holding of a summit conference in Switzerland in early summer.

Summit Conference in Geneva, 1955. For six months after the conclusion of the Austrian State Treaty, a new spirit of good will seemed to sweeten East-West relations. In July, the first high-level Soviet delegation to tour Britain arrived to inspect British farming methods. Soviet Defense Minister Zhukov praised President Eisenhower in a message to the Overseas Press Club in Washington. Chancellor Adenauer was invited in June to pay a visit to Moscow to discuss the establishment of diplomatic relations. Conciliatory gestures to Finland culminated in the return of the naval base of Porkkala in September, even though the Russian lease still had forty-two years to run. In June Khrushchev visited Belgrade and attempted to restore good relations with Tito by blaming the 1948 excommunication of Yugoslavia on Beria, who had been executed two years earlier. Even in the UN disarmament subcommittee set up in 1953, progress was made toward an agreement on control of nuclear weapons. This atmosphere of *détente* persuaded the American, British, and French governments that a meeting of heads of governments would be useful, especially in dealing with the problems of disarmament, European security, German reunification, and East-West contacts.

On July 18–23, 1955, Marshal Bulganin accompanied by Party Secretary Khrushchev met with President Eisenhower, Prime Minister Eden, and Premier Faure in Geneva. The reunification of Germany, which the Western powers regarded as the primary item for discussion, and European security, which the Russians emphasized, were discussed together. The Western proposals again required the holding of free elections throughout Germany, the right of Germany to be a member of NATO, and the inclusion of a reunified Germany in a general European security treaty. Bulganin suggested the conclusion of a fifty-year treaty on collective security, in which the United States and both West and East Germany would participate; the Paris Agreements, the NATO treaty, and the Warsaw Pact would become ineffective after a transition period. Deadlock was reached when it became clear that the Russian government was not willing to risk the elimination of the Communist regime in East Germany, and that the Western powers were equally determined not to give up the Paris Agreements or NATO. On July 21, Eisenhower made his startling "open-skies" proposal, by which the Soviet Union and the United States would "give to each other a complete blueprint of our military establishments, from one end of our countries to the other" and would permit aerial photography by the other. The two would thus make a surprise attack extremely unlikely. The Russians promised to study the plan, but soon adopted Khrushchev's view that it was no more than an attempt to spy on the U.S.S.R. Finally, it was decided to study the increase of communication and trade between the two blocs. At the end of the conference, the foreign ministers were directed to meet for a more detailed study of the proposals that had been discussed in general terms by the heads of government.

The Two-Year Détente. It became clear, when the foreign ministers met at Geneva on October 27–November 16, that the summit meeting had achieved a relaxation of tension but no substantive agreements. Although Adenauer, on his visit to Moscow on September 9–13, had agreed to establishment of diplomatic relations between Soviet Russia and West Germany in return for the freeing of German prisoners of war still held in Russia, no progress was made on the German question by the foreign ministers. The disarmament question was finally referred back to the UN subcommittee; and Molotov blocked Western attempts to begin an exchange of ideas and information between the peoples of the two blocs. The so-called Geneva spirit had cooled considerably by the end of 1955. Already, the conclusion of the Soviet arms agreement with Egypt, the visit of Indian Prime Minister Nehru to Moscow in June 1955, and the visit of Bulganin and Khrushchev to India and Burma in November, indicated that the next goal of Soviet policy was penetration of the Middle East and south Asia.

Between 1956 and 1958, the Soviet government was occupied in retaining its hold over its restive satellites in Eastern Europe, and in profiting from the discomfiture of Britain and France in the Middle East. Britain and France, after their abortive attempt to bring about the downfall of Nasser, were forced to concentrate on overcoming the economic difficulties at home that their intervention had produced. The

United States government, feeling that a fairly stable situation existed in Europe, concentrated on blocking Communist expansion into the Middle East by the Eisenhower Doctrine of January 1957, by the dispatch of the Marines to Lebanon in July 1958, and by the use of the Seventh Fleet in August 1958 to break the Chinese Communist blockade of the Nationalist-held islands of Quemoy and Matsu off the mainland of China. The one source of East-West tension in Europe was the decision of the NATO Council in May 1957 to equip NATO forces in Europe with nuclear warheads, followed by the decision in December to set up bases in NATO countries for Intermediate Range Ballistic Missiles. Several tactics were tried by the Soviet government to counter this increase in the striking power of NATO. At first, the smaller powers of Europe were unsuccessfully urged of the danger of American hegemony. Then the Soviet government espoused the Rapacki Plan, suggested in the United Nations on October 2, 1957 by the Polish foreign minister, for the creation of a zone in Central Europe, including Poland and the two Germanies, where the production and stockpiling of nuclear and ballistic weapons would be forbidden. In March, the Soviet Union carried out a series of nuclear tests in the atmosphere, in which bombs of megaton size were exploded, while simultaneously proposing the end of nuclear testing. Finally, efforts were made to persuade the Western powers to hold another summit meeting. These moves had little effect on the members of NATO, and missile bases were soon established in Britain, Turkey, West Germany, and other NATO countries.

The Opening of the Berlin Crisis. Khrushchev thereupon decided on a double coup—to bring disarray into the NATO alliance, and to rid East Germany of the problem of West Berlin. On November 10, 1958, in a speech to a Soviet-Polish meeting in Moscow, he declared that the time had come to "renounce the remnants of the occupation regime in Berlin and thereby make it possible to create a normal situation in the capital of the German Democratic Republic." On November 27, a Soviet note to the United States, Britain, and France declared that the Soviet government intended to hand to the East German government its functions in Berlin, including supervision of access to West Berlin, and suggested that West Berlin might become a free, demilitarized city, possibly under United Nations supervision. The Western powers were given six months to reach agreement. Khrushchev's principal motive in thus precipitating a new Berlin crisis was to rid the East German regime of the increas-

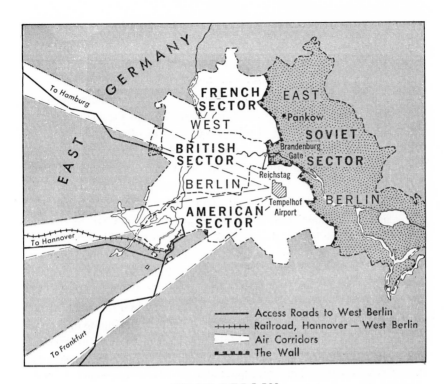

Access Roads to West Berlin
Railroad, Hannover — West Berlin
Air Corridors
The Wall

WEST BERLIN

ingly damaging influence of West Berlin. West Berlin was a showcase
for the Western way of life, where East Germans could read Western
newspapers and books, see the working of a multiparty system of democratic government, and enjoy some of the luxuries of a consumer-
oriented society. After 1950, when production in West Berlin was only
32 per cent of that in 1938, West Berlin began to enjoy some of the
benefits of the West German economic miracle, and by 1958 its production was 18 per cent higher than in 1938. Beautiful modern shops and
offices lined its main streets; its parks were replanted, its palaces newly
painted, its suburbs rebuilt. Close to the boundary of the Soviet sector,
in the Hansa Viertel, one of the most glittering displays of modern housing was erected after a competition in which the most famous architects
of the world competed. This show of prosperity, which the East German
regime regarded as deliberate incitement of disaffection in the East German population, subsidized by the West German and American governments, was accompanied by more irritating, and perhaps unwise, at-

tempts on the part of the West Berlin government to proclaim that West Berlin was an integral part of West Germany and, moreover, was the capital of all Germany—*Hauptstadt Berlin*. Even the West Germans whittled away at the four-power status of the city by summoning the joint session of parliament to elect the West German president there in 1954, and holding the first regular session of the Bundestag there in 1955. Symbolically, the burnt-out ruins of the Reichstag were slowly being refurbished as the future home of the German parliament. These gestures made the East Germans and the Russians more than ever determined to force the West into recognition of the German Democratic Republic and into renunciation of its claim that the West German government possessed the legal right to speak for all Germans. Finally, through West Berlin, the vital manpower of East Germany was fleeing to the West. Throughout the 1950's an average of 230,000 East Germans a year crossed into West Berlin to fly to refuge in West Germany. Although a rise in living standards in East Germany in 1959 reduced the flow to 143,000, it rose again the next year with the beginning of a drive to complete the collectivization of farming. Half of these refugees were under twenty-five, and three-quarters were under forty-five; and they included large numbers of professional classes, like teachers and doctors. Probably about three million people left East Germany between 1949 and 1961, leaving its population at sixteen million compared with West Germany's fifty-three million.

Geneva Foreign Ministers' Conference, 1959. While promising a remedy to most of the disadvantages of West Berlin, Khrushchev's proposal also had the effect of throwing the Western powers into disarray. Whereas President de Gaulle of France immediately gave firm support to Chancellor Adenauer's refusal to countenance any change in the status of West Berlin or to recognize the legality of the East German regime, he was not willing to support the German claim to the Oder-Neisse territories taken by Poland. The British, who had distrusted the American doctrine of massive retaliation and Dulles' call for "liberation" of satellite peoples, were little disposed to get involved in a war for the defense of Berlin and pressed for negotiations with the Russians, without, however, suggesting any form of concession that might be offered. The United States government, which had been accepting without significant protest the growing powers of the East German regime in Berlin, such as control of civilian and goods traffic into West Berlin and the right to issue transit visas to foreign civilians, declared its willingness to negotiate if Russia dropped its six-month ultimatum, and agreed that a foreign ministers' conference should precede a summit meeting. This flexibility worried the French and Germans, who were, however, reassured by the total failure of the Foreign Ministers' Conference in Geneva on May 12–June 19 and July 13–August 5, 1959. The aim of Soviet Foreign Minister Gromyko was to persuade the West to agree to write separate treaties with the two German states, to leave negotiations on reunification to them, and to make West Berlin a "free, demilitarized city." The NATO powers were to withdraw their troops and bases from foreign territory, and in return the Soviet Union would withdraw its forces from East Germany and Hungary. American Secretary of State Herter proposed a "Western Peace Plan," by which the reunification of Germany would be carried out in four carefully regulated steps, during which a mixed German commission would draft an electoral law and elections would be held under international supervision. Each side rejected the other's proposal. The only Western gain from the meeting was that Khrushchev's six-month ultimatum passed unheeded; the only Communist gain was acceptance of an East German delegation as "advisers" at the conference.

Khrushchev's American Tour and the Paris Summit Conference. On August 3, tension was dissipated with the announcement that Khrushchev had accepted an invitation from President Eisenhower that he had long coveted, to visit the United States. On a ten-day tour of the country between September 15–25, Khrushchev made his ebullient way through the film studios of Hollywood, an IBM plant near San Francisco, and the corn fields of Iowa, gaining, American observers felt, a deep impression of the productive capacity of the United States and of the determination of the American government to avoid a military showdown. At the presidential retreat of Camp David in the Catoctin Mountains on September 25–27, it was agreed that talks on Berlin would be resumed and that "these negotiations should not be prolonged indefinitely but there could be no fixed time limit for them." President Eisenhower would visit the Soviet Union in the spring of 1960, and a summit meeting would be held the following May. On May 1, however, two weeks before the opening of the summit conference in Paris, an American U-2 reconnaissance plane was shot down 1,300 miles inside Russia, its pilot captured, and photographic equipment for espionage found on board. In moves of great clumsiness, the American administration first declared that the plane lost its course on a meteorological mission and then admitted its explanation was a lie, that the spy flights had been going on since 1956, and that they would continue. Eisenhower himself took personal responsibility and thus forced Khrushchev into a difficult political position at home, as he had claimed, since the Camp David talks, that the American President could be trusted to follow a policy of peaceful coexistence. At Paris, Khrushchev demanded a personal apology from Eisenhower and a promise that no flights would be undertaken in the future, and revoked the invitation to visit Russia. Eisenhower promised that no further flights would take place during his administration, but Khrushchev refused to be placated and broke up the conference before the German question had even been discussed.

The Berlin Wall. For the next year, harassment of West Berlin was left by the Soviet authorities to the East Germans. In September, West Germans were required to apply for special permits to visit East Berlin, and West Berliners were informed that their West German passports would not be recognized in East Germany. In return, the West German government canceled the interzonal trade agreement. Khrushchev suddenly inaugurated a new phase of the Berlin crisis by presenting to the new American President, John F. Kennedy, at their meeting in Vienna on June 4, 1961, an *aide-memoire* demanding a German treaty, an end to occupation rights, and the establishment of West Berlin as a free city. In a television speech on June 15, Khrushchev declared that the settlement would have to be reached before the end of the year. On July 25, Kennedy replied that the West would defend Berlin by force if necessary, and announced an increase of $3 billion in defense expenditure, much of it for increasing conventional forces. Meanwhile the Soviet government canceled its planned reduction of its armed forces, and Khrushchev boasted in August that the U.S.S.R. was in possession of a 100-megaton bomb. The people of East Germany, suspecting that a final showdown was near, fled in extraordinary numbers—22,000 between August 1 and August 12. Then, at two o'clock in the morning of August 13, East German troops and police began erecting barbed-wire barriers along the whole border of East and West Berlin, and an East German decree required special permits of East Germans traveling into West Berlin. Within five days, a hideous concrete-and-barbed-wire barrier cut off all physical access from East to West Berlin, except through a small number of closely guarded check points. The Western commandants in Berlin and the Allied governments protested; Western garrisons in Berlin were increased; Vice-President Johnson flew to West Berlin to assure the population of American support; the attempt of the East Germans to create a "safety zone" of 100 meters on the western side of the wall was prevented by Western troops. For a few weeks, the world seemed to be on the brink of war. Kennedy recalled 76,000 reservists. Khrushchev began a series of nuclear tests in the atmosphere on an unprecedented scale. American and Soviet tanks faced each other across the sector boundary. But the occupying powers in West Berlin made no attempt to destroy the Wall, and very little harassment occurred of Western military convoys on the autobahn or of military access to East Berlin. In fact, it slowly became clear that the Wall had temporarily solved the Berlin problem from the Soviet point of view. Although the Wall was a terrible confession of failure and tangible evidence to the uncommitted world of the prison-like conditions of East Germany, it cut the refugee flow to about 6,000 a year. Khrushchev dropped any attempt to impose a deadline for settlement and on June 12, 1964 signed a treaty with East Germany, which, although recognizing its sovereignty, did not attempt to change the status of West Berlin.

Thus, in spite of many professions of interest in German reunification, both the Soviet Union and the Western powers seemed reconciled to the continuing existence of two Germanies. In Cold War conditions, a *modus vivendi* had come to take the place of a peace treaty.

WESTERN EUROPE'S READJUSTMENT: FIRST STEPS TOWARD UNIFICATION

The crises of decolonization and of the Cold War made the people of Western Europe increasingly frustrated and disturbed at their political and military impotence and at their slow economic progress. As a result, they became receptive to the idea preached throughout the interwar years by federalist enthusiasts like Count Coudenhove-Kalergi, that Europe could only maintain its distinctive culture and way of life by unification of its nation-states.

The Value of Integration. The most obvious argument in favor of integration was simple addition. In 1962, the population of Russia was 221 million and that of the United States 186 million, whereas the population of the largest European state, West Germany, was only 54 million. Together, however, the "Inner Six"—West Germany, France, Italy, Belgium, the Netherlands, and Luxembourg—had 173 million, and the "Outer Seven"—United Kingdom, Norway, Sweden, Denmark, Switzerland, Austria, and Portugal—another 90 million. Coal production of Russia in 1961 was 395 million tons and that of the United States 379 million; the Inner Six produced 263 million, and the Outer Seven 198 million. Steel production of Russia in 1962 was 76 million tons, and that of the United States 90 million tons; the Inner Six produced 72 million tons, and the Outer Seven 28 million tons. The Inner Six alone approached the population and productive capacity in certain basic industries of Russia and the United States. With the addition of the United Kingdom only, population and many sectors of production would exceed that of the giants; and the military capacity of a unified Europe, in both armaments and manpower, would be correspondingly larger.

The supporters of integration argued, however, that the creation of economic unity of the European nations would have results far greater than simple addition. The success of the United States in creating the highest productivity ever known, both in gross national product and per capita, was due above all, they claimed, to the fact that the writers of the American Constitution had envisaged the new state as an integrated economic community. From its birth, the United States of America possessed the three primary characteristics of such a community—free movement of goods, labor, and capital. The European states were restricting their own expansion by use of tariff barriers, quotas, discriminative freight rates, cartels, and immigration controls. If goods were to move freely in a united Europe, manufacturers would be able to reap the economies of large-scale production; specialization would be encouraged; production would not be dictated by autarkic national governments but by the most rational use of the Continent's resources. Labor would move to the jobs, as in the United States. Capital would be invested where it would be most productive and would not be hindered in jumping national boundaries. Integration, its supporters concluded, would produce a multiplication of economic activity within the community. Moreover, the shocks inevitable when free competition replaces national protection could be mitigated by institution of a community administration charged with the task of aiding the relocation and training of unemployed workers, the foundation of new industries in areas harmed by more efficient competitors, and the planned development of the economically backward sections of the Continent.

A third argument was that the nation-state had become a dangerous anachronism in Europe. Whereas in the nineteenth century, nationalism had sometimes been a liberating and progressive force, the Franco-Prussian War and the two World Wars convinced many Europeans that the existence of rival nation-states was in itself a cause of war. Such feelings were natural in the inhabitants of areas like Alsace-Lorraine or the Saar, which were the territorial prizes over which wars had been fought. They were shared by many who felt that such international systems as a "balance of power" had been unsuccessful in preventing aggressive nations from seeking hegemony, whether it was France in the seventeenth century or Germany in the twentieth. In particular, integration was seen as a way of solving the German problem, by merging Germany in a wider European nationalism. The peoples of Europe outside the Iron Curtain, it was argued, were emotionally ready for such a European patriotism. The process of decolonization was rapidly destroying the belief of the citizens of the former colonial powers that their loyalty lay in such groupings as the French Union or even the British Commonwealth rather than in Europe. Visits to neighboring countries, whether by students, soldiers, workers, or tourists, were fostering an awareness of what the different peoples of Europe had in common, while acquaintance with Americans or Russians confirmed the sense of the distinctiveness of being Europeans. The fostering of a European patriotism came to be regarded by many as a double benefit—a protection of the European heritage from the superpowers, and an enrichment of each nation's inheritance by deeper acquaintance with that of its European partners.

Possible Methods of Integration. Unfortunately, there was no simple formula for achievement of these political, military, economic, or cultural goals. In the immediate postwar years, several alternatives presented themselves. The first, and in some ways the most appealing, was to consider the Americans and Canadians as the children of Europe and the sharers in a common cultural inheritance that would be safeguarded by formation of an Atlantic Community of some kind. This community could be a loose partnership of equals between North America and Western Europe, in which economic and military cooperation might perhaps lead to a formulation of common policy for certain problems affecting both partners. President Kennedy envisaged such a relationship when he spoke in Independence Hall in Philadelphia on July 4, 1962, of a "Declaration of Interdependence" and of "Atlantic partnership." When applied in practice, Kennedy's plans involved closer trade relations and the establishment of a common nuclear-defense force, the Multilateral Nuclear Force (MLF). Even these moves aroused considerable opposition in Europe. A more integrated Atlantic Community would run into more serious difficulties, both from statesmen like General de Gaulle, who claimed that "a colossal Atlantic Community under American dependence and leadership . . . would soon completely swallow up the European Community," and from more cynical critics who felt that the United States would never permit the free movement of European immigrants into the American labor market nor would the European states allow unrestricted investment of American capital. Thus, for at least fifteen years after the war, the Atlantic partnership was in fact an alliance under the leadership of the United States, which provided the financing for OEEC and a large share of the weapons and manpower for NATO. When Western Europe finally began to regain a position of equality, its leaders were divided between those who sought interdependence with, and those who sought independence from, the United States.

A second approach, which was seductively noncommital, was to form a consultative federation in Europe. This proposal was favored by neutral countries like Switzerland, Sweden, and Austria; by Britain because of its Commonwealth ties and its supposedly "special relationship" with the United States; and by countries like Portugal that opposed foreign interference in their domestic affairs. A consultative federation would possess a parliament composed of members of the national parliaments of the participating states, whose debates would in theory serve to create a European consensus on problems of common interest. Similar meetings of cabinet ministers would take note of the debates of the parliament, and individual ministers would report to their governments on the results of the consultations. The Council of Europe, founded in 1949, was intended as a model of this approach; but its institutionalized procrastination quickly disillusioned the more enthusiastic supporters of supranationalism.

For leaders like Belgian Foreign Minister Spaak, progress toward integration could be achieved only by the grant to a supranational authority of powers exercised previously by the governments of the nation-states. Only by the abrogation of national sovereignty to a European government could a United States of Europe be created. To achieve this goal, there were again several routes. For the most impatient, the fastest method was to elect a European parliament by European suffrage—one member for every million Europeans, Paul Reynaud suggested—and to permit that parliament to set up a European executive with the widest possible powers. Since such a suggestion was obviously utopian, a second possibility was to divide up the activities of the national governments into such broad areas as economic, military, or political competence, and to hand to a European authority control over one or more of these areas. To begin even more modestly, it was possible to subdivide even these areas of government control, by dividing, for example, economic activity into coal and steel production, atomic energy, communications, and so on, and to give to a European authority control over one or more of these subdivisions. This so-called functional approach eventually proved to be the most effective.

The European Federalist Movements. Many different groups favored integration. The wartime Resistance movements voiced the first demands that Europe unite. The common experience of opposing the Nazi tyranny, contacts with other Europeans in the underground or the concentration camp, and conviction of the insensate suffering inflicted by wars among Europeans, led Henry Frenay, leader of the Combat group in the French underground, and Eugen Kogon, a German Resistance leader who had spent several years in Nazi concentration camps, to found the European Union of Federalists, which soon had branches in most European countries. Similar federalist groups were founded by supporters of political parties, such as the Socialist Movement for the United States of Europe or the Christian Democratic Nouvelles Equipes Internationales. Coudenhove-Kalergi revived his European Parliamentary Union. Liberal-minded businessmen and politicians formed the European League for Economic Cooperation. In England, the United Europe Movement was set up in June 1947. By 1947, most of the prominent statesmen of Europe were vociferously proclaiming their commitment to the unification of Western Europe. At Zürich on September 19, 1946, Winston Churchill, freed of the responsibilities of office, called for the reconstitution of the European family in a United States of Europe, whose foundation would be the reconciliation of France and Germany; and Spaak in Belgium, Schuman in France, De Gasperi in Italy, and Adenauer in Germany were all calling for decisive action before Western Europe should suffer the fate that was overtaking Eastern Europe.

The Council of Europe. So great was the proliferation of federalist groups and so varied were their aims that under Churchill's leadership, a Congress of Europe met at The Hague in May 1948 to federate the federalists. The Congress, attended by a glittering array of 750 European statesmen, agreed to the formation of the European Movement, as a union of the federalist groups, and of a European Assembly. On May 5, 1949, ten countries approved the foundation of the Council of Europe, whose Consultative Assembly held its first meeting in Strasbourg in August 1949. Its members, chosen by the national parliaments but not including any Communists, sat alphabetically, and later formed transnational political parties—the Christian Democrats, Socialists, and Liberals. A pleasant, permanent "House of Europe" was built in Strasbourg the next year for the Assembly meetings and the secretariat. Regular, often impassioned, debates were held; a European Convention for the Protection of Human Rights was drawn up; and intergovernmental cooperation within the Council led to the establishment of minimum standards for old-age pensions and other social security benefits. But within two years, the Council demonstrated that consultative federation would not lead inevitably to political integration because the limiting of national sovereignty was wanted neither by the neutral powers nor by Great Britain and the Scandinavian countries. The Committee of Ministers of the Council of Europe was able to block the efforts of the Assembly to win real power because the majority of the Council's member governments refused any form of supranational authority in Europe. A completely new approach was needed.

The European Coal and Steel Community. On May 9, 1950, French Foreign Minister Robert Schuman announced in a press conference that the French government proposed "to place all Franco-German coal and steel production under a common High Authority, in an organization open to the participation of the other countries of Europe." A merger of the coal and steel industries would "mean the immediate establishment of common bases of industrial production, which is the first step toward European Federation and will change the destiny of regions that have long been devoted to the production of war armaments of which they themselves have been the constant victims." The author of this plan was Jean Monnet, head of the French planning commission and the most influential advocate of supranational administration. Monnet's dramatic coup lay in linking the reconciliation of France and Germany with a scheme in which German heavy industry would be supervised by its neighbors and in which the institutions of a European union would be forged. The treaty, creating a European Coal and Steel Community, was signed on April 18, 1951, and, after ratification by the parliaments of France, West Germany, Italy, Belgium, the Netherlands, and Luxembourg, came into force on July 25, 1952.

The purpose of the treaty was to create a common market for coal and steel among the six members. Within two years, coal, iron ore, and steel were to circulate freely, free of tariffs and import quotas. Discriminatory freight rates were to be abolished. Monopolies and cartels restricting trade in coal and steel were to be broken up. The practice of charging different prices at home and abroad for identical products was forbidden. Different systems of taxing imports and exports of coal and steel were to be harmonized. Where free competition forced the closing of mines or factories, the workers were to be given financial aid for relocation, or new enterprises were to be aided in establishing themselves in areas of unemployment. A High Authority of nine members, chosen by the member governments but responsible to the community as a whole, was empowered to act as the first supranational governmental body in Europe, carrying out the provisions of the treaty even against the wishes of individual countries. It was aided by a secretariat, which eventually numbered over two thousand, and was permitted to impose a tax of up to 1 per cent of the coal and steel production of the members. The interests of the member countries were to be represented by a Council of Ministers. Both private individuals and governments could appeal to a Court of Justice against the actions of the High Authority. A parliament of seventy-eight members, known as the Common Assembly, was to be picked by member countries and was given the power of forcing the resignation of the High Authority if it voted disapproval of the Authority's annual report by a two-thirds majority. After considerable argument, it was decided that the Community would have four official languages—French, German, Italian, and Dutch; that the High Authority would set up offices in Luxembourg; and that the Common Assembly would use the Council of Europe's parliament buildings in Strasbourg. Jean Monnet was named first president of the High Authority.

Monnet brought tremendous enthusiasm to the task of making the common market in coal and steel a reality, and of ensuring that the Coal and Steel Community would expand into a European federal state. "Our Community is not an association of producers of coal and steel," he declared. "It is the beginning of Europe." Within two years, tariffs and import quotas on coal and steel had been removed; a dispute on the nature of turnover taxes was resolved in favor of the French; France's monopolistic coal-import agency, ATIC, was forced to shed many of its powers; GEORG, the Ruhr's centralized coal sales agency, was split into two companies after a long dispute with the High Authority. By 1962, loans of $312 million had been given to aid modernization, and the building of 75,000 homes was subsidized. When relocation payments failed to persuade French workers to move out of their native Cévennes region, attempts were made to support new industry there.

The first results of the creation of the Community were very encouraging. At the end of the five-year transitional period, trade between the six members in coal had increased 21 per cent, in iron 25 per cent, and in steel 157 per cent. Coal production reached a peak in 1956, when the Community produced 249 million tons. Competition with oil as a source of power ended the need for increased coal production after 1956; but modernization of the mines increased the output per man by almost 50 per cent between 1953 and 1962. Steel production soared from 39 million tons in 1953 to 72 million tons in 1962. The operation of the common market for coal and steel justified the belief that integration made possible economies of scale, modernization, higher productivity, reduction of social dislocation, and rationalization of investment. The High Authority's tactful dealings with the national governments and with individual enterprises persuaded them that a supranational authority was by no means so obnoxious as they had feared. The development of European political parties in the Common Assembly and the useful work of supervision exercised by the Assembly's standing committees proved that a European assembly with limited but real powers was more valuable than so innocuous a body as the Council of Europe. Even the weaknesses of the Community indicated the need for more rather than less integration. Since the High Authority was not empowered to deal with all sources of power, especially oil and electricity, it was unable to prevent the frictions due to uncontrolled competition between suppliers of different forms of fuel. The inability of the inefficient Belgian mines to sell their overpriced coal and the resulting unemployment demonstrated the need of a common energy policy for Europe. Similarly, the need was felt for common transport, commercial, and social policies. The answer appeared to be a common market extending to all economic activity, and a proposal for the establishment of such a community was made by the Belgian, Dutch, and Luxembourg delegations at a meeting of the foreign ministers of the European Coal and Steel Community, at Messina on June 1–3, 1955.

The Abortive European Defense Community. Before this meeting, however, an attempt to further the integration of the Six by creation of a European army had been proposed and rejected. In the summer of 1950, faced with American pressure for the rearmament of West Germany, the French decided to capitalize on the enthusiastic reception of the Schuman Plan for pooling of the European coal and steel industries, by suggesting the pooling of European armies, including the forces with which Germany might be armed. In this way, Premier Pleven told the French parliament on October 24, West Germany would contribute to the defense of the West, but would not have an autonomous national army nor a General Staff, and at the same time the integration of Western Europe would be rapidly advanced. After two years of negotiation it was agreed that the armies of France, West Germany, Italy, Belgium, the Netherlands, and Luxembourg would be fused into a European army. The component national units would be the size of an army corps. The General Staff would be completely integrated. Administration would be in the hands of a Commissariat modeled on the High Authority of the Coal and Steel Community. This European Defense Community would have the same Court of Justice as ECSC, and its parliament would be the Common Assembly with the addition of a few more members. The treaty was signed in Paris on May 27, 1952. The federalists, seizing their chance, argued that a common army would have to receive its orders from a European government. A European Political Community was therefore planned, and a draft treaty instituting a European Executive Council with powers over foreign affairs was drawn up. In France, however, many important groups were opposed to the EDC Treaty. The Communists feared the rearmament of West Germany; the Gaullists and other right-wing groups were determined not to replace the French national army, as de Gaulle said, with a "denationalized jumble," governed by a "countryless government, a technocracy." Certain federalists felt that they were damaging their own cause by building

Europe around an army. Many moderates, like the old Radical states-man Edouard Herriot, opposed union with a country like Germany that had three times invaded France in the past seventy years. On August 30, 1954, the National Assembly defeated the EDC Treaty, and thereby killed the European Political Community as well.

Western European Union. A month later, to the surprise and chagrin of EDC's opponents, at a conference in London of the Six, Great Britain, the United States, and Canada, it was agreed that West Germany should be given an autonomous national army, that West Germany and Italy should become members of a revived Western European Union, originally founded by the Brussels Pact of 1948, and that West Germany should become a member of NATO. These decisions were embodied in the Paris Agreements of October 23, 1954 and were approved by the French Assembly in December. Welcomed by the American government and guaranteed by the British, the Agreements came into force on May 5, 1955. West Germany became an independent state authorized to set up an army of twelve divisions. The Western European Union never became a significant international organization, in spite of regularly scheduled meetings of its Council of Ministers, Permanent Council of Ambassadors, and Assembly, and the maintenance of a Standing Armament Committee and Agency for the Control of Armaments. It was little more than a device for linking Britain with the Six in yet another consultative federation, but one whose functions were duplicated in NATO and the Council of Europe.

The Messina Resolution. Far more significant for the integration of Europe was the Messina resolution of June 3, 1955. Defeat of the European Defense Community and the European Political Community, the lack of supranational features in Western European Union, and the resignation of Jean Monnet from the High Authority had thrown the federalists into despair in the winter of 1954. With the French and Germans deeply discouraged, Dutch Foreign Minister Beyen and Belgian Foreign Minister Spaak joined with Luxembourg Premier Bech in an attempt to give a new drive to the unification movement. At Messina, the Benelux ministers persuaded the others to agree to the appointment of a committee of governmental delegates, under the dynamic leadership of Spaak, which would report on methods for creation of a common market for all sectors of the European economy, common institutions, and coordinated commercial and social policies. "We must work toward the establishment of a united Europe," the final resolution declared, "through the development of common institutions, the gradual merger of national economies, the creation of a common market, and increasing harmonization of social policies." Drawing upon the experience and personnel of ECSC, Spaak's committee proposed the creation of a European Economic Community or Common Market, and a European Atomic Energy Community (Euratom). At Venice, on May 29–30, 1956, the foreign ministers authorized the negotiation of treaties creating the two Communities, which were signed on the Capitol Hill in Rome on March 25, 1957.

Euratom. Euratom was created to help solve Europe's long-term needs for power, its original goal being set at the production of 15 million kilowatts from nuclear reactors by 1967. The actual results of the Community's activity were far more modest. Through agreement with the United States, a $350 million program for the building of power stations equipped with American reactors was begun, but by 1964 only three plants with a capacity of 700,000 kilowatts were under construction. Research was advancing rapidly, however, on new types of reactors, the high-temperature gas-cooled and the fast breeder reactor, which might eventually lower the cost of producing nuclear energy. Four important research centers were set up in Belgium, the Netherlands, Germany, and Italy where nuclear scientists could be trained, new materials and plants tested, and large-scale projects of research sponsored; and further research was sponsored by contracts with private firms or universities. A system of control of fissionable materials within the Community was instituted, and a strict code of health standards was drawn up. The five-member Commission has worked quietly and in effective collaboration with the national governments, with the one exception of President Etienne Hirsch whose Europeanism was so vigorous that President de Gaulle refused to support his reappointment in 1961.

Organization and Achievements of the Common Market. The Common Market was a far more ambitious undertaking than either the European Coal and Steel Community or Euratom. Its basic aim was to fuse the six countries into an economic unit, in which goods, labor, and capital would circulate freely. The administrative machinery was modeled upon the ECSC. A nine-member Commission was appointed to carry out the provisions of the treaty. A Council of Ministers, consisting of representatives of the governments of each of the member states, was given the task of the final policy decisions necessary for application of the treaty. The technical preparation for the meeting of the Council was to be made by a Committee of Permanent Representatives composed of the heads of the national delegations at the Common Market headquarters in Brussels; but the proposals upon which the Council was to vote were to be prepared by the Commission. Voting procedure in the Council of Ministers was laid down in the treaty in such a way as to reduce the veto power of any one nation progressively. The Court of Justice of ECSC was to act as a common court for all three Communities. The Common Assembly of ECSC, expanded from 78 to 142 members, was to become the parliament of the three Communities. Since usually only the convinced "Europeans" wanted to serve in the new Assembly, which demonstrated its ambitions by changing its title to European Parliament, it tended to act as a goad, both to the Council of Ministers and to the Commission, in reducing national powers within the Community. Through its committee, it exercised critical supervision of the most detailed aspects of the Commission's work.

The first task of the Community was the dismantling of the customs barriers between the member states, which was to be done in three 4-year periods. During each of the first two stages, tariffs were to be reduced 30 per cent; during the third, they were to be completely eliminated. So successful were the first reductions in increasing trade between members that this program was accelerated, and by 1968 tariffs were to disappear completely. Import quotas within the Community were abolished by 1961. As a corollary to the ending of internal tariffs, the treaty required the six states to establish identical tariffs on goods imported from nonmembers. A great deal of bargaining was necessary before this Common External Tariff could be agreed upon, since low-tariff countries like Germany and the Netherlands were required to raise their tariffs on goods they imported from trading partners outside the Community. Nevertheless, by 1963 national tariffs were within 40 per cent of the Common External Tariff, and were due to be aligned by the end of the transitional period. By setting up such a customs barrier against nonmembers, the Common Market deliberately gave preference to its own members, making it more difficult, for example, for British manufacturers of agricultural machinery to compete with the French or the Germans in winning the Dutch market. Rulings were made in 1961 and 1964 to facilitate the free movement of workers within the Community; but the labor shortage was so great that large numbers of workers were brought into the Community from outside, and it was not necessary to give priority to citizens of member countries. Movement of capital was hindered by the nature of the national banking systems, which were not well adapted to making large international investments. On the other hand, the success of the Common Market provided a direct stimulus for increased American investment, and over 600 American companies established themselves in the Community between 1958 and 1961, bringing American investments in the Six to more than $3 billion. To ensure that freedom of trade would lead to "fair" or "normal" competition, the EEC treaty required the Commission to establish controls over the market, to prevent restrictive agreements between companies for sharing markets or lowering production. The general effect of freeing trade within the Community, however, was to encourage closer ties within different industries. A very large number of federations of different branches of industry were created and set up headquarters in Brussels near the EEC offices. Mergers of firms were frequently used to increase specialization of production or to meet competition by adopting large-scale production, and were approved by the Commission as proof that the Common Market was compelling rationalization of production.

While it is incorrect to attribute all economic progress within the Community to institution of the Common Market, it is indisputable that an extraordinary productive boom occurred after 1958. In 1958–62 France's industrial production rose 30 per cent, Germany's 39 per cent. Whereas Luxembourg trailed with an increase of only 13 per cent in industrial production, the Netherlands increased 44 per cent, and Italy achieved the astounding increase of 73 per cent. Trade among members increased far more rapidly than with nonmembers, rising 130 per cent above the level of 1958, whereas imports from nonmembers increased only 52 per cent. Although trade within the Community was less than 40 per cent of the Community's total trade, the trend to creation of a self-sufficient, protected Community caused considerable misgivings among other European countries and in the United States, whose own economic prosperity was dependent to some degree upon finding markets for its own products in the Community.

The Common Agricultural Policy. The success of integration of industrial activity caused the agricultural producers within the Community, particularly the French, to demand implementation of the vague section of the EEC Treaty requiring the institution of a common agricultural market. The writers of the Treaty had recognized that it was impossible to have free trade in agricultural produce as in industrial products. It was hoped that the family basis of European farming would be maintained, although efficiency would be increased through a consolidation of holdings. Price supports and protection from external competition had to be continued in some form, partly because the farmer was such a potent force in politics, and partly because no European country wished to see its agriculture wiped out by imports of cheap food bought on the world market. Moreover, a common agricultural market would be of benefit principally to the French, who possessed 40 per cent of the arable land of the Community and produced large surpluses of cereals, beef, dairy products, and wine. The Italians were interested in finding a market for their fruit, vegetables, and wine, but wanted to protect their high-cost cereal producers. The Germans imported $2.5 billion of agricultural produce annually, particularly in cereals and meat, but they were unwilling to throw the German market open to French production because the inefficient German farmer, strongly represented by the German Farmers' Union and in the Christian Democratic party, wanted to maintain high prices and government subsidies, while German business wanted to keep open markets in South America and northern Europe for German industrial goods by importing agricultural goods in return. The struggle over formulation of a common agricultural policy thus became mainly a battle between the Germans and the French, who were supported by the Commission. In 1960, it was decided to make a system of levies on agricultural imports from outside the Community the keystone of the common policy. For the following two years, negotiations dragged on over application of the system to different classes of agricultural production, such as cereals, poultry and eggs, fruit and vegetables, and wine. The French finally declared that if sufficient progress had not been made by the end of 1961, they would not agree to the beginning of the second four-year stage of the Treaty for industrial products. In a marathon meeting lasting two hundred hours, during which the clock was stopped to pretend that it was still 1961, the negotiators agreed on the principles of a common agricultural policy. By instituting a complicated series of "target prices," "intervention prices," "threshold prices," and "sluicegate prices," during the coming seven and a half years, prices within the Community would be harmonized, levies would raise the price of imports from nonmembers and thus provide protection, and export subsidies would be paid to enable producers to sell on the world market. Germany was forced to give up national protection of its farmers; but the German government prepared for a major battle with the French over the price to be charged for cereals, which was the standard for all agricultural prices, and over the use to be made of the levies on imports; in 1964–66, this struggle almost destroyed the Common Market.

External Relations of the Common Market. On the insistence of the French and the Belgians, their colonial territories in Africa were to be associated with the Community in a free-trade area, although those territories were permitted to protect infant industries by imposing duties on imports from the Six. Moreover, a Development Fund of $581 million was to be made available during the five-year period of association for stimulating economic growth and raising living standards, and assistance was to be given in training economic and agricultural administrators. This association proved very successful, and all the African states, who gained their independence by 1960, asked for it to be renewed.

Relations with the nonmember countries in Europe presented difficulties to the Community. The British, who had refused to join ECSC in 1950, had refused to join EEC on the grounds that membership in such an economic union was incompatible with its Commonwealth ties. Fearing the loss of its markets within the Six with the raising of a Common External Tariff, the Conservative government retaliated by demanding the creation of a free-trade area between the Six and the other members of the Organization of European Economic Cooperation. Since their proposal was favored by the German government and firmly opposed by the French, it appeared to be a somewhat insidious method of shipwrecking EEC at its inception. In November 1958, the new French government of de Gaulle peremptorily broke off negotiations. The British then joined Denmark, Sweden, Norway, Switzerland, Austria, and Portugal in forming a European Free Trade Association (EFTA) on November 20, 1959. For the Outer Seven, EFTA would have none of the inconveniences of the Common Market, since it would not have a Common External Tariff, nor would it include agriculture. The Seven simply agreed to abolish all tariff and quota restrictions on trade with other members of EFTA within ten years. By 1964, tariffs had been reduced 60 per cent, and trade among members had increased by over 50 per cent. But EFTA was only a moderate success. During its first four years, its gross national product increased only 16 per cent compared with the Common Market's 25 per cent; and the lack of progress was particularly evident in Britain, EFTA's most important member. Its attractive power was small compared with the Common Market. In 1959, both Greece and Turkey asked for association with EEC. On July 31, 1961, British Prime Minister Macmillan told the House of Commons that his government was opening negotiations with the Six for British membership in EEC. EFTA at once began to fall apart. Denmark and Norway also applied for membership, while the three neutrals, Austria, Sweden, and Switzerland, asked for association, and Portugal asked for an agreement. It thus appeared by 1961 that the success of the Common Market was bringing about the early unification of all Western Europe, that—in Jean Monnet's words—the United States of Europe had begun. The hope that Western Europe had readjusted its conception of its world role to the realities of the postwar world was to be dashed when, on January 14, 1963, General de Gaulle placed his personal veto on British entry into the Common Market.

Chapter Eight

RESURGENCE, 1953-1960

THE *détente* in East-West relations that followed the death of Stalin in 1953 was reflected in the internal development of the European states. Stalin himself had declared that the revolutionary flood of the early postwar years would be followed by a period of revolutionary ebb, during which Russia would consolidate its gains; and Khrushchev's one confrontation with the West over Berlin was probably regarded by the Soviet government as aiming at the stabilization of the European situation by eliminating the anomaly of the persistence of a Western outpost behind the Iron Curtain. Under both Malenkov and Khrushchev, the Soviet Union adopted the New Course, in which the Stalinist autocracy was relaxed and the Russian people began to receive a few of the benefits of a consumer society. In Eastern Europe, the system of Soviet controls was lightened to permit slight variations from the Russian norm. The successful Polish attempt to adapt communism to certain national imperatives and the unsuccessful Hungarian attempt to challenge the principle of Soviet supremacy indicated the limits within which national roads to communism would be tolerated by the new Soviet leadership. The West European powers accepted the division of Europe by the Iron Curtain as a *fait accompli* and made almost no attempt to interfere in the internal affairs of the Communist bloc. They tended to turn to moderately conservative governments who would concentrate on increasing national economic prosperity and in solving the bitter problem of decolonization. In this atmosphere of prosperous conservatism, both Franco's Spain and Salazar's Portugal moved slowly toward international acceptance and economic revival.

RUSSIA FROM MALENKOV TO KHRUSHCHEV

Collective Leadership. The death of Stalin on March 5, 1953 marked the end of an era in Russia. His leading associates, who have been accused of hastening his end, lost no time in making known to the Russian people that they intended an immediate break with the forms of Stalinist government. In place of what was later called the "cult of personality," there was to be "collective leadership" in the state and the party. Power lay principally in the hands of the Presidium, the ten-member body that controlled the Central Committee of the Communist party; and in the Presidium were old-line Bolsheviks, like Molotov and Mikoyan; Lavrenti Beria, who as head of the Ministry of Internal Affairs controlled a private police army of half a million men; Nikita Khrushchev, who had been appointed by Stalin in 1952 to reform the party and who, on March 21, became senior party secretary; and Georgi Malenkov, Stalin's apparent choice as heir and the spokesman of the new industrial bureaucracy of the sixty ministries centered in Moscow. As chairman of the Council of Ministers, Malenkov was the official head of the government; and he at once made a bid for popular support by pledging an increase in consumer goods and foodstuffs "within two or three years." The "doctors' plot" was declared to be a fabrication of a deputy minister of the secret police, and the thousands arrested during the last months of Stalin's life for implication in the plot were released. Stricter respect for constitutional liberties of Soviet citizens was promised. In foreign affairs, relaxation of tension with the West was to be sought.

The Rise of Khrushchev. Behind the façade of good will that the collective leadership was determined to display, there was, however, a bitter struggle for power. Beria had massed secret-police units in Moscow after Stalin's death and had made himself the spokesman of those who demanded widespread legal and economic changes in the satellites as well as in Russia itself. After winning the support of the army by calling Marshal Zhukov to become deputy defense minister, the rest of the collective leadership suddenly had Beria arrested and shot in June 1953, although the news of his execution was not made public until December. Zhukov and the army leaders seemed satisfied to act as arbiters of the continuing power struggle, rather than to seize political control themselves; and for the next two years a duel continued between Khrushchev and the party hierarchy and Malenkov and the industrial bureaucracy. Khrushchev's ascendency was slow but sure. In September 1953, he took the official title of "first secretary" of the Communist party. Shortly afterward, he contradicted Malenkov's statement that the Soviet Union had solved its agricultural problems and declared that, in many ways, the situation was worse than it had been under the Tsars. Khrushchev himself began to run agriculture from September 1953, promising incentives while demanding greater output per man and increasing party controls in the Machine Tractor Stations and on the collective farms. In February 1954 he announced a scheme to reclaim for arable farming about 90 million acres of waste or virgin soil in Kazakhstan and southwestern Siberia; about half a million young people, army recruits, and workers from the collective farms were sent out to raise grain. At the end of 1954, Khrushchev finally struck at Malenkov's call for increased production of light industry and consumer goods, in language so rough that it was evident the showdown was near. On February 8, 1955, Malenkov told the Supreme Soviet that he was resigning as premier because of his "inexperience" and because he was responsible for Soviet shortcomings in agriculture. Khrushchev proposed that Malenkov's successor be Marshal Bulganin, a military technician who at once assured the army's acceptance of the change of leadership by appointing Zhukov minister of defense. The change of mores in the Soviet Union was illustrated by the appointment of Malenkov to the post of minister of electric power stations, and by his retention of membership in the party Presidium.

For the rest of 1955, Khrushchev and Bulganin concentrated on easing relations with the West while opening up new avenues for Soviet influence in the nonaligned countries. On May 15, the State Treaty gave Austria its independence, and the occupying troops of Russia, the United States, Britain, and France were withdrawn. In July, the summit conference at Geneva created an aura of good will at no expense to any of the participants. In September, the Soviet government announced that it intended to return the naval base of Porkkala to Finland; and, in the same month, Chancellor Adenauer was told, during his visit to Moscow, that the Soviet Union would give diplomatic recognition to West Germany and would return the German prisoners of war still in Soviet hands. Relations with Tito were re-established by the visit of Bulganin and Khrushchev to Belgrade in May. Soviet arms were promised to Egyptian President Nasser during the summer. And in December, Bulganin and Khrushchev paid a highly successful visit to India, Burma, and Afghanistan, after which the Soviet Union promised aid in constructing steel and aluminum plants and hydroelectric works in India, aid for construction of industrial plants in Burma, and a $100 million credit for Afghanistan. Meanwhile, at home, there were few signs that

Khrushchev intended to alter the policies established under Malenkov. The increase in production of consumer and light industrial goods continued. The plans for agriculture were left unchanged. The lightening of controls over intellectual and cultural life, known as the "Thaw," which had been briefly halted in 1954, again continued. The most notable break with Stalinism occurred, however, at the Twentieth Party Congress in Moscow on February 14–25, 1956.

De-Stalinization at the Twentieth Party Congress. For Khrushchev, the Congress provided the opportunity to disassociate himself from Stalin's unpopularity by denouncing the leader whom he had served for three decades. At open sessions of the Congress, Mikoyan declared that "the cult of the individual" had had "extremely adverse" results; at a secret session on February 24, Khrushchev went much further, giving in extraordinary detail a description of the crimes Stalin had perpetrated against the party faithful. Lenin himself, Khrushchev revealed, had suggested that Stalin should be removed from power, but Stalin had in fact created a "despotism." Whoever opposed him "was doomed to removal from the leading collective and to subsequent moral and physical annihilation"; the government apparatus was turned against honest Communists who were treated as enemies of the people; confessions were extorted by physical violence; and mass arrests and executions were made of thousands of innocent party members. The reason why none of the close associates of Stalin could stand up against him lay in his dictatorship: "Possessing unlimited physical power, he indulged in great willfulness and choked a person morally and physically. A situation was created where one could not express one's own will." To remedy the situation left by Stalin, Khrushchev continued, thousands were being rehabilitated. Decentralization of both industry and agriculture would give greater responsibility to the local administrators. Individual liberty would be increased by improvements in the legal system and by controls over the police and administration. Although ties with the countries of the Communist bloc would be strengthened, the possibility of different "forms of transition to socialism in different countries" would be recognized. With the West, peaceful coexistence would lessen the danger of nuclear war.

Khrushchev's Defeat of the "Anti-Party Group." Although Khrushchev's speech shocked those still faithful to Stalin's memory, it undoubtedly strengthened his popularity with the mass of the party members and with the people at large. Molotov was replaced as foreign minister in June 1956 by the more flexible Shepilov, shortly after the decision had been taken to dissolve the Cominform. Relations with Tito improved when the Yugoslav president paid a triumphant visit to Moscow in June; and closer links with the West seemed promised by the visits of French President Auriol and Premier Mollet to Moscow in March and May and especially by the trip of Bulganin and Khrushchev through Great Britain in April. De-Stalinization proved to have its dangerous consequences for the Soviet regime, however, with riots in Tbilisi in Soviet Georgia in February, in Poznan in Poland in June, and especially with the Hungarian uprising in October. The need to use force against the people of a satellite nation undoubtedly strengthened Khrushchev's opponents who had distrusted de-Stalinization from its inception; and their criticism redoubled when the Soviet Union's economy began to suffer from the cost of propping up the East European regimes, granting more favorable trade relations, abandoning the joint-stock companies in the satellites, and revising Comecon's plans to the disadvantage of Russia. By the end of 1956, many branches of Russian production were failing to meet the goals of the Five-Year Plan, which had to be lowered by the Central Committee. To restore local initiative and at the same time to bring local factory managers under party control, Khrushchev ordered the abolition of 33 of the central industrial ministries in Moscow and their replacement by 104 Regional Economic Councils, the increase in the power of the trade unions, and new rights to factory councils and committees. At the same time, he abolished compulsory food deliveries, handed over to the collective farms the property of the Machine Tractor Stations, and promised the farmers more material rewards for increased production. The economic crisis following the political crises of the previous year brought together, in opposition to Khrushchev, Malenkov and the industrial managers, Molotov and the Stalinists, and even some former supporters of de-Stalinization like Shepilov. In June 1957, Khrushchev was deposed as first party secretary by a vote of seven to four in the party Presidium. He fought back, however, by demanding that the issue be submitted to a full meeting of the Central Committee, which not only kept him in office but expelled Molotov, Malenkov, Kaganovich, and Saburov from the Presidium. Leonid Brezhnev was appointed a new member of the Presidium and Aleksei Kosygin a candidate-member. Thus, with the defeat of the so-called anti-party group, Khrushchev brought into power the two men who were to oust him in 1964. Khrushchev's predominance seemed assured in 1957, however. Molotov was exiled as ambassador to Outer Mongolia; Malenkov was sent to run a power station in Kazakhstan; Zhukov, who had apparently given Khrushchev the army's support against the "anti-party group" was dismissed as minister of defense in October, for encouraging the "cult of personality" in the army, and he was soon afterward dropped from the Presidium; in March 1958, Bulganin was demoted to be head of the State Bank, and Khrushchev replaced him as premier, thus like Stalin combining the roles of head of the government and of the party.

Soviet Industry under Khrushchev. For seven years after the defeat of the "anti-party group" in June 1957, Khrushchev's control of Russia was largely undisputed; he was free to dictate policy according to his personal impulses. Khrushchev was undoubtedly serious in his vision of the good life that communism would bring to every Russian citizen. As early as February 1959, the Twenty-First Party Congress had been told that the Seven-Year Plan, which was to replace the last two years of the sixth Five-Year Plan adopted in 1956, would bring Russian production close to that of the United States, would harmonize emphasis on heavy and consumer industry, and would make possible the introduction within ten years of a 30–35 hour work week. Natural gas and gasoline were to provide up to 60 per cent of the country's energy needs. Meat production was to increase 70 per cent, milk products 120 per cent, plastics 500 per cent, artificial fibers 400 per cent. Moreover, the gap between high and low incomes was to be reduced progressively, In October 1961, the Twenty-Second Party Congress was told that the material basis for the transition from socialism to communism would be completed by 1980, by which time every city family would have its own apartment and Russia's gross national product would be two and a half times that of the United States in 1961. Finally, in March 1963, Khrushchev brought in a new plan in place of the last three years of the Seven-Year Plan, after which Russia was to return to a Five-Year Plan (1966–70). To carry through these programs Khrushchev continued to order far-reaching changes in Soviet industrial administration. In 1957, he had adopted decentralization through Regional Economic Councils. In 1960, he removed from Gosplan (the State Planning Commission) the power of long-term planning, leaving it with the role of coordinating the Regional Economic Councils, and in its place gave a State Economic and Scientific Council the task of making long-term plans. Since neither of these reforms worked satisfactorily, in 1963 the number of Regional Economic Councils was reduced to fifty, Gosplan was again given control of long-term planning, and a new Supreme Economic Council given the job of supervising all the other economic organizations. These constant changes convinced many party leaders that Khrushchev's attitude to economic planning was impulsive and irresponsible; and the desire to restore some stability to economic administration was a principal reason for his ouster. Nevertheless, under Khrushchev Soviet industry made extraordinary progress. Between 1958 and 1962, industrial production increased 47 per cent; steel production rose to 76 million tons; 11.7 dwellings were built for each thousand of the population, compared with 7.4 in the United States and 6.0 in Britain.

Khrushchev's Agricultural Policy. In agriculture, Khrushchev's plans were far less successful, in the long run. The Virgin-Lands scheme did provide a bumper harvest for its first three years of operation and prevented food shortages when drought ruined the Ukraine grain crop. The amalgamation of the collective farms, the *kolkhoz,* from 1953 on certainly increased efficiency and made it possible to introduce into the country a few of the amenities of urban living, which he had promised would be normal when all the rural population would be gathered into agricultural cities (*agrogoroda*). The increase in corn production, which won him the nickname of *kukuruza* ("corn crazy"), made it possible to raise the number of cattle from 65 million in 1954 to 74 million in 1960. After 1958, production slipped badly, however. In 1962, food prices had to be raised 25–30 per cent; and in the following years the failure of the grain harvest sent Soviet trading teams abroad, notably to the United States, to make vast purchases of wheat. By 1964, official Communist journals were reporting that dust-bowl conditions existed in the Virgin Lands, where production had fallen almost by half in the past three years. The great drive for rapid increase in chemical production in 1963 was itself due to Khrushchev's belief that a final answer to the agricultural problem lay in artificial fertilizer. Since Khrushchev had taken personal responsibility for Russian agriculture since 1953, its failure was blamed directly upon him, and added a second reason for his ouster.

Continued De-Stalinization. In spite of the arbitrary power that he possessed, Khrushchev pressed on with the de-Stalinization of many sides of Soviet life, although not always with desirable results. He was most concerned to revitalize the Communist party which, under Stalin, had become a vested-interest group divorced from the mass of the people. Between 1956 and 1959, over a million new members were brought into the party, mostly peasants or workers. The Twenty-First Party Congress was told that the inefficient "who cannot cope with the job entrusted to them and lag behind life," would be weeded out. To break the social predominance of the growing Communist bourgeoisie—the "New Class" of industrial administrators and party officials—a new education law in December 1958 required university students to put in two years of manual labor in the factory or the fields, made greater educational opportunity available to adults, and played down the role of the humanities in the universities. A new Criminal Code brought considerable improvement in judicial procedure, forbidding the police to try or deport citizens, reducing penalties, and putting an end to such categories as "enemy of the people" or guilt by association. In 1959, Khrushchev claimed that the "withering away of the state" would be advanced by giving new powers to "public organizations" rather than to instruments of the state, and he cited as examples the maintenance of order by groups of one's neighbors in so-called Comrade's Courts or the punishment of hooligans by volunteer groups from the Communist Youth. Whereas this might have been regarded as a way of encouraging private initiative previously lacking in Soviet life, it resulted in arbitrary local interference in the life of one's neighbors, or in officially approved beatings administered by roughnecks from the party youth groups. Finally, in the cultural field, the Thaw was of very uncertain duration. In 1956, the Soviet artist appeared to have gained wide freedom of self-expression and of criticism, with the publication of Vladimir Dudintsev's *Not By Bread Alone,* a year after the genetical theories of Lysenko had been officially renounced. Younger poets like Yevtushenko wrote openly of anti-Semitism in Russia or of "Stalin's Heirs," some of whom "in retirement, cultivate roses,/And secretly believe,/That their retirement is temporary." Yet there were very clear limits to the extent to which criticism of the basis of Communist society would be tolerated. When the great poet Boris Pasternak published his only novel, *Dr. Zhivago,* in Italy in November 1957, it was hailed as a masterpiece throughout the West; in Russia, however, he was told that the novel offended because of its "non-acceptance of the socialist revolution." When awarded the Nobel Prize for Literature in 1958, it was made clear to him that if he accepted, he would not be permitted to return to Russia. He chose to remain in solitude at his country home near Moscow until his death two years later. After the condemnation of *Dr. Zhivago,* controls over writers tightened for several months, but by the 1960's it was possible for Alexander Solzhenitsyn to publish a novel of life in a Soviet concentration camp, *One Day in the Life of Ivan Denisovich,* which appeared the same year that Stalin's body was removed from the mausoleum in Red Square. During his last two years in office, Khrushchev reimposed cultural controls, requiring Socialist Realism as the standard for the Soviet artist.

Khrushchev's Ouster. By 1964, Khrushchev's "cult of personality" had become intolerable to his leading associates. The sudden changes of policy both in industry and agriculture, a succession of unfavorable crises from the Hungarian uprising to the confrontation with the United States over the Cuban missiles, his desire for a showdown with the Chinese Communists, and the peasant rudeness of his political style, could no longer be tolerated. Led by Brezhnev and Kosygin and profiting from Khruschev's absence on a vacation, the Presidium announced on October 15, 1964, that Khrushchev had been removed from his positions as premier and first party secretary on grounds of age and health. He was permitted to retire to his country home, and all official reference to the man who had been dictator of Soviet Russia for the past nine years ceased abruptly.

THAW AND REFREEZE IN THE EAST EUROPEAN SATELLITES

Between 1945 and 1953, all the East European satellites evolved in fairly similar stages toward the consolidation of Communist control. After Stalin's guiding hand was removed, however, control from the Soviet Union lacked coherence, and the basic principle imposed on the satellites, de-Stalinization, was accepted with varying degrees of subservience by regimes in whom the Soviet dictator still found influential adherents. The diversity of evolution of the East European countries, which became a major factor of European affairs after 1960, became evident in the manner in which de-Stalinization was applied. The implications for the Soviet bloc as a whole of the crisis in Poland and

Hungary provoked by de-Stalinization were considered in Chapter Seven. The implications of de-Stalinization for the internal development of the East European states will now be considered.

Novotny's Czechoslovakia. The country least affected by the Thaw was Czechoslovakia. The coup d'état of February 1948 had been followed by five years of efficient repression, both inside and outside the Communist party, which cowed any potential opposition. Although Klement Gottwald, who had been Communist premier since 1946, died a few days after returning from Stalin's funeral, two of his closest collaborators, Antonin Zápotocki and Viliam Siroky, became president and premier, while the first party secretaryship was taken by a cold, sharply efficient younger party man, Antonin Novotny. After a harsh currency reform on May 30 provoked riots in Pilsen, the new regime followed the Malenkov line of promising a slowdown in industrialization, higher wages, and more consumer goods. Without giving up their goals of ending private ownership of industry and agriculture and of building the country's heavy industrial base, the government succeeded in alleviating immediate economic discontent, and to the end of the decade the Czechs retained the highest standard of living of the satellites. Novotny was able to survive the impact of Khrushchev's secret speech to the Twentieth Party Congress by making only one major concession; in April 1956, the hated minister of defense, Alexei Cepička, was dismissed. None of those executed in the purges of 1952 were rehabilitated, although it was announced that the crimes of Rudolf Slansky, minister of the interior, had been in support of Beria rather than emulation of Tito. In June, the writers who had called for the resignation of the government, were severely rebuked, and sharper controls were imposed over cultural life. In October, the Czech Communist party went to great lengths to point out its support for the Soviet Union against the demands of Gomulka. The next year, Czechoslovakia and East Germany were given the predominant industrial role as suppliers of industrial equipment to the Communist bloc in the plans of Comecon; and long-term agreements were signed with the Soviet Union for harmonization of industrial planning. Soviet ties with Czechoslovakia were closer and more beneficial than with any other satellite. Through 1960, the Novotny regime's record was of political stability and steady economic progress. By 1959, Czechoslovakia, with a population of 13.6 million, was producing 58.7 million tons of coal and 6.1 million tons of steel. With its farming almost totally collectivized, Czechoslovakia continued to cover its traditional imports of foodstuffs with exports of industrial and consumer goods. Unaware that a devastating economic crisis would break the next year, the Czech government declared that it was the second state, after Russia, to have completed the transition to "socialism," issued a new constitution, and changed its official title to the Czechoslovak Socialist Republic.

Ulbricht's East Germany. East Germany rivaled Czechoslovakia in its lack of enthusiasm for de-Stalinization. Although an old-time Communist, Wilhelm Pieck, was president from 1949 to his death in 1960 and a former left-wing Socialist, Otto Grotewohl, was premier from 1949 to 1964, power was in the hands of the first party secretary, Walter Ulbricht. Apparently enjoying Stalin's favor from 1923 on, Ulbricht supported the pro-Russian rather than the nationalist wing of the German Communist party throughout the interwar years, served with the Comintern in Moscow, and was brought back into Germany with Zhukov's armies in 1945. He was primarily responsible for the nationalization of industry in the Soviet zone of occupation, and for the great land reforms. A tough, brilliant, and inhumane administrator, he carried out the purges of 1950–53 efficiently, without staging any show trials like those in Hungary and Czechoslovakia. In spite of being regarded as one of the most convinced Stalinists, he immediately accepted the first recommendations of the Soviet collective leadership in 1953, declared that living conditions would be improved, and, after the suppression of the June uprising, cut investment in heavy industry and raised wages. No major changes of policy or personnel were made, however; and even after Khrushchev's denunciation of Stalin at the Twentieth Party Congress, Ulbricht merely granted a partial amnesty to innocuous political prisoners and made a few speeches denouncing the cult of personality. The regime was critical of both the Poles and the Hungarians for seeking national communism and welcomed the attempt to integrate the economies of the East European countries through Comecon, particularly as it was given the key role in producing machinery, precision instruments, and electrical equipment. The eastward orientation of the economy of East Germany had stimulating effects on economic growth. With about 90 per cent of its trade conducted with the Communist bloc, an expanding market largely protected from Western competition lay open. A pipeline was constructed to bring Soviet oil to

Frankfurt on the Oder, and the canals and railroads were renovated to carry goods eastward. Research scientists succeeded in making the poor-quality coal suitable for coking and in creating the world's sixth largest chemical industry. In spite of the refugee flow to the West, the East German economy reached the 1936 level of per capita production by 1953 and continued throughout the 1950's to maintain a growth rate of at least 4 per cent annually. The contrast with West Germany, however, both in personal freedom and in economic prosperity, remained blatant, while the ease with which East Germans could flee through Berlin and, perhaps more important, find employment on arriving in West Germany, was a constant justification in Ulbricht's view of the maintenance of political repression. The erection of the Berlin Wall was to mark a completely new stage in the evolution of East Germany because, by stopping the flow of East Germans to the West, it made possible realistic economic planning, reinforced the sovereign character of the East German state, and compelled the discontented to seek remedy for their grievances by changes in the Ulbricht regime rather than by flight to the West.

Bulgaria from Chervenkov to Zhivkov. In 1953, the Communist regime in Bulgaria was well entrenched. Benefiting from the traditional sympathy for Russia and from the undoubted need for wide-reaching economic and social reforms, the party had made rapid progress in the socialization of Bulgarian society. Almost two-thirds of agricultural land was collectivized by 1953, and almost all industry was state-owned. A vigorous purge of 90,000 party members and the execution of Deputy Premier Traicho Kostov was carried out after 1949 by Vulko Chervenkov, a Moscow-trained Communist favored by Stalin. From 1950 to 1956, when he was ousted from the premiership, Chervenkov exercised supreme power in Bulgaria. He adjusted to the New Course by making the usual promise of lowering the goals for development of heavy industry and of increasing consumer goods. His own nominee, forty-two-year-old Todor Zhivkov, was chosen first party secretary in March 1954, with the task of maintaining Chervenkov's hold over the party hierarchy. Chervenkov, however, was the object of Tito's enmity, and his support in the Kremlin rapidly dwindled, particularly after the Twentieth Party Congress. In April 1956, he was demoted from premier to deputy premier; his place was taken by Anton Yugov, who, as minister of the interior in 1944–48, had carried out much of the repression during the establishment of Communist control. Although Kostov was rehabilitated, the regime remained Stalinist in character. It condemned the Polish and Hungarian disturbances, appointed Chervenkov minister of culture and education in 1957 to curb criticism by professors and writers, and purged three "revisionists" shortly after Khrushchev's attack on the "anti-party group" in Russia in 1957. Collectivization covered 92 per cent of the arable land by 1958; and Bulgaria appeared resigned to the role of food producer of the Soviet bloc.

Shortly after the third Five-Year Plan had been approved, however, the Bulgarian government revised upward all its goals, both industrial and agricultural, declaring in emulation of Communist China that it was embarking on a "Great Leap Forward." The volume of agricultural production was to be tripled by 1960; that of industrial output was to be more than tripled by 1965. To make this possible, collective farms were merged into huge units of over 10,000 acres; the whole population, including housewives, students, and government officials, was called upon to give "voluntary" labor; economic administration was decentralized; and even education was reorganized, to permit students to spend a third of their time in manual labor. The goals were obviously unattainable, and discontent was widespread even within the highest party ranks. Within a year it was clear that the "Great Leap Forward" had totally failed. At the end of 1959, agricultural production was two-thirds below the planned increase; goals for 1960 were greatly reduced; and the government admitted that raw materials and human resources were insufficient for the tasks set. Since Zhivkov had personally taken responsibility for the overambitious program in his "theses" of March 1959, he preserved his predominance only by attacking his rivals. In November 1961, Chervenkov was dismissed from the Politburo and from his deputy premiership; and exactly a year later, Premier Yugov, who had been capitalizing upon economic discontent to gather together the conservative elements within the party in opposition to Zhivkov, was dismissed from all government and party positions. Two other former ministers of the interior were expelled from the party at the same time. Thus, by 1962 Zhivkov had defeated all his principal rivals; and, firm in the favor of Khrushchev, he seemed prepared to embark upon a period of very moderate reforms.

Gheorghiu-Dej's Rumania. Between 1953 and 1960, Rumania carried out the remarkable feat of maintaining the outward appearances of a loyal Soviet satellite while preparing itself for the successful assertion of its independence. After the purge in 1952 of the Moscow-trained group within the Rumanian Communist party, of whom the most redoubtable was Ana Pauker, leadership of the regime lay with "home" Communists. The dominant personality was Gheorghe Gheorghiu-Dej, who from 1945 alternated between, and sometimes combined, the posts of first party secretary, premier, and head of state, until his death in March 1965. Possible rivals were summarily dealt with. Lucretiu Pătrăşcanu, a loyal Communist who had been imprisoned for his nationalism in 1948, was tried secretly and executed in 1954; and in 1957, Gheorghiu-Dej dismissed from the Politburo both the last important Pauker supporter and the leader of a reform wing of the party. Around him, Gheorghiu-Dej gathered an able group of young native Communists, including Chivu Stoica, premier in 1955–61, and Ion Gheorghe Maurer, a middle-class lawyer who had made his name defending Communists in the interwar years. Maurer became a personal friend of Gheorghiu-Dej and his choice as premier in 1961. This group retained power with remarkable stability from 1952 on, so that Soviet efforts in 1963–64 to find rivals willing to oust Gheorghiu-Dej were a failure.

The Rumanian party was thus able to go through the crises of de-Stalinization without major upset. In 1952, even before Stalin's death, the Rumanian Politburo had scaled down the goals of the first Five-Year Plan (1951–55), which had envisioned an increase of 244 per cent in industrial production, and promised not to force the collectivization of agriculture, which in 1952 constituted only 19 per cent of the country's arable land. Even by 1958, only half had been collectivized. The goals of the second Five-Year Plan (1955–60) were also revised downward within a year, probably as a result of the Hungarian revolution, and more consumer goods were produced. In spite of incoherence in planning, poor worker morale, the low level of technical training, and even theft of factory property, Rumania made great economic progress by 1960. Steel production rose from 353,000 tons in 1948 to 1,806,000 tons in 1960, and over-all industrial output had increased almost fivefold. Probably in 1958–59, the Rumanian government decided that it could aim for "rapid and all-round industrialization" rather than specialize within the bounds allotted it by Comecon. Premier Stoica hinted that Rumania was willing to spend $100 million on machinery in the United States. British, French, and American claims for compensation for property lost or confiscated at the end of the war were partially settled in 1959, and an important trade delegation made a large volume of purchases, including a British tire factory, from six West European countries. The strength of Rumania's economy gave the regime self-confidence in its moves away from the Russian orbit. Finally, the Rumanians succeeded, in an unexplained diplomatic triumph, in persuading the Soviet government to remove all Russian troops from Rumania in July 1958. The basis had thus been laid for the regime's assertion of Rumania's national road to communism.

Hoxha's Albania. Albania, the smallest and most backward of the East European satellites, had seized the chance of ridding itself of Yugoslav tutelage at the time of Tito's quarrel with Stalin in 1948. Party leader Enver Hoxha dismissed the pro-Yugoslav minister of the interior, Koçi Xoxe, and in 1949 had him tried and executed. Hoxha's fidelity to Stalin was rewarded with Soviet economic support for the second Two-Year Plan (1949–50); Soviet technicians and educators were sent to replace the Yugoslavs whom Tito had withdrawn; and a Soviet submarine base was constructed at Valona on the Adriatic. The adoption of the New Course in Russia after the death of Stalin placed Hoxha in a difficult position, especially when Khrushchev made overtures of friendship to Yugoslavia in 1955. Hoxha compromised to the extent of giving up the premiership, but he retained effective control as party secretary. Even after the Twentieth Party Congress he refused to rehabilitate Xoxe or those purged with him; and the Hungarian uprising gave him the opportunity to resume his arrest and execution of Yugoslav "spies," openly to praise Stalin as a "great Marxist-Leninist," and to hold Tito responsible for all the troubles in the satellites. Collectivization continued, in spite of the opposition of the peasantry, until by 1960 86 per cent of the arable land was collectivized. An attempt was made to develop heavy industry, with gifts from the Soviet Union of 422 million rubles, but as an underdeveloped country, Albania found it necessary to concentrate on the export of raw materials like nickel, iron ore, and copper.

Khrushchev's renewed attempt to come to agreement with Tito in 1959 probably forced the Albanians into the arms of the Chinese Communists, who had become the greatest critics of the Yugoslav brand of communism as well as of Khrushchev's policy of "peaceful coexistence" with the West; but undoubtedly the main reason for the development of a close alliance between Albania and Communist China was the reverence of both regimes for the methods of Stalinism. Throughout 1959, relations with China were furthered, by foundation of an Albanian-China Friendship Society, exchange of visits between leading party members, and by coordination of ideological opposition to Soviet Russia. In 1960, Hoxha did not attend the satellite summit meeting in Bucharest in June, nor did he appear with Khrushchev at the United Nations in September. At the world conference of eighty-one Communist parties in Moscow in November, however, Hoxha sharply criticized Khrushchev, as "a traitor to the communist idea, a weakling, and a revisionist," and was vilified by Khrushchev in return. An open break was close.

Gomulka's Poland. In Poland, it appeared that de-Stalinization had been extended, with the return of Gomulka to power in October 1956, to permit the Poles to find their national road to socialism. Yet Gomulka was rapidly to disappoint those who saw in him another Tito. By 1960, Gomulka had embarked upon the "retreat from October," in which he gradually whittled away many of the concessions that had been granted in October 1956. Two outstanding reforms were not withdrawn, however. The peasants had been permitted to dissolve the collective farms, and about 8,500 out of 10,500 were returned to private ownership, reducing the area of arable land under collective ownership from 24 to 14 per cent. With other governmental concessions, the peasant found that his income rose 21 per cent in 1956–57; private investment in agriculture jumped by 50 per cent; and production remained high. Police repression, from which Gomulka himself had suffered, was severely curtailed. Although considerable freedom of political discussion was tolerated after October, it was not permitted to interfere with Gomulka's exercise of power through the Communist party hierarchy. In the elections of January 1957, only one list of candidates was presented, although the voters were free to cross off the ballot any names they wished. The workers' councils, which had sprung up spontaneously in the October events, were deprived of political rights within a month, and in 1959 they were abolished. The universities succeeded in retaining much of their freedom from state control, including the rights to elect their own officers, to purchase some Western journals and newspapers, and to abandon compulsory courses in Marxism-Leninism. Nevertheless, strict controls over publication, especially in the humanities, were imposed, and in 1959 the liberal-minded minister of education, Wladislaw Bienkowski, and the presidents of the Writers' Union and of the Journalists' Union, were removed. Perhaps the most outstanding example of a relaxation of Communist pressure in 1956 came in relations with the Catholic Church. Wyszynski and several bishops were released from detention, and in December 1956 a Church-State agreement was reached in which the Church agreed to encourage citizens to support the Gomulka programs; in return it was given greater freedom of religious and educational activity. Wyszynski was even permitted to go to Rome to be made a cardinal and again to take part in the election of Pope John XXIII in 1958. Within a year, however, government propaganda against the Vatican was resumed; Catholic publications were censored; and riots provoked in 1960 in the new industrial city of Nowa Huta by cancellation of the grant of a site for a large Catholic Church. The enormous support for the Church among the peasantry and even among the workers, the large number of people entering the clergy as priests, monks, and nuns, and the wealth of the Church were increasingly intolerable for Gomulka, as his hold over the party strengthened. After 1960, he clearly felt strong enough to challenge the Church with increasing intensity. Gomulka had thus created his own particular brand of national communism, a middle course between the "dogmatists" in his party who wished to return to the days of Stalin and the "revisionists" who wanted total independence of the kind the Hungarians had demanded under Imre Nagy.

Kádár's Hungary. While the Poles were surprised to find Gomulka destroying the gains of the Polish October, the Hungarians were equally astonished to find János Kádár granting many of the benefits they had hoped to win by their revolution. For two years after the failure of the revolution, Kádár applied a policy of harsh repression. The Hungarian Writers' Union was banned in January 1957 and the Workers' Councils in November 1957. Writers who had supported the revolution, like Tibor Dery, were jailed. In March 1957, Kádár agreed, during a visit to Moscow, that Soviet troops should remain in Hungary "as long as necessary." A new attack was launched against the old democratic parties, which had reappeared during the revolution; and the Communist party was reconstituted under the title of Hungarian Socialist Workers' party, with some 300,000 new members. In the first difficult months after the revolution, when Hungary was receiving food supplies from both the Soviet bloc and the West, Kádár made no attempt to force the peasantry back into collective farms. But between 1959 and 1961, when his position seemed secure, he embarked upon so vigorous a program of socialization of agriculture that the percentage of arable land collectivized rose from 23 per cent to 80 per cent. Pressure against the Catholic Church was renewed. Cardinal Mindszenty remained in refuge in the American Embassy, but three bishops were arrested, and by 1961 only five bishops were allowed to carry out their duties fully. The months of deportation, imprisonment, and execution of those implicated in the uprising reached their climax with the execution in June 1958 of Nagy and his closest associates.

After 1958, however, Kádár began to attempt to win popular support, or at least tolerance, for his regime. He himself had been imprisoned and tortured by the Nazis, and in 1951–54 by the Rákosi government, and the secret police were not given the same powers they had under Rákosi. An amnesty for some political prisoners and the closing of the internment camps was announced in 1960, and some imprisoned writers were released. To make use of the professional classes and the intellectuals, some important positions in industry and administration, and even seats in parliament, were opened to non-party members and to people not of proletarian origins. Kádár summed up his new policy in December 1961, in the famous phrase, "He who is not against us is with us." A lessening of tension became apparent when the new line was accompanied by a rise in living standards. The Five-Year Plan of 1956–60 achieved its goal of an over-all increase of 20 per cent in national production. Large loans were received from Russia and several other satellite countries. Workers were given a share in the profits of their factories after 1958; a fund to establish technical development was established; and a start was made in earning hard currency with the opening of the country to Western tourists in 1960. This relaxation was to continue through the early 1960's, with the surprising result that Hungarians who had detested Kádár for his role in the suppression of the revolution had come to accept him as the least bad ruler they could hope for as long as Hungary remained a Soviet satellite.

Tito's Yugoslavia. In 1953–60, Yugoslavia, while not returning to the Soviet bloc, renewed amicable relations with the Khrushchev regime in Russia and with most of the East European satellites. Internal developments, however, indicated that the Yugoslav government was developing

"Titoism" into a distinctive ideology. After 1950, party theorists like Dedijer, Kardelj, and Djilas attacked the Soviet Union for adopting a form of state capitalism controlled by a top-heavy, privileged bureaucracy, which resulted in social inequality and injustice. In June 1950, the Yugoslav government declared that "ownership" of industry was being turned over to the workers, whose Workers' Councils would elect Management Committees. Industrial enterprises would have a large amount of autonomy; profits would be shared between the federal state, the provinces, and the workers; and competition between enterprises would be permitted to encourage quality in production. The state would lay down only the basic goals, leaving detailed planning to the local enterprises. At the same time, the powers of the police were reduced, a new criminal code was brought in, and special privileges of party members were canceled. Collectivization of agriculture continued until 1953, when its palpable failure forced the regime to change its stand completely, by allowing peasants to withdraw from the Cooperatives. Three years later, the area of arable land under collective ownership had fallen from 24 to 9 per cent. Agricultural production, which had been slowly declining before 1953, spurted by an average of 4.1 per cent annually in 1953–56 and by 10.5 per cent annually in 1957–60. In 1955, Tito admitted that the economic situation of Yugoslavia was dangerously threatened by inflation, low worker productivity, speculation, waste, and arbitrary price policy of certain enterprises; and he sought to remedy the situation by allowing greater production of consumer goods and higher investment in agriculture. The Five-Year Plan (1957–61) proved a great success, its goals being achieved a year early; strengthened by this justification of their course, the Yugoslav leaders issued a 100,000 word program, at the party congress of March 1958, in which they claimed that Yugoslav socialism was the synthesis that emerged out of the conflict of the thesis of Western capitalism and the antithesis of Stalinist bureaucratism. Their solution, they claimed, had a universal validity in the inevitable movement of the world to socialism. This deliberate challenge to Soviet leadership produced a bitter denunciation from Moscow, but Khrushchev refused to be forced into an open break, and a few months later most normal relations were resumed. By 1960, therefore, Tito seemed to have successfully profited from his break with Stalin. He had restored diplomatic and economic relations with the Communist bloc while receiving large-scale American military and economic aid and conducting growing trade with Western Europe. He had entered a mutual defense pact in 1953 with Greece and Turkey; and in October 1954 he had settled his quarrel with Italy by agreeing to permit Italy to take the city of Trieste while Yugoslavia took the southern, rural portion of the peninsula of Venezia Giulia. Above all, Tito had begun to court the growing number of neutralist powers in Asia and Africa, seeing in himself the obvious leader of the uncommitted nations.

THE ADENAUER ERA IN WEST GERMANY

Adenauer's Kanzlerdemokratie. The character of the West German Bundesrepublik (Federal Republic) was already formed by the time of the second federal election in September 6, 1953. Konrad Adenauer, who at the age of seventy-three had barely been elected chancellor on September 15, 1949 by a vote of 202 out of 402, had established virtually unchallenged authority not only within his own Christian Democratic party but within the Bundestag and over the powerful federal bureaucracy. While adamantly refusing to share power with the second largest party, the Social Democrats, he had brought into his government the small, business-oriented party of the Free Democrats, and was to govern in close cooperation with them until his resignation on October 15, 1963. His cabinet was dependent upon his wishes, partly because he retained personal control of foreign policy until 1955 and partly because he remained chairman of the Christian Democrats and thus managed party appointments himself. President Theodor Heuss, an amiable, dignified professor and author, was kept strictly within the ceremonial duties of his office, especially after Adenauer forced him to give up his attempt in 1953 to interfere in the struggle over German rearmament. The only cabinet member with strong prestige was Professor Ludwig Erhard, who was widely regarded as the author of the German economic miracle. Adenauer never hid his dislike and distrust of Erhard, nor his determination that Erhard should not succeed him as chancellor; but the uneasy alliance between the two was maintained by Germany's continuing prosperity. The prestige of Adenauer and Erhard was a major factor in giving the Christian Democratic party (and its ally the Bavarian Christian Social Union) electoral victory with 139 seats in 1949 and 243 in 1953; but the Christian Democratic party's deliberately nondenominational Christian program, its offer of social-welfare programs combined with support of a free-enterprise economy, its belief in

European integration, and its agrarian protectionism won it a faithful body of voters among the farmers, the middle classes, and many workers. The small parties that contested the 1949 elections, such as the Bavarian party, the Refugee party, and the German party, quickly lost their supporters to the Christian Democrats. With the banning of the neo-Nazi Socialist Reich party in 1952 and of the Communist party in 1956, the number of parties represented in the Bundestag fell from seven in 1949, to five in 1953, four in 1957, and three in 1961. The Free Democrats, with their appeal to big business and their opposition to the extension of government controls, were able to muster a small but constant body of support to the right of the Christian Democrats, receiving between 7 and 13 per cent of the vote. The Socialist party, in spite of the vigorous leadership until his death in 1952 of Kurt Schumacher and the efficient organization of Erich Ollenhauer, suffered by the separation from East Germany where its traditional strength lay. In West Germany, its program of anticommunism, German reunification, and social reform won it a solid following of about 30 per cent of the voters; but throughout the 1950's, it was unable to throw off the label of being a party for the workers alone and of being consistently negative in its approach, the party of the *Neinsager* (Nay-sayers). West Germany thus became a Chancellor-Democracy (*Kanzlerdemokratie*), with a center-right government whose tenure of power promised to be of long duration.

The Basis of the German Economic Miracle. The basis of West German economic policy had also been laid by 1953. By then, the occupying powers had ceased to interfere in the German economy. The International Authority for the Ruhr, which had controlled the allocation of German coal production, was disbanded in 1952. Dismantling of factories for reparations had ended. The great monopolistic companies in coal and steel, chemicals, and banking had been partially broken up. The one remaining burden was the payment of occupation costs of just under $2 billion annually for maintenance of the occupying forces in West Germany. Economics Minister Erhard, free of Allied controls, helped stimulate business expansion by encouraging free competition, giving tax privileges to those companies that reinvested their profits, and reducing to a minimum government controls over foreign trade. According to Erhard, an increase in the standard of living would follow from the encouragement of production. After two years of difficulty, when Germany ran a deficit in its foreign trade and suffered from unemployment at home, the Korean War boom provided a great stimulus to heavy industry. Exports rose drastically. By 1952 the balance of trade was favorable. Unemployment had fallen in 1950–52 from one and a half to one million; the trend continued until, in 1956, it became necessary to import workers from Italy. By 1953 production was 58 per cent higher than before the war. Moreover, Erhard's optimism that the benefits of the "social market economy" would be shared by the whole population seemed to be justified. While the cost of living remained fairly stable, the average weekly wage almost doubled in 1948–53. In 1950–54, 1.5 million houses were built. In 1952, a "burden equalization" law passed the Bundestag, requiring everyone to give half of his possessions (as of 1948–49) for redistribution to many categories of persons who had suffered from the Nazi regime, the war, or the occupation. While payments could be stretched over thirty years, the income from this tax reached $690 million in 1953 alone. A vigorous effort was begun to help refugees and expellees to settle in West Germany, and in 1953 special financial aid was made available through the Law on Matters Affecting Expellees and Refugees. The small number of strikes, the opposition of the trade-union federation to the occupying powers' attempts to break up the great industrial combines, and the ubiquitous evidence of a rising standard of living were already proof by 1953 that Erhard's doctrines appealed to the workers as well as to the employers.

Westward Orientation of Adenauer's Foreign Policy. Finally, the orientation of West German foreign policy was also laid down by 1953. Although Adenauer constantly emphasized his desire for the reunification of Germany, he set higher priority on his other goals—the independence of West Germany, a reconciliation with France, and the unification of Western Europe within an Atlantic alliance. By constant battles with the Allied High Commission, which from 1949 to 1955 exercised supervision on behalf of the three occupying powers over the activity of the federal government, he gradually won the full attributes of sovereignty—freedom of tax legislation, the right to conduct its own foreign affairs, and, through the European Defense Community, the right to rearm. An independent Germany, he felt, should end its "hereditary enmity" with France. In 1950, he abruptly proposed the complete unification of the two countries, but found his proposal ignored. He seized upon Robert Schuman's offer of May 9, 1950 to fuse the coal and steel industries of the two countries in a European federation, and forced the treaty creating the European Coal and Steel Community through the Bundestag against the opposition of German business and of Economics Minister Erhard. He refused to allow the fusion of the Saar in an economic union with France to cause the alienation of the two countries and even agreed that West Germany and the Saar would become members of the Council of Europe at the same time. In the European Defense Community treaty, he saw a method by which all three of his goals would be furthered. In return for German rearmament, the occupation would be ended; by the integration of the French and German armies in a European army, war between the two nations would be made impossible; and the capping of the Defense Community with a supranational political organization would bring about the unification of Western Europe. Achievement of these goals, Adenauer urged, would strengthen the North Atlantic alliance, and enable reunification negotiations to be undertaken from a position of strength.

On September 6, 1953, the electorate warmly endorsed Adenauer's programs. The Christian Democratic share of the vote rose from 31 to 45.2 per cent; the Free Democrats fell from 11.9 to 9.5 per cent; the Social Democrats remained stable, falling only 0.4 to 28.8 per cent; and several small parties disappeared from the Bundestag. After re-forming his coalition with the Free Democrats, he applied great pressure on the members of the coalition to amend the Federal constitution by a two-thirds majority in both houses of the legislature, in order to permit German rearmament; and, after recalling deputies from as far away as Ethiopia and bringing others from hospitals, he won the required majority to amend the constitution on March 30, 1954. The defeat of the European Defense Community treaty by the French Assembly five months later was a personal blow to him, seeming at the time to be destroying all his work toward reconciliation with France and ensuring that the Allied occupation would continue indefinitely. He was therefore delighted when, in September, it was agreed at the London and Paris conferences that West Germany should be permitted to set up its own national army, become a member of NATO, and be freed of occupation controls. To win these concessions, Adenauer paid what he regarded as a small price: He agreed that Germany would not manufacture atomic, biological, or chemical weapons and that the future status of the Saar should be settled by a plebiscite.

The Saar Problem. The Saar territory, an important coal-mining basin on the border of France and Luxembourg, with about one million German-speaking inhabitants, had been occupied by France from 1919 to 1936, under the provisions of the Treaty of Versailles. In 1948, after its inhabitants had voted overwhelmingly in favor of a constitution providing for economic fusion of the territory with France, it was separated from the rest of the French zone and was brought within the French currency and customs area. A complaisant government led by Johannes Hoffmann worked closely with the regally mannered French military governor, Gilbert Grandval, in developing economic ties with France and even agreed to permit France to exploit the Saar coal mines until the signature of a German peace treaty. In West Germany, however, France's intention to separate the Saar permanently from the German *Heimat* (homeland) met increasing opposition from exiled Saarlanders, from the leaders of the neighboring state of Rheinland-Pfalz, and from politicians of all parties who argued that acquiescence in the loss of the Saar would imply German recognition of loss of the Oder-Neisse territories. Within the Saar, pro-German parties were forbidden; and an underground agitation, financed by the Bonn government's Ministry of All-German Affairs, produced a growing Francophobia directed against Grandval and his Saar collaborators. The French government decided to save its privileges in the Saar by supporting proposals originally instigated by Adenauer for the Europeanization of the territory. At Paris, in September 1954, Adenauer and Mendès-France agreed to ask the Saarlanders in a plebiscite if they wished their territory to receive political autonomy within the framework of the Western European Union, and thus to be politically independent of both France and Germany while joining in an economic union with both. On October 23, 1955, after a prolonged, vituperative campaign, the Saarlanders amazed both the French and German governments by giving a vote of 67.72 per cent against Europeanization. The French at once agreed that the Saar should be reunited with Germany politically on January 1, 1957 and economically on January 1, 1960. In return, the Germans agreed to finance jointly with France and Luxembourg the canalization of the Moselle River from the French border to the Rhine, thereby giving the Lorraine iron and steel industry an important transport link with the rest of the Common Market. The canal, which involved the building of thirteen dams and sluices and eleven hydroelectric stations, cost about $192 million, and was opened to traffic in February 1964.

Summit and Decline of Adenauer's Prestige. In the elections of September 15, 1957, Adenauer attained the height of his popularity, sweeping the Christian Democrats back into power with an absolute majority of the vote, 50.2 per cent, and of the seats in the Bundestag, 270 out of 497. The economy was maintaining its extraordinary growth rate, the gross national product increasing 186 per cent during the 1950's to a total of $88 billion. The new army, strictly supervised by committees of the Bundestag and democratically organized by the first defense minister, Theodor Blank, numbered 180,000 by 1958; it had also received rockets armed with atomic warheads from the United States. Entry into the Common Market on January 1, 1958 promised a new stimulus to the whole economy. Even the Soviet Union recognized the new state after Adenauer's Moscow visit in September 1955, and had sent Deputy Premier Mikoyan to sign a commercial and consular treaty in April 1958 that substantially increased Soviet-West German trade. In the spring of 1959, seemingly prepared to lay down power while his reputation was undimmed, Adenauer declared that he would be a candidate for the presidency, but shortly afterward changed his mind and retained the chancellorship. The avuncular tradition of the presidency was continued with the choice of the Christian Democratic candidate, Heinrich Lübke. Adenauer's popularity suffered a severe decline, however. Members of his own party were discontented at his authoritarianism, and especially at his open attacks on Erhard. The Ruhr coal mines faced a crisis of overproduction and the possibility of unemployment, as increased importations of oil lessened the need for coal. Above all, the erection of the Berlin Wall on August 13, 1961 emphasized the failure of the West German government to make any progress toward reunification. On September 17, 1961, the Christian Democrats won only 242 seats and 45.4 per cent of the vote; the Social Democrats, led by the personable and dynamic mayor of West Berlin, Willy Brandt, raised their number of seats to 190 and their percentage of the vote to 36.2; and the Free Democrats regained their position of arbiter with 67 seats and 12.8 per cent of the vote. To put together his coalition, Adenauer was forced to sacrifice his minister of foreign affairs, Heinrich von Brentano, and he himself was invested as chancellor only after agreeing to step down before the next elections.

With his days as chancellor numbered, Adenauer pressed on with realization of his external goals. Adamantly refusing to give in to pressure from both Social Democrats and Free Democrats to engage in direct negotiations with the Soviet Union, he continued to strengthen the Federal Republic's ties with the West. German armed forces rose to 375,000 in 1962, constituting about one-third of NATO's land forces in Europe. The German government accepted measures to strengthen the Common Market as a whole, even where, as in the acceleration of the timetable of customs reductions and especially in establishment of a common agricultural policy, sacrifices would be required from sectors of the West German economy. Above all, Adenauer sought to keep close relations with French President de Gaulle. He supported de Gaulle's plans for European political union, even though they did not provide for creation of a supranational authority, accepted his veto on British membership in the Common Market, and joined him on January 22, 1963 in signing the Franco-German Treaty of Cooperation, which provided for harmonization of policy on matters of mutual interest by frequent consultation between the governments. On October 15, 1963, after unsuccessfully pronouncing Erhard unfit to be his successor as chancellor, Adenauer finally resigned, at the age of eighty-seven.

Erhard's Failure as Chancellor. Erhard proved as unsuccessful as Chancellor as Eden had been as Prime Minister. Although he led the CDU to electoral victory in 1965, both the economic and political situation got out of hand. Tight money policies intended to curb chronic inflation, labor costs that rose faster than productivity, and falling industrial investment, cut West Germany's economic growth rate by half in 1966 and tripled unemployment. Erhard's coalition allies, the Free Democrats, provoked a government crisis in October 1966 by withdrawing from his cabinet. At once Erhard's rivals within the CDU, making great play not only of the economic downturn but of the worsened relations with France resulting from Erhard's pro-American foreign policy, forced his replacement as chancellor by Kurt Georg Kiesinger, the dignified minister-president of Baden-Württemberg. The Kiesinger government, composed of an unprecedented coalition of Christian Democrats and Socialists, promised friendship with France, wider contacts with Eastern Europe, and constitutional and economic reform at home.

POLITICAL INSTABILITY AND ECONOMIC PROGRESS IN INNER EUROPE

In 1945–53, Belgium, the Netherlands, Luxembourg, Italy, and France went through a similar process of political and economic reconstruction that was largely completed by the time the Marshall Plan ended. Whereas the industrial advances of the 1950's showed that the economic foundation had been well laid, the chronic governmental instability proved that political reconstruction had been much less successful.

Continuing Political Unrest in Belgium. In Belgium, the quarrels between Walloons and Flemings, Catholics and non-Catholics, and the Social-Democratic and Christian-Social parties continued unabated. As a result of unemployment in the coal mines and of its decision to raise to two years the period of compulsory military service, the Christian-Social government, which had been in office since 1945, was ousted at the 1954 elections, and replaced by a Socialist-Liberal coalition government, under Van Acker. While gaining popularity by reducing military service to eighteen months, the new government aroused Catholic opposition by reducing subsidies paid to private schools. Catholic teachers resigned, the minister of education was burnt in effigy, and mass Catholic demonstrations were held. After the elections of June 1958, a Christian-Social government under Eyskens, heavily weighted in favor of the Flemings, annoyed the Walloons by considering a redistribution of parliamentary seats to give greater representation to the rapidly expanding Catholic population in Flanders. The royal family further embittered relations between Walloon and Fleming. Leopold had continued to live in the Royal Palace of Laeken after his abdication, where it was suspected he dictated royal policy, but he was finally forced to leave in 1959. The same year, Baudouin's brother, the heir to the throne, further annoyed the Walloons by marrying an Italian Catholic princess in the Vatican without a preliminary civil ceremony in Belgium. The sudden grant of independence to the Belgian Congo on June 27, 1960 endangered the Belgian currency and brought immediate economic dislocation, which the government proposed to meet by passage of an austerity program, called the *Loi unique* (Single Law). The Walloons of the southern industrial regions went on strike, and the Walloon deputies petitioned the king to introduce decentralization of the Belgian political administration. Although the elections of March 1961 gave the Christian-Social party an increased majority, the Socialist Paul-Henri Spaak became foreign minister in the new government. The hostility of the French-speaking and Flemish-speaking Belgians did not lessen, however, and the passage of a law shifting the linguistic frontier only heightened passions.

Political Tension in the Netherlands. Although the Netherlands had only two premiers between 1946 and 1959, Dr. Beel of the Catholic party (1946–48, 1958–59) and W. Drees of the Labor party (1948–58), the inability of either of the two major parties to win more than a two-to-five-seat majority in parliament caused constant friction in the formation of coalition cabinets. It took Drees ten weeks in 1952 and sixteen weeks in 1956 to form his cabinet; and there was constant dispute within the coalition government, particularly over the method of dealing with the Indonesian independence movement, the danger of inflation, the increase in the length of military service, and above all over the influence of the Catholic Church on policy-making. Although the Catholic party decided to govern without the support of the Labor party after 1959, disagreement continued with the smaller parties in the governmental coalition, and Protestant criticism compelled the resignation of Premier De Quay and the remodeling of his government after a ten-day crisis. Only in Luxembourg was there relative calm on the political scene. Grand Duchess Charlotte continued to reign until 1961, when she handed over a share of her powers to her son, while the government was dominated for most of the decade by the jovial figure of Joseph Bech, premier, foreign minister, and wine minister, who took Luxembourg into Benelux, NATO, ECSC, and the Common Market, and who won for Luxembourg city the choice as the seat of the High Authority of ECSC.

Immobilism in Italy. After the overthrow of De Gasperi on July 28, 1953, no political leader emerged in Italy with the personal stature or political support necessary to assure governmental continuity. The four-party coalition of Christian Democrats, Social Democrats, Republicans, and Liberals through which De Gasperi had ruled between 1948 and 1953 had only a bare majority in the two houses of parliament, and was strongly challenged not only by the Communists and the left-wing Socialists but also from the right by the neo-Fascists and a newly strengthened Monarchist party. Moreover, the Christian Democrats themselves were divided into factions, a right wing sympathetic to big business, a center that emphasized political liberty, and a left wing desirous of social reform. Between 1953 and 1958, the premiership alternated between these three tendencies. The result was a period of "immobilism" similar in character to that in France. The principal achievements of the governments of these years were two—the passage of a ten-year program for economic development and the ratification of Italy's participation in the Common Market and Euratom.

The elections of May 25, 1958 again demonstrated the disorder of the Italian political system. Even though the Communist party suffered from the Soviet suppression of the Hungarian revolt, it still received almost 7 million votes and 140 seats in the Chamber of Deputies. The Socialists remained split. Three right-wing parties polled almost 3 million votes, including 659,000 for the Popular Monarchists. The Republicans and Liberals polled about 1.5 million votes; and the Christian Democrats, who had hoped for an absolute majority, received only 273 seats out of 596. Government by coalition remained imperative; but a renewed series of cabinet crises compelled the Christian Democratic leadership to reconsider the whole basis of its political power. In the summer of 1960, Fernando Tambroni personally and unexpectedly decided to experiment with an opening to the right, by accepting neo-Fascist support. He was brought down by widespread rioting among the working classes of the northern cities. The only remaining alternative was the "opening to the left," the wooing of the left-wing Socialists of Pietro Nenni to win them away from their increasingly unrewarding alliance with the Communists.

The Opening to the Left. Until 1958, the Papacy had firmly rejected any alliance of the Christian Democrats with the strongly anticlerical followers of Nenni. The accession of Pope John XXIII transformed the official attitude of the Church to such a move, for John, with a simple kindliness that extended to all human beings, seemed determined to destroy the barriers the Church had erected against political and religious faiths of which it disapproved. Culminating in the encyclical *Pacem in Terris,* the Pope's moving plea for international reconciliation, the Vatican's change of approach helped DC Party Secretary Aldo Moro rally the disparate wings of his party to collaboration with Nenni. Meanwhile, the left-wing Socialists were detaching themselves from their Communist allies. Nenni had denounced the 1934 Unity of Action Pact with the Communists after the Hungarian uprising, and his party had campaigned against the Communists in the 1958 elections. In 1960, the Nenni Socialists had united with the Christian Democrats rather than with the Communists in fighting the municipal elections, and together they won control of a number of local administrations. In March 1962 they pledged themselves to support a reform program to be initiated by a new government under Christian Democrat Amintore Fanfani. During the next year, Fanfani introduced measures that taxed real-estate speculation and dividends on shares, increased pensions, reorganized the school system, pressed on with the economic development of the south, and nationalized the electricity industry. The elections of April 28, 1963 gave the four parties favoring the opening to the left and the new reform program 60 per cent of the vote. In December, Moro put together a coalition that satisfied the left-wing Socialists, and the opening to the left became a reality. Nenni himself became vice-premier. The new government promised decentralization of administration, education reform, a program of home building, and a change in agrarian tenure. Parliamentary stability was not assured by the coalition, however, for Moro was overthrown in July 1964 when the Nenni Socialists refused to support him on a minor issue. He returned to power with a re-formed cabinet that showed considerable resilience in surviving several new crises, including a much-contested presidential election and the flamboyant resignation of Fanfani as foreign minister in 1965. By 1966, the opening to the left had begun to show solid successes; and as a result the two Italian Socialist parties, which had been divided since 1947, constituted once more a united Socialist party.

French Politics and the Algerian Rebellion. After the ouster of Mendès-France in February 1955, the French Assembly invested the satisfactorily unadventurous Radical Edgar Faure as premier. He returned to the conservative economic and social policies inaugurated by Queuille and Pinay. The 1956 elections showed that even this conservatism did not satisfy a large element in French society, since the small shopkeepers and small farmers gave 52 seats to the party of a demagogue, Pierre Poujade, who preached against big government, taxation, planning, and Europeanism. The Communists won 145 seats and 27 per cent of the vote. The parties in the center were hopelessly fragmented; and a government coalition of Socialists, MRP, Radicals, and Independent-Peasant deputies so broad as to be almost impotent faced the worst crisis of the whole period of the Fourth Republic, the rebellion in Algeria. The inability of the Mollet government and its almost indistinguishable successors to solve the Algerian problem destroyed the Republic itself.

The French had barely given up control of Indochina when, in October 1954, a series of coordinated attacks on government buildings, outposts, farms, and policemen was launched by a secret revolutionary committee formed within the Moslem Movement for the Triumph of Democratic Liberties. The French government, which regarded Algeria as an integral part of France rather than as a colony sent air and artillery forces to crush the revolt in its infancy. Repression failed, however, and throughout 1955 the rebels, led by the National Liberation Front (FLN) grew more daring. Mollet, after first promising reforms, bowed to the pressure of the European settlers in Algeria and to the army, which was determined not to repeat the debacle of Indochina, increased French forces in Algeria to 500,000 men, and acquiesced in the kidnapping of five rebel leaders, including the future premier Ben Bella while en route from Morocco to Tunisia by plane. At home newspapers were censored, critics were hauled into court, and suspects were jailed without trial. To end Egyptian aid to the rebels, the French government entered secret negotiations with the British and the Israelis, which culminated in the disastrous Suez invasion of November 1956; and French planes caused an international scandal by bombing a Tunisian border village, Sakhiet, where the international Red Cross was aiding Algerian refugees.

The Return of de Gaulle. By 1958, the government was being attacked from all sides—by the European settlers, the army officers, and the right-wingers in France, for considering a political settlement through gradual concessions; by the French Communists and by the majority of Moslem Algerians for being unwilling to accept the inevitability of independence; and by a growing number of liberal and intellectual leaders in France for condoning the terroristic methods of "revolutionary war" that the army had learned from the Viet Minh and introduced into Algeria. The nomination as premier of Pierre Pflimlin, a well-known moderate in colonial affairs, presented the dissidents in Algeria with the opportunity for direct action. On May 13, the day of Pflimlin's investiture, a huge demonstration in Algiers turned into a riot, in which the main government building was seized and a Committee of Public Safety was formed under the presidency of a tough paratroop general, Jacques Massu. Several groups of conspirators then came into the open, among them a group of Gaullists who were determined to engineer the return to power of General de Gaulle—who continued writing his memoirs in his country home without either supporting or disclaiming them. In Algeria, plans were prepared for the seizure of Paris by paratroops, and the takeover of Corsica on May 24 appeared a first step to invasion of the mainland. De Gaulle, who had declared on May 15 that he was "ready to take over the powers of the Republic," increasingly appeared to be the only alternative to chaos and civil war; and he reassured his opponents by asking scornfully, "Do you think that at sixty-seven I am going to begin a career as a dictator?" Pflimlin resigned on May 28, and the next day President Coty announced that he had "turned to the most illustrious of Frenchmen" as Pflimlin's successor. De Gaulle was invested as premier on June 1, opposed only by the Communists, half of the Socialists, and the followers of Mendès-France, and was given the power to govern for six months by decree and to rewrite the constitution.

De Gaulle set to work with great vigor to put an end to the disasters he believed the "régime des partis" had brought upon France. A new constitution was quickly drawn up by his long-time supporter, Michel Debré, and received an 80 per cent vote of approval when presented to the people in a referendum in September. The constitution provided for a powerful president, with the right to choose the premier, dissolve the Assembly, and in cases of emergency, to govern by decree. The Assembly's power to overthrow the government was drastically reduced, its sessions shortened, and its members forced to resign their seats if appointed to the cabinet. A new electoral law restored single-member constituencies, a provision that favored the new Gaullist party, the Union for the New Republic (UNR), which with its allies won more than half the seats in the elections in December, and worked against the Communists, who won only ten seats. However, the elections also showed that France had joined de Gaulle in rejecting both the practices and the politicians of the Fourth Republic, since only 131 of the deputies of the last assembly were re-elected. De Gaulle was chosen president in December by vote of the deputies, senators, and delegates of the local electoral bodies; and he at once named Michel Debré as his first premier. To tackle France's economic problems, he appointed a conservative as minister of finance to reassure the business community, brought in a series of stabilization measures, including a freeze of salaries for the military and public-service employees, and in December, devalued the franc by 17.5 per cent, increased taxes, and cut social security payments. In spite of his often-voiced contempt for European integration, he declared that France would accept all its obligations within the Common Market, including the immediate reduction of tariffs by 10 per cent; and he brusquely broke off negotiations with Britain for the establishment of a Free Trade Area that might weaken the initial impact of economic unification within the Common Market.

De Gaulle's Treatment of the Algerian Problem. He had been called back, however, primarily to deal with the Algerian problem. He first procrastinated, attempting to give both the European Algerians and the Moslems the impression that he favored their cause. The Committees of Public Safety were disbanded, and a civilian administration restored. The Constantine Plan was drawn up in 1959 to raise Moslem living standards and to speed Algerian economic development. But he refused to deal with the rebel leaders, who had organized a Provisional Government of the Algerian Republic, and permitted new programs of military "pacification." On September 16, 1959, he suggested for the first time that the Algerians be given the choice of seceding from France, of being totally integrated with France through a process of "Francisation," or of creating a close "association" with France. When protest demonstrations were held in Algeria, de Gaulle began transferring disaffected army officers, including General Massu, back to France; and when open insurrection broke out among the European civilians and some of the military in Algiers in January 1960, it was put down by force. By June, de Gaulle realized that no alternative existed to negotiations with the FLN; yet when Ferhat Abbas came to Melun, near Paris, to open talks, both sides were so intransigent that the talks were quickly broken off. The effect was disastrous. Assassinations were carried out by Moslem terrorists in both Algeria and France; reprisals and counterreprisals caused the deaths of thousands of innocent Algerian villagers; and vast numbers fled for safety across the Moroccan and Tunisian borders. The French people were bitterly divided between the adherents of *Algérie Française* and those who wanted a negotiated settlement with the FLN. With his prestige weakened by the inability to bring peace to Algeria, de Gaulle went to the French people to ask for a massive vote of confidence in his policy of giving Algeria self-determination, and received a 75 per cent vote of approval in a referendum in January 1961. The European Algerians and the leading French officers in Algeria concluded that de Gaulle had become a traitor to the very elements whose uprising in May 1958 had brought him back to power. On April 22, 1961, Generals Salan, Challe, Zeller, and Jouhaud announced that the army had taken control of Algeria in order to keep it French. Panic in France was increased when Premier Debré called upon the civilian population to take up arms against possible paratroop invasion; the trade unions called out eleven million workers on a general strike; and de Gaulle, dressed in his general's uniform, appeared on television in both France and Algeria to use his personal influence to order the army to obey the legally constituted government. The revolt collapsed within four days, and its leaders were arrested. Terrorism continued unabated, however; and a number of army deserters formed the Secret Army Organization, used plastic explosives against supporters of Algerian independence, and made several attempts to assassinate de Gaulle himself. In a situation of growing chaos, new talks began with the FLN in February 1962, and agreement was finally reached on March 18. The Algerians were to decide by plebiscite if they wished independence; France was to retain the right to exploit the oil deposits of the Sahara, and would give financial aid to a new Algerian state; after independence, any Algerian citizen would be free to return to France with his possessions. The OAS went on a rampage in Algeria when the agreements were announced, burning schools and libraries, setting off bombs in the Moslem quarters, and seizing bank deposits and weapons. The violence of the OAS was returned by the Moslems, and the Europeans began to flee to France by the thousands. Within a few months, four-fifths of the European population had fled, posing the French government the enormous problem of resettling some 800,000 refugees, many of whom had never set eyes on France. Nevertheless, the end of the Algerian War was greeted with enormous relief in France, which found itself at peace for the first time since 1939.

French Economic Expansion. De Gaulle, far from regarding his task as over, considered that he had merely completed the liquidation of the problems bequeathed him by the Fourth Republic, and that he could now turn to the more important task of making France capable of playing a major role in world affairs. He was fortunate in inheriting from the much-maligned Fourth Republic a renovated economic system. The Monnet Plan of 1947–53 had concentrated on the development of six basic sectors—coal, steel, electricity, cement, transport, and agricultural machinery. The later Plans turned to wider economic development, becoming more supple as the newly developed techniques of national income accounting made possible accurate projections of the behavior of different areas of the economy, the avoidance of bottlenecks in production, and the identification of growth areas that would stimulate the rest of the economy. The elite group of French bureaucrats, many of them graduated from the new National School of Administration or from the more traditional Parisian colleges, according to Andrew Shonfield, maintained "voluntary collusion" with senior managers in business, while "the politicians and representatives of organized labor were both largely passed by." French business was shaken out of its emotionally based opposition to change and its traditional belief in the moral values of smallness and stability. The new approach was especially evident in industries requiring large capital investment and wide markets, such as steel or petroleum, and in enterprises using new productive methods, such as rubber, metal processing, and synthetics. Unfortunately, older industries like textiles refused to adapt to the doctrine of expansion, and France found its economy increasingly split into static and dynamic sections; Alsace-Lorraine and the area between Paris and the Belgian border made rapid economic progress, while the rest of the country fell far behind. Monnet's bright young men at the Commissariat du Plan had linked with the federalists among French politicians in bringing France into the European Coal and Steel Community and the Common Market, as a method of forcing French industry to modernize by opening it to the harsh pressure of foreign competition; and much of French industry had profited from the challenge. The sudden upswing in the size of the French population, which began in 1946 after a century of decline, was undoubtedly favored by the social security measures of the first de Gaulle administration and of the Fourth Republic, while it in itself stimulated economic growth by creating a vast need for schools and universities, hospitals, and homes, and eventually for new jobs. Whereas the French population had increased by only 2 million between 1900 and 1946, even with large foreign immigration, it jumped 3.5 million between 1946 and 1958. The young people brought a new attitude of mind, especially to mobility in employment, social class, and place to live, thus aiding France's adaptation to the requirements of a competitive economy.

Under the Fifth Republic, expansion was considerably accelerated. Devaluation of the currency, accompanied by deflationary measures at home, enabled French industry to compete successfully in international trade. Exports rose 88 per cent in 1958–65, while the foreign debt was almost wiped out and French monetary reserves rose to $5.5 billion. The planners turned to those sections of the economy neglected by the Fourth Republic, notably by attempting to modernize France's anachronistic distribution system and by taking steps to stimulate the economic growth of France's static geographical areas. The tax structure was revamped, the budget was balanced, and improvements were made in the banking system to encourage saving and productive investments. Agriculture benefited from the two Agricultural Orientation Laws of 1960 and 1962, which increased government spending in aid to the farmer to over $1 billion annually. French pressure compelled its Common Market partners to formulate a common agricultural policy that would open their markets for the sale of the vast French surpluses of beef and wheat. With the departure of 800,000 redundant farm workers for the factory, the merger of small farms, the improvement of agricultural education, and the reform of market organization, productivity increased greatly. With industrial production increasing at 6 per cent annually, workers saw their standards of living rising rapidly; by 1964, 45 per cent of French homes had an automobile, 40 per cent a television set, and 52 per cent a refrigerator. Three hundred and fifty thousand houses were built annually compared with 190,000 annually during the last seven years of the Fourth Republic. France was more prosperous than at any time in its history, and that well-being filtered down to the working classes to a far greater extent than ever before.

The Italian Economic Miracle. Italy too had enjoyed the benefits of a belated economic miracle. The Italian gross national product increased by an average of 6.3 per cent in 1952–62, which was one of the highest rates of growth in Europe. The opening of the Common Market provided an almost revolutionary stimulus, however, for in the first seven years Italian industrial production rose by an amazing 107 per cent. Slender skyscrapers in Milan, the steel complex of Taranto in the south, the network of freeways, and the intolerable traffic jams of Rome were all symbols of the vast changes that Italy was undergoing. The causes of the great economic boom were numerous. Postwar Italy did not waste its substance on military aggression and colonial expansion. It possessed a vast reservoir of surplus labor, particularly in the south. Until the mid-1960's, wages did not rise faster than productivity, thus making it possible for Italian goods to compete successfully in foreign trade and for Italy to avoid a balance-of-payments problem that would have restricted investment at home. Among the legacies of the Fascist and pre-Fascist eras were the existence of a number of large, semimonopolistic companies, like Fiat, Montecatini, and Olivetti, accustomed to long-term investment and to the benefits of an expanding economy; state ownership of a large sector of the economy, through the Institute for Industrial Reconstruction, whose 120 companies included the major Italian steel producers, state airline Alitalia, most of the freeways, and the nationalized broadcasting company; and a highly developed system of public works in the south, in the form of roads, public buildings, and harbors. The Institute for Industrial Reconstruction became a major factor in furthering the industrialization of southern Italy as envisaged in the Vanoni Plan adopted by the Chamber of Deputies in 1955, especially after 1957 when it was compelled to make two-fifths of its investments in the south. Perhaps the most notable example of state intervention in the economy was the formation in 1953 of the Ente Nazionale Idrocarburi (ENI), the nationalized company controlling oil and natural gas, which was run as a private fief by the crusading Enrico Mattei. The ENI company developed newly discovered sources of natural gas in north Italy so fast that production increased eightfold, and for the first time Italian companies enjoyed unlimited supplies of cheap domestic fuel. Mattei sought new sources of oil in the Middle East, Morocco, and Sinai and contracted to buy large quantities of Russian oil, fighting vigorously against what he regarded as a combine of the world's large petroleum companies organized to keep prices up and outsiders out.

The Italian economic miracle did, however, have many shortcomings. Expansion in the south, in spite of government efforts, was slower than in the north, and the division between the two parts of the country grew rather than lessened. Socially, the boom increased the differences between classes, for the well-to-do enjoyed luxury homes, automobiles, and travel, while real-estate speculation prevented the erection of much-needed inexpensive housing, especially for the thousands of southern workers moving into the northern cities. Inflation ate into the value of wages; unemployment remained serious (623,000 in 1962). The over-centralized and poorly financed administrative system of the country proved totally ineffective in meeting the problems of mass migration, exorbitant rise in real-estate costs, inadequate schools, and rise in crime. Above all, agriculture remained a depressed area of the economy. Although production had increased 40 per cent in 1950–62, real income had only gone up 1.5 per cent; many agrarian reform projects already begun were rendered valueless by depopulation of large rural areas in the south and the Apennines, as the peasants sought urban life as the only alternative to rural misery. Not until 1964 was a determined effort begun to destroy the system of *mezzadria*, or sharecropping. Agricultural reform remained a major task of the governments of the opening to the left.

Economic Problems of Benelux. The Benelux countries did not enjoy the same boom conditions as Italy and France after 1953. Whereas Belgium had been one of the most prosperous countries in the world in the immediate postwar years, its growth rate during the 1950's was just over 3 per cent annually. Its coal industry found itself unable to meet the competition of the more efficient mines of Germany and France within the Coal and Steel Community, and the closing of uneconomic pits caused violent outbreaks of labor discontent. Exploitation of the copper, rubber, and uranium of the Belgian Congo helped prevent a major decline during the 1950's, and the loss of the Congo in 1960 was offset by the advantages Belgium received from membership in the Common Market. Indeed, Brussels, chosen as the seat of the EEC Commission, began to vie for the position of capital of a future United States of Europe. The Dutch maintained a growth rate of about 5 per cent throughout the 1950's, with slowly rising living standards and a minimum of unemployment. Grave problems tested the strength of the economy, however, especially the rapid increase in population, the loss of Indonesia and the reabsorption of the returning Dutch colonists, and the devastating storms of 1953 in which many of the Dutch polders were destroyed and vast areas were flooded by the North Sea. To meet these difficulties, the government favored foreign investment; natural-gas and oil deposits were exploited; and a successful effort was made to increase manufacture of finished and semifinished products. Membership in Benelux, ECSC, and the Common Market stimulated both industry and agriculture. Luxembourg's economy advanced slowly during the 1950's, although its living standards remained good, foreign labor had to be imported, and 40 per cent of national production was reserved for export. The opening of ECSC was especially useful to the Grand Duchy's steel industry, while the construction of the Moselle Canal promised it a competitive advantage in the German and overseas markets.

CONSERVATIVE BRITAIN AND
LABOUR'S RETURN

Victory in the elections of October 25, 1951 brought the Conservative party to power in Britain for thirteen years under four prime ministers—Winston Churchill, 1951–55; Anthony Eden, 1955–57; Harold Macmillan, 1957–63; and Lord Home (who, on giving up his peerage, became Sir Alec Douglas-Home), 1963–64.

Churchill's Last Government, 1951–55. In Churchill's cabinet, the most important posts were given to the party stalwarts who had served with him during the war years. Eden was foreign secretary; R. A. Butler, chancellor of the exchequer; and Harold Macmillan, minister of housing. The Conservatives had promised, in a manner unprecedented in British politics, to undo the Labour government's nationalization of steel and road transport and to restore the initiative to business that state intervention had supposedly been crushing. No attempt was made to interfere in the highly popular social services, except to impose slight additional charges for medical supplies. The rationing system was finally abolished in 1954, but the reduction in food subsidies helped raise the cost of the foodstuffs that were available in virtually unlimited quantities for the first time since 1939. The most popular achievement of the government, due largely to Macmillan, was the annual construction of over 300,000 houses; and Conservative support slowly increased as a fall in world prices for raw materials aided the export drive and helped end the era of austerity. By 1955 the Conservatives felt sure enough of their chances to risk a new general election. Churchill, who had suffered a stroke in 1953, had handed over power to Eden in April 1955; and the new prime minister decided to make an appeal especially to the lower middle classes and the skilled workers by asking for a mandate to create "a property-owning democracy." The Labour party entered the campaign gravely hindered by internal divisions between the moderate majority, led by Clement Attlee and Hugh Gaitskell and the radical wing that followed Aneurin Bevan and Harold Wilson. The campaign roused little public enthusiasm, and turnout on election day was low; but a swing of 1.6 per cent to the conservatives gave them 324 seats to Labour's 277.

The Errors of Eden, 1955–57. Eden's two years as prime minister were probably the least illustrious of his career, and when he retired from ill-health in January 1957 it seemed likely that his mistakes would drag the Conservative party out of office with him. Major errors crept into Conservative economic policy from 1955 on. Reduction of the income tax just before the election brought on an inflation of 4–5 per cent; attempts to restore the full convertibility of sterling caused a run on the pound. A series of repressive measures resulted in the stagnation of the economy throughout 1956. The basic problem facing Britain was the failure of both management and labor to meet the need of greater productivity. British business was slow to seek and exploit foreign markets. Labor pressed for a more rapid increase in wages than was justified by productivity, and workers went on strike to win their demands, over 8 million working days being lost in 1957 alone. The education system failed to provide the skilled workers and especially the technologists needed. As a result, the average productivity per man in Britain between 1955 and 1963 rose only 1.9 per cent compared with 4.1 per cent in Italy and 4.2 per cent in West Germany. The mistakes that began under Eden were carried on by his successors and were finally exposed to the public by an outraged Harold Wilson when as prime minister in 1964 he realized the full extent of Britain's difficulties.

Eden's worst errors lay in his foreign and colonial policy. Although he took great credit for suggesting the Western European Union as an organization within which German rearmament might be permitted after the French Assembly had defeated EDC, he never recognized that a British promise to maintain four divisions on the Rhine, which he made in support of the Western European Union, might have saved EDC if it had been made before the French Assembly debated the EDC Treaty. In March 1956, Eden exacerbated the situation in Cyprus, where the Greek majority of the population was using terrorism to bring about the island's union with Greece against the wishes of both the British and of the Turkish minority, by deporting to the Seychelles Islands the Greek Orthodox Patriarch Makarios. The invasion of Suez in November 1956 was the culmination of what world opinion regarded as a reversion to the worst features of colonialism. Eden, seeing in Nasser a new Hitler, attempted to overthrow him by force as he had demanded unsuccessfully that Hitler be overthrown two decades earlier, but his action showed extraordinary misunderstanding of Britain's new position in the world. The cost of the invasion, coupled with the interruption of Middle East oil supplies, brought a perilous fall in British gold reserves and a new threat to the pound, and was a major factor in forcing Eden to call off the attack. The United States, whose benevolent neutrality Eden had confidently expected, joined the Russians in the United Nations in opposing the British action; and Russia brought home to Britain the ignominy of the status of a second-class power by threatening it with rockets. Even the violence of public opposition to the invasion was unexpected by the government; and only five weeks after the invasion, Eden gave way to the suave and imperturbable Macmillan.

Unstable Prosperity under Macmillan, 1957–63. Macmillan decided to ride out the storm over Suez before going to the polls. British ships were permitted to pay Suez Canal tolls to the nationalized Egyptian company, although Macmillan did not intend to disavow the Suez adventure, of which he had originally been an enthusiastic supporter. Archbishop Makarios was permitted to return to Greece, but not to Cyprus, and he played a significant role in the negotiations that culminated in the grant of independence to the island in 1960. The grant of independence to Ghana (the former colony of the Gold Coast) and to the Federation of Malaya in 1957 indicated Conservative intention to continue with the process of decolonization. Macmillan's government even succeeded within a few months in overcoming the economic difficulties caused by the Suez crisis. Meanwhile, Macmillan had established himself as a world figure. He had toured the Commonwealth countries in January–February 1958, the first British prime minister to do so; in February 1959 he visited Khrushchev in Moscow and returned with a commercial treaty; and he had made headlines by pressing for a summit conference to ease world tension. To his prestige as the apostle of peace, Macmillan added the claim to be the bringer of prosperity; and the Conservatives fought the campaign for the election of October 8, 1959 with the slogan, "You're having it good—Have it better—Vote Conservative." The Labour party, led after Attlee's retirement in 1955 by Hugh Gaitskell, was still weakened by the revolt of a number of left-wing members who demanded unilateral nuclear disarmament, a loosening of the American alliance, and more nationalization. The swing to the Conservatives continued for the fourth successive election, giving them 366 seats to Labour's 258 seats.

After 1959, the economic situation deteriorated dangerously, as British export industries found themselves facing stiffer competition and saw their markets in the Common Market countries threatened by the establishment of the common external tariff. Tinkering with the interest rate merely slowed the rate of investment in industry and further hindered increase in productivity. The establishment of the European Free Trade Association in 1959 was a desperate and unsuccessful attempt to compensate for expected losses in exports to the Common Market countries. In July 1961, the government called for a "pause" in wages and salaries until productivity had increased, but was faced by a go-slow strike in the post office and by wage hikes for railroad workers, many civil servants, and engineers. Macmillan read the signs with grim realism and moved ruthlessly against those he regarded as incapable of remolding their economic attitudes. In July 1962, he dismissed one-third of his cabinet, and he brought in younger party members more attuned to the necessity of government intervention and planning for economic growth. The vitally important, and exceedingly tradition-bound, Treasury was completely reorganized to compel it to make long-term projections for the economy as a whole. A central planning authority and a body to formulate incomes policy were created. A tough administrator was called in from private business to reorganize the ailing nationalized railroads. Most important of all, Macmillan decided to force British industry to modernize by throwing open the protected British market to the competition of the Common Market countries; and, picking a moment just before the parliamentary vacation when his right-wing critics would be disorganized, he told the House of Commons on July 31, 1961 that his government had decided to apply for membership in the Common Market.

The negotiations with the Six dragged on for eighteen months, since the British government needed to protect the interests of the Commonwealth, of its partners in the European Free Trade Association, and of the highly subsidized British farmer. At home, the government had to face the criticism both of the left, which regarded entry into EEC as endangering the welfare benefits of labor, and of the right, which objected to Britain giving up its imperial position to submerge itself in a European union. Progress was slow but, in view of the complexity and importance of the negotiations, satisfactory. British defense policy, which was never discussed in the negotiations, was, however, to cause their failure. In December 1962 Macmillan accepted the American government's offer of Polaris missiles, to be mounted on British submarines as part of a NATO multilateral nuclear force. To French President de Gaulle, this decision completed Macmillan's subservience to American policy-makers and was proof that Britain would be little more than the mouth-piece of the United States if admitted as a member of the Common Market, an American "Trojan Horse." On January 14, 1963, he told his press conference that Britain was "insular, maritime, and linked by trade—both by markets and suppliers—to the most diverse and faraway countries," was set apart from the continental countries by distinctive habits and traditions, and was not yet ready for membership in the Common Market. Macmillan's great gamble had thus embittered relations with the Commonwealth, roused distrust among its EFTA partners, and alienated the right wing of his own party. When in 1963, his secretary of war was compelled to resign after a much-publicized scandal, Macmillan's health broke down, and in October he resigned the prime ministership. The obvious candidates as his successor were pushed aside in favor of Macmillan's own choice, the innocuous and uninspiring Douglas-Home.

Ministry of Douglas-Home and the Conservative Legacy. Throughout 1963–64 the Labour party gathered strength. After the untimely death of Gaitskell in January 1963 at the age of fifty-six, a leader of intellectual and oratorical brilliance was found in Harold Wilson, a former Oxford Economics lecturer, Bevanite, and hero of the party's rank and file. Wilson reunited the party's leadership, spelled out a forward-looking program emphasizing science, higher education, and economic growth, and indulged in scintillating attacks on Prime Minister Douglas-Home. By midsummer of 1964, a huge Labour victory seemed assured, but Douglas-Home wisely postponed elections until the last possible moment, on October 15. Profiting from the best summer weather of the century, from Labour's weariness after nine months of campaigning, and from Douglas-Home's newfound popularity, the Conservatives regained much of their strength. On election day, Labour received 44.1 per cent of the vote with 317 seats, while the Conservatives won 43.4 per cent and 304 seats. Labour's majority over all other parties was only four.

The results of thirteen years of Conservative rule were not encouraging. There had been external-payments crises in 1951, 1955, 1956, 1957, 1961, and 1964. Britain's share in world exports of manufactured goods, of vital importance to a country importing half of its food supply, had fallen steadily. Wages had risen three times faster than productivity. Long-established markets had been lost to the competition of Germany,

Italy, and Japan. Educational opportunities had been developed far too slowly, so that half the children prepared for college were unable to find places. The hold of the "establishment"—the exclusive upper social class—on most of the important positions in education, government, and business, combined with the universal unwillingness to reward initiative, had led thousands of Britain's most qualified scientists and intellectuals to seek employment in the Commonwealth or in the United States, creating the urgent problem of a "brain drain." Immigration from the Commonwealth of unskilled workers created a totally new problem of racial discrimination and conflict. Steady inflation had lowered living standards for older people living on pensions and fixed incomes, while most of the population was enjoying a large increase in consumption. Yet there was a brighter side to the picture. The Conservative economic reforms of 1961–64 had made possible modernized economic planning. Negotiations for entry into the Common Market had forced both the administration and industry to undertake a new appraisal of their attitudes and goals, and even after de Gaulle's veto Britain's trade with the Common Market continued to expand faster than with any other part of the world, while a reorganization of agriculture brought the British system more in line with the European. A program for the foundation of new universities was begun with the creation of the University of Sussex in 1961, and the Robbins Report in 1963 envisaged a revolutionary increase in universities and institutes of technology and business administration. Decolonization continued with relatively little friction, with the grant of independence in 1956 to the Sudan, in 1957 to Ghana and Malaya; in 1960 to Nigeria, British Somaliland, and Cyprus; in 1961 to Sierra Leone and Tanganyika; in 1962 to Western Samoa, Jamaica, Trinidad and Tobago, and Uganda; in 1963 to North Borneo, Sarawak, Kenya, and Zanzibar; and in 1964 to Northern Rhodesia, Nyasaland, and Malta. British influence remained strong in all these countries, and in many cases British economic investment and often even the number of British residents increased after independence.

For Harold Wilson's new government, however, the Tory legacy was a sharp economic crisis culminating in a severe run on the pound, which continental experts regarded as a preliminary to devaluation. Wilson chose instead to reinforce the pound with overseas credits of $3 billion, a 15 per cent surcharge on imports that broke Britain's treaty obligations to its EFTA partners, and higher taxes on goods and income, but canceled charges for prescriptions on the National Health Service and raised pensions. By December, the pound was out of danger, but inflation at home was still increasing dangerously. Chancellor of the Exchequer James Callaghan therefore brought in a deflationary budget in April 1965, raising income and consumer taxes, introducing a capital-gains tax of 30 per cent, and promising higher company taxes. A program of long-term regional development was drawn up. In May 1965 a government white paper outlining plans for the renationalization of the steel industry was approved in the Commons by a majority of four. By the time of the parliamentary summer recess in 1965, Wilson had established himself as a confident, able leader and as the master debater in Parliament. The Conservatives became increasingly discontented with the leadership of Sir Alec Douglas-Home, who was continually worsted in his jousts with Wilson; and, on Douglas-Home's resignation on July 22, the Conservative MP's, choosing their leader by democratic ballot for the first time, picked Edward Heath, an urbane bachelor of middle-class background, who had distinguished himself as Britain's negotiator for entry into the Common Market. Wilson refused to gratify Conservative demands that he call an election in 1965, while his own popularity was still uncertain, and decided to profit from the grudging admiration aroused by his ability to govern with so narrow a margin in Parliament. By March 1966, with a marked upswing to Labor indicated in the by-elections and the opinion polls, and disunion in Conservative leadership, Wilson called a new election for April. After a dull campaign in which both sides attempted in vain to interest the public in entry into the Common Market, nuclear defense, and industrial productivity, the Labour party was swept back into power with 363 seats to the Conservatives' 253. From a majority that had sunk to three before the election, Wilson could look forward to governing with an absolute majority of 97. The real test of his program lay ahead.

THE ENDURING AUTHORITARIANISM OF SPAIN AND PORTUGAL

In the Iberian Peninsula, the authoritarian regimes of Francisco Franco, leader of Spain since 1939, and of Antonio de Oliveira Salazar, ruler of Portugal since 1932, survived through all the vicissitudes of the Second World War, international isolation, political and social unrest, and finally even, in the 1960's, of economic progress. The longevity of regimes based upon an alliance of the army, the Church, the landowners, and a semi-Fascist political party was due in large measure to the political acumen of Franco and Salazar themselves.

Emergence from International Isolation. During the Second World War, both Spain and Portugal were ostensibly neutral. Franco refused to let Hitler inveigle him into war with Britain in 1940, other than at a price Hitler would not pay, although he did send the 14,000 man Blue Division to fight on the Russian front in 1941. Once the Anglo-American invasion of French North Africa in November 1942 brought the Allies to his doorstep, he carefully shifted the bias of his neutrality, permitting Frenchmen to escape across Spain to join the Free French in North Africa but refusing to allow German troops to cross in order to attack Gibraltar; and Franco even made overtures to Britain and the United States, suggesting special understandings between the three countries in view of the threat of world communism. Although Salazar had been openly sympathetic to Franco during the Spanish Civil War, and had concluded the Iberian Nonaggression Pact with Spain in 1943, he was more favorable to Britain and the United States during the war. In spite of Portugal's official neutrality, Salazar permitted the Allies to use the Azores as a naval base and to conduct espionage from Lisbon. Both the Spanish and Portuguese governments made superficial gestures of relaxing the authoritarian nature of their regimes at war's end. Franco introduced a charter of the citizen's rights, declared that a monarchical regime would eventually be needed to perpetuate his movement, and favored the Catholic Action group at the expense of the Fascist Falange party in a cabinet remodeling. Salazar renamed his propaganda agency the "National Secretariat of General Information and Culture," lessened the censorship, and permitted national elections in November 1945, which were boycotted by the opposition parties. Neither country was accepted for membership in the United Nations at its founding, however; and between 1945 and 1950 the United Nations endorsed ostracism of Spain in the hope of ousting Franco. The French government closed the Pyrenees border; several governments withdrew their ambassadors; and Spain was refused foreign loans and to a large extent isolated from international trade. On the urging of Britain and France, Spain was not permitted to receive Marshall Aid. Salazar fared much better with the Western powers, since his regime had not been installed with the direct aid of Hitler's and Mussolini's armies. The Azores bases were handed back to Portugal in 1946; Marshall Aid brought British and American technical assistance and large-scale public works for irrigation and hydroelectric power; and Portugal was admitted to NATO with the guarantee that its bases would not be used by foreign powers in time of peace.

The isolation of Spain was gradually ended after 1950. Salazar had declared, on joining NATO, that Spain was a necessary part of the Western defense system, and had renewed the Iberian Pact. A strong Spanish lobby in the American Congress had joined Pentagon officials in pressing the Truman administration to profit from Spain's anticommunism at the time of the Korean War, and in September 1950 Truman authorized private American banks to make loans to Spain. In November, the UN General Assembly withdrew its recommendation that ambassadors be recalled from Madrid. Finally, since the West European powers were still unwilling to enter a military agreement with Spain, the American government decided to act unilaterally, by concluding a series of economic and defense agreements that would give the United States the use of military bases in Spain in return for large-scale economic aid. Franco's terms were harsh, and the negotiations dragged on for two years; but on September 26, 1953, three agreements, known as the Pact of Madrid, were signed. The United States was permitted to build and maintain air bases for the use of medium-range bombers at Zaragoza, Torrejón, and Seville, and a naval-and-air base at Rota, near Cadiz, as well as a 485 mile oil pipeline linking the bases, and seven radar sites. By 1959, the bases had cost over $400 million, and were manned by 6,000 men. The 400,000 man Spanish Army was to be modernized with American equipment; and by 1960, Spain had received $374,236 in military aid. Spanish economic development was to be furthered with American assistance that by 1960 totaled almost $1 billion.

Slow Economic Progress. In spite of American aid, the economic progress of Spain and Portugal before 1960 was very slow. Both Franco and Salazar based their support upon the great landowners and did little to carry out urgently needed land redistribution. In Spain, 9,000 families owned more than one-seventh of the total farmland. Mechanized agricultural equipment and fertilizer were lacking, and vast irrigation works were desperately needed. The rapid population growth helped nullify the small gains in productivity that were made. Although the Spanish government failed to make investments in roads and railways, it embarked upon an industrialization program in the 1950's that brought increases in production of machinery, chemicals, metals, and electric power, stimulated particularly by the activity of the huge state-owned National Institute of Industry. Inflation resulted from the excessive haste of industrialization, and the conditions of life of the working classes remained very poor. Although strikes were illegal and state controls over both employers and workers was exercised through the syndicates that both must join, dissatisfaction was expressed by sabotage, slowdowns, street demonstrations, and frequent strikes. The situation in Portugal was even worse, after a brief flurry of overseas purchasing had exhausted the currency reserves built up during the war. Salazar's swollen bureaucracy discouraged economic initiative by private businessmen, although attempts were made to speed up industrialization and the modernization of agriculture through six-year plans, the first of which was introduced in 1953. Yet in 1960, the Portuguese standard of living was still the lowest in Western Europe. Average food consumption was 2,460 calories a day compared, for example, with 3,060 in Norway and 2,950 in Greece; there were only 7,864 tractors in the whole country; and only 34,000 houses a year were completed.

Political Opposition in Spain. Throughout the 1950's economic dissatisfaction stimulated the demand for a lightening of the dictatorships. The greatest opposition to Franco lay in the Basque provinces of the northeast and in Catalonia, where the desire for cultural autonomy increased the industrial workers' annoyance at their poor living conditions. The small but efficient Communist party, well financed by Moscow and supported by broadcasts of the Radio España Independiente, made great efforts to throw off the reputation for cruelty and arrogance it earned during the Civil War, but failed to gain any significant support when it called for general strikes in 1958 and 1959. The Socialists were weakened by the flight of most of their leaders to exile in the south of France, where, from their center in Toulouse, they had difficulty in maintaining the loyalty of the Socialists remaining in Spain. Franco's secret police was effective in hunting down the underground Socialist groups; in November 1958, eighty Socialist leaders were arrested in a nationwide sweep. With the political parties they had formerly followed thus shackled, the Catalan and Basque workers and students showed their opposition by ignoring elections, although voting was compulsory, by strikes, and by boycotting the Barcelona transport system in 1957. The opposition groups in the other parts of the country were varied. A small group of Christian Democrats attempted to organize a party like those of Adenauer and De Gasperi. The monarchists found themselves joined by an increasing number of Franco's opponents, who saw in a restoration of the pretender Don Juan de Bourbon, or of his son Don Juan Carlos, a peaceful way of destroying the power of the Falange and of edging Franco out of office. Don Juan settled in the Portuguese resort of Estoril with a crowd of aristocratic hangers-on; but Franco met the monarchist threat by espousing the cause of monarchy himself, permitting Don Juan Carlos to be educated in Spain, but refusing to declare which pretender he considered to be his successor. At the same time, he attempted to divert discontent by reviving Spanish demands for the restoration of Gibraltar, and he declared August 4, the anniversary of the loss of the Rock, to be a day of national mourning. Finally, he continued to rely upon close ties with the Catholic Church as a guarantee of the regime's stability. He had been permitted in 1941 to have the final say in appointment of bishops; in 1953, a new Concordat was at last signed with the Vatican, by which the Church was given exemption from taxation, the clergy were to be tried only in ecclesiastical courts, and religious education in all schools was placed under its control; and several members of the influential Catholic lay organization, Opus Dei, were brought into the cabinet. The vested interests of army, Church, great landowners, big business, and Falange in continuance of the regime thus provided Franco with the power to crush the forces of opposition.

Maintenance of Salazar's Supremacy. Like Franco, Salazar was determined to prevent the organization of any political opposition. In 1945, he briefly permitted the Republican, Socialist, and Communist parties to unite in the Movement of Democratic Unity, but soon suppressed it for attacking the regime. The next year, army officers who attempted a coup d'état received little popular support, and were arrested and given jail terms. When eighty-year-old General Norton de Martos challenged incumbent President Carmona in the 1949 elections and demanded a restoration of political liberties, he was declared to be a Communist tool, and his candidature was withdrawn. Carmona died two years later, and in the new presidential elections the governmental candidate was elected after his opponent was disqualified as a Communist instrument for openly regretting that Portugal was a dictatorship. The presidential elections of 1958 provided a great rebuff to Salazar. Two opposition candidates withdrew before the polling, but General Humberto Delgado, the director of civil aviation, campaigned vigorously for the freeing of political prisoners, the restoration of democratic government, and the dismissal of Salazar from the premiership. Many of Delgado's supporters were arrested; rioting occurred during the elections; and 23 per cent of the electorate wrote in Delgado's name on the ballot. His supporters claimed that he actually won the election, but that the government falsified the results. Delgado himself, pursued by the police, took refuge in the Brazilian Embassy, from where he was given a safe-conduct pass to Brazil. Shortly afterward, the constitution was changed to transfer election of the president to parliament. Twenty-five of Delgado's supporters, led by Captain Henrique Galvão, determined to dramatize their opposition to Salazar's regime by hijacking the Portuguese luxury liner "Santa Maria" in the Caribbean in January 1961. The romantic adventure, in which these few lightly armed men took possession of the pride of the Portuguese Merchant Marine, with 600 passengers and 350 crew members on board, roused universal interest in conditions in Portugal; and when the ship put in to Recife in Brazil, Delgado and Galvão were able to make their case before reporters from all over the world. Conditions in Portugal changed little, however. A new attempted uprising in southern Portugal, in January 1962, led by some army officers and Catholic leaders, was easily put down; the police opened fire on a workers' demonstration in May; and students demonstrating in Lisbon, Coimbra, and Oporto were arrested.

Economic Advances in the 1960's. The 1960's brought hope of economic and political improvements in both Spain and Portugal. The foundation for Spain's great economic boom was a harsh stabilization and austerity plan, introduced in July by Minister of Commerce Alberto Ullastres. Based upon the recommendations of experts from OEEC and the International Monetary Fund, and of private Spanish banking and industrial leaders, the plan called for devaluation of the peseta, reduction of government expenditure, encouragement of foreign investment, linking of wage raises to productivity, and abolition of price controls. A loan of $420 million, mostly from the United States and the International Monetary Fund, was to be used for furthering industrial expansion. While the deflation produced unemployment of one million during the first winter, the plan soon brought impressive results. Currency reserves rose to over $1 billion; foreign investment rose sharply; large public works, such as the Aldeadavila Dam and hydroelectric plant and the Badajoz irrigation projects, have been carried out; and a very successful effort has been made to attract tourists. Throughout the 1960's, more tourists visited Spain than any other country in the world—36 million in 1961–65. The presence of so many American and West European tourists undoubtedly forced a lightening of police controls and the more obvious aspects of totalitarianism. In 1965, strikes were finally legalized, and an end of censorship was promised. Supervision of cultural activity was eased; and freedom of speech was increased. With housing construction booming, television sets in two-fifths of Spanish homes, and per capita income above $500 a year, Franco's regime had at last provided some of the social benefits that might smooth away the remaining tensions of the Civil War and the dictatorship that followed.

Portugal too experienced the first flush of material prosperity in the 1960's. The jet plane brought the isolated coasts of Portugal within reach of the tourist. From a mere 70,000 in 1950, the number of foreign tourists reached 353,000 in 1960. Public-works projects included the great dam on the Rabagão River near Lisbon, completed in 1966 at a cost of $49 million, and the first bridge across the Tagus at Lisbon, the longest suspension bridge in Europe, intended to open up southern Portugal to industrial development. With the gross national product growing at over 5 per cent annually, a slow but steady rise in exports, particularly of textiles, wines, and canned foods, and with the beginning of a diversification of the industrial base, Portugal appeared to have the chance of throwing off the torpor of the past four centuries. Colonial revolt, however, threatened this incipient prosperity. While the great European powers were relinquishing hold on their colonies, the Portuguese government was determined not to give independence to any part of its colonial territories, which included Angola and Mozambique in southern Africa, Portuguese Guinea on the West African coast, part of Timor in the East Indies, Goa on the west coast of India, and Macao off the coast of China. Indian Premier Nehru finally wearied of Salazar's refusal to negotiate the return of Goa and used Indian troops to seize the enclave on December 17, 1961. Rebellion broke out in Angola in March 1961 and was repressed after atrocities by both sides. Supported especially by Algeria and the Congo Republic (Léopoldville), the Angolan National Liberation Army then embarked upon a new guerrilla campaign that brought 43,000 Portuguese troops to Angola. The burden of the war was quickly felt in Portugal, where special taxes had to be applied; and, in spite of the government's slogans, such as "Portugal Is Not for Sale" and "Mozambique and Angola, Portuguese for Five Centuries," it was clear that a long, expensive war would be extremely damaging to the Portuguese economy.

Chapter Nine **THE BREAKING OF THE BLOCS, 1960-**

IN the 1960's international politics ceased to be dominated by the confrontation of the Western bloc of powers headed by the United States and the Communist bloc led by the Soviet Union; and some political analysts claimed that the Cold War, during which all the countries of the world except for a few neutralist powers were aligned in one or the other of two armed camps, came to an end. Several factors characterized this change. First, as a result of the acceleration of the process of decolonization, a large number of new states swelled the ranks of the nonaligned, giving them a majority in the General Assembly of the United Nations Organization and a more significant role in modifying the conflicts between the blocs. Second, the Soviet Union's hegemony over the Communist bloc was challenged by Communist China, which not only broke away from Moscow's tutelage but also began to put together a power bloc of its own composed of defectors from the Soviet camp and to extend its influence among the nonaligned powers of Asia and Africa. Third, the Soviet satellites in Europe, led by Rumania, successfully asserted their right to greater autonomy, profiting from the Soviet Union's need for support in its struggle with Communist China. Finally, the Western bloc itself began to disintegrate. Western Europe failed to solve the problem of its division between the Inner Six of the European Economic Community and the Outer Seven of the European Free Trade Association. Prosperous Western Europe became a dangerous competitor for the United States in the markets of the world, the American government finding itself for the first time faced by a serious balance-of-payments crisis which it sought West European help in ending. And French President de Gaulle, after first demanding a wider role for the European powers in NATO's decision-making, became the first defector from the alliance.

NONALIGNMENT IN ASIA AND AFRICA

The European powers quickly discovered that the grant of independence to their colonies in Asia and Africa was far from ending their involvement in the affairs of those continents. In the first place, most of the newly independent countries, following the lead set by India's Nehru, attempted to exercise their influence in a positive manner upon the affairs of the two blocs by grouping together under the banner of nonalignment. This influence was tenuous at best because of the tremendous problems, both internal and international, that these powers found themselves facing. Secondly, the weakness of these countries, due above all to the so-called underdevelopment of their economies, encouraged the Communist powers to foment revolution among the poverty-stricken masses of those countries, and thereby induced the involvement of the Western powers as a result of their desire to prevent a Communist takeover. Consequently, every newly independent country became more or less of a battlefield where, by means ranging from material blandishments to open war, the Communist and the Western powers confronted each other. Thirdly, the extreme poverty of most of Asia and Africa, contrasting with the wealth of the developed countries, both Western and Communist, indicated that the world was divided not only into ideological blocs, but between the haves and the have-nots. Both Eastern and Western Europe were compelled to face the problem of helping the underdeveloped countries to attain a better standard of living. After two decades of insufficient effort, very little progress had been made.

Organization of the Nonaligned Nations. As early as September 2, 1946, Jawaharlal Nehru laid down the principles of nonalignment that he was to follow for seventeen years (1947–64) as premier of India: "We hope to develop close and direct contacts with other nations and to co-operate with them in the furtherance of world peace and freedom. We propose, as far as possible, to keep away from the power politics of groups, aligned against one another, which have led in the past to world wars and which may again lead to disasters on an even vaster scale." The refusal to enter any military alliance made India a positive force in the world, he added in 1949. "If by any chance we align ourselves definitely with one power group we may perhaps from one point of view do some good but I have not the shadow of a doubt that from a larger point of view, not only of India but of world peace, it will do harm. Because then we lose that tremendous vantage ground that we have of using such influence as we possess—and that influence is going to grow from year to year—in the cause of world peace." While the Western powers often took exception to the constant tongue-lashings to which Nehru subjected them, they admitted that on several occasions India's position of nonalignment permitted it to play a constructive role. As chairman of the Neutral Nations Repatriation Commission, the Indian representatives supervised the exchange of prisoners after the Korean armistice in 1953. In 1954, following the Geneva Conference on Indochina, Indian representatives sat on the International Supervisory Commissions in Vietnam, Cambodia, and Laos; and Indian troops were sent as part of the United Nations' forces to the Gaza Strip in 1957 and to the newly freed Belgian Congo in 1960.

In Indonesian President Sukarno, Nehru found another outspoken advocate of nonalignment and anticolonialism. In 1954 India and Indonesia joined Ceylon, Pakistan, and Burma in the Colombo Conference in denouncing the continuance of colonialism; and in 1955 the five Colombo powers took a major step toward the creation of an Afro-Asian grouping by inviting to a conference at Bandung, Indonesia, twenty-five "countries in Asia and Africa which have independent Governments." The twenty-nine countries that attended the Bandung Conference (April 18–24, 1955) were a disparate group, who were far from constituting an "Afro-Asian bloc." At one extreme were the Communist states—China and North Vietnam; at the other extreme were the states linked in military alliances with the United States or Britain—Turkey, Iraq, Iran, Pakistan, Thailand, and the Philippines. It was, however, the views of the nonaligned nations, led notably by Nehru, Sukarno, and Nasser that predominated in the conference's final pronouncement, which condemned colonialism "in all its manifestations," called for prohibition on the production and testing of nuclear weapons, and declared that "all nations should have the right freely to choose their own political and economic systems and their own way of life in conformity with the purposes and principles of the Charter of the United Nations."

In 1961, Yugoslav President Tito made a vigorous attempt to take the leadership of the nonaligned nations. After a seventy-day trip through North and West Africa, in which he persuasively presented the Yugoslav brand of socialism as ideally suited to the emerging nations of

Africa and Asia, he acted as host in Belgrade to a Conference of Non-aligned Nations on September 1–6, 1961. Attended by the leading statesmen of twenty-five countries, the conference was the scene of an open duel for predominance between Nehru and Tito, but ended in agreement on the principles of nonalignment—condemnation of military blocs, the need for "active coexistence," and aid to colonial peoples seeking independence. No progress was made toward Ghana President Nkrumah's "non-nuclear third force," which would act as "a war-preventing force between the two blocs of the so-called East and West," since, as Nasser pointed out, if a third nonaligned bloc were formed, "we should then have to apply our policy of nonalignment to all three blocs." The Afro-Asian powers thus agreed only on the need for national independence, the end of colonialism, their right to receive economic aid from both Western and Communist countries, and on their role in moderating conflicts between the blocs.

Nonalignment in Africa. Partly in reaction against their Asian partners, the independent states of Africa south of the Sahara began to give nonalignment a distinctively "Africanized" interpretation. In the view of Kwame Nkrumah of Ghana, the peoples of Africa should seek to form an integrated African state that could remain independent of other continents. Under the slogan of Pan-Africanism, he determined to use the resources of Ghana, which in 1957 became the first colony south of the Sahara to be given its independence, to win for himself the leadership of a united Africa. In April 1958, the first Conference of Independent African States was held in Accra, and a start was made in discussion of common African problems and of the development of Africanism. The following December, a broader group of delegates from twenty-five independent and colonial states of Africa met in Ghana for the first All-African People's Conference, which established its own secretariat to organize cooperation among the African powers. The grant of independence to the French colonies in Africa did not bring Nkrumah the allies he had hoped for. Only in left-leaning Guinea's President Sékou Touré did he find an ally; in November 1958 a Ghana-Guinea Union was formed as a largely symbolic nucleus for a future Union of African States. The rest of the former French colonies in Africa, which had all negotiated their independence by 1960 chose to follow Félix Houphouet-Boigny, the dynamic premier of the Ivory Coast, and Léopold Senghor, president of Senegal and poet of the virtues of *"négritude,"* in relying

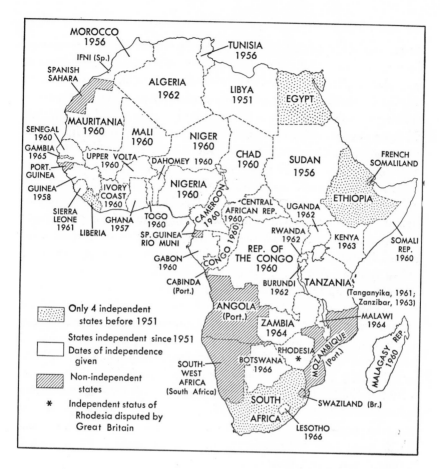

MOROCCO
1956
IFNI (Sp.)
SPANISH
SAHARA
ALGERIA
1962
TUNISIA
1956
LIBYA
1951
EGYPT
SENEGAL
1960
MAURITANIA
1960
MALI
1960
NIGER
1960
GAMBIA
1965
UPPER VOLTA
1960
DAHOMEY 1960
CHAD
1960
SUDAN
1956
FRENCH
SOMALILAND
PORT.-
GUINEA
GUINEA
1958
IVORY
COAST
1960
NIGERIA
1960
CAMEROON 1960
CENTRAL
AFRICAN REP.
1960
UGANDA
1962
ETHIOPIA
SIERRA
LEONE
1961
GHANA
1957
LIBERIA
TOGO
1960
SP. GUINEA
RIO MUNI
RWANDA
1962
KENYA
1963
SOMALI
REP.
1960
GABON
1960
CONGO
REP. OF
THE CONGO
1960
BURUNDI
1962
TANZANIA
CABINDA
(Port.)
(Tanganyika, 1961;
Zanzibar, 1963)
ANGOLA
(Port.)
ZAMBIA
1964
MALAWI
1964
RHODESIA
*
MOZAMBIQUE
(Port.)
MALAGASY REP.
1960
SOUTH-
WEST
AFRICA
(South Africa)
BOTSWANA
1966
SOUTH
AFRICA
SWAZILAND (Br.)
LESOTHO
1966

Only 4 independent
states before 1951

States independent since 1951
Dates of independence
given

Non-independent
states

* Independent status of
   Rhodesia disputed by
   Great Britain

THE NEW AFRICA, 1968

upon continued partnership with France. In 1960, they joined together in
the Brazzaville group, consisting of Ivory Coast, Senegal, Upper Volta,
Dahomey, Niger, Chad, the Central African Republic, the Congo Re-
public, Gabon, Mauritania, Togo, and Malagasy (Madagascar). Only
Mali decided to join the Ghana-Guinea Union. When this Union joined
Egypt and Morocco in denouncing the Brazzaville group as the support
of neocolonialism and formed a rival Casablanca group, it appeared that
Africa itself had split into two opposed blocs.

The grant of independence to the large and relatively wealthy state of
Nigeria in October 1960 and to the East African states of Tanganyika in
December 1961 and of Kenya in December 1963 brought new pressure

for reconciliation among the African states. Under the sponsorship of the Emperor Haile Selassie of Ethiopia, an Inter-African Conference of thirty African heads of state or government was held in Addis Ababa on May 22–23, 1963. While the majority of the leaders rejected Nkrumah's wish for establishment of a political authority for a united Africa, they did agree to the ultimate desirability of unity and to the immediate formation of an Organization of African Unity. Its charter set up the machinery of the organization—an Assembly of Heads of State or Government, a Council of Ministers, a General Secretariat, and a Commission of Mediation, Conciliation and Arbitration. The final resolutions of the conference expressed the determination of the participants to cooperate in the economic development of the continent, to work for general disarmament, to remain nonaligned, and to act as a group in the United Nations. Above all, the continuance of colonialism and the rule by a white minority in Southern Rhodesia, South Africa, and the Portuguese colonies of Angola and Mozambique was condemned; and all African states were called on to break diplomatic relations with South Africa and Portugal, to boycott their trade, and to help finance a special fund for aid to national liberation movements, for which a coordinating committee was to be established in Dar es Salaam in Tanganyika.

By the 1960's, therefore, the nonaligned powers of Asia and Africa had made some progress in organizing themselves into groupings that would be independent of both the Communist and Western blocs. But the influence these governments could exert on world events was small in comparison with the dangers they faced.

External Aggression and Internal Subversion. In the first place, the desire for nonalignment was no guarantee that a nation would be safe from external aggression or internal subversion. As restated by the Declaration of the eighty-one Communist parties that met in Moscow in December 1960, the Communist movement continued to regard its final goal as the extirpation of capitalism and the extension of communism to every country in the world. In the newly independent countries, Communists were warned that the Western powers were continuing to maintain their hold through "neo-colonialism," the control of the economy through "foreign monopolies," and the maintenance in power of puppet regimes dependent on Western arms and financing. Communist policy within these countries was to work within the existing governmental system to end its capitalist orientation, to seek control of its mass organizations, like labor unions and youth groups, and, where necessary, to organize guerrilla insurrection and ultimately open war. Both the Soviet Union and China advocated these tactics. To meet them, the Western powers sought to bolster both pro-Western and neutralist governments with economic and military aid, and, when insurrection threatened the existence of the government itself, with direct military intervention.

Southeast Asia was the most notable victim. After the Geneva Conference in 1954, both Laos and Cambodia attempted to follow a policy of nonalignment. The premier of Laos, Prince Souvanna Phouma, was opposed by the Communist forces of the Pathet Lao led by his half-brother, and by right-wing forces under General Phoumi Nosavan, who after 1958 was supported by the American government. In 1960–62 Laos was the scene of chaotic fighting between Phoumi Nosavan's forces and the combined armies of the Pathet Lao and neutralist Captain Kong Lee; but both the Soviet Union and the United States sought to avoid a major trial of strength in the jungles of Laos and agreed at a fourteen-nation Geneva Conference (May 1961–July 1962) to the representation of all three Laotian groups in a "government of national union" headed by Prince Souvanna Phouma and to the neutralizing of the country. A temporary respite was thus granted, but by 1964 open fighting was again taking place between the Pathet Lao and their former ally, Kong Lee, who had joined forces with General Phoumi. By 1966, the Pathet Lao held half the country, while Prince Souvanna Phouma maintained the fiction that his government of national union was still functioning. In Cambodia, Prince Sihanouk had become one of the most vociferous neutralists and had been careful to prevent the subversion of his personal rule by infiltrators from North Vietnam. He declared openly, however, that China would eventually dominate Southeast Asia and moved to better his own relationship with the Chinese regime. He reacted to the widening of the civil war in South Vietnam by permitting the North Vietnamese regulars and the Viet Cong guerrillas to ship supplies through Cambodia and to regroup on Cambodian territory. Furious at the refusal of Britain and the United States to accept his proposal for an international conference that would guarantee the neutrality of Cambodia and for not closing down radio stations in South Vietnam that were beaming into Cambodia criticism of his regime, he cut off the receipt of American economic aid and in December 1963 broke diplomatic relations with both Britain and the United States.

The governments of Thailand and South Vietnam made no pretense of nonalignment. Thailand, rich in rice, rubber, sugar, jute, and teak, had never known colonial rule, and felt little of its neighbors' animosity to the West. Ruled by a military autocracy since 1932, the country had boomed during the vigorous regimes of General Sarit Thanarat (1957–63) and his successor Thanom Kittikachorn. Development programs for the poverty-stricken northeastern area had begun to lessen the appeal of Communist propagandists; agriculture and industry were diversified, the growth rate reaching 7 per cent annually, and illiteracy was reduced to 29 per cent. Bangkok became a flourishing modern city, a tourist paradise on the new jet routes around the world. Thailand was a founding member of the Southeast Asia Treaty Organization. It sought American aid in May 1962, when Phoumi Nosavan was defeated in Laos, and was sent both Marines and Army forces. The United States government sent advisers for the police force, helped the Thais develop effective local administration in the remote provinces, constructed highways to the border areas, and built a series of small airfields. The Thai government permitted the United States to build a radar network along its borders with Laos and Cambodia, to fly from Thai airfields after its decision to intervene in the South Vietnamese civil war, and to construct a new port and airfield at Sattahip, on the Gulf of Siam.

In South Vietnam, the government was headed by Ngo Dinh Diem from June 1954 until his murder in 1963, a tough anti-Communist whose corrupt and brutal regime was dominated by members of his own family. Diem did, however, break the control of Saigon's crime and police by a gangster group called the Binh Xuyen; 900,000 refugees from the North were resettled; the army was reorganized and well equipped. Communist-led insurrection broke out in 1958, with a campaign of assassinations of provincial officials. Control by the Communist guerrillas, or Viet Cong, was extended over the rural areas of the country, half of which was in Viet Cong control by 1962. In December 1960, the National Front for the Liberation of South Vietnam was created as the political authority commanding the guerrillas. From 1961, when a mission under General Maxwell Taylor reported to President Kennedy on the need for increased American military participation on behalf of the South Vietnamese government, American involvement in the war grew rapidly. In 1962, American forces in South Vietnam numbered 15,000; in 1967, they were planned to reach 475,000. A decisive change occurred in 1964 when, under President Johnson, the United States Air Force retaliated, after attacks by North Vietnamese torpedo boats on the Seventh Fleet in the Gulf of Tonkin, by bombing the torpedo boats and their bases in North Vietnam itself. By 1966, American planes were bombing North Vietnam daily. A trial of wills had begun, which appeared likely to end in the decimation of the Vietnamese people.

That even the strongest of the nonaligned powers was not safe from foreign intervention was graphically illustrated in 1962, when Chinese forces invaded Ladakh and the North East Frontier Agency in northern India. Nehru had consistently denied the existence of a potential threat to India from China, had developed close cultural and economic relations, and in 1954 had even recognized Chinese sovereignty in Tibet, four years after China had occupied the country. In 1958–60, however, the Chinese government had laid claim to large areas of Indian territory, and had begun a piecemeal annexation. In 1959, after a revolt in Tibet had been savagely repressed, India gave refuge to the Tibetan religious leader, the Dalai Lama, and to thousands of refugees. After good relations had been temporarily restored between the two countries, China suddenly mounted a large-scale invasion of India in October 1962, crossed the passes of the Himalayas, and seemed about to threaten the Indian capital of Delhi itself. Nehru requested, and almost immediately received, military aid from Britain, the United States, and the Soviet Union; and after a month the Chinese withdrew from their positions in the North East Frontier Agency but held on to about 12,000 square miles of territory in Ladakh. A troubled cease-fire prevailed, while India sought to bolster up its defenses against the possibility of a new attack. Similar Chinese claims against Burma were settled in 1961, by Burmese recognition of China's sovereignty over the Wa area it had seized in 1955–56. Pakistan, deeply perturbed at the vast armaments being sent to India by the United States and Britain, sought a reconciliation with the Communist Chinese regime, and was rewarded by the return of 750 square miles of territory in Kashmir that the Chinese had occupied, as well as by the grant of a $60 million loan.

Conflicts among the Nonaligned Peoples. The nonaligned powers were also dangerously embroiled in conflicts among themselves, in most of which the European powers found themselves involved, on one side or the other, or occasionally as mediator. The most lasting quarrel was the dispute of India and Pakistan over possession of Kashmir. The cease-fire line drawn in 1949 under UN auspices had not altered Pakistan's claim to possession of the Indian-held section where, it was convinced, the Moslem majority would vote for union with Pakistan if a plebiscite were held. India, however, refused to permit a plebiscite, completed the constitutional fusion of Kashmir with India in 1957, and under Prime Minister Shastri began to place Indian civil servants in charge of the Kashmir administration. Border incidents became common, not only in Kashmir, but in the barren coastal area on the Arabian Sea known as the Rann of Kutch, where hostilities were stopped only by the intervention of British Prime Minister Wilson in June 1965. In August 1965, infiltration of Indian Kashmir by Pakistan-trained saboteurs brought open war, in which both India and Pakistan fought largely with planes, tanks, and guns supplied by the United States, Britain, and France. In this unique instance, the Soviet Union successfully mediated the dispute, in the Tashkent meeting of Soviet Premier Kosygin with General Ayub Khan and Prime Minister Shastri.

Indonesian President Sukarno's ambitions were aimed first at acquisition of West New Guinea, or West Irian, the one portion of the former Dutch East Indies still in Dutch hands. Although West New Guinea was inhabited by Papuans with no racial ties to Indonesia, Sukarno sent paratroops against the Dutch occupation forces. Largely under the pressure of President Kennedy, the Dutch avoided another struggle with Indonesian forces, accepting a face-saving compromise by which the United Nations would supervise the transfer of administration of West New Guinea from the Dutch to Indonesia, while after five years of Indonesian rule, the inhabitants would be asked by plebiscite to choose between independence or incorporation in Indonesia. The Indonesians thus acquired an unwilling population of 700,000, and a territory so rough that its exploitation had defied the strongest efforts of the Dutch. Shortly afterward, Sukarno began to lay claim to the Portuguese-held section of the island of Timor. His ambitions in Borneo were blocked by the creation in 1963 of the Federation of Malaysia, which joined to Malaya and Singapore the British colonies on Borneo of North Borneo, Brunei, and Sarawak. From Indonesian-held South Borneo, guerrillas moved into the jungles of Sarawak in 1963, and the following year small groups of infiltrators were shipped across the Malacca Strait into Malaya itself where most of them were immediately captured. The British, however, retaliated by sending 50,000 troops to the defense of Malaysia; and Sukarno built up a war fury among the underfed masses of Indonesia, pulled out of the United Nations Organization in January 1965 when Malaysia was seated in the Security Council, and promised his forces would "crush Malaysia." Although Malaysia was suffering from its own internal divisions—Singapore, with its predominantly Chinese population, broke away from the federation in 1965, and the sultan of Brunei withdrew his agreement to join at the last moment—Sukarno's forces made little headway; and in May 1966, after Indonesian Army leaders had taken power in Djakarta, they called off the dispute with Malaysia. The price of the confrontation had been paid by the masses of Indonesia who had seen their country's economy collapse so that an army of 350,000 men could be maintained as an instrument of Sukarno's imperial ambitions.

Even Africa was not immune to struggles between the new states, often culminating in war, although their pitifully poor peoples could little afford the luxury of mutual destruction. Algeria fought Morocco in 1963 in a dispute over possession of the desert area near Colomb Béchar. Somalia, formed in 1960 by a union of British Somaliland with the Italian-administered Somalia, maintained a vigorous campaign for annexation of the eastern area of Ethiopia inhabited by 500,000 Somalis and for annexation of northeastern Kenya, where another 100,000 Somalis lived. Togo, the former French Togoland, was in constant dispute with Ghana because it had hoped British Togoland would vote to unite with it rather than with Ghana and because Nkrumah hoped to annex Togo itself to Ghana. The continuance of colonial or white-minority rule in Africa was also a source of tension. All independent African states were united in demanding independence for, and many of them in subsidizing rebellion in, the colonies of Spanish Guinea and Spanish Sahara, and especially in Portuguese Angola and Mozambique. South Africa, where a policy of racial segregation, or *apartheid,* was institutionalized, and all political power and most of the wealth lay in the hands of the Europeans, mostly of British and Dutch origin, who constituted one-fifth of the population, was attacked by the African states in the United Nations where a trade boycott was endorsed and shipments of arms were banned. When Botswana (Bechuanaland) and Lesotho (Swaziland) received their independence from Britain in 1966, they found themselves dependent on the good-will of neighboring South

Africa, while under pressure from the newly independent states to the north to cooperate in efforts to overthrow South Africa's *apartheid* regime. Southern Rhodesia, while still legally a British colony, became self-governing in 1923, although power lay largely in the hands of the white settlers who constituted only one-sixteenth of the population; African opposition parties, especially the African National Congress, were suppressed; the Central African Federation, in which Southern Rhodesia had been linked since 1953 with Northern Rhodesia and Nyasaland, broke up in 1963, with the coming to power of African governments in Northern Rhodesia (independent as Zambia in October 1964) and in Nyasaland (independent as Malawi in July 1964). Faced with British demands that power be shared with the African majority before independence would be granted, the Southern Rhodesia government of Ian Smith declared itself independent of Britain in November 1965. The Labour government of Harold Wilson applied economic sanctions, cutting off Rhodesia's exports to Britain and Rhodesia's vitally needed imports of oil, while the African states quarreled among themselves between the advocates of military intervention and the supporters of economic pressure.

Political Instability. A third problem of the newly independent states was their own political instability. Since their boundaries were often the artificial creations of the colonial powers, many of them had separatist problems. Uganda, which gained its independence from Britain in October 1962, was faced by separatist demands from the king, or *Kabaka,* of Buganda, the country's richest province, and Prime Minister Milton Obote sent troops against the rebellious province in May 1966, compelling the *Kabaka* to flee for his life. In September 1963 the Berbers of the Kabyle Mountains of Algeria revolted and were suppressed by force. The most bloody example of unsuccessful secession occurred in the Belgian Congo, shortly after the grant of independence on June 30, 1960. Belgium had developed the raw materials of the Congo, especially the copper deposits of Katanga Province, had given good technical training to the African population, had built several fine modern cities, but had made almost no preparation for granting independence. There were few university graduates or trained administrators, and Africans had no experience in politics. The government of President Kasavubu and Premier Patrice Lumumba collapsed within two weeks, when faced with the flight of most European administrators and professional classes, revolt in the army against its white officers, and the attempted secession of Katanga led by Moise Tshombe and undoubtedly supported by the Belgian copper trust. The central government, faced with universal chaos and murder, called for help from the United Nations, which in an unprecedented decision, sent military, economic, and medical aid. The UN Army, composed of forces from nonaligned countries in Asia and Africa and from Scandinavia, forced the Belgian troops sent at the opening of the crisis to leave, and fought a long, tough battle against Katanga, for which it was bitterly criticized by Belgium and France. In 1963, Katanga's secession was ended; but a year later, by a curious reversal of roles, Tshombe, whose forces had murdered Lumumba in 1961, was called in as prime minister with the role of ending a new secession in Kivu Province. As the United Nations forces were withdrawn, Tshombe used white mercenaries against the rebels, who received Russian and Chinese military equipment supplied through the Casablanca group. In 1966, when comparative order had been restored, Kasavubu dismissed Tshombe, only to be ousted in his turn by the army commander, General Mobutu. Independence had thus brought to the Congo chaos, violence, economic decline, and eventually military rule.

In Nigeria, the Eastern province attempted to secede in June 1967 as a new state called Biafra; and in the resulting civil war, the Soviet Union intervened by supplying arms to the federal government.

In Asia, secessionist movements also threatened stability. In Indonesia, the Sukarno government on Java was occupied in bitter fighting from 1958 to 1961 with a rival government set up in Sumatra and strongly entrenched in the Celebes. West Pakistan faced a campaign by Pathan tribesmen encouraged by neighboring Afghanistan to form a separate state of Pakhtunistan or Pathanistan, a move that was supported by the Soviet Union in 1955. Finally, racial tensions existed even where no demands for independence were made. The presence of 16 million Chinese outside China was a source of racial unrest in Malaya, Thailand, Burma, and Indonesia. Fighting broke out in 1958 and 1961 on Ceylon between the Sinhalese majority and the South Indian (Tamil) minority. The Indian government was compelled to create a new province of Nagaland in 1963 to satisfy the aspirations of Naga tribesmen, many of whom wished to join Burma; and the attempt to satisfy Sikh aspirations by creating a separate state of West Punjab caused more communal rioting in 1966. And throughout Africa, tribal rivalries remained a potent source of friction.

In so turbulent a situation, democracy had little chance of survival; and one-man or one-party rule became almost the accepted practice for the newly independent states, most of whom lacked sufficient trained personnel to afford the luxury of a legal opposition. Most of the African states were the personal domains of one strong politician or hereditary ruler. The pattern had been set by President Tubman in Liberia and Emperor Haile Selassie in Ethiopia, but Nkrumah in Ghana added a new refinement by making Ghana a one-party state in a constitutional referendum in 1964. The French-speaking states ran the gamut from radical Sékou Touré in Guinea through the poet-philosopher Léopold Senghor in Senegal and the mildly conservative Félix Houphouet-Boigny in the Ivory Coast. The English-speaking states had the leonine Jomo Kenyatta in Kenya, formerly accused of heading the savage Mau Mau uprising against British rule, the subtle African Socialist Julius Nyerere in Tanganyika (and later President of Tanzania, the union of Tanganyika and Zanzibar formed in April 1964) and ambitious Milton Obote of Uganda. In Asia, the picture was similar. Synghman Rhee in South Korea, Ngo Dinh Diem in South Vietnam, Sukarno in Indonesia, Bandaranaike in Ceylon, U Nu in Burma, Nehru in India—all in different ways maintained a form of one-man rule. With very few exceptions, these rulers showed themselves oppressive and inefficient, a combination that proved intolerable to the one force capable of providing alternative leadership—the officers of the army. In 1958 General Ayub Khan moved to end the political chaos that had plagued Pakistan since the death of Jinnah the same year that General Ne Win overthrew the government of U Nu in Burma; two years later, after student riots, the South Korean Army ousted Synghman Rhee, and in 1963 General Park was elected president; Ngo Dinh Diem was murdered in 1963, and the South Vietnamese government passed unsteadily from one military leader to another for the following three years; in 1966, the Indonesian Army, again after student riots, took control of the government, imprisoned or executed most leaders of the huge Communist party, and reduced Sukarno to the position of a figurehead. Between November 1965 and February 1966 alone, the army seized power in six African states—the Congo, Dahomey, the Central African Republic, Upper Volta, Nigeria, and even in Ghana.

The Problem of Underdevelopment. Yet, in spite of all these national, racial, tribal, and political frictions, the principal source of the weakness of the states and the misery of the peoples of Asia and Africa was economic backwardness, or, in a more hopeful term, underdevelopment. Whereas some members of the Western bloc and all the Asian members of the Communist bloc were underdeveloped countries, the nonaligned countries were almost without exception underdeveloped. Their economic activity was primarily concerned with the production of agricultural goods and raw materials, rather than with industrial goods or with services. Productivity per capita was extremely low, even in agriculture averaging about one-tenth of that in Western Europe. Income per capita was very small, usually less than $100 a year; in 1954, per capita income in the United States was $1,850, while in Kenya it was $50, and in Indonesia $30. Consequently, very little capital was accumulated at home for investment, while political instability discouraged foreign capital from seeking investments in the newly independent countries. American investment in Asia increased by only $60 million annually in 1949–54. Food supply was low, rarely reaching 2,000 calories daily and consisting mainly of cereals; few people were healthy or capable of continued heavy work; illiteracy made the training of skilled workers difficult; and general poverty prevented the establishment of good schools and universities. Even improved medical care, especially in the prevention of endemic diseases like malaria or cholera, thrust a new burden on the economy by creating a vast increase in population. In fact, after the Second World War, overpopulation became one of the most frightening of all dangers faced by the underdeveloped countries. India's population grew 3 per cent a year, from 320 million at independence to 480 million in 1966 and was expected to reach one billion by the end of the century. Its gross national product increased at a lower rate, however, and in times of drought, as in 1960–63 and 1965, food production either remained static or fell. In 1966, widespread famine was avoided only by vast imports of American surplus grain and by strict rationing. In a very few countries, such as Thailand, it was still possible to bring more land under cultivation; but for most of the countries of Asia agricultural production could be raised only by consolidation of landholdings, by use of chemical fertilizer, by the mechanization of farming, and by improvement in transportation. But most underdeveloped countries saw agricultural improvements and increase in sale of raw materials as merely a palliative, and industrialization as their only hope for higher living standards in the future. The only possible source of capital was from the advanced countries, either in the Western or the Communist bloc; and thus the so-called revolution of rising expectations in the nonaligned countries forced both groups to reassess their policies toward foreign aid in a period of peaceful coexistence.

Aid Programs. For the United States, the needs of Europe had received first priority in foreign-aid programs until 1955, when 60 per cent of the aid funds was allocated to Asian countries, particularly, in President Eisenhower's words, "to the so-called 'arc of freedom' that stretches from Japan to Pakistan." Although under President Truman's Point Four Program of 1949, $488 million had been given in technical assistance to thirty-eight underdeveloped countries in 1950–56, much larger sums were made available during the late 1950's. Most of the funds were used for subsidizing the military forces of Formosa, South Korea, and South Vietnam, and little went to subsidize the economic development of India or of any of the African countries. Through the Development Loan Fund set up in 1957, annual sums of over $300 million were made available, to be repaid in local currencies; and in 1960 the United States persuaded Canada, Japan, and most of the countries of Western Europe to provide financing for an International Development Association that would offer low-interest loans to underdeveloped countries. President Kennedy attempted to rationalize the aid programs by bringing both the Point Four Program and the Development Loan Fund together in the Agency for International Development in 1961; and the same year, he promised that the United States would provide the major share of a $20 billion fund to be spent over the coming decades in Latin America under an Alliance for Progress. In spite of the vast sums involved, American aid was so widely spread among the underdeveloped countries that little improvement could be seen as the direct effect of American programs, except to the extent that surplus food had prevented millions from starving. Far too little had been achieved in laying the foundations for long-term economic development.

Of the West European countries, both Britain and France made large contributions to the economic progress of their former colonies. Most of Britain's colonies received a large loan with their grant of independence; and under the Colonial Development and Welfare Acts and through the Colonial Development Corporation, Britain provided over $750 million to the colonies and Commonwealth countries. In 1950, the foreign ministers of the British Commonwealth met at Colombo, Ceylon, where they approved the Colombo Plan for mutual assistance and cooperation. The plan was later joined by several non-Commonwealth countries, including the United States and Japan; and technical assistance and financial aid was channeled through the plan's administrators to most of the countries of south and southeast Asia. France had begun an impressive development program for the French empire in 1946, with the establishment of two investment funds, which by 1957 had spent over $1.5 billion. Under the Fifth Republic, an even greater effort was made to help the Brazzaville group of states in Africa, which received $341 million in direct aid from France annually. French pressure compelled the Common Market countries to set up the European Development Fund, with a capital of $581 million to aid the Belgian and French African colonies, both before and after independence. Foreign aid cost France more per capita than the United States; and, being carefully channeled to a selected group of countries already oriented toward France economically, was of more immediate effectiveness.

The Communist bloc began to offer aid to the nonaligned nations in 1954, with a loan to Afghanistan; but such grants did not begin on a large scale until the 1955 visit of Khrushchev and Bulganin to India, which received $259 million in loans during the following two years. By 1961, the Communist bloc as a whole had extended credits of about $4.6 billion, of which only a quarter had been used; at the same time, military aid totaling $1.8 billion had been given to ten countries, particularly to Egypt and Syria. Soviet loans were generally regarded favorably because of their low interest rate, usually 2.5 per cent, while much propaganda value was gained by the construction of showpieces of heavy industry, such as a steel mill in India and especially the Aswan High Dam in Egypt.

Finally, aid was made available through the various agencies of the United Nations, such as the Bank for Reconstruction and Development, the International Development Association, and the International Finance Corporation. Interest was high, however, and most of the projects had to show a clear economic result. In order to provide financing for such substructure investments as in roads or schools, the underdeveloped countries pressed for establishment of a Special United Nations Fund for Economic Development, which would remove much foreign aid from the influence of the blocs. The donor countries found the proposed machinery unsatisfactory; and as a result, of the $8 billion provided in aid to underdeveloped countries annually at the beginning of the 1960's, barely 10 per cent was provided through the United Nations.

In spite of this aid, the underdeveloped nations continued during the 1960's to become poorer in relation to the advanced countries. The population explosion increased the population of the underdeveloped countries in relation to the advanced, while their economic growth rate barely reached 2 per cent in comparison with 5.6 per cent for the Common Market countries and 3 per cent for the United States. Experts predicted that the advanced countries would be compelled to allot between 7 and 13 per cent of their national income in provision of aid to the underdeveloped countries merely in order to maintain a 2 per cent growth rate in per capita income. The dangerous division of the world between the haves and the have-nots seemed likely to continue with explosive consequences, from which the Communist powers would profit. The situation was complicated, however, by the discovery in the 1960's that the Communist world itself was split between the industrially advanced nations led by the Soviet Union and the underdeveloped countries that followed China.

THE DISINTEGRATION OF
THE COMMUNIST BLOC:
THE SINO-SOVIET RIFT

The breakup of the Soviet bloc may be said to have begun with the death of Stalin, although the expulsion of Tito had already been marked by the same conflict of ideology and of national interest that later typified both the Sino-Soviet quarrel and the reassertion of the autonomy of the East European satellites. "The death of Stalin in 1953," according to Richard Lowenthal, "foreshadowed the abandonment of a historically unique enterprise—the attempt to transfer the centralism of a ruling totalitarian party to an international movement." The Sino-Soviet conflict was major proof of that failure. By 1960, the Chinese Communist leaders felt confident enough in themselves and sufficiently contemptuous of the post-Stalin leadership of the Soviet Union to challenge Russia's dominance of the Communist nations.

Internal Development of Red China. In October 1949, the establishment of Communist control over the whole of mainland China vindicated Mao Tse-tung in his refusal to follow Soviet advice and example. He had based his revolution upon the peasant masses, had carried it out with almost no help from Russia, and had ignored Stalin's recommendation that he compromise with Chiang Kai-shek. "Mao's Road" was already in 1949 regarded by the Chinese as a better guide to the communization of the underdeveloped countries of Asia and Africa than Stalin's. China, however, had enormous work of reconstruction and reform at home as its immediate task. Party dictatorship was at once established and was institutionalized in the Constitution of 1954, which created a National People's Congress chosen by indirect election from a single list of candidates, a Permanent Committee corresponding to the Russian Presidium, and a Council of State. Party members, who in 1958 numbered about 14 million, held the important administrative posts. An immediate attack was made on the feudal structure of landownership by confiscation in 1950–51 of all property not worked by its owners, the land being redistributed in 110 million small plots among the peasantry. In 1953–57, however, collectivization was pushed rapidly, the number of collective farms rising from 114,000 in 1953, to 8 million in 1957. The peasants fought back, as they had done in Russia, by killing their livestock and by passive resistance, so that food production fell while the population continued to grow by 15 million a year. Industrial changes were more successful. Heavy industry and foreign trade was nationalized at once; and private ownership had virtually disappeared by 1957. Three major steel complexes were developed. Oil was exploited in Sinkiang. New railroads were built to open up the western parts of the country where settlement was encouraged. According to official statistics, industrial production rose 10 per cent annually. In this ambitious program, Soviet aid was vitally necessary. A trade and communications treaty was concluded in June 1950, and by 1960 half of China's trade was with Russia. One hundred and sixty-six basic projects in the First Five-Year Plan (1953–58) were built with Russian aid, and over 10,000 Soviet technicians were sent to China. After 1956, scientific cooperation was extended, including work on nuclear energy. Chinese leaders lost no opportunity of praising the Soviet Union as "the most faithful friend of the Chinese people."

Origins of the Sino-Soviet Conflict. Khrushchev's denunciation of Stalin at the Twentieth Party Congress in February 1956 did not immediately disturb the Chinese Communists, although later they claimed that the "secret speech" caused their conflict with Khrushchev. The Chinese pressed Khrushchev to permit Poland some leeway in making its own way to socialism, but they advocated ruthless repression of the Hungarian uprising and took credit later for the return of the Russian Army into Budapest. Their distrust of Khrushchev's handling of the Hungarian situation turned to personal grievance when the Soviet government was compelled to reduce its economic aid to China in order to cover the $1 billion expense of its new aid program for the East European regimes. In China, Mao had been disturbed by the vast upswelling of discontent in February 1957 that had followed his invitation to the people to criticize: "Let a hundred flowers bloom, and let a hundred schools of thought contend." He had clamped down on the critics within a few weeks. The causes of the discontent were obvious— collectivization, food shortages, rationing, lack of fuel, and suppression of intellectual freedom. To deal with them, the Chinese leadership decided upon a radical new approach to economic development that would cast aside the Soviet model. Announced in 1958 as the "Great Leap Forward," the program called for maximum use of labor through dispersal of industry, encouragement of tiny production units such as "backyard furnaces" for steel production, ideological rather than material rewards, and above all for the regrouping of the rural population in "people's communes." The communes, in which over 90 per cent of the rural population were concentrated in semimilitary groupings of 5,000 families, were presented as Mao's method for building a Communist society in underdeveloped countries with a vast peasant population, and thus were an ideological challenge to the Russians. The prolonged debate within the Chinese government over this program had probably been settled in favor of the radicals when the Chinese attended the Moscow Conference of Communist Parties in November 1957; and while Khrushchev spoke of peaceful coexistence, Mao told the party leaders that "the international situation has now reached a new turning-point. . . . I think the characteristic of the situation today is the East wind prevailing over the West wind. That is to say, the socialist forces are overwhelmingly superior to the imperialist forces." To Mao, peaceful coexistence was unnecessary.

The next year, the Chinese began the Great Leap Forward. At the same time, they began bombarding the Nationalist-held offshore islands of Quemoy and Matsu, and threatened imminent invasion; and when American Marines moved into Lebanon and British planes into Jordan in August, they demanded that Khrushchev take action for the defense of the newly installed regime of General Kassim in Iraq. On all three matters, the Russian attitude was unsatisfactory. The Soviet government warned the Chinese of the economic risks they were taking in the commune program and advised caution. By the end of the year, their warnings were justified because a series of natural disasters had combined with peasant resistance to lower food production and to prevent achievement of the industrial goals. The retreat began in December 1958, with an official warning against "behaving like Utopians"; cereal production continued to fall from 250 million tons in 1959, to 160 in 1960, and meat and eggs became almost unobtainable. In 1961 and 1962, China was compelled to buy vast quantities of cereals from Canada. In the Quemoy dispute, Russian support for the Chinese position came only after Mao had expressed willingness to negotiate, an offer that itself followed Secretary of State Dulles' threat to invade the Chinese mainland if Quemoy were attacked. It is possible that Mao may have regarded his failure to take the offshore islands as due to lack of support from his Russian ally. Finally, Khrushchev's call for a summit conference to end the Middle East dispute appeared to the Chinese to be a retreat before Western aggression. Krushchev's visit to the United States in September 1959 and his warm endorsement of President Eisenhower completed the Chinese disillusionment; and Khrushchev received an ostentatiously chilly welcome when he appeared in Peking a few days later for the celebration of the tenth anniversary of the Chinese Communist victory.

Sino-Soviet Ideological Battles. The break between the two powers became public in 1960. In February, at a meeting of the Warsaw Pact powers, Khrushchev attacked the policies of the Chinese regime. In April, the Chinese published a series of articles in *Red Flag* in which they argued, in opposition to Khrushchev, that coexistence was a temporary expedient, that local wars at least were inevitable, and that the revolution could be carried out only by civil war. In June, at the

Rumanian Party Congress in Bucharest, attended by fraternal delegates from all over the world, the Russians circulated a long letter exposing their ideological position in the dispute with China; and at a secret session, Khrushchev excoriated the Chinese leaders, accusing Mao himself of becoming "an ultra Leftist, an ultra dogmatist, indeed, a left revisionist!" In July, in a significant parallel with Stalin's quarrel with Tito, the Russians complained about the attitude of the Chinese to the Soviet technicians in China, and the next month most Soviet experts returned home, taking with them the plans for the half-finished factories and power stations they had been constructing. In November, a major confrontation occurred at the Moscow Conference of eighty-one Communist parties, which argued for two weeks in secret over the text of a long Declaration dealing with the origin of authority in the Communist bloc and the strategy to be adopted toward the West. The Declaration spoke of the Communist party of the Soviet Union as "the universally recognized vanguard of the world Communist movement," but not as "the head"; the Chinese rejected even this position of Soviet superiority and claimed a position of equality with Russia in making policy for the bloc. "How can there be equality between fraternal parties if everything the Soviet Party decides at its own Congresses is binding on the rest?" a Chinese delegate asked the conference. "Or must we admit a new concept—'father' Parties and 'son' Parties? . . . We shall not yield." The Russians insisted that the "character of the epoch" was marked by the growing preponderance of the "Socialist world system" over the capitalist system, making it possible "to settle the major problems of our own age in a new manner, in the interest of peace, democracy and socialism." The Chinese retorted that local wars were inevitable and probably desirable, particularly in underdeveloped countries, and would be unlikely to develop into world war; and they sharply criticized Khrushchev's dealings with the "imperialists." The break became more vituperative when Albanian President Enver Hoxha criticized Khrushchev personally for misunderstanding Lenin, for "underhand trickery" against the Chinese, for whitewashing Tito, and for blackmailing Albania. The conference closed with a compromise endorsement of the Soviet position on all essential matters, and with the virtual isolation of the Chinese, the Albanians, and a few small Asian and Latin American parties.

China's Albanian Ally. China's befriending of Albania marked the opening of its attempt to win the allegiance of Russia's satellites. Albanian President Enver Hoxha had his own grievances against Khrushchev, for pressuring the Albanian regime to embark upon de-Stalinization, courting Yugoslavia, and even suggesting to Greece that Russia might countenance its annexation of part of southern Albania; and Khrushchev's belated visit to Hoxha at Tirana in 1959 failed to calm Albanian apprehensions. Throughout 1960 the Albanian leaders supported the Chinese rather than the Soviet position on peaceful coexistence and praised the experiment of the People's Communes and the Great Leap Forward. Pro-Soviet party leaders and military officers were purged, and a show trial was held of officials accused of plotting a pro-Soviet coup d'état against Hoxha. At the conference in Moscow in November, Hoxha declared that the Soviet Union had already begun to take punitive action against Albania, cutting off its wheat shipments at a time when the country was faced with mass starvation. He left the conference a week early and never returned to Moscow. Both the Russians and the East European satellites attempted to win Albania back into the fold with tempting offers of trade treaties, and a new Soviet ambassador was appointed to Tirana. The Albanians dispatched an economic mission to Peking instead, and at the Party Congress in February 1961 the Albanians again backed the Chinese against Soviet criticism, giving the Soviet delegates a cold reception and feting the Chinese. In March, the Albanians boycotted a meeting of the Warsaw Pact powers. The Russians thereupon began to apply the same pressures on Albania that had previously failed to end Yugoslavia's defection. Russian submarines were withdrawn from their Mediterranean base at Valona in June; technicians from Russia and the East European countries were called home, and credits were canceled; Albanian officers receiving military training were sent back, and the programs were ended. At once, the Chinese filled the vacuum. A credit of $125 million was granted in April, and Chinese technicians were sent to Albania in growing numbers. Khrushchev reserved his reply for the Twenty-Second Party Congress in Moscow in October 1961. Although the Albanians did not attend, the Chinese sent an important delegation headed by Premier Chou En-lai, who was apparently taken by surprise at Khrushchev's open attack on the Albanian leaders. Chou, after making clear that he was aware that criticism of Albania was simply a euphemistic manner of criticizing China, attacked Khrushchev's policies before the Congress, laid a wreath "To the great Marxist-Leninist, Joseph Stalin" in the Red Square mausoleum, and walked out of the Congress a week early. After his departure, Khrushchev attacked the Albanian leaders far more viciously, accusing them of "despotism and misuse of powers," and of "malicious, dirty attacks" on communism "such as not even our enemies, open or concealed" had indulged in. Khrushchev thereby read Albania out of the Soviet bloc. Diplomatic relations were broken in December 1961, and it was forced out of Comecon. Albania, however, survived this isolation, providing an important lesson to other countries considering defection. Its trade with China increased rapidly; the East European countries, but not Russia, resumed their economic relations; and a small increase in trade with Italy and Greece was negotiated.

Soviet Reaction to the Chinese Challenge. After 1961, the Soviet government and its satellites no longer felt it necessary to attack China indirectly through Albania. Chinese demands for a new conference of the world Communist parties to settle the differences of opinion were not taken up. The Chinese press criticized the new program of the Soviet Communist party as "economic heresy." The victory of the radicals within the Chinese Communist party was seen in the invasion of India in October 1962, which occurred almost simultaneously with Khrushchev's withdrawal of Soviet missiles from Cuba. Chinese criticism of Khrushchev for bowing before the imperialists had, however, little effect at a time when almost no country in the world—Communist, non-aligned, or Western—expressed anything but disgust at its aggression in India. Apart from Albania, which remained loyal, the Chinese made no progress in winning the allegiance of the Soviet satellites. Moreover, the Soviet government pressed its offensive against the Chinese by wooing Ho Chi Minh of North Vietnam, as well as Outer Mongolia and North Korea, whereas Chinese attempts to influence the African countries were being checked by the establishment of military regimes. Even the overthrow of Khrushchev did not bring the expected reconciliation between Moscow and Peking. Brezhnev and Kosygin remained adamantly opposed to Chinese "dogmatism," particularly in the refusal of peaceful coexistence. Kosygin visited North Korea in February 1965 and re-stored Russian economic aid, which had been cut off two years before. Russian antiaircraft missiles were supplied to North Vietnam after the beginning of American raids in 1964. After a brief period of Chinese ascendancy in Cuba, the Russians succeeded in re-establishing their control, largely by grant of economic aid of $350 million annually. The vast internal disturbances provoked throughout China from 1965 by Mao's Great Proletarian Cultural Revolution, an attempt to restore the fanatical puritanism of the early days of Chinese Communism by loosing on the population indoctrinated hordes of youthful Red Guards, not only threatened chaos for the Chinese economy but weakened Mao in his challenge of Russian leadership of the Communist world. Thus, by 1966, the Russians seemed to have parried the Chinese blow to their position of supremacy, both within the Communist movement and as a source of influence in the nonaligned countries. Preoccupation with the Chinese challenge had, however, made the Russians extremely vulnerable to another challenge—"polycentrism," the desire of the satellites and of the Communist parties in the nonaligned and Western countries to exert greater control over their own road to communism.

THE NEW EASTERN EUROPE, 1960–

While Khrushchev was engaged in his bitter dispute with the Chinese leaders, he was compelled for the first time to bid for the support of the East European regimes. Although the satellites, with the sole exception of Albania, supported the position of the Soviet Union, they were able to exact a price for that support—increased autonomy. As in their attitude to de-Stalinization in 1953–60, however, the regimes varied greatly in the degree to which they sought, or even desired, to modify their status as satellites of the Soviet Union.

Libermannism in East Germany. East Germany remained the most obedient satellite because it was dependent upon Soviet support in holding down its discontented population. The Berlin Wall could be maintained only with Soviet acquiescence; East Germany profited from its position within Comecon as the foremost industrial producer; growing contacts of the other East European countries with West Germany made Ulbricht fear the sacrifice of the interests of his regime. He was outspoken in his criticism of the Chinese attitude after 1960, although he probably sympathized with the Chinese praise of Stalin, and he accepted, though with ill-grace, the visit of Khrushchev's son-in-law to Bonn in July 1964. At home, under pressure from Moscow, he began to relax political and cultural restrictions in 1963. More freedom of discussion was permitted. Professors and writers criticized by the regime could still lose their posts, but in several notable cases they were not imprisoned. Ten thousand prisoners were released in an amnesty on September 1964, on the celebration of the fifteenth anniversary of the founding of the Republic. The most notable sign of change was in economic administration. Taking their cue from the famous article, "The Plan, Profits and Bonuses," published in *Pravda* on September 9, 1962, by Economics Professor Evsei Libermann, East German economists proposed decentralization through some eighty Associations of State-owned Enterprises, borrowing of capital by factories on a commercial basis, price reform to end hidden state support of unprofitable goods, and acceptance of profits as the principal indicator of economic efficiency and level of wages. In this way, Ulbricht made a skillful attempt to enlist the aid of the managerial and technical elite of East Germany. The reforms had been widely instituted by 1965, were on schedule, and were already showing proof of success.

Economic Problems in Czechoslovakia. Like Ulbricht, Czechoslovak President and First Party Secretary Antonin Novotny had shown little enthusiasm for de-Stalinization during the 1950's, and he was dismayed at Khrushchev's new attack on Stalin at the Twenty-Second Party Congress in October 1961. Novotny again found stirrings of rebellion within the Communist hierarchy against his own personal control and was forced to act promptly to subdue this discontent. His most obvious rival, Minister of the Interior Rudolf Barak, was first removed from his office; in February 1962 he was tried on criminal charges of theft and embezzlement and condemned to fifteen years of imprisonment. He was unable to prevent the Party Congress in 1962 from demanding an inquiry into the political trials held in 1949–54; and as a result of the findings was compelled to dismiss two former Stalinists. Agitation in Slovakia, where the intellectuals had been demanding greater autonomy and in particular the rehabilitation of Foreign Minister Clementis, a Slovak who had been hanged in 1952, forced Novotny to give way. Clementis was quietly cleared, and two leading Slovaks were released from jail. Finally, in September 1963 Novotny made a major gesture to appease Slovak patriotism by dismissing Premier Viliam Siroky, a Slovak who was regarded as both a conservative and a centralizer, and replacing him by a moderate reforming Slovak, Jozef Lenart. Novotny's willingness to compromise with the reformers was due to a large extent to the disastrous economic situation in Czechoslovakia in 1961–63. Overinvestment in heavy industry had produced a shortage of raw materials and labor. Communications were antiquated, productivity was low, and waste through shoddy workmanship and poor planning was enormous. The harsh winter of 1962–63 completed the damage, leading to an over-all fall in production and universal shortages of food and consumer goods. The Czech economists led by Professors Ota Sik and Josef Gold-mann also found the solution to the economy's troubles in "Liberman-nism," which Novotny himself officially endorsed in 1965. Central planning was to be greatly reduced, the profitabilty of investment was to become the guideline, and trusts controlling local groupings of factories were to become the principal arbiters of production planning. Moreover, moves were made to re-establish Czechoslovakia's traditional contacts with the West. Restrictions on tourists were sharply reduced, and the number of foreign tourists rose from 40,000 in 1960 to 744,000 in 1964. A British company agreed to set up a fertilizer plant on a twelve-year credit. An American company undertook to market precision tools made by the Skoda Factory. Thus, by the mid-1960's, the Novotny regime, if it had not yet joined the ranks of the "revisionists," had at least ceased to be Stalinist.

Middle-of-the-Road Communism in Bulgaria. Bulgarian Premier and First Party Secretary Todor Zhivkov had fought off a challenge to his position in 1961–62 by dismissing from the Presidium the old-time Stalinist Chervenkov and the conservative Premier Yugov. Lining up closely with Khrushchev against the Chinese and, after Khrushchev's fall, with his successors, Zhivkov attempted to hold down internal opposition through his close ties with the Soviet Union. He was op-posed, however, by groups sympathetic to China and by more powerful nationalist forces who wished to see Bulgaria pursuing a course similar to that of Rumania or even of Yugoslavia. In April 1965, these na-tionalist groups unsuccessfully planned a coup d'état, which was dis-covered by Soviet counterespionage agents. Zhivkov did respond to the forces of Libermannism by adopting a modified experimental form of competition among factories, interest charges for use of state-owned capi-tal, and linking of wages to profits. The Bulgarian, like the Rumanian, Polish, and Hungarian governments, concluded a trade agreement with the government of West Germany, permitted the establishment of a trade mission in Sofia, provided for increase in trade, and, over East Ger-man protests, accepted the West German stipulation that West Berlin be explicitly included as part of the West German currency area. With the development of the Black Sea beach resorts of Varna and Zlatni Piassatsi, the Bulgarian state tourist agency, *Balkantourist,* succeeded in raising the number of foreign tourists from 8,000 in 1960 to 400,000 in 1964. Bulgaria thus maintained a prudent and unadventurous middle-of-the-road course in keeping with the cautious character of President Zhivkov himself.

Disappointing Character of Polish National Communism. In Poland, First Party Secretary Wladislaw Gomulka continued to pursue his own conception of a distinctively Polish communism. He remained independent of Moscow in intrabloc negotiations, defending revisionism and demanding that Khrushchev avoid a split with China. Relations with the West remained quite good. In 1960, the Eisenhower administration granted Poland "most favored nation" treatment for exports to the United States; and by 1964, 29 per cent of Poland's trade was with Western countries. At home, however, Gomulka's firm discipline was further strengthened. After 1960, a group of tough, conservative-minded party leaders, known as the Partisans for their work in the underground in Poland during the war, began to win greater influence over policy. Gomulka successfully reduced their power by manipulation of party appointments and reduction of the powers of the Ministry of the Interior. But he willingly accepted the Partisans' demand for restriction of cultural freedom, cut down the newsprint available to liberal magazines, closed down two of the most lively reviews, and in 1965 brought to trial several writers who had published anonymously in the West. He also continued his conflict with the Catholic Church, headed by Cardinal Wyszynski, whom the regime attempted to present as an obstacle to a new understanding between Church and State that Pope John XXIII might be prepared to accept. A minor campaign of harassment was conducted against the clergy, who were liable to special taxes, prevented from giving religious instruction in the schools, and hindered in the organization of pilgrimages. The great celebrations of the thousandth anniversary of the founding of Polish Christianity were frowned upon, and the Pope was refused a visa to attend. In one respect, Gomulka was unable to remain conservative in the 1960's. Unemployment, lack of capital, failure to exploit raw materials adequately, and bureaucratic inefficiency brought the economy to a state of stagnation by 1963, and the party leadership turned, at the Fourth Party Congress in June 1964, to some of the reforms that had been rejected in 1957, including study of profits, interest rates, realistic pricing, and a decentralization of decision-making. In contrast with the Czech and East German reforms, this program was not very far-reaching. Ten years after the Polish October, Gomulka's regime was looking increasingly old-fashioned.

Slight Liberalization in Kádár's Hungary. By contrast, the Hungarian regime of János Kádár continued its policies of liberalization. Kádár remained close to Khrushchev in aims and ideology and was a firm supporter of the Russian line in foreign policy. By pursuing this course, he earned the right to permit Hungary its own "national peculiarities." Rákosi supporters were demoted without ceremony or victimization, the powers of the secret police were further restricted, and in 1963 a general amnesty was proclaimed. A more flexible attitude to the Church led to the conclusion of an agreement with the Papacy in 1964, by which a number of vacant bishoprics were filled; but no agreement was reached on the future of Cardinal Mindszenty, who had been living in the American Embassy since 1956, and the state continued to arrest priests who were too outspoken before young people. Kádár's greatest hope was that a growing economic prosperity would reconcile the vast majority of the population to communism. Living standards did rise slowly after the 1956 uprising and many of the economic reforms introduced in the other East European countries in the comprehensive plans of the 1960's, such as profit-sharing by workers, decentralization of planning, and the revolutionary step of charging 5 per cent interest on capital, were introduced piecemeal in Hungary before 1962. Hungarians found themselves able once again to travel abroad, over 100,000 visiting the West in 1964; fashions and antiques were again on display in Budapest's Vaci Utca; the burnt-out shell of the Royal Palace on the summit of the Buda Hill was rebuilt; and flower-studded parks filled the gaps in city blocks left from the fighting in 1956. By the mid-1960's, Hungary wore a new and slightly more contented face.

Rumania's National Road to Communism. Nowhere, however, was the reassertion of national independence more evident than in Rumania. The first step was to refuse the role of agricultural and petrochemical producer assigned to it by Comecon in 1962. From 1958 on, when Gheorghiu-Dej's control over the Communist party in Rumania became unassailable, and when the Rumanian economy gave first indications of a "miracle" in the making, the Rumanian leaders determined to establish "rapid and all-round industrialization" as their goal. They decided to scrap the Five-Year Plan in progress (1956–61) and to begin a Six-Year Plan in 1960 that would turn Rumania into a major industrial power. The Plan was approved in June 1960, and an extensive trade agreement concluded in November provided for the purchase from the Soviet Union of raw materials and machinery costing half a billion dollars that would make possible the diversification planned for the Rumanian economy. In December 1959, however, the Comecon countries had drawn up a Charter proclaiming the purpose of Comecon to be the "international socialist division of labor and the specialization and cooperation of production." To the Czechs and East Germans, this division implied their privileged position as the powers best fitted to control the heavy industry of the group, while countries like Rumania and Bulgaria would supply them with raw materials and food. In 1962, Khrushchev himself espoused the cause of economic integration, perhaps influenced by the startling successes of the Common Market in Western Europe, and even proposed the institution of a supranational planning authority. The battle was fought through a series of Comecon meetings between June 1962 and July 1963, when Khrushchev admitted defeat, dropped the plans for integration, and accepted bilateral consultations as an alternative. Rumania pressed on with its plans for rapid industrial growth. Between 1960 and 1965, the growth rate ran between 12.5 and 16.4 per cent annually; a great steel complex was constructed at Galati; trade with the West expanded to more than a third of Rumania's total; and Western investment by such firms as Siemens, Krupp, Pechiney, and even Pepsi-Cola was encouraged. The Black Sea beaches, the Carpathian Mountains, and the pink-and-cream rococo towns of Cluj and Braşov in Transylvania welcomed 200,000 Western tourists in 1965.

Gheorghiu-Dej was not satisfied with mere economic independence. From 1962, he began to remove the remaining signs of Russian influence in Rumania. Rewritten history books played up the role of native Communists rather than the Red Army in the overthrow of the Antonescu regime in August 1944. Russian-language study was no longer required in the schools, and the Soviet cultural center, the Maxim Gorky Institute in Bucharest, was closed. Even street names were changed, and popular agitation for the return of Bessarabia, annexed by Russia in 1940, was permitted. Gheorghiu-Dej profited to the utmost from the Sino-Soviet dispute, increasing Rumanian trade with China while the other East

European states were reducing theirs; Premier Maurer twice visited Peking in 1964 and offered to mediate the dispute; and in the Central Committee Declaration of April 1964, which was Gheorghiu-Dej's final testament and indeed declaration of independence, the rejection of supranational integration was justified in terms almost identical with the words of the Chinese at the Moscow conference of 1960: "There does not and there cannot exist a 'father' party and a 'son' party." To complete Moscow's discomfiture, the Rumanians even concluded a new trade agreement with Albania in March 1963.

Nicolae Ceausescu, who became First Party Secretary on the death of Gheorghiu-Dej in March 1965, was an even more determined nationalist. The son of peasants, he spent his whole life from the age of fifteen as a Communist organizer, was with Gheorghiu-Dej in Doftana Prison during the war, and later rose rapidly in the party as Gheorghiu-Dej's protégé. Aged only forty-seven in 1965, he was the youngest of all the East European leaders and was able to appeal to some extent to the younger generation of Rumanians. He showed that he was willing to innovate by ordering the writing of a new party history describing the facts "as they happened and in accordance with ethical truth." His most important departure was, however, to question the value of the Warsaw Pact. In May 1966, Ceausescu told his party leaders that "military blocs and the existence of military bases and troops [in foreign countries were] an anachronism incompatible with the independence and national sovereignty of the peoples and normal relations between states," and shortly afterward he proposed that most Russian troops be withdrawn from Eastern Europe. Coming after the Gomulka Plan of 1964 for the freezing of nuclear weapons and bases in the countries of the Warsaw Pact and NATO and de Gaulle's announcement of France's withdrawal from NATO, Ceausescu's proposal made clear that the disintegration of both blocs would, in the opinion of some leaders in both Eastern and Western Europe, be of benefit to Communist and non-Communist powers alike.

DISUNITY IN THE WEST

While the cohesion of the Soviet bloc was greatly weakened by the Sino-Soviet rivalry and by the self-assertion of the East European countries, the Western bloc also began to disintegrate. Territorial disputes flared up between individual nations; the French veto on British entry into the Common Market prevented a rapprochement between the Outer Seven of EFTA and the Inner Six of EEC; Belgium opposed de Gaulle's conception of the political unification of the Common Market countries while French pressure for acceptance of a common agricultural policy almost destroyed the Common Market itself; and American supremacy in the Atlantic Community became increasingly galling to the newly prosperous countries of Western Europe, particularly to French President de Gaulle, who climaxed a series of challenges to American authority by withdrawing French troops from the NATO alliance.

Territorial Disputes in Western Europe. Most of the national disputes arose from territorial changes resulting from past European wars. Britain had captured the Rock of Gibraltar in 1704 during the Spanish Succession war and had retained it at the Treaty of Utrecht in 1713. To Franco, the continuance of a British colony on Spanish soil was both an affront to national dignity and a suitable pretext for diverting national discontent from problems at home. He applied economic pressure on the colony during the late 1950's by refusing work permits to Spaniards and by imposing annoying customs formalities at the border. In October 1964, the Spanish government appealed to the UN Special Committee on Colonialism and ordered a total economic blockade of Gibraltar. The British reacted with legislation encouraging industry to settle in the colony, with a show of air power, and with the conciliatory gesture of a clampdown on smuggling. They made it clear, however, that since the majority of the Rock's inhabitants were not of Spanish origin but were from various parts of the Mediterranean seaboard, they would not consider returning Gibraltar to Spain.

At the opposite end of the Mediterranean, the island of Cyprus presented the British with a far more difficult problem. Occupied in 1878 by special agreement with the Turkish Empire at the Congress of Berlin and annexed outright in 1914, Cyprus was for Britain an important link in the sea route to India through Suez and, after the evacuation of the Suez Canal zone in 1956, Britain's sole remaining military and air base in the eastern Mediterranean. Whereas 80,000 islanders were of Turkish origin, about 400,000 were of Greek origin and easily won to the support of union with Greece, or *Enosis,* which was proclaimed as a slogan by Greek Cypriot leaders from the 1930's. In the 1950's, the Greek government took up the cause of *Enosis;* in 1956, following the breakdown of a conference in London of the British, Greek, and Turkish governments, the Greek government withdrew its ambassador from Britain. Rather than accept NATO mediation, the Greeks appealed to the United Nations General Assembly, where the issue was debated during the following two years. Meanwhile, Cyprus suffered from ugly terrorist outbreaks, by both the Greek Cypriot forces of (EOKA) and by Turkish armed bands. The British were unable to keep order, in spite of the temporary exile of the leader of the Greek Cypriot community, Archbishop Makarios, to the distant Seychelles Islands; anti-British and anti-Turkish rioting broke out in Athens; in Turkey, crowds demonstrated in favor of partition. Finally, in 1959, a compromise agreement was reached between Britain, Greece, Turkey, and the leaders of the Greek and Turkish Cypriot communities, by which Cyprus was to become an independent republic, with a Greek president and a Turkish vice-president, minority rights were to be guaranteed, and both Greek and Turkish military units stationed on the island. Britain retained its military bases. Independence, achieved on August 16, 1960, did not however solve the dispute on Cyprus. General Grivas, leader of the EOKA underground, continued to agitate in Athens and on Cyprus itself for the fusion with Greece for which he fought for four years. Makarios, as president, failed to keep the agreement on minority rights, maintained a police force that was largely Greek Cypriot, and in 1963 announced his intention of amending the constitution to abolish Turkish rights of special representation in the police and town councils. Civil war broke out almost immediately between secret armies that both communities had been training since independence. Greek and Turkish Army contingents on the island took up positions facing each other. With the threat of war between two NATO members, the British intervened to head off a Turkish invasion; and a neutral area in Nicosia was established. More incidents at the beginning of 1964 led the British and American governments to propose a NATO peace force, but it was rejected by Makarios in favor of a United Nations force. After Turkey had again threatened to invade in March 1964, a UN peace force, composed largely of British, Canadian, Irish, and Scandinavian troops, was formed. By the end of the year, the Greeks were in virtual control of the island, and the lives of the Turks were safeguarded by the presence of this tiny UN force.

Britain also became involved in a quarrel with Iceland over fishing rights. The Iceland government claimed exclusive rights over waters within four miles of its coasts; when from 1952 it kept out British trawlers, their owners replied by procuring a boycott in Britain of fish caught by Icelanders. The loss of its best customer forced Iceland to turn to Russia, which obligingly accepted a large share of the fish exports upon which Iceland depended for its livelihood. Coming at a time when the Icelanders were demanding the removal of the large American manned NATO base at Keflavik, Iceland's new ties with the Soviet Union worried the British and American governments. After the repression of the Hungarian rebellion, the Iceland parliament withdrew its demand for the removal of the base, and a temporary compromise was reached in the fisheries dispute. In 1958, however, Iceland extended its territorial waters to twelve miles from its coasts, excluding its competitors from some of the richest waters in the North Atlantic. Britain refused to recognize the new limits and sent naval patrols to escort its trawlers. No agreement was reached by international negotiation in 1960, but the following year Britain accepted the twelve-mile claim and was given in return provisional rights to fish between six and twelve miles from shore.

Finally, relations between Italy and Austria were embittered by Austria's demand that Italy grant autonomy to the South Tirol region, which had been annexed by Italy in 1919 and had a German-speaking minority of 250,000 people. Austria took its protests against violation of the rights of the German-speaking minority to the UN General Assembly in 1959, which recommended direct negotiation between the two governments. From 1962, extremist elements in the South Tirol dramatized their grievances by terrorist attacks, the Italians claiming that Fascist groups from Austria were responsible for these outrages. The Italian parliament recommended greater autonomy for the region in 1964, but the situation remained inflammable.

De Gaulle's Veto on British Membership in the Common Market. Convinced federalists had believed during the 1950's that Western Europe was making rapid progress toward solution of such national disputes as these by integrating the nation-states in a supranational community. The attractive power of the prosperous Common Market would, it was felt, persuade all the countries of non-Communist Europe to seek entry, while the completion of economic integration would require increasing political integration. Many of these hopes were dashed in the 1960's.

The creation of EEC in 1958 and EFTA in 1959 threatened to divide Western Europe into two competing economic blocs, whose existence exacerbated national disputes. Between 1959 and 1961, for example, the British sought to establish themselves in the place previously held by the Germans in the Scandinavian markets, while the French saw an opening for their agricultural produce in Germany by exclusion of products hitherto imported from Denmark. Even the timetables of tariff reduction of EEC and EFTA were calculated as moves in the rivalry between the groups. This unhealthy situation seemed to have been resolved when British Prime Minister Macmillan opened negotiations in October 1961 on British entry into the Common Market. Great excitement and good will was expressed in all six Common Market countries at the British decision. Even General de Gaulle declared that the Six had "always desired that others, and Great Britain in particular, accept the Treaty of Rome, assume its obligations and reap its advantages. . . . I can only be pleased not only from my country's point of view but also, I think from that of Europe, and, at the same time, of the whole world." The negotiations did not proceed smoothly, however; the problems proved more complex than expected, particularly since Britain demanded special privileges for the Commonwealth countries in EEC trade and a long transition period in remodeling the British system of agricultural supports. For many months, the EEC negotiators felt that the British delegate Edward Heath was not even negotiating seriously, but was introducing minor problems, such as tariffs on Indian cricket bats, to delay decisions. The opposition of right-wing Conservatives and of the Labour party in Britain also seriously disturbed the members of EEC who tended to forget the opposition within their own countries at the time of the negotiation of the Treaty of Rome. Nevertheless, after eighteen months of talks in Brussels, there was hope that in 1963 Britain would be able to enter the Common Market, and would be followed by several other members of EFTA.

Failure of de Gaulle's Plans for European Political Union. In his press conference of January 14, 1963, however, President de Gaulle declared that Britain could not yet be permitted to enter the EEC, and the French representatives forced their partners to break off negotiations at the end of January. De Gaulle's motives for this action, which infuriated and grieved not only the British but the other five EEC members, were complex, deriving more from de Gaulle's conception of the role of

France in Europe than from his objections to Britain's attitude. De Gaulle believed that in the postwar world French greatness, without which France would not be herself, could only be achieved within a united Western Europe whose peoples had realized their "complementary character—from the geographical, strategic, economic, cultural and other points of view." The Common Market represented a necessary start in economic integration, which, in his opinion, Britain was unable to accept, owing largely to the nature of its trade with the Commonwealth and of its agriculture. But de Gaulle believed that the Six must unite politically, not under a supranational government, but by institutionalized consultation between the governments of the states which alone "are valid, legitimate and capable of action." This form of political union was proposed by the French government in 1960, and negotiations dragged on among the EEC partners until 1962. A consultative union of this kind was in the traditional line of British policy, and would have been supported by the British government. It was turned down in May 1962, however, by the Belgian and Dutch foreign ministers, who were the strongest supporters of British membership in the Common Market. As de Gaulle realized, the Belgians and Dutch would accept his schemes if Britain was present in the Community to counterbalance the French; without Britain, they would press for a supranational union, which he would not tolerate. The veto on British membership thus made achievement of de Gaulle's aims for political union of the Six unlikely, and he turned instead to the bilateral treaty of friendship and cooperation with Germany in January 1963. The success of this treaty would, he hoped, eventually attract the other four EEC partners into the political union he had offered them in 1960. The achievement of political and economic union of the Six would bring into being a "European Europe" guided by France. Britain's close ties with the United States would prevent it from sharing in this Europe, which de Gaulle believed, was necessary in the 1960's because "the division of the world into two camps led by Washington and Moscow, respectively, corresponds less and less to the true situation. With regard to the slowly splitting totalitarian world, or the problems posed by China, or the attitude to be adopted toward many countries of Asia, Africa and Latin America, or the reshaping of the United Nations Organization which ought to follow, or the adjustment of world trade of all kinds, and so on, it appears that Europe, provided it wants to do so, is henceforth called upon to play a role that is its own." In short, the Europe of the Six would, in de Gaulle's view, stand independent of the United States and would not be "dissolved in a system of some kind of 'Atlantic Community' which would be only a new form of that famous integration."

De Gaulle wrecked the chances of British entry into EEC without winning over his partners to his concept of a European Europe. The Franco-German Treaty, which was the keystone of his plans, proved a further divisive factor. The Benelux countries and Italy immediately suspected the establishment of a new Bonn-Paris axis for the domination of Western Europe. The German Socialists and many Christian Democrats opposed so tight a link with de Gaulle so soon after his autocratic and unilateral decision to keep Britain out of Europe. Neither Erhard, who succeeded Adenauer as chancellor in October 1963, nor his foreign minister Gerhard Schröder, desired to break Germany's close bonds with the United States. Hence, within a year, the Franco-German Treaty was moribund; and de Gaulle himself admitted ruefully, "Treaties are like maidens and roses. They each have their day!" Meanwhile, his veto had virtually brought the Common Market to a standstill. In the European Parliament, de Gaulle was vigorously criticized, the sense of mutual trust that had prevailed in the Commission headquarters was dissipated, and negotiations became more and more an open form of national bargaining. Above all, France's partners became more stubborn about accepting de Gaulle's ultimatums on agricultural policy.

Battles over Agricultural Policy in EEC. De Gaulle had forced his partners to draw up regulations for cereals, pork, eggs and poultry, fruit and vegetables, and wine in the marathon negotiation session of January 4–14, 1962, by refusing to agree to the beginning of the second four-year stage of the treaty until these agricultural problems were settled. In a second ultimatum, he demanded that regulations for beef, rice, and dairy products be drawn up before the end of 1963; he was again gratified in the marathon negotiation of December 18–23, 1963 that drew up market regulations for these important products, which exceeded in value the total production of the Community's metal working industries, including shipbuilding and automobile manufacturing. In 1964, the Germans were pressured into accepting a common cereal price for the Community considerably lower than the price the German farmer had been receiving at home. The way seemed to be open for a vast expansion of French agricultural exports to Germany. In June 1965, however, France's partners refused to accept the financial regulations of the agricultural common market, which were largely in France's favor, unless the French agreed to increase the supranational powers of the European Parliament and of the EEC Commission. Faced with tactics he himself had successfully used on many occasions, de Gaulle reacted violently, withdrawing all French representatives from the policy-making bodies of EEC, Euratom, and the European Coal and Steel Community. Not before January 1966 did the French resume the negotiations, and then it was only to demand that the EEC Commission's powers be reduced and that the individual states retain their right of veto on EEC policy, thus effectively ending any hope of turning the Common Market into a supranational government. In running for re-election as president in December 1965, however, de Gaulle was not re-elected by an absolute majority on the first ballot, his fall in popularity being due in part to annoyance of French farmers and businessmen at his attitude to the Common Market. After his election on the second ballot, de Gaulle became slightly more conciliatory toward his EEC partners; and in May 1966, the French delegate agreed to financial regulations for agriculture, which would give the French farmer over $60 million annually in subsidies but accepted the German demand that EEC abolish all internal tariff barriers by July 1, 1968. At the same time, the Commission brought out a medium-range plan for the Common Market that envisaged a growth rate of 4.3 per cent in the gross national product through 1970. The Common Market had thus survived its most serious crisis, although the prospects of further political integration remained slim. The slowdown in the West European economic growth rate after 1964, especially in West Germany, was not conducive to major political decisions. The fusion in July 1967 of the executive bodies of EEC, Euratom and ECSC was largely a consolidation of bureaucracies. And General de Gaulle made clear that he had no intention of accepting the new British application for EEC membership made in 1967.

   Disorder in the Atlantic Alliance. The disunity within Western Europe was of less significance than the disorder within the Atlantic alliance. In the 1960's, the virtual hegemony exercised by the United States within the Western bloc was criticized more or less vigorously by almost every member of the bloc. Portugal, for example, was affronted by the refusal of the American government to seize the "Santa Maria" and surrender to Portuguese justice Salazar's political opponents who had hijacked the ship; by the lack of United States support when India

annexed Portuguese Goa; and by the American vote in favor of the UN resolution proposing an inquiry into conditions in Portuguese Angola. The Belgians objected to the American pressure in favor of a strong UN force for reunification of the former Belgian Congo at the time of Kantanga's secession under Moise Tshombe. Many Germans were disappointed that the American forces did not tear down the Berlin Wall within a few hours of its erection. Strong elements within the British Labour party were loudly in favor of the Rapacki Plan, proposed in 1957, for the creation of a denuclearized zone in Central Europe, and vociferous radical groups among young people called for British unilateral disarmament and demonstrated against the establishment of a base for American nuclear submarines in Scotland. Only de Gaulle, however, considered that the interests of Europe would be served by the breakup of NATO.

In de Gaulle's view, Europe's relation to the United States was radically different in the 1960's from that of the immediate postwar years, when the ravaged European states were dependent upon America for economic support and military security, and when as a result "America was seen to take over the conduct of political and strategic affairs in all areas where the free world found itself in contact with the direct or indirect activity of the Soviets." This situation was transformed by Russia's acquisition of the atomic bomb and intercontinental ballistic missiles, which introduced a balance of deterrence between the two world powers, by the breakup of the Communist bloc, by the appearance of a large number of independent but underdeveloped, states, and by the revival of the strength and prosperity of Western Europe. France in particular, under the Fifth Republic, had restored its economy, granted most of its colonies independence, and equipped its modernized army with an independent nuclear force. "Since the division of the world between the two great powers, and therefore into two camps, obviously does not further liberty, equality and fraternity of peoples, a different order, a different balance is necessary for peace." France was to be the instrument for the maintenance of that new order.

To extend the influence of France, de Gaulle made a long tour of Latin America in 1965, where he proclaimed the virtues of Latinity in implied contrast with the culture of the Anglo-Saxons; and he provoked an international incident during his visit to Canada in July 1967 by endorsing the French-Canadian separatist movement in Quebec. He established

warm relations with Rumanian Party Secretary Ceausescu and signed a commercial treaty with Rumania in December 1964. In June 1966, he paid a state visit to the Soviet Union; and in 1964, in a calculated attempt to profit from the disunity within the Communist bloc and to force the American government into a new appraisal of its Asian policy he recognized the Communist regime as the legal government of China. While thus making clear that France intended to be independent of American influence in its diplomatic relations, de Gaulle began breaking down the Western military alliances. French representatives boycotted the meetings of the Southeast Asia Treaty Organization from 1965, and de Gaulle disassociated himself from the other SEATO powers by publicly condemning President Johnson's policy in Vietnam. In September 1958, he unsuccessfully demanded that Britain, the United States, and France should share the leading role in planning NATO's political and military strategy. He refused to agree to the integration of the French fighter force into the NATO defenses in Europe and withdrew French ships from the NATO forces in the Mediterranean. Furious that the United States would not share its nuclear technology with France, he refused to allow American missiles on French soil and went ahead with the development of the French *force de frappe*. After meeting with Prime Minister Macmillan on December 15–16, 1962, he apparently believed that the British and French had agreed to work together toward creation of a European nuclear force. He was therefore deeply disappointed when Macmillan agreed in the Bahamas meeting with Kennedy three days later to accept American Polaris missiles and to share in a multilateral nuclear force (MLF). This fury partly explained his veto on British entry into EEC. Finally, in March 1966 he demanded that all NATO troops in France be placed under French command, and failing that, leave France by April 1967. The cost of the movement, which the French government refused to pay, was expected to be $700 million. French troops would be withdrawn from NATO command on July 1, 1966, and France would cease to take part in the NATO military structure, although it was willing to remain in the political alliance. In June 1966, the remaining NATO allies decided to move the NATO command administration from Paris to Brussels. Once again, de Gaulle had compelled his allies to undertake a major reconsideration of their strategy.

Thus, two decades after the end of the Second World War, Europe entered a new era of self-respect and independence. In many ways, the Europeans could look back upon the period with a certain pride. The Continent had emerged from the terrible destruction of the war to build a prosperity that was greater and more widely shared than ever before in Europe's history. From being minor, and in many cases unwilling partners of the two great continent-states of the Soviet Union and the United States, the countries of Europe were again able to a considerable degree to control their own internal and external policies. With very few exceptions, the great drama of decolonization was over, and the former colonial powers had suffered few of the expected ill-effects of loss of their overseas territories. A new sense of responsibility for the well-being of the inhabitants of the underdeveloped countries of Asia and Africa was evident in the foreign-aid programs and in support of the police actions of the United Nations Organization. Yet the future remained distinctly overcast. The threat of nuclear war was becoming greater as more and more nations developed their own atomic arsenals. The confrontation of the Communist and Western ideologies, quiescent but by no means ended in Europe, was becoming more vicious in Asia; and even the recent slight advances toward freedom and prosperity in the Communist countries of Eastern Europe were far from bridging the gap in ideology and living standards between them and Western Europe. Perhaps of even deeper significance for the future, the contrast between the wealth of the developed countries and the poverty of the under-developed countries was becoming greater; and the aid programs hitherto supported had been quite inadequate in relation to the need of the recipients. Even Western Europe's progress toward integration of the nation-states within a supranational community seemed to have come to a halt with the resurgence of nationalism, which was encouraged by the new prosperity and magnified by anachronistic politicians.

In short, while living better than ever before, the European had never been faced by greater problems. Threatened by atomic war, involved in the clash of ideologies, enjoying the benefits of prosperity in a world of poverty, the European could not help but feel the precariousness of his blessings.

Additional Reading

UNTIL quite recently, the student of contemporary history was regarded by more orthodox, or perhaps one might say conservative, historians as a dabbler in ephemera. It was implied that until government archives were opened, usually fifty years after the events with which they dealt, and until the passage of time had allowed the truly significant events to emerge in perspective, the historian should leave the exposition of the recent past to the newspapers. Yet the standard works dealing with the more remote past were themselves outmoded within a few years by the introduction of new methods of inquiry if not of new documentation; and the great historians tended to survive as literary giants rather than as historians. Moreover, the contemporary historian possesses greater wealth of source material in parliamentary papers, government publications, personal memoirs, statistics, journalistic revelations, labor and industrial publications, and so on, than ever before. There is a sense of freshness in dealing with events and documents that have not been handled many times and a feeling of significance in interpreting events whose aftereffects may still be in the future. The challenge of contemporary history lies in understanding the past without the benefit of long perspective; its reward lies in its immediacy in the first generation threatened by the dangers of total war.

BIBLIOGRAPHICAL AIDS: The most useful bibliographical tools are the book reviews published in the *American Historical Review, The Journal of Modern History,* the *American Political Science Review,* the *Annals of the American Academy of Political and Social Science, Foreign Affairs,* and *World Politics;* and in the valuable series, R. G. Woolbert, ed., *Foreign Affairs Bibliography, 1932–1942* (New York, 1945), H. L. Roberts, ed., *Foreign Affairs Bibliography, 1942–1952* (New York, 1955), and *Foreign Affairs Bibliography, 1952–1962* (New York, 1965). Detailed surveys of events year by year are given for France, in *L'Année politique économique, sociale et diplomatique en France* (Paris, 1946–), which is a model yearbook; for Britain in the *Annual Register* (London, 1758–); for Italy in *L'Annuario politico italiano* (Milan, 1964–). Comparable volumes are badly needed for other countries, particularly for the United States, but world events can be pieced together by use of the loose-leaf *Keesing's Contemporary Archives,* or *Facts on File.* The *Political Handbook of the World,* published annually by the Council on Foreign Relations, gives a short, factual survey of cabinets, parliaments, parties, and the press of all countries. *The Statesman's Yearbook* is a famous reference book giving more detailed data on each country's political and economic system. Authoritative articles on recent events will be found in *International Affairs*, published in London by the Royal Institute of International Affairs and in *Foreign Affairs*. The behavioral scientist's approach to international relations can be sampled in *World Politics*, especially in the important issue of October 1961 devoted to systems theory.

I. THE ORIGINS OF THE SECOND WORLD WAR

Good surveys of the interwar years are: G. M. Gathorne-Hardy, *A Short History of International Affairs, 1920–1939* (London, 1950); E. H. Carr, *The Twenty Years' Crisis 1919–1939* (London, 1939); Elizabeth Wiskemann, *Europe of the Dictators, 1919–1945* (New York, 1966); A. J. P. Taylor, *From Sarajevo to Potsdam* (New York, 1966); and Maurice Baumont, *La Faillite de la Paix, 1918–1936* (Paris, 1946). Gordon A. Craig and Felix Gilbert, eds., *The Diplomats* (New York, 1963) has excellent essays on interwar diplomatic leaders.

The classic denunciation of the Treaty of Versailles is John Maynard Keynes, *The Economic Consequences of the Peace* (New York, 1920), which still sparkles today, although Keynes's conclusions have been cogently questioned by Étienne Mantoux, *The Carthaginian Peace* (New York, 1952). Paul Birdsall presents a balanced account of the peace conference in *Versailles Twenty Years After* (New York, 1941).

The birth of the new states of Eastern Europe is described in Ivo J. Lederer, *Yugoslavia at the Paris Peace Conference: A Study in Frontiermaking* (New Haven, 1963); Nina Almond and Ralph H. Lutz, *The Treaty of Saint-Germain* (Stanford, 1935); Thomas G. Masaryk, *The Making of a State* (New York, 1927); and Hugh Seton-Watson, *Eastern Europe between the Wars* (Cambridge, 1946).

On the Russian revolution, see the standard work by E. H. Carr, *A History of Soviet Russia* (New York, 1951–64). The relations of Lenin, Trotsky, and Stalin before the revolution are analyzed by Bertram D. Wolfe, *Three Who Made a Revolution* (New York, 1960). Isaac Deutscher's biographies, *Stalin: A Political Biography* (New York, 1949) and, on Trotsky, *The Prophet Armed: Trotsky, 1879–1921* (New York, 1954), *The Prophet Unarmed: Trotsky, 1921–1929* (New York, 1959), and *The Prophet Outcast: Trotsky, 1929–1940* (New York, 1963) are first-rate. Lenin's belief that the revolution would spread westward in the aftermath of the war led him into a diplomatic duel with Wilson, described in Arno Mayer, *Political Origins of the New Diplomacy, 1917–1918* (New Haven, 1959) for the allegiance of the peoples of Eastern Europe. On the attempt to foment revolution in Germany, see Ruth Fischer, *Stalin and German Communism: A Study in the Origins of the State Party* (Cambridge, Mass., 1948); on the Comintern, see Franz Borkenau, *World Communism: A History of the Communist International* (Ann Arbor, 1962). Merle Fainsod, *How Russia Is Ruled* (rev. ed.,

Cambridge, Mass., 1965) is the basic account of the Soviet political system; economic development is described in Maurice Dobb, *Soviet Economic Development since 1917* (London, 1960) and Harry Schwartz, *Russia's Soviet Economy* (Englewood Cliffs, N. J., 1961).

Major documents of both communism and fascism are compiled in Michael Oakeshott, *Social and Political Doctrines of Contemporary Europe* (Cambridge, 1939). Anti-Fascist accounts of Mussolini's Italy are presented by Gaetano Salvemini, *Under the Axe of Fascism* (New York, 1936) and Herman Finer, *Mussolini's Italy* (New York, 1935); perceptive biographies of the Duce are Sir Ivone Kirkpatrick's, *Mussolini: A Study in Power* (New York, 1964) and Laura Fermi's *Mussolini* (Chicago, 1961). Far better is Alan Bullock's *Hitler: A Study in Tyranny* (New York, 1962). A useful symposium on Nazi Germany was published under the auspices of UNESCO, Maurice Baumont *et al., The Third Reich* (New York, 1955), the German contributions being particularly revealing. Nazi theory is best studied in Adolf Hitler, *Mein Kampf* (New York, 1939) and Rohan d'O. Butler, *The Roots of National Socialism* (London, 1941), and Nazi practice in Franz Neumann, *Behemoth: The Structure and Practice of National Socialism* (New York, 1944) and Eugen Kogon, *The Theory and Practice of Hell* (New York, 1950).

The policy of the United States during the interwar years is sharply criticized in William Appleman Williams, *The Tragedy of American Diplomacy* (New York, 1962), and more calmly discussed in Selig Adler, *The Uncertain Giant: 1921–1941; American Foreign Policy Between the Wars* (New York, 1965) and Jean-Baptiste Duroselle, *From Wilson to Roosevelt: Foreign Policy of the United States, 1913–1945* (Cambridge, Mass., 1963). Britain's economic problems are succinctly described in W. Arthur Lewis, *Economic Survey, 1919–1939* (London, 1949), and its social divisions in the first volume of Alan Bullock's life of the future foreign minister, *The Life and Times of Ernest Bevin* (London, 1960). Conservative foreign policy is indicted by A. L. Rowse in his scintillating *Appeasement: A Study in Political Decline, 1933–39* (New York, 1963) and by Sir Lewis Namier, in *Diplomatic Prelude, 1938–39* (London, 1948) and in *Europe in Decay: A Study in Disintegration* (London, 1950). Chamberlain's policy is mildly defended by Keith G. Feiling's, *The Life of Neville Chamberlain* (London, 1946), and explained by F. S. Northedge, *The Troubled Giant: Britain among the Great Powers, 1916–1939* (New York, 1966). The weakness of France is chronicled by British journalist Alexander Werth in *France in Ferment* (London, 1934) and *The Twilight of France, 1934–1940* (London, 1942). Charles A. Micaud, *The French Right and Nazi Germany, 1933–39* (Durham, N. C., 1943) explains the appeal of appeasement; the weakness of the French elites is seen by Marc Bloch as the cause of the French collapse in 1940, in *Strange Defeat* (New York, 1949). Léon Blum is admirably characterized in Joel Colton, *Léon Blum: Humanist in Politics* (New York, 1966).

For general histories of Asia in the interwar years, see Indian historian

K. M. Panikkar, *Asia and Western Dominance* (London, 1953); Kenneth S. Latourette, *A Short History of the Far East* (New York, 1964); and Claude A. Buss, *The Far East* (New York, 1955). C. P. Fitzgerald, *The Birth of Communist China* (London, 1964), by an outstanding Australian Sinologist, is excellent. A good short history of recent Japan, by a Harvard historian turned ambassador, is Erwin O. Reischauer, *The United States and Japan* (Cambridge, Mass., 1957); another reliable general survey is Hugh Borton, *Japan's Modern Century* (New York, 1955). Stewart C. Easton competently describes the last century and a half of Western colonialism in *The Twilight of European Colonialism* (New York, 1960) and *The Rise and Fall of Western Colonialism* (New York, 1964). On the British Commonwealth, see Nicholas Mansergh, *Survey of British Commonwealth Affairs: Problems of External Policy, 1931–1939* (London, 1952); on French Indochina, see John F. Cady, *Southeast Asia: Its Historical Development* (New York, 1964); on the Dutch East Indies (Indonesia), see L. H. Palmier, *Indonesia and the Dutch* (London, 1962). Two classic condemnations of colonialism are required reading for an understanding of the colonial revolt: John A. Hobson, *Imperialism: A Study* (London, 1902; rev. ed., 1938) and V. I. Lenin, *Imperialism: The Highest Stage of Capitalism* (rev. ed., New York, 1934).

Germany's relations with Italy during the 1930's are soundly analyzed in Elizabeth Wiskemann, *The Rome-Berlin Axis* (New York, 1949); with Japan, by Ernest L. Presseisen, *Germany and Japan* (The Hague, 1958); with Russia, in E. H. Carr, *German-Soviet Relations Between the Two World Wars, 1919–1939* (Baltimore, 1951); with Britain and France, in William M. Jordan, *Great Britain, France, and the German Problem, 1919–1939* (New York, 1943) and Arnold Wolfers, *Britain and France Between Two Wars* (New York, 1940). Hugh Thomas, *The Spanish Civil War* (New York, 1961) is magnificently written; the political intricacies of the conflict are analyzed in Gerald Brenan, *The Spanish Labyrinth* (New York, 1943) and David T. Cattell, *Communism and the Spanish Civil War* (Berkeley, Calif., 1955). The American attitude to the coming conflict is studied in William L. Langer and S. Everett Gleason, *The Challenge to Isolation, 1937–1940* (New York, 1952) and *The Undeclared War, 1940–41* (New York, 1953).

Stimulating reappraisals of the causes of the Second World War are to be found in A. J. P. Taylor, *The Origins of the Second World War* (New York, 1962) and Burton H. Klein, *Germany's Economic Preparations for War* (Cambridge, Mass., 1959). Both should be approached with a salutary cynicism.

II. THE TRIUMPHS OF THE AXIS, 1939–42

GENERAL: Winston Churchill and Charles de Gaulle have written accounts of the war and of the part they played, which are literary masterpieces; the former's is the six--volume *The Second World War* (Boston, 1948–53), and the latter's is the three-volume *War Memoirs* (New York, 1958–60). Other useful memoirs by participants are Dwight D. Eisenhower, *Crusade in Europe* (New York, 1948); Viscount Montgomery of Alamein, *Memoirs* (Cleveland, 1958); Marshal Jean de Lattre de Tassigny, *The History of the French First Army* (London, 1952). Two good short secondary accounts are Cyril Falls, *The Second World War: A Short History* (London, 1948) and F. J. C. Fuller, *The Second World War, 1939–1945: A Strategical and Tactical History* (New York, 1949).

NAZI VICTORIES, *1939–41:* The partition of Poland by Germany and Russia is described in Gerhard L. Weinberg, *Germany and the Soviet Union, 1939–41* (Leiden, 1954); the Russo-Finnish War in C. Leonard Lundin, *Finland in the Second World War* (Bloomington, Ind., 1957) and John H. Wuorinen, *Finland and World War II, 1939–1944* (New York, 1948); and the campaigns against Norway, Denmark, and Western Europe in Arnold and Veronica M. Toynbee, eds., *The Initial Triumph of the Axis* (London, 1958), which is part of the invaluable war coverage of the *Survey of International Affairs* published by the Royal Institute of International Affairs. The reasons for the fall of France in 1940 have been much debated. Paul Reynaud's own account of how it happened is given in *In the Thick of the Fight, 1930–1945* (New York, 1955), while the attitude of Pétain and Weygand is justified in Jacques Benoist-Méchin, *Sixty Days That Shook the West* (London, 1963).

BATTLE OF BRITAIN: On the projected invasion of Britain, see Ronald Wheatley, *Operation Sea Lion* (Oxford, 1958) and Walter Ansel, *Hitler Confronts England* (Durham, N.C., 1960); on the air battles, see Basil Collier, *The Battle of Britain* (London, 1962).

CONQUEST OF THE BALKANS AND THE INVASION OF RUSSIA: On the advance through the Balkans, see C. A. Macartney and W. W. Palmer, *Independent Eastern Europe: A History* (London, 1962), and through Russia, see Trumbull Higgins, *Hitler and Russia: The Third Reich in a Two-Front War, 1937–1943* (New York, 1966). British journalist Alexander Werth, who was in Russia during most of the war, gives a detailed, lively account in *Russia at War, 1941–1945* (New York, 1964). The sufferings of the German soldiers at Stalingrad are still vivid in *Last Letters from Stalingrad* (New York, 1962) and of Russian soldiers in Mikhail Soloviev's *My Nine Lives in the Red Army* (London, 1956).

FROM PEARL HARBOR TO MIDWAY: Japanese political struggles are elucidated in the important study by Robert J. C. Butow, *Togo and the Coming of the War* (Princeton, 1961), while the controversy over Pearl Harbor, raised in Charles A. Beard's impassioned *President Roosevelt and the Coming of the War, 1941* (New Haven, 1948), is temperately reviewed in Roberta Wohlstetter, *Pearl Harbor: Warning and Decision* (Stanford, 1962). The American road to war is charted by Herbert Feis, *The Road to Pearl Harbor* (Princeton, 1950) and William L. Langer and S. Elliott Gleason, *The Un-*

declared War, 1940–1941 (New York, 1953). For a robust history of the Pacific campaigns, see Samuel E. Morison, *The Two-Ocean War* (Boston, 1963).

FORMATION AND AIMS OF THE GRAND ALLIANCE: Wartime relations of the three major allies are described, with wide documentation, in Herbert Feis, *Churchill, Roosevelt, Stalin: The War They Waged and the Peace They Sought* (Princeton, 1957) and William H. McNeill, *America, Britain and Russia: Their Co-operation and Conflict, 1941–1946* (London, 1953). Robert Sherwood uses the role of Roosevelt's confidant, Harry Hopkins, as a means of portraying intimately the diplomatic background in *Roosevelt and Hopkins* (New York, 1950). A rather controversial account of the Casablanca Conference is given by Anne Armstrong, *Unconditional Surrender: The Impact of the Casablanca Policy upon World War II* (New Brunswick, N.J., 1961). For a heavily documented account of British policy, see Sir Llewellyn Woodward, *British Foreign Policy in the Second World War* (London, 1962).

III. THE AXIS NEW ORDER IN EUROPE AND ASIA

WARTIME GERMANY: On conditions in Germany, see William L. Shirer, *Berlin Diary* (New York, 1941) and *The Rise and Fall of the Third Reich* (New York, 1960). A French journalist, Georges Blond, described the chaos of the last few months of the war in *The Death of Hitler's Germany* (New York, 1954); H. R. Trevor-Roper, *The Last Days of Hitler* (New York, 1962) makes fascinating reading. Economic policy is analyzed in Karl Brandt, *Germany's Agricultural and Food Policies in World War II* (Stanford, 1953). On the treatment of the Jews, see Gerald Reitlinger, *The Final Solution: The Attempt to Exterminate the Jews of Europe, 1939–1945* (New York, 1953) and Raul Hilberg, *The Destruction of the European Jews* (Chicago, 1961); on the German resistance, a standard short account is Hans Rothfels' *German Opposition to Hitler* (Chicago, 1948). A masterly account of the role of the army in the German state is John W. Wheeler-Bennett's *The Nemesis of Power: The German Army in Politics, 1918–1945* (New York, 1954). Eugene Davidson sketches biographies of the major Nazi leaders in *The Trial of the Germans: Nuremberg, 1945–1946* (New York, 1966).

WARTIME ITALY: Mussolini's subordination to Hitler is documented in F. W. Deakin's *The Brutal Friendship: Mussolini, Hitler and the Fall of Italian Fascism* (New York, 1962) and in the diary of Foreign Minister Count Galeazzo Ciano, *The Ciano Diaries, 1939–1943* (New York, 1945). Norman Kogan's *Italy and the Allies* (Cambridge, Mass., 1956) deals with the Badoglio and Bonomi governments' difficulties after the fall of Mussolini. On the Italian resistance movement, see Charles F. Delzell's authoritative survey, *Mussolini's Enemies: The Italian Anti-Fascist Resistance* (Princeton, 1961).

WESTERN EUROPE UNDER THE NAZI YOKE: Arnold and Veronica M. Toynbee, eds., *Hitler's Europe* (London, 1954) is first-rate. For more detailed treatment, see Werner Warmbrunn, *The Dutch under German Occupation* (Stanford, 1963) and Jan A. Goris, ed., *Belgium under Occupation* (New York, 1947). Robert Aron's, *The Vichy Regime, 1940–1944* (New York, 1956), in spite of its irritating style, provides much useful information on the Pétain administration, as does the similarly frustrating grab-bag by Alexander Werth, *France, 1940–1955* (New York, 1956). Paul Farmer's *Vichy: Political Dilemma* (New York, 1955) is better organized but lacks immediacy. Robert O. Paxton uses much new material in *Parades and Politics at Vichy: The French Officer Corps under Marshal Pétain* (Princeton, 1966). De Gaulle's early career and the founding of the Free French are well described in Paul-Marie de la Gorce, *De Gaulle entre deux mondes: Une Vie et une époque* (Paris, 1964) and in a deliciously adulatory reminiscence by François Mauriac, *De Gaulle* (Paris, 1964). David Thomson, *Two Frenchmen: Laval and De Gaulle* (London, 1951) thinks de Gaulle was a revolutionary Jacobin. Arthur L. Funk, *Charles de Gaulle: The Crucial Years, 1943–1944* (Norman, Okla., 1959) explains the mutual incomprehension of de Gaulle and Roosevelt. Henri Michel, *Histoire de la résistance* (Paris, 1950) provides an admirable little survey of the French underground. No one should miss reading the superb sketches of de Gaulle by underground leader Emmanuel d'Astier, *Seven Times Seven Days* (London, 1958).

EASTERN EUROPE: Hugh Seton-Watson, *The East European Revolution* (New York, 1956) gives a comprehensive and thoroughly reliable account of Eastern Europe from 1939 to 1955. Robert L. Wolff, *The Balkans in Our Time* (Cambridge, Mass., 1956) provides a basic survey. On individual countries, the best works deal with Poland. The Warsaw uprising is described by its leader, T. Bor-Komorowski, *The Secret Army* (London, 1951); the leader of the London Poles, Stanislas Mikolajczyk, tells his story in *The Rape of Poland: Pattern of Soviet Aggression* (New York, 1948); the diplomatic tangle over Poland is unraveled by Edward J. Rozek, *Allied Wartime Diplomacy: A Pattern in Poland* (New York, 1951). On Greece, during world war and the civil war several incisive studies are available: William H. McNeill, *The Greek Dilemma: War and Aftermath* (Philadelphia, 1947); L. S. Stavrianos, *Greece: American Dilemma and Opportunity* (Chicago, 1952); Edgar O'Ballance, *The Greek Civil War, 1944–49* (New York, 1966); and Bickham Sweet-Escott's analysis for the Royal Institute of International Affairs, *Greece: A Political and Economic Survey, 1939–1953* (London, 1954). The atmosphere of wartime Yugoslavia is ably re-created in Brigadier Fitzroy Maclean's life of Tito, *The Heretic* (New York, 1957) and in Stephen Clissold, *Whirlwind: An Account of Marshal Tito's Rise to Power* (New York, 1949). Alexander Dallin's *German Rule in Russia, 1941–1965* (London, 1957) is indispensable.

THE GREATER EAST ASIA CO-PROSPERITY SPHERE: On Japanese occupation policies, see: F. C. Jones, *Japan's New Order in East Asia: Its Rise and*

Fall, 1937–45 (Cambridge, Mass., 1953); F. C. Jones, Hugh Borton, and B. R. Pearn, *The Far East, 1942–1946* (London, 1955); and Harry J. Benda, *The Crescent and the Rising Sun: Indonesian Islam Under the Japanese Occupation, 1942–1945* (The Hague, 1958). The rise of nationalism in the Japanese-occupied colonies of the European powers is detailed in Willard H. Elsbree, *Japan's Role in Southeast Asian Nationalist Movements, 1940 to 1945* (Cambridge, Mass., 1953).

IV. THE DEFEAT OF THE AXIS POWERS, 1943–45

THE ALLIED OFFENSIVE IN EUROPE: Interesting memoirs by German officers include: Erich von Manstein, *Lost Victories* (Chicago, 1958); Hans Speidel, *Invasion 1944* (Chicago, 1950); Heinz Guderian, *Panzer Leader* (New York, 1952). Cornelius Ryan's *The Longest Day: June 6, 1944* (New York, 1959) vividly re-creates the minutiae of D-Day. The Soviet view is presented in Mathew P. Gallagher, *The Soviet History of World War II: Myths, Memories, and Realities* (New York, 1963). Chester Wilmot, *The Struggle for Europe* (New York, 1952), by an Australian journalist, provides a detailed military and diplomatic history of the later stages of the war, with pronounced bias in favor of Churchill's proposed Balkan strategy.

THE DIPLOMATIC FRONT FROM TEHERAN TO POTSDAM: In addition to Herbert Feis's *Churchill, Roosevelt, Stalin,* see his *Between War and Peace: The Potsdam Conference* (Princeton, 1960). The U. S. State Department has published documentary collections on the major conferences: *The Conferences at Cairo and Teheran, 1943* (Washington, 1961), *The Conferences at Malta and Yalta, 1945* (Washington, 1955), and *The Conference of Berlin (The Potsdam Conference), 1945* (Washington, 1960). Works by participants in the conferences include: James F. Byrnes, *Speaking Frankly* (New York, 1947); Edward R. Stettinius, *Roosevelt and the Russians: The Yalta Conference* (New York, 1950); and Cordell Hull, *Memoirs* (New York, 1948). Two articles by Philip E. Mosely give the most coherent account of the negotiations on occupation boundaries in Germany: see his "The Occupation of Germany: New Light on How the Zones Were Drawn," *Foreign Affairs,* XXVIII (July 1950), 589–97 and "Dismemberment of Germany: The Allied Negotiations from Yalta to Potsdam," *Foreign Affairs,* XXVIII (April 1950), 487–98. The symposium edited by John L. Snell, *The Meaning of Yalta: Big Three Diplomacy and the New Balance of Power* (Baton Rouge, 1956), is illuminating, as is Snell's own study, *Wartime Origins of the East-West Dilemma over Germany* (New Orleans, 1959) and his short survey, *Illusion and Necessity: The Diplomacy of Global War, 1939–1945* (Boston, 1964).

THE DEFEAT OF JAPAN: Herbert Feis is again a sure guide, in *Japan Subdued: The Atomic Bomb and the End of the War in the Pacific* (Princeton, 1961). Robert J. C. Butow's *Japan's Decision to Surrender* (Stanford, 1954) is thoroughly documented.

V. THE OPENING OF THE COLD WAR IN
EUROPE AND ASIA, 1945–53

RESULTS OF THE WAR: On the refugee problem, see Malcolm J. Proud-foot, *European Refugees: A Study in Forced Population Movement* (London, 1957). The relief work of UNRRA is described in Arnold and Veronica M. Toynbee, eds., *The Realignment of Europe* (London, 1955), which also gives a comprehensive account of the political transformation of the continental European states in the last months of the war.

THE OPENING OF THE COLD WAR: On Stalin's postwar foreign policy, see: Marshall D. Shulman, *Stalin's Foreign Policy Reappraised* (Cambridge, Mass., 1963); J. M. Mackintosh, *Strategy and Tactics of Soviet Foreign Policy* (New York, 1962), a good survey from 1944 to 1961; collected essays of Philip E. Mosely, *The Kremlin and World Politics* (New York, 1960). On American policy, see Harry S Truman, *Memoirs* (New York, 1955–56); Martin F. Herz, *Beginnings of the Cold War* (Bloomington, Ind., 1966); Richard L. Walker, *E. R. Stettinius*, George Curry, *James F. Byrnes* (New York, 1965), both in one volume; and George F. Kennan, *American Diplomacy* (Chicago, 1951). On British policy, see Matthew A. Fitzsimons, *The Foreign Policy of the British Labour Government, 1945–51* (Notre Dame, Ind., 1953); Leon Epstein, *Britain—Uneasy Ally* (Chicago, 1954); and C. M. Woodhouse, *British Foreign Policy Since the Second World War* (London, 1961); on French policy, see Alfred Grosser, *La IVᵉ République et sa politique étrangère* (Paris, 1961).

The making of the satellite peace treaties is adequately covered in Amelia C. Leiss and Raymond Dennett, eds., *European Peace Treaties after World War II* (Boston, 1954). A largely economic appraisal of the Marshall Plan is given by Harry B. Price, *The Marshall Plan and Its Meaning* (Ithaca, 1955). Marshall's diplomacy is reviewed in Robert Ferrell, *George C. Marshall* (New York, 1965). On NATO, see Lord Ismay, *NATO: The First Five Years, 1949–1954* (Utrecht, 1954) and Alvin J. Cottrell and James E. Dougherty, *The Politics of the Atlantic Alliance* (New York, 1964).

DECOLONIZATION IN ASIA, 1945–1949: British Prime Minister Clement Attlee chats briefly about presiding over the dissolution of the British Empire in *Twilight of Empire* (New York, 1962). On the end of British India, see Michael Edwardes, *The Last Years of British India* (London, 1963); W. Norman Brown, *The United States and India and Pakistan* (Cambridge, Mass., 1953); A. K. Majumdar, *Advent of Independence* (Bombay, 1963); and Ian Stephens, *Pakistan: Old Country New Nation* (London, 1963). On the other British colonies in Asia, see Frank N. Trager, *Burma—From Kingdom to Republic: A Historical and Political Analysis* (New York, 1966), and the excellent study by the Smuts Professor of Commonwealth History at Cambridge, Nicholas Mansergh, in: *Survey of British Commonwealth Affairs: Problems of War-time Co-operation and Post-War Change* (London,

1958). The achievement of Indonesian independence is covered in detail in the Royal Institute of International Affairs's annual *Survey of International Affairs* and in Palmier's *Indonesia and the Dutch,* cited earlier. The evolution of Dutch thinking on decolonization is exhaustively chronicled in Arend Lijphart, *The Trauma of Decolonization: The Dutch and West New Guinea* (New Haven, 1966). On the sufferings of Indochina, see Brian Crozier's brilliant little paperback, *South-East Asia in Turmoil* (London; 1965) and his earlier study, *The Rebels* (London, 1960).

The rise of communism in East and Southeast Asia is documented in J. H. Brimmel, *Communism in South-East Asia* (Oxford, 1961); Gene D. Overstreet and Marshall Windmiller, *Communism in India* (Berkeley, Calif., 1959); Frank N. Trager, *Marxism in Southeast Asia: A Study of Four Countries* (Stanford, 1959), which deals with Indonesia, Vietnam, Thailand, and Burma; Arnold C. Brackman, *Indonesian Communism: A History* (New York, 1963); Donald Hindley, *The Communist Party in Indonesia, 1951–1963* (Berkeley, Calif., 1964); and Ruth T. McVey, *The Rise of Indonesian Communism* (Ithaca, 1965).

COMMUNIST VICTORY IN CHINA; KOREAN WAR; FRENCH DEFEAT IN VIETNAM: Indispensable reading: Mao Tse-tung, *On Guerrilla Warfare* (New York, 1961) and Vo Nguyen Giap, *People's War, People's Army: The Viet Cong Insurrection Manual for Underdeveloped Countries* (New York, 1962), which are well-tried prescriptions for victory in "revolutionary war." On the Communist victory in China, see: Herbert Feis, *The China Tangle* (Princeton, 1953); U.S. State Department, *United States Relations with China, with Special Reference to the Period 1944–1949* (Washington, 1949); and Robert C. North, *Moscow and the Chinese Communists* (Stanford, 1953). For the Korean War, consult R. Leckie, *Conflict: The History of the Korean War, 1950–1953* (New York, 1962) and William H. Vatcher, Jr., *Panmunjon: The Story of the Korean Military Armistice Negotiations* (New York, 1958). On the French defeat in Indochina, see the documentary collection edited by Allan B. Cole, *Conflict in Indo-China and International Repercussions, 1945–1955* (Ithaca, 1956); Bernard Fall, *The Two Viet-Nams* (2nd ed., New York, 1963); Ellen J. Hammer, *The Struggle for Indo-China* (Stanford, 1954); and Donald Lancaster, *The Emancipation of French Indochina* (London, 1961).

VI. and VIII. DIVIDED EUROPE, 1945–53; THE RESURGENCE OF THE EUROPEAN NATIONS, 1953–60

For bibliographical purposes, the chapters dealing with internal events in the individual European countries have been grouped together.

SOVIET UNION FROM STALIN TO KHRUSHCHEV: Soviet politics and government are ably presented in: John A. Armstrong, *The Politics of Totalitarianism: The Communist Party of the Soviet Union from 1934 to the Present* (New York, 1961); Zbigniew K. Brzezinski, *The Permanent Purge:*

Politics in Soviet Totalitarianism (Cambridge, Mass., 1956); W. W. Kulski, *The Soviet Regime—Communism in Practice* (Syracuse, 1959); Julian Towster, *Political Power in the U.S.S.R., 1917–1947* (New York, 1948); and particularly in Merle Fainsod, *How Russia Is Ruled* (rev. ed., Cambridge, Mass., 1965). The transition after Stalin's death is covered soundly by Wolfgang Leonhard, *The Kremlin Since Stalin* (New York, 1962) and by Edward Crankshaw, *Khrushchev's Russia* (London, 1959). On Khrushchev, see: Lazar Pistrak, *The Grand Tactician: Khrushchev's Rise to Power* (New York, 1961); Bertram D. Wolfe, *Khrushchev and Stalin's Ghost* (New York, 1957), which analyzes the "secret speech" to the Twentieth Party Congress; Konrad Kellen, *Khrushchev: A Political Portrait* (New York, 1961); and Edward Crankshaw, *Khrushchev: A Career* (New York, 1966). Robert Conquest analyzes the circumstances of Khrushchev's fall in *Russia after Khrushchev* (New York, 1965).

On the Soviet economy, consult: Walt W. Rostow *et al., The Dynamics of Soviet Society* (New York, 1953); Harry Schwartz, *Russia's Soviet Economy* (rev. ed., Englewood Cliffs, N. J., 1961); Alec Nove, *The Soviet Economy: An Introduction* (New York, 1961).

SOVIET SATELLITES IN EASTERN EUROPE: The standard work covering 1945–60, with stress on bloc ideology, is Zbigniew K. Brzezinski, *The Soviet Bloc: Unity and Conflict* (New York, 1961). The later chapters of Hugh Seton-Watson, *The East European Revolution* (New York, 1956) cover the Communist seizure of power. Other general studies of the whole area include: Richard V. Burks, *The Dynamics of Communism in Eastern Europe* (Princeton, 1961); Nicholas Spulber, *The Economics of Communist Eastern Europe* (New York, 1957); Stephen D. Kertescz, ed., *East Central Europe and the World* (Notre Dame, Ind., 1962); and Stephen A. Fischer-Galati, ed., *Eastern Europe in the Sixties* (New York, 1963), an unusual attempt at "area" analysis. Michael Kaser's *Comecon: Integration Problems of the Planned Economies* (London, 1965) is sound and factual.

On POLAND, see: Oscar Halecki, ed., *Poland* (New York, 1957), for reference; Richard Hiscocks, *Poland: Bridge for the Abyss?* (London, 1963), thoroughly useful; Hansjakab Stehle, *The Independent Satellite: Society and Politics in Poland since 1945* (New York, 1965); and Richard Staar, *Poland 1944–1962: The Sovietization of a Captive People* (Baton Rouge, 1962), which concentrates on political organization. On HUNGARY, see: Ernst C. Helmreich, ed., *Hungary* (New York, 1957), for reference; Paul E. Zinner, *Revolution in Hungary* (New York, 1962), the best account of the Hungarian uprising; Paul Kecskemeti, *The Unexpected Revolution: Social Forces in the Hungarian Uprising* (Stanford, 1961); Ferenc A. Váli, *Rift and Revolt in Hungary* (Cambridge, Mass., 1961), which covers the years 1945–61. On CZECHOSLOVAKIA, see: Joseph Korbel, *The Communist Subversion of Czechoslovakia, 1938–1948: The Failure of Coexistence* (Princeton, 1959) and Edward Taborsky, *Communism in Czechoslovakia, 1948–1960* (Princeton, 1961). On RUMANIA, see: Stephen Fischer-Galati, ed., *Rumania* (New York, 1957), for reference; Ghita Ionescu, *Commu-*

nism in Rumania (London, 1964); and David Floyd, *Rumania: Russia's Dissident Ally* (New York, 1965), a useful explanation of Rumania's evolution toward national autonomy. On BULGARIA, see: L. A. D. Dellin, ed., *Bulgaria* (New York, 1957). On ALBANIA, see: Stavro Skendi, ed., *Albania* (New York, 1956) and Harry Hamm, *Albania—China's Beachhead in Europe* (New York, 1963).

GERMANY UNDER OCCUPATION: Beate Ruhm von Oppen has edited an excellent collection of documents for the Royal Institute of International Affairs, entitled *Documents on Germany Under Occupation, 1945–1954* (London, 1955). Also valuable are volumes VI–VIII of the German documentary collection edited by Johannes Hohlfeld, *Dokumente der deutschen Politik und Geschichte von 1848 bis zur Gegenwart* (Berlin, n.d.). Of the few attempts to write a history of the four-power occupation as a whole, the best is Michael Balfour and John Mair, *Four-Power Control in Germany and Austria, 1945–1946* (London, 1956). Most works on the American zone of occupation were polemics by disillusioned military government officers; one can more profitably consult Eugene Davidson, *The Death and Life of Germany: An Account of the American Occupation* (New York, 1959); Harold Zink, *The United States in Germany* (Princeton, 1957); Hajo Holborn, *American Military Government: Its Organization and Policies* (New York, 1947); and especially General Lucius D. Clay's excellent memoir, *Decision in Germany* (New York, 1950). On the French zone, see F. Roy Willis, *The French in Germany, 1945–1949* (Stanford, 1962); and on the Soviet zone, J. P. Nettl, *The Eastern Zone and Soviet Policy in Germany, 1945–1950* (New York, 1951). On Berlin, see: Frank L. Howley, *Berlin Command* (New York, 1950), by the commander of the American sector; and W. Phillips Davison, *The Berlin Blockade: A Study in Cold War Politics* (Princeton, 1958). On the Four-Power occupation of Austria, consult William B. Bader, *Austria Between East and West, 1945–1955* (Stanford, 1966).

WEST GERMANY: Two good accounts of West Germany by British journalists are: Terence Prittie, *Germany Divided: The Legacy of the Nazi Era* (Boston, 1960) and Alistair Horne, *Return to Power: A Report on the New Germany* (New York, 1956). For two particularly good surveys by a French political scientist, see: Alfred Grosser, *La Démocratie de Bonn* (Paris, 1958) and a much shorter, updated English version, *The Federal Republic of Germany: A Concise History* (New York, 1963). Richard Hiscocks comments on West German political and economic development in *The Adenauer Era* (Philadelphia, 1966). Two studies explain the creation of the West German Republic: John F. Golay, *The Founding of the Federal Republic of Germany* (Chicago, 1958) and Peter H. Merkl, *The Origin of the West German Republic* (New York, 1963). Ludwig Erhard has commented on the economic miracle in *Germany's Comeback in the World Market* (New York, 1953) and in *Prosperity Through Competition* (New York, 1958); his economic views are endorsed by Patrick Madigan Boarman, *Germany's Economic Dilemma: Inflation and the Balance of Pay-*

ments (New Haven, 1964); Konrad Adenauer, aged ninety, has published the first volume of his acute and caustic *Memoirs* (New York, 1966); Adenauer's ablest opponent, SPD leader Kurt Schumacher, is portrayed in Lewis J. Edinger, *Kurt Schumacher: A Study in Personality and Political Behavior* (Stanford, 1965), and his party in D. Childs, *From Schumacher to Brandt* (Long Island City, 1966). The Saar problem is well synthesized by Jacques Freymond, *The Saar Conflict 1945–1955* (New York, 1960), which summarizes the findings of an international group of political scientists. On German foreign policy, see: Hans Speier and W. Phillips Davison, eds., *West German Leadership and Foreign Policy* (Evanston, Ill., 1957); Wolfram F. Hanrieder, *West German Foreign Policy, 1929–1963: International Pressure and Domestic Response* (Stanford, 1967); and F. Roy Willis, *France, Germany and the New Europe, 1945–1963* (Stanford, 1965). A good study of East Germany is badly needed.

FRANCE: See the studies of de Gaulle listed under Chapter II, and the bibliography to F. Roy Willis, ed., *De Gaulle: Anachronism, Realist or Prophet?* (New York, 1966). On the Fourth Republic, see the standard work by English political scientist Philip Williams, *Crisis and Compromise: Politics in the Fourth Republic* (Hamden, Conn., 1964); Jacques Fauvet, *La IVᵉ République* (Paris, 1959), by a leading Parisian political commentator; and George Lichtheim, *Marxism in Modern France* (New York, 1966). For suggestive interpretations of the weakness of the Fourth Republic, see: Herbert Lüthy, *France Against Herself* (New York, 1955); Ronald Mathews, *The Death of the Fourth Republic* (New York, 1954); John Stewart Ambler, *The French Army in Politics, 1945–1962* (Columbus, Ohio, 1966); and the essays collected in Stanley Hoffmann *et al.*, *In Search of France* (Cambridge, Mass., 1963). On the fall of the Fourth Republic, James H. Meisel gives a vigorous account in *The Fall of the Republic: Military Revolt in France* (Ann Arbor, 1962), while Philip Williams and Martin Harrison unravel the complex pattern of Algerian events in *De Gaulle's Republic* (London, 1961). On the Fifth Republic, see: Roy C. Macridis and Bernard E. Brown, *The de Gaulle Republic: Quest for Unity* (Homewood, Ill., 1960) and Dorothy Pickles, *The Fifth French Republic* (New York, 1962); and W. W. Kulski, *De Gaulle and the World: The Foreign Policy of the Fifth Republic* (Syracuse, 1966). The French system of economic planning is appreciatively analyzed in Andrew Shonfield's important study, *Modern Capitalism: The Changing Balance of Public and Private Power* (Oxford, 1965) and in J. and A.-M. Hackett, *Economic Planning in France* (London, 1963); the plight and prospects of the French peasant are described in Gordon Wright, *Rural Revolution in France* (Stanford, 1964).

ITALY: Three good surveys of the postwar years are: H. Stuart Hughes, *The United States and Italy* (Cambridge, Mass., 1965); Norman Kogan, *A Political History of Postwar Italy* (New York, 1966); and Giuseppe Mammarella, *Italy after Fascism: A Political History, 1943–1963* (Montreal, 1964), a series of lectures given at Stanford in Florence. On Italy's two most important parties, see: Mario Einaudi and François Goguel,

Christian Democracy in France and Italy (Ithaca, 1955) and Mario Einaudi, Jean-Marie Monenach, and Aldo Garosci, *Communism in Western Europe* (Ithaca, 1951). Italian pressure groups can be studied in Joseph La Palombara, *Interest Groups in Italian Politics* (Princeton, 1964) and Norman Kogan, *The Politics of Italian Foreign Policy* (New York, 1963). The problem of the south is best understood by reading Danilo Dolci's *Report from Palermo* (New York, 1959) and Carlo Levi, *Christ Stopped at Eboli* (New York, 1963). For more factual treatment, see: Sergio Barzanti, *The Underdeveloped Areas Within the Common Market* (Princeton, 1965); Muriel Grindrod, *The Rebuilding of Italy: Economics and Politics, 1945–1955* (London, 1955); and Vera Lutz, *Italy: A Study in Economic Development* (London, 1962).

BENELUX: There are no good histories in English of postwar Belgium, the Netherlands, or Luxembourg. For an excellent economic study of Benelux, see: J. E. Meade, H. H. Liesner, and S. J. Wells, *Case Studies in European Union: The Mechanics of Integration* (Oxford, 1962).

THE PAPACY: Non-polemical literature on the nature of the Papacy is scarce. Carlo Falconi, an avowed critic, is nevertheless informative if one-sided in *I Papi del ventesimo secolo* (Rome, 1967) and *Il Pentagono vaticano* (Bari, 1958). A. Carlo Jemolo's classic *Chiesa e stato in Italia negli ultimi cento anni* (Turin, 1952) unfortunately ends in 1948. Gianfranco Poggi, *Catholic Action in Italy: The Sociology of a Sponsored Organization* (Stanford, 1966), describes the major layman's movement. George Bull looks behind the scenes in *Vatican Politics at the Second Vatican Council, 1962–65* (New York, 1966). Indispensable to an understanding of the changing Papacy are the two great encyclicals, John XXIII's *Pacem in Terris* and Paul VI's *Populorum Progressio*.

BRITAIN: There are several good surveys: Francis Boyd, *British Politics in Transition, 1945–1963* (London, 1964); Alfred F. Havighurst, *Twentieth-Century Britain* (2nd ed., New York, 1966); and David Thomson, *England in the Twentieth Century* (London, 1965). British political life continues to be enriched by outstanding personalities. See: Michael Foot's first volume in his biography, *Aneurin Bevan* (London, 1962); Bullock's life of Bevin, cited earlier; Earl of Woolton, *Memoirs* (London, 1962) and *The Reckoning* (Boston, 1965). British economic planning does not get good marks in Andrew Shonfield, *British Economic Policy Since the War* (London, 1958); Shonfield, *Modern Capitalism*, cited above; and Samuel Brittan, *The Treasury Under the Tories, 1951–1964* (London, 1964). On nationalization of industry, see: A. A. Rogow, *The Labour Government and British Industry, 1945–1951* (Oxford, 1955); on nationalized medicine, see: Harry Eckstein, *The English Health Service: Its Origins, Structure and Achievements* (Cambridge, Mass., 1958). The defects of contemporary Britain are nicely characterized by Anthony Sampson, *Anatomy of Britain* (New York, 1962). The Commonwealth is discussed under Decolonization in Asia and Africa.

SCANDINAVIA: See two short surveys by American scholars: John H.

Wuorinen, *Scandinavia* (Englewood Cliffs, N.J., 1965), which has an excellent bibliography; and Franklin D. Scott, *The United States and Scandinavia* (Cambridge, Mass., 1950). On Finland, see Wuorinen's *A History of Finland* (New York, 1965).

THE ENDURING DICTATORSHIPS OF SPAIN AND PORTUGAL: Biographies of Franco and Salazar can hardly be impartial. Nevertheless, one might glance at S. F. A. Coles, *Franco of Spain* (London, 1955) and Christine Garnier, *Salazar* (New York, 1954), *faute de mieux*. Fortunately, Arthur P. Whitaker, *Spain and the Defense of the West: Ally and Liability* (New York, 1961), and Benjamin Welles, *Spain: The Gentle Anarchy* (New York, 1965) are very sound. Henrique Galvão gives a short sketch of the Salazar regime before describing how he hijacked the "Santa Maria," in *Santa Maria: My Crusade for Portugal* (Cleveland, 1961). Richard Pattee, *Portugal and the Portuguese World* (Milwaukee, 1957) gives detailed information on the Portuguese colonies.

VII. CRISES AND READJUSTMENT, 1953–60

THE MIDDLE EAST: Pierre Rondot, *The Changing Patterns of the Middle East* (New York, 1961) is a stimulating survey by a French scholar; Elizabeth Monroe, *Britain's Moment in the Middle East, 1914–1956* (Baltimore, 1963) presents an excellent analysis of British aims in the Arab world and of reasons for postwar failures. Another British scholar, George Kirk, draws on firsthand knowledge in *A Short History of the Middle East from the Rise of Islam to Modern Times* (6th ed., London, 1961) and in *Survey of International Affairs: The Middle East, 1945–1950* (Oxford, 1954). Sydney N. Fisher, *The Middle East, a History* (New York, 1959) is a good textbook. For a suggestive, journalistic discussion, see Jay Walz, *The Middle East* (New York, 1965). On the Suez crisis, see: Guy Wint and Peter Calvocoressi, *Middle East Crisis* (London, 1957). On Nasser's Egypt, see: Jean and Simon Lacouture, *Egypt in Transition* (New York, 1958) and Charles D. Cremeans, *The Arabs and the World: Nasser's Arab Nationalist Policy* (New York, 1963). On Soviet expansion into the Arab world, see: Walter Z. Lacqueur, *Communism and Nationalism in the Middle East* (New York, 1956) and *The Soviet Union and the Middle East* (New York, 1959). The Royal Institute of International Affairs in London has issued two penetrating essays on Arab politics, Patrick Searle, *The Struggle for Syria: A Study of Post-War Arab Politics* (New York, 1965), and Malcolm Kerr, *The Arab Cold War, 1958–1964: A Study of Ideology in Politics* (New York, 1965). A useful compendium on oil finances is Zuhayr Mikdashi, *A Financial Analysis of Middle Eastern Oil Concessions, 1901–1965* (New York, 1966).

CRISIS IN CENTRAL EUROPE: See books listed under Chapter VI and VIII under Soviet Satellites in Eastern Europe.

THE CONTINUING EAST-WEST CRISIS: BERLIN: East-West relations after the death of Stalin are discussed in: Jacques Freymond, *Western Europe since the War: A Short Political History* (New York, 1964); Frederick H. Hartmann, *Germany Between East and West: The Reunification Problem* (Englewood Cliffs, N.J., 1965); W. W. Kulski, *Peaceful Coexistence* (Chicago, 1959); Frederick L. Schuman, *The Cold War: Retrospect and Prospect* (Baton Rouge, 1962). On the Berlin crisis, see: John Mander, *Berlin: Hostage for the West* (London, 1962).

WESTERN EUROPEAN INTEGRATION: For a good over-all view, see: Richard Mayne, *The Community of Europe* (New York, 1962), by an associate of Jean Monnet; Ernst H. Van Der Beugel, *From Marshall Aid to Atlantic Partnership: European Integration as a Concern of American Foreign Policy* (New York, 1966); Michael Curtis, *Western European Integration* (New York, 1965); and Arnold J. Zurcher, *The Struggle to Unite Europe, 1940–1958* (New York, 1958), which contains a good survey of the federalist groups. On ECSC, see: Louis Lister, *Europe's Coal and Steel Community: An Experiment in Economic Cooperation* (New York, 1960), a mine of statistical information; Ernst B. Haas, *The Uniting of Europe: Political, Social and Economic Forces, 1950–1957* (Stanford, 1958); Stuart A. Scheingold, *The Rule of Law in European Integration* (New Haven, 1965), on the Court of Justice of ECSC; and William Diebold, Jr., *The Schuman Plan: A Study in Economic Cooperation* (New York, 1959). On EEC, see: Uwe Kitzinger, *The Politics and Economics of European Integration: Britain, Europe, and the United States* (New York, 1963); Michael Shanks and John Lambert, *The Common Market Today—and Tomorrow* (New York, 1963); and Emile Benoit, *Europe at Sixes and Sevens: The Common Market, The Free Trade Association, and the United States* (New York, 1961). On Britain's relations with EEC, see the masterly study by Miriam Camps, *Britain and the European Community, 1955–1963* (Princeton, 1964) and the scintillating attack on de Gaulle in Nora Beloff's *The General Says No* (London, 1963); and two careful studies of the impact on Commonwealth countries of possible membership in EEC, H. G. Gelber, *Australia, Britain and the EEC, 1961–1963* (New York, 1967), and Dharma Khumar, *India and the European Economic Community* (New York, 1966).

IX. THE BREAKING OF THE BLOCS, 1960–

INDEPENDENT STATES OF AFRICA: For a general survey of decolonization and its aftermath, see: John Hatch, *A History of Postwar Africa* (New York, 1965); Gwendolen M. Carter, *Independence for Africa* (New York, 1960); and Brian Crozier's vivid *The Morning After* (New York, 1963). On Pan-Africanism, see the works of Kwame Nkrumah, *I Speak of Freedom* (New York, 1961) and *Africa Must Unite* (New York, 1963); the highly critical study by Henry L. Bretton, *The Rise and Fall of Kwame Nkrumah: A Study of Personal Rule in Africa* (New York, 1966); and Claude E.

Welch, Jr., *Dream of Unity: Pan-Africanism and Political Unification in West Africa* (Ithaca, 1966), which shows that local forces are likely to remain stronger than the movement to unification. Useful for reference are Colin Legum's *Pan-Africanism: A Short Political Guide* (New York, 1965) and Helen Kitchen, ed., *A Handbook of African Affairs* (New York, 1964).

On West African states, see: David E. Apter, *Ghana in Transition* (New York, 1963); W. E. F. Ward, *A History of Ghana* (New York, 1963); John E. Flint, *Nigeria and Ghana* (Englewood Cliffs, N. J., 1966); and Frederick A. O. Schwarz, Jr., *Nigeria: The Tribes, the Nation, or the Race —The Politics of Independence* (Cambridge, Mass., 1965). On Central and East Africa, see: Richard Greenfield, *Ethiopia: A New Political History* (New York, 1965); I. M. Lewis, *The Modern History of Somaliland: From Nation to State* (New York, 1965); Michael F. Lofchie, *Zanzibar: Background to Revolution* (Princeton, 1965), the revolution in question being that of January 1964; Richard I. Rotberg, *The Rise of Nationalism in Central Africa: The Making of Malawi and Zambia, 1873–1964* (Cambridge, Mass., 1965), detailed and scholarly; Richard Hall, *Zambia* (New York, 1965); Colin Legum, *Congo Disaster* (London, 1961); Crawford Young, *Politics in the Congo: Decolonization and Independence* (Princeton, 1965), very reliable; Richard L. Sklar *et al.*, *National Unity and Regionalism in Eight African States: Nigeria; Niger; The Congo; Gabon; Central African Republic; Chad; Uganda; Ethiopia* (Ithaca, 1966); and Virginia Thompson and Richard Adloff, *The Malagasy Republic: Madagascar Today* (Stanford, 1965). South Africa is bitterly criticized in Brian Bunting, *The Rise of the South African Reich* (London, 1962), whereas John Cope, *South Africa* (New York, 1965) provides a sound introductory survey. Two interesting studies of the aftermath of colonialism are Richard Symonds' documented account of how the British prepared their colonial subjects for independence, *The British and Their Successors: A Study in the Development of the Government Services in the New States* (Evanston, Ill., 1966) and Teresa Hayter's study of the French aid program to its former colonies, *French Aid* (London, 1966). On the Arab states of North Africa, consult Charles A. Micaud, *Tunisia: The Politics of Modernization* (New York, 1964); Clement Henry Moore, *Tunisia since Independence: The Dynamics of One-Party Government* (Berkeley, Calif., 1965); Douglas E. Ashford, *Political Change in Morocco* (Princeton, 1961); Dorothy Pickles, *Algeria and France: From Colonialism to Cooperation* (New York, 1963); and David C. Gordon, *The Passing of French Algeria* (New York, 1966).

NEUTRALISM AND NONALIGNMENT: Theodore Geiger provides a wide survey in *The Conflicted Relationship: The West and the Transformation of Asia, Africa and Latin America* (New York, 1967). Two useful symposia are: Kurt London, ed., *New Nations in a Divided World: The International Relations of the Afro-Asian States* (New York, 1964), and Laurence W. Martin, *Neutralism and Nonalignment: The New States in World Affairs* (New York, 1962). For an Indian viewpoint, see G. H. Jansen, *Nonalign-*

ment and the Afro-Asian States (New York, 1966). Hugh Seton-Watson, *Neither War Nor Peace: The Struggle for Power in the Postwar World* (New York, 1960) gives a penetrating analysis of the forces of revolution in the underdeveloped world, whose problems are wisely discussed in Barbara Ward, *The Rich Nations and the Poor Nations* (New York, 1962), and in John Pincus, *Aid, Trade and Development: The Rich and Poor Nations* (New York, 1967). W. W. Kulski's textbook on international relations, *International Politics in a Revolutionary Age* (New York and Philadelphia, 1964) gives special emphasis to the problems of the Third World. Philip M. Hauser, ed., *The Population Dilemma* (Englewood Cliffs, N. J., 1963) discusses the most basic problem of the underdeveloped countries.

THE SINO-SOVIET DISPUTE: Donald S. Zagoria, *The Sino-Soviet Conflict, 1956–1961* (Princeton, 1962) is heavily documented; Klaus Mehnert, *Peking and Moscow* (New York, 1963) ranges wider and more suggestively; Edward Crankshaw, *The New Cold War: Moscow v. Peking* (London, 1963) is very lively. Richard Lowenthal, *World Communism: The Disintegration of a Secular Faith* (New York, 1964) relates the Yugoslav, Chinese, and East European defection from Russian-imposed orthodoxy. Raymond Aron *et al., Marxism in the Modern World* (Stanford, 1965), has good essays on Maoism, Khrushchevism, and Castroism.

THE NEW EASTERN EUROPE: In addition to the books listed under Chapters VI and VIII, see: J-F. Brown, *The New Eastern Europe: The Khrushchev Era and After* (New York, 1966), a thorough study by a British expert on East European affairs drawing upon the documentation of Radio Free Europe; Kurt London, ed., *Eastern Europe in Transition* (Baltimore, 1966); and Adam Bromke, ed., *The Communist States at the Crossroads: Between Moscow and Peking* (New York, 1965). Zbigniew Brzezinski has some important suggestions for American policy-makers in *Alternative to Partition: America's Role in Europe* (New York, 1965).

DISUNITY IN THE WEST: De Gaulle's foreign policy has outraged, among many, John Pinder, *Europe against de Gaulle* (New York, 1963); Paul Reynaud, *The Foreign Policy of Charles de Gaulle* (New York, 1964); and Roger Massip, *De Gaulle et l'Europe* (Paris, 1963). De Gaulle's aims are explained in his own words in Roy C. Macridis, ed., *De Gaulle: Implacable Ally* (New York, 1966). On NATO, see Alistair Buchan, *NATO in the 1960's—The Implications of Interdependence* (New York, 1963); Timothy W. Stanley, *NATO in Transition: The Future of the Atlantic Alliance* (New York, 1965); and Henry A. Kissinger, *The Troubled Partnership* (New York, 1965). On the Cyprus problem, see: Charles Foley, *Legacy of Strife: Cyprus from Rebellion to Civil War* (London, 1964). A good companion in studying contemporary history is Andrew Boyd, *An Atlas of World Affairs* (5th ed., New York, 1964).

Finally, for a stimulating reappraisal of the whole period, read the highly interpretive sketch by the distinguished historian Geoffrey Barraclough, *An Introduction to Contemporary History* (New York, 1965).

Index